DATE DUE

e-Business, e-Government & Small and Medium-Sized Enterprises: Opportunities and Challenges

Brian J. Corbitt
Deakin University, Australia

Nabeel A. Y. Al-Qirim
Auckland University of Technology, New Zealand

IDEA GROUP PUBLISHING
Hershey • London • Melbourne • Singapore

Acquisitions Editor:	Mehdi Khosrow-Pour
Senior Managing Editor:	Jan Travers
Managing Editor:	Amanda Appicello
Development Editor:	Michele Rossi
Copy Editor:	Bernard J. Kieklak, Jr.
Typesetter:	Sara Reed
Cover Design:	Jennifer Jones
Printed at:	Yurchak Printing Inc.

Published in the United States of America by
    Idea Group Publishing (an imprint of Idea Group Inc.)
    701 E. Chocolate Avenue, Suite 200
    Hershey PA 17033
    Tel: 717-533-8845
    Fax: 717-533-8661
    E-mail: cust@idea-group.com
    Web site: http://www.idea-group.com

and in the United Kingdom by
    Idea Group Publishing (an imprint of Idea Group Inc.)
    3 Henrietta Street
    Covent Garden
    London WC2E 8LU
    Tel: 44 20 7240 0856
    Fax: 44 20 7379 3313
    Web site: http://www.eurospan.co.uk

Library of Congress Cataloging-in-Publication Data

E-business, e-government & small and medium-sized enterprises :
opportunities and challenges / Brian J. Corbitt, editor, Nabeel A.Y.
Al-Qirim, editor.
       p. cm.
Includes bibliographical references (p.) and index.
  ISBN 1-59140-202-6 (h/c) — ISBN 1-59140-264-6 (s/c) — ISBN
1-59140-203-4 (ebook)
  1. Electronic commerce—Government policy. 2. Small
business—Technological innovations. I. Corbitt, Brian J. II. Al-Qirim,
Nabeel A. Y., 1966-
  HF5548.32.E17375 2004
  338'.064—dc22

                               2003022605

British Cataloguing in Publication Data
A Cataloguing in Publication record for this book is available from the British Library.

e-Business, e-Government & Small and Medium-Sized Enterprises:
Opportunities and Challenges

Table of Contents

Preface

There has been increased research investigating e-commerce adoption and diffusion in Small to Medium-Sized Enterprises (SMEs) in different parts of the world. What could be synthesized from this research is that in comparison with large enterprises, SMEs would always be positioned in a lagging position in terms of adopting or using e-commerce strategically in business. The reasons which have led to this conclusion were attributed to different contextual causes relating to the SME's weak structure and resources, to technology, to individuals in SMEs (e.g., the CEO) and to their susceptibility to different environmental forces.

With the recent emergence of e-commerce technologies in the early 1990s and their role in encouraging global interconnectedness, there have been increased concerns amongst researchers and professionals that SMEs would always be locked in a position where they could not progress any further with e-commerce or fail to spot the strategic importance of e-commerce to their survival in the long term. Of course, the situation is further aggravated in developing or least-developed countries and isolated economies.

Such implications motivated the editors to look at the role of governments in different parts of the world in order to investigate their role in assisting their SMEs to embrace and benefit from e-commerce. Since the 1970s, most of the countries in the world have deregulated most of the business approaches and policies in order to encourage efficiency, free and cross-trade, and competition in the business environment. An era witnessed the growing economical importance of SMEs in these countries.

This edited book attempts to highlight the e-commerce initiatives of different governments in the world with respect to e-commerce adoption and usage in SMEs. By reviewing the e-commerce policy of different countries in the world, as one focus here, this edited book emphasizes the importance of bridging the divide between e-commerce and SMEs and the importance of devising means and measures where e-commerce could be progressed more strategically in SMEs. It is worth noting here that e-commerce may not be the magical solution for many SMEs in the world. However, what is important in this edited book is to emphasize the importance of introducing the varied and multi-faceted perspectives of e-commerce to the different SME communities in the world and to give them the opportunity to judge the effectiveness of e-commerce in their businesses. This objective could be of great interest to other parties interested in SMEs, such as policymakers, professionals and researchers.

This edited book has policy implications for e-commerce adoption and diffusion in SMEs in different parts of the world and this focus should appeal to different stakeholders, policymakers, researchers and professionals interested in SMEs. The SME sector is of significant economical and social importance to countries all over the world and this focus should resemble a contribution to the literature targeting SMEs and e-commerce. It also raises the attention of governments in different parts of the world about the importance of focusing their strategies on this weak, yet very formidable, sector.

CONTRIBUTIONS IN THIS EDITED BOOK

Despite the apparent enthusiasm among the different governments in the world about e-commerce and their interest in developing policies and initiatives aiming at encouraging e-commerce uptake and use of their business communities, what could be understood from the different contributions in this edited book highlights the following main issues:

1) Most of the governments in the world and in developed countries specifically acknowledge the importance of e-commerce to their countries and to the survival of their businesses in the long term. Most of these governments have actively engaged in setting out initiatives and policies to investigate the status of e-commerce in the business environment and to put in place plans where e-commerce could be introduced and diffused amongst the overall business community in their countries.

2) The e-commerce policies of the different governments were set broadly and, hence, were not concentrating on SMEs as such.

3) The lack of awareness among the SMEs about e-commerce in general and about their government's e-commerce initiatives and policies would further widen the e-commerce divide mentioned above. The lack of detailed knowledge amongst the SMEs about e-commerce and its different business models would further aggravate the gulf between e-commerce and SMEs. Most probably SMEs would adopt e-commerce based on factors that do not necessarily relate to government initiatives or policies.

4) The SMEs should play more proactive role in exploring the multi-faceted perspectives of e-commerce and in devising means where they could

benefit from the different opportunities provided by e-commerce. This is essential for any governmental e-commerce initiative to succeed.

5) The importance of establishing networked SMEs for the purpose of driving efficiencies in operations and reduced costs, increasing the effectiveness of the decision-making process or gaining competitive advantage. This objective becomes very important to SMEs in order to face their limited resources and/or to withstand global competition.

6) Developing countries are still facing different infrastructure issues pertaining to technological and telecommunication infrastructure. Their e-commerce policy/initiatives seemed to be incomplete.

7) The importance of reviewing the government e-commerce initiatives and monitoring progress.

The contributions in this edited book are divided into three main parts. The contributions in the first part attempt to investigate broad and different e-commerce policies in different countries in the world (developed and developing). The aim of these chapters is to investigate these policies in relation to e-commerce uptake and use in SMEs. Authors belonging to the first part provide rich insights about: the e-commerce policy and initiatives in their countries, the status of e-commerce in SMEs and the possible solutions and recommendations which could assist policymakers in bridging the existing gulf between e-commerce and SMEs in their countries.

The contributions in the second part look at a specific focus of the e-commerce policy. Such a focus is highly emphasized here as it attempts to overcome the different inherent contextual weaknesses in SMEs by encouraging them to join forces. Policies aiming at encouraging networking amongst the SMEs are of great importance to SMEs' existence in the long term.

The last part looks at an interesting policy focus represented here by the challenges facing governments in providing effective information strategies supported by online resources (portals) and program that aims at accelerating the adoption of e-commerce through the provision of seed funding to online projects proposed by industry-based consortia. Providing effective information-based portals to support export development amongst SMEs represents a climax here for two reasons. Firstly, it encourages the SMEs belonging to a certain sector or industry (exporting here) to network and create a community which could be further utilized to the benefit of the different SMEs belonging to this cluster. Secondly, this focus embarks on important features of e-commerce, the global nature of e-commerce. Features such as the global interconnectedness, convenience, marginal costs, 24X7, etc., could introduce unique and different opportunities to SMEs. Networked SMEs would be in a much better position to face such global competition. Easily said, it is clear that the road to the full realization of e-commerce opportunities is indeed a long one and not any easy one. The amount of variables introduces by the recent emergence of this innovative technology (e-commerce) is indeed beyond the scope of this book.

E-commerce impacts organizations immensely and holistically in an unprecedented manner and challenges many researchers and standing theories — theories that withstood scrutiny for many years. For example, researchers were struggling or spent a long time investigating whether SMEs were witnessing any real or tangible benefits out of their e-commerce initiatives in the light of their adopted e-commerce technologies (Internet, email and Web sites). Recent research reported limited usage and benefit realization by SMEs. Addressing issues pertaining to the SMEs themselves, represented here by their CEOs and internal processes/structure, are vital to the large-scale success of e-commerce in SMEs. Indeed, looking on how SMEs run their daily business activities could shed essential light into their practices and how they behave when they are confronted with e-commerce technology. Attempting to review processes and attempting to eliminate waste and obstacles, optimize processes and then attempting to streamline certain processes represent a great gain here for SMEs and indeed, represents a vital step for SMEs to take in the e-commerce direction.

Some of the concepts, models and frameworks such as the information-based portals discussed in this edited book are not new. Indeed, different researchers investigated these issues from different perspectives and contexts. What is unique in this edited book is that it attempts to focus on the main issues that are of importance to SMEs. The aggregate of the contributions in this edited book serves two objectives. Firstly, it highlights the research direction and status of e-commerce in SMEs. This could represent a good starting point for countries (researchers, professionals) interested in moving their SMEs in the e-commerce direction at various levels of sophistication. Secondly, these contributions allow researchers and professionals interested in this area to observe and monitor the progress of e-commerce policy in different countries in the world and this could assist such researchers in judging whether they are in the right track in addressing the main issues that are of importance to their SMEs. This edited book raises the awareness of different governments about the importance of e-commerce to their SMEs and this book could assist such governments fine-tune their policies with respect to e-commerce SMEs.

Finally, what is observed from the different contributions in this edited book is the continued concentrating on the B2B business model, more than B2C. It seems that most of the SMEs and, hence, researchers are more focused on this type of business interrelationship. Thus, addressing this perspective first could resemble a good starting point for researchers and professionals in targeting this important sector (SMEs) in their countries. On the other hand, it is worth investigating why B2C attracted such limited attention.

SECTION I

Electronic Commerce Initiatives and Policy Implications in Different Countries in the World

Chapter I attempts to link findings of recent e-commerce research in SMEs in New Zealand with the Government's e-commerce strategy. The research stresses the need for the Government to bridge the existing gap between small business and e-commerce strategy. The strategy emphasizes the Government's role in providing leadership, in building the capability of New Zealanders, and in providing an enabling regulatory environment. Recent progress on this strategy is reviewed and its significance to small business in New Zealand is discussed. However, this chapter points to the importance of prioritizing the implementation of certain strategies and of addressing impending e-commerce issues relevant to the small business sector in New Zealand. The chapter provides different suggestions and ways to bridge such divide between SMEs and e-commerce.

Chapter II introduces government support model for e-commerce readiness in SMEs. The authors contend that a knowledge and innovation-based economy is the desired outcome of such a model. They effectively build six important components in the model and conceptualize dependencies in the model at a high level and provide visibility in Canada's work in building each component. Common to these six components are the profound effects that government policies and actions can have on each component in terms of creation and subsequently diffusion. The model could be useful to describe government's role in preparing SMEs to adopt e-commerce.

Chapter III discusses the role of the Dutch Government in engaging their SMEs in the digital economy. This chapter provides detailed information about the policies of the Dutch government for the development of the information society and, in particular, for the diffusion of electronic commerce in SMEs. The chapter also presents the current situation of the Dutch SMEs with respect to the adoption of e-commerce and their opinion about the governmental policies. One of the main targets of this chapter is to help branch originations and their members to get a grasp on the use of electronic marketplaces and application service providing. In achieving such targets, the chapter finally highlights some of the objectives, approaches and outcomes of different projects in the Nederland such as the in iASPect and iMPact.

In line with the above theme, **Chapter IV** provides a comprehensive coverage about SMEs and e-commerce initiatives in Singapore and investigates the status of e-commerce developments in SMEs. Singapore has put in place an advanced digital telecommunications network as well as the necessary regulatory and policy frameworks for the support of e-commerce. The chapter introduces different impediments toward e-commerce adoption by SMEs. The authors note that, while SMEs have still quite a way to go in terms of emulating e-commerce practices, market developments will force many of them to adopt e-commerce practices in due course. State intervention strategies are also especially imperative in getting promising enterprises as well as others in growth sectors to come on board the e-commerce bandwagon. However, this chapter emphasizes the importance of the private sector efforts in driving the e-commerce growth in SMEs in Singapore.

Chapter V presents a framework that explores the factors and problems that account for the apparent lack of benefit derived from e-commerce activity in SMEs. This framework is based upon a detailed qualitative data analysis of 34 Australian SMEs utilizing e-commerce. The combined results provide interesting insights pertaining to the reality of e-commerce for most SMEs. The chapter highlights policy implications including issues of costs, critical mass, and standards of technology service as critical elements that need to be addressed to create the best environment to support continued SME e-commerce utilization.

Chapter VI describes the key factors that are hindering SMEs' participation in e-commerce in the Asian Pacific region. It covers SMEs in countries such as Thailand, Singapore, Philippines, Malaysia, Cambodia, China and Vietnam and provides qualitative analysis pertaining to their adoption experience of e-commerce. The chapter highlights different obstacles to e-commerce adoption facing Asian Pacific SMEs and suggests different measures and changes to policy to overcome such barriers. The chapter concludes by depicting a strategic grid of e-commerce potential for SMEs made of four broad dimensions. This grid could prove useful to SMEs and policymakers in portraying a path where they could make real progress with their e-commerce initiatives and policies.

Due to the significant importance of the SMEs in the Asian Pacific Economic Cooperation (APEC) regions, this chapter (**Chapter VII**) examines the use of IT in SMEs and the role that the APEC has played in encouraging increased trade by SMEs. In particular, a study of six successful micro and small businesses in APEC economies that was commissioned by APEC examines their attitudes toward trade and e-commerce. Conclusions are drawn as to the role that IT and e-commerce has to play in small business trade. The chapter concludes with the recommendations made to APEC by the study and a summary of the SME policy initiatives announced by APEC as a result of the study and other APEC activities.

Chapter VIII discusses the European Union (EU) innovation policy initiatives for SMEs and the UK innovation policy. The chapter examines the strategic implications of the adoption and implementation of e-commerce by two successful start-up SMEs in the UK in the light of the EU policy initiatives. Findings reveal that SMEs, and start-ups particularly, find themselves having to operate without role models and tested business plans within an increasingly complex and competitive environment. Pure-player start-ups are driven by the "market focus" as a main driver to adopt e-commerce and they are not aware of projects or policy initiatives in this regard. The chapter provides guidelines for policymakers in the UK based on its findings from the two case studies.

SECTION II
Policy Implication for Networked SMEs in Supply Chain

Chapter IX investigates the key infrastructure factors affecting the success of small companies in developing economies that are establishing B2B e-commerce ventures. The factors were identified through an extensive literature review and a pilot study carried out in two organizations. The results of the pilot study and literature review reveal five factors that contribute to the success of B2B E-Commerce. These factors were later assessed for importance using a survey. The chapter provides interesting comparisons with some developed countries such as the US.

Chapter X provides comprehensive literature about the nature and role of formal networks in SMEs. The chapter examines the nature and role of formal networks on e-commerce adoption by SMEs in Sweden. The chapter presents data gathered from 350 regional SMEs in Sweden. This chapter presents a set of comparisons between formally networked and non-networked SMEs that have both adopted or not adopted EC technology. These comparisons focus on the criteria for adoption, perceived benefits of EC and perceived disadvantages of EC adoption for those SMEs that have adopted the technology; and the perceived barriers for those that have decided against EC adoption. The chapter introduces interesting comparisons between networked and non-networked SMEs, highlighting policy implications for SMEs in Sweden.

Chapter XI contends that SMEs have always been under pressures from large firms to implement B2B e-commerce information systems. However, these SMEs have faced various challenges to do so in the supply chain. This chapter explains the role of Taiwanese government in supporting SMEs in implementing e-commerce by analyzing the interactions of government teams with current projects, and challenges of Taiwanese SMEs. Discussions and analyses focus on the government help in setting up infrastructure, B2B e-commerce implementation, and interfirm interactions among SMEs and larger firms. The Taiwanese government has been promoting its global logistics strategy for economic development which stresses supply chain integration by bridging information flows among overseas enterprises, domestic large firms, and local SMEs. Government projects related to this strategy are intended to anchor SMEs' growing needs in linking B2B e-commerce with large firms. The chapter explains how government can further bridge the gaps between the intrinsic barriers of SMEs and the interactions with larger firms in B2B e-commerce implementation.

SECTION III
Policy Push and Monitoring

In line with the above policy implications from the SME's perspective, this chapter (**Chapter XII**) looks at ways where government policies could assist the SMEs in adopting and using e-commerce effectively. Specifically this chapter: (a) outlines the challenges that governments face in providing effective information strategies supported by online resources, (b) discusses research relating to the information strategy of one Australian government agency to support export development among small business, (c) sets out a framework for government online information provision in a diverse industry context. The authors contend that the development of well-designed strategies can improve the usability of online information and the efficiency of government information services.

In a similar sense, **Chapter XIII** provides an overview to date of 81 projects funded by the Australian Government initiative: Information Technology On-Line (ITOL) program — a program that aims to accelerate the adoption of e-commerce through the provision of seed funding to online projects proposed by industry-based consortia. The chapter highlights the reasons behind the success and the failure of some of these projects. The chapter then proposes some interesting critical success factors for such governmental initiatives to succeed in Australia.

SECTION I:

ELECTRONIC COMMERCE INITIATIVES AND POLICY IMPLICATIONS IN DIFFERENT COUNTRIES IN THE WORLD

Chapter I

The Government and eGovernance:
A Policy Perspective on Small Businesses in New Zealand

Nabeel A. Y. Al-Qirim, Auckland University of Technology, New Zealand

Brian J. Corbitt, Deakin University, Australia

ABSTRACT

This chapter reviews e-Commerce research in Small to Medium-Sized Enterprises (SMEs) in New Zealand. The chapter then attempts to review the Government's e-Commerce strategy highlighting commonalities and gaps with respect to e-Commerce adoption and diffusion research in SMEs in New Zealand. The chapter found the strategy emphasising the role of the Government in providing leadership, in building the capability of New Zealanders and in providing an enabling regulatory environment. The strategy is set out to be a complete partnership between Government, business, and the broader community to achieve these objectives. Recent progress on this strategy is reviewed and its significance to SMEs is discussed. This chapter points to the importance of prioritising the implementation of certain strategies by the New Zealand Government in order for e-Commerce to succeed in SMEs.

INTRODUCTION

Small business Internet commerce (e-Commerce) is defined as "the use of Internet technology and applications to support business activities of a small firm" (Poon, 1999). Recent research in Small to Medium-Sized Enterprises (SMEs) in New Zealand (Al-Qirim, 2003; Al-Qirim & Corbitt, 2002) revealed that organisational size emerged as a strong motivator for e-Commerce adoption. Thus making it quite clear that larger SMEs are more capable than smaller SMEs in adopting e-Commerce technologies. The innovative Chief Executive Officer (CEO) was needed to guarantee the shift to the e-Commerce arena. The compatibility of e-Commerce in the business environment of SMEs appeared to be highly significant. Hence, in order to move to the e-Commerce arena, potential adopters highlighted the need to overcome compatibility issues such as security and legal concerns and the compatibility of e-Commerce with their earlier practices and customers. In addition, the SMEs would adopt more e-Commerce technologies as a result of pressure from their competitors. However, those adopters highlighted the negative effect of technology vendors in New Zealand on their adoption decision of more e-Commerce technologies. Other factors such as the relative advantage of e-Commerce, cost of adopting e-Commerce, information intensity of products, pressure from suppliers/buyers, and CEOs' involvement were not significant in Al-Qirim's (2003) and Al-Qirim's and Corbitt's (2002) research suggesting that adopting SMEs were not witnessing many advantages out of their e-Commerce initiatives. It is worth noting that most of Poon's (2000) and Poon and Swatman's (1997, 1998, 1999a, b) research focused on whether SMEs were realising any real advantage from having e-Commerce. They found that most SMEs were not witnessing tangible advantages from e-Commerce and the advantages sought from having e-Commerce were perceptions only (Poon, 1999, 2000; Poon & Swatman, 1997, 1999a). Poon and Swatman (1997, 1998) found that SMEs did not use the Internet strategically to gain a competitive advantage. Poon and Swatman (1998, 1999a) related these lower advantages to the different perceptions about e-Commerce advantages and found that most of the SMEs did not anticipate real benefits (direct sales and tangible profits) in the short term due to difficulties in selling their products over the Internet.

Recent survey research in New Zealand confirmed the same and provided significant insight into the level, value, growth and extent of e-Commerce among high adopters (ACNielsen, 2001). The survey targeted businesses with commercial websites (taking orders via their website) and included 800 respondents (e-traders). Although commercially oriented sites were targeted, 50% of those surveyed currently are selling less than $NZ 10,000 per annum over the Internet. Overall, this study reported that Internet sales are a small percentage of total sales volume for most e-traders. Fifty-eight percent (58%) of the businesses do not anticipate significant growth in their Internet business or profit levels in the next 12 months.

While the New Zealand Government reported the widespread adoption of technologies that enable e-Commerce, it suspected little depth in their penetration to support fully integrated electronic business systems (MOED, 2000). It also found a relatively low level of understanding of the opportunities offered by e-Commerce and the Information and Communications Technology (ICT) revolution and varying ICT literacy in the community as a whole. The New Zealand Government suspects that many businesses in New Zealand have recognised the advantages of electronically integrating all their business systems from the front end (e.g., website), through integrated management and planning systems, to their supply and distribution chains. This requires a comprehensive assessment of processes and internal systems (MOED, 2000). Other research

Table 1. Inhibitors and accelerators for Internet use in small business.

NZ SMEs (Abell & Lim, 1996; Abell & Black, 1997)	APEC countries including New Zealand (PWHC, 1999)	Australian SMEs (Poon & Swatman, 1999b)
Advantages:		
- Effectiveness in information gathering (3) - Availability of expertise regardless of locality - Better service and support from suppliers (3) - Increased productivity (3) - Better awareness of business environment (competition (3)) - Ability to reach international markets (3) - Faster delivery from suppliers - Greater customer satisfaction (3) - Opportunity to be seen at the forefront of technology	- Improved customer service - Enhanced company Image (1) - Customer information exchange (1) - Improved competitive position - Increased customer loyalty - Access to international markets - Increased revenue - Reduction in costs of information - Supplier information exchange (1) - Attraction of new investment - Reduction in procurement costs	- Time saving in finding resources - Useful expertise from Net - Savings in communication costs - Better company image - Better customer relationships - More extensive business network - Increased knowledge about competitors - Better advertising and marketing - Significant increase in business opportunities - Better opportunity to make well-informed business decisions - Improved trade in virtual marketplace - Significant sales increase through Net - Better supplier relationships
Disadvantages:		
- Connection and/or usage charges too high (2) - Target customers not connected (3) - Lack of expertise or personnel (3) - Technical limitations in hardware and software - Benefits not always evident (2, 3) - No guarantee of message delivery - Enforceability of contracts - Concerns about security (2, 3): tampering with network messages, unauthorised access to internal network, authenticity, and misuse by employees. - Difficulty in locating information	- Low customer e-Commerce use - Concerns about security - High cost of technology - Legal and liability concerns - Low supplier e-Commerce use - High cost of technology - Limited knowledge - Concern about telecom services - Y2K concerns - Firm computerisation too low - Low investment in computers	- Low supplier e-Commerce use - High cost of technology

(1) Adam and Deans (2000); (2) Deloitte (2000); (3) MOED (2000a)

highlighted different perceived motivators and inhibitors of e-Commerce in SMEs (Table 1).

At a broader level, the New Zealand Government (MOED, 2000) highlighted other weaknesses:

1.   An uneven distribution of infrastructure capability at reasonable cost, particularly in rural communities.
2.   A lack of integration or connectivity to global business networks.
3.   The short supply of technical graduates from tertiary institutions.
4.   The emigration of skilled New Zealanders, in particular IT personnel with a high degree of technical skill who are attracted by the pay and opportunities overseas.
5.   A lack of good quality information to support policy formation and inform how we are portrayed in the wider world.

These results suggested the weakness of the e-Commerce phenomenon in SMEs. Other research found that barriers concerning the adaptation of business processes were hardly expressed among adopters and non-adopters of the Internet in SMEs (Walczuch et al., 2000), demonstrating that SMEs use e-Commerce on an experimental level.

STATUS OF ELECTRONIC COMMERCE IN NEW ZEALAND

The CEO's innovativeness appeared consistently as a significant factor in e-Commerce adoption in Al-Qirim's (2003) and Al-Qirim and Corbitt's (2002) research. Addressing this perspective in managers of different SMEs in New Zealand could encourage adoption. However, this is not sufficient alone to guarantee adoption. E-Commerce requires different expertise in different technical and business areas to guarantee its adoption and its diffusion in the business environment of SMEs. Therefore, it is unlikely that the CEO/owner alone would be able to manage the whole adoption process of e-Commerce. "Resource poverty" (Thong et al., 1994) — the lack of both financial and human resources — may influence the CEO's behaviour and force a minimum and multi-staged commitment process. Limited human resources may mean either fewer available employees or employees without the appropriate skills. In either case, the CEO of the small business will be limited to what activities he/she can initiate or complete. Hence, there will be a focus on the near term, with an emphasis on allocating these scarce resources only to what is considered a top priority activity. Indeed, developing a long-term plan for IS (and e-Commerce) and a large one-time commitment of both financial and human resources would represent the greatest challenge for the manager of a small business in New Zealand.

Despite the high representation of the SME sector within New Zealand, there exists a counter-argument that points to the existence of a high degree of inter-subjective agreement that New Zealand culture is more oriented towards the non-entrepreneurial end of the continuum (Harper, 1992). In comparison with other developed nations, New Zealand has a weaker scientific culture and generally the division of labour has not been scientifically and extensively applied to management in New Zealand, largely because of the relatively small size of most New Zealand businesses and the low levels of formal education and specialist skills of most owner-managers of small businesses (Harper, 1992). These managers rarely have any functional specialisation: the manager is usually responsible for production, finance, sales, personnel, and purchasing.

This research highlights that it might turn out that further e-Commerce opportunities to exploit by certain businesses do not exist or the identified opportunities are not financially justifiable or the nature of the product or industry does not encourage adoption. However, the issue here is whether the SMEs are willing to undertake the consultative investment or learn about the technology to bridge the existing gap between their business knowledge and their lack of knowledge about e-Commerce. The New Zealand Government points to weaknesses in business innovation (MOED, 2000), as highlighted earlier. The domestic market provides a small economic base for businesses and while technology uptake is high, the benefits are not necessarily reflected in business profits and growth. This weakness in business innovation could be easily remedied by increasing the investment in research and development (MOED, 2000). Bridge and Peel (1999) emphasise that the wide success of information, its analysis and applications in SMEs do not rely on educating the SMEs about the benefits of IT adoption only, but also on fostering a planning orientation, which will encourage management to utilise their existing capabilities more fully. Waiting for e-Commerce to diffuse widely in the business environment and for the numbers of online buyers and competitors to increase is cautioned and SMEs would indeed miss the different opportunities provided by e-Commerce.

It is worthy recalling here the need for the small business to think about e-Commerce differently and the fact that e-Commerce requires a change (compatibility) in the way business is conducted for it to be successful and to be able to transform to the marketplace transparently. It is only when the SMEs reassess their products and processes in the light of the new emerging technology (e-Commerce) that they can operate their e-Commerce initiatives more effectively. Thus, breaking from the current paradigm dictated mostly by traditional business practices and processes is highly emphasised here. A participant in recent research in New Zealand confirmed the same and commented, "at the beginning we had a big picture plan but as you do the next thing eyes become open to the situation. Every time we take the next step we'll be saying, what is the next step after that? You've got to live it, to experience it … (however), if you say to (an SME owner) go out and make a website and sell to the world, and they don't know how to make today work, how are they possibly going to comprehend it" (Chapple, 2002). This mindset is holding businesses back from progressing with e-Commerce (Chapple, 2002).

On the other hand, issues pertaining to small business such as the inadequate financial, and human resources, time, and expert knowledge about e-Commerce, would indeed widen the existing gap between their simple initiatives and their envisioned advanced e-Commerce initiatives. It seems that the SMEs would be locked in that vacuum for a long time unless concerned or interested stakeholders in SMEs such as the Government do something to help the SMEs bridge this gap. Recent research in New Zealand emphasises that the Government could do more to promote technology to SMEs, either financially or through a mentoring programme (Chapple, 2002). The outcomes of Al-Qirim's (2003) and Al-Qirim and Corbitt's (2002) research raise the following significant issues, which could assist the Government in addressing the main impending issues pertaining to e-Commerce in SMEs in New Zealand:

1. Due to the high significance of the CEO's innovativeness, the existing electronic divide between adopters and non-adopters in SMEs could be bridged alongside the entrepreneurial perspective in New Zealand. Issues pertaining to the characteristics and personal traits of the manager/owner of the SMEs and their knowledge and understanding of e-Commerce as a technology and as an enabler for business innovations needs to be addressed. Other issues pertaining to leadership, business practices and strategic planning could be addressed as well.

2. Unveiling the varied perspectives and advantages of e-Commerce could further attract SMEs to e-Commerce. The cost as highlighted in the current research is not significant in that if the SMEs are able to realise the opportunity (advantages) out of e-Commerce, cost should not be a problem. Cost could become a problem if the SMEs invest in e-Commerce projects with unknown ends or results (risky e-Commerce initiatives). Simply, they will not invest in something they know nothing about (risk averse). The New Zealand Government reported a tendency among businesses and financial institutions in New Zealand to be risk averse such as ignoring critical intangible factors and a failure to appreciate the changing strategic environment and the opportunities it offers (MOED, 2000).

3. The performance of technology vendors in New Zealand needs to be addressed as well. Providing a "trusted third party," which could introduce some performance indicators (benchmarks) and put measures in place (e-Commerce code of practices for technology vendors), could further

encourage interested SMEs in moving ahead with their e-Commerce initiatives. Interestingly, CICA (2001) found the Canadian SMEs struggling with e-Commerce and found that accountants were the professionals most trusted to give advice on e-Commerce strategy, not technology vendors or consultants! This might be another option for SMEs to consider.

4.   Regulatory, security, and electronic-payment issues need to be addressed and bridged at least within the New Zealand perspective. However, such broad issues need to be addressed at the global level as well as most of the e-Commerce opportunities are of global nature.

In the following, the Government's e-Commerce strategy in New Zealand is reviewed and recent progress on this strategy is introduced. These policies are then compared with the above findings with respect to e-Commerce adoption in SMEs in New Zealand.

ELECTRONIC STRATEGY OF NEW ZEALAND GOVERNMENT

In November 2000, the Government launched its e-Commerce strategy for New Zealand (MOED, 2000). The strategy set out the Government's vision to build New Zealand's knowledge economy (MOED, 2001). "New Zealand will be world class in embracing e-Commerce for competitive advantage" (MOED, 2000, p. 2). The Strategy recognises the opportunities and risks associated with the e-Commerce and the information technology revolution and sets out the goals and principles to guide the Government's response. It detailed the Government's commitment to provide leadership and work in partnership with business and the broader community to build the e-Commerce capability of New Zealanders. Implementing the e-Commerce strategy is a priority for the Government in this drive for economic transformation (MOED, 2001). The strategy identified three broad roles for the Government (MOED, 2000):

Leadership and communication in partnership with the private sector (shared responsibility):

1.   Raise awareness and champion e-Commerce through leadership in communication (e.g., workshops, publications, develop websites, national awards, support through Government agencies such as Industry NZ, Trade NZ, and Technology NZ, develop key networks between businesses, professional services providers, and the financial community).
2.   Be informed about e-Commerce capability through quality information and research. Identify research and development (R&D) programmes aiming

at providing better statistics on the penetration of information and communication technology (ICT) and ICT skills, improving the understanding of the constraints on the adoption of e-Commerce by businesses to inform policy response, and benchmarking New Zealand against the rest of the world.

3.   Deliver better quality, cheaper, secure, and faster services to its customers through the introduction of online services, and lead by example through e-Government and e-procurement. Developing New Zealand Government Online (NZGO) as the primary Internet portal into Government agencies and services, and Web-based access to forms, with 40% of all public service forms available online by June 30, 2001. Information and online payment systems will be in place by June 30, 2001; and identifying activities where New Zealanders will be encouraged to interact with Government agencies online, and providing incentives for them to do so.

4.   Ensure the continuing supply of skilled resources either nationally (training) or internationally (supply of skilled people in New Zealand through review of immigration policies).

Helping to build human capability in business and the broader community including Maori[1] and rural businesses:

1.   Facilitate building business e-Commerce skills by working with business to build strategic, management, and technology skills. Focusing on SMEs is an immediate priority.

2.   Work to ensure that all New Zealanders have access to life-long learning opportunities to develop ICT skills for the 21st century through leadership in the education sector and by promoting the integration of ICT across the curriculum.

3.   Build broader ICT literacy and capability in the community including rural areas.

Ensuring an enabling regulatory environment for e-Commerce (domestic and international). It embraces trade policy, tax policy, industry specific regulation and consumer policy:

1.   Ensure flexible and timely legislative responses by passing the Electronic Transaction Bill, Crimes Amendment Bill No. 6 to deal with cyber crimes, amend the Privacy Act of 1993 to meet with the European directive on data protection, progress the development of the evidence code (communications used as evidence), and review other legislation including intellectual property.

2.   Facilitate the development and protection of telecommunication infrastructure.

3. Encourage appropriate self-regulation of industry by developing industry codes of practice in areas such as consumer protection and Internet services.
4. Ensure an appropriate tax environment that takes into account the growth of e-Commerce.
5. Promote New Zealand's interests internationally alongside the above points.

The strategy identified a significant number of both broad and specific commitments and actions for Government under this framework. The strategy identified how and where Government would focus its efforts to ensure that all citizens have access to new technology and it outlined initiatives to support an enabling regulatory environment in which e-Commerce can flourish. It is agreed that achieving the above objectives and principles could happen in stages. However, addressing these broad objectives is indeed a very complex task and requires the cooperation/collaboration of the different entities in the Government.

The strategy contained 60 commitments and actions. The Government's progress report in 2001 (MOED, 2001) reported different achievements alongside the different issues highlighted in the strategy (full details in MOED, 2001). This research highlights some of the main issues:

Leadership and Communication

One of the most important achievements in this strategy was the establishment of the E-Commerce Action Team (ECAT) in March 2001 to assist in implementing the e-Commerce strategy. It is made up of industry and business leaders and experienced e-Commerce individuals. It has worked on raising awareness of e-Commerce issues across the broader community represented by its members and identifying ways of meeting specific sector needs. ECAT consists of three main entities (Figure 1): (1) The ECAT core group, a leadership team appointed by the Minister for Information Technology; (2) A largely self-selected ECAT network of sector or community groups and individuals (the ECAT Network); and (3) A website (ECAT, 2001).

A key objective of ECAT is to promote the establishment of additional regional or sector-based ECATs and to support existing groups. Several "mini-ECATs" have formed, including a research ECAT; an Education ECAT (EduCAT); a rural ECAT lead by Federated Farmers; the Waikato ECAT (WECAT) and the Hawkes Bay E-Commerce Development Committee. Six regional e-Commerce events have been held in different parts of the country to assist in building awareness of the opportunities afforded by e-Commerce and in helping businesses learn from each other. Most importantly they have acted as catalysts for the establishment of local groups and e-Commerce initiatives.

Figure 1. Structure of the ECAT

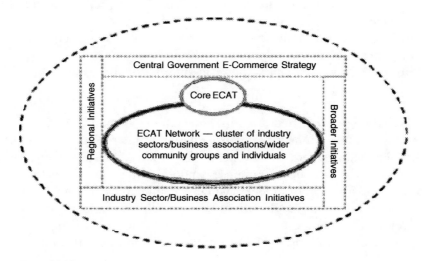

Source: ECAT (2001)

The ECAT website is being developed (launched recently and hosted by the Government[2]) as a key instrument to support business and the wider community to build their e-Commerce capability and develop support networks. It contains links to a wide variety of information including the e-Commerce guide, case studies, current research and statistics, ECAT Network member pages, a calendar of e-Commerce events and training and e-Commerce news.

One significant achievement of the ECAT is the launch of the ECAT Network in June 2001. It provided a channel for businesses, non-profit organisations and individuals to share their experience and interest in e-Commerce. Members contribute to the resources on the ECAT website through their member pages. Anyone may join the network and the e-Commerce-contacts mailing list. This list is used to notify members about updates to the ECAT website, publicise events and stimulate feedback on practical e-Commerce questions and issues.

The E-Government Strategy was released in April 2001 with the mission that by 2004 the Internet will be the dominant means of enabling ready access to Government information, services and processes (e-Commerce.govt.nz). Work continues on a comprehensive range of projects including implementation of secure e-mail, development of a new Government portal, the e-procurement pilot and work on establishing interoperability and standards. An enhanced NZGO website will be implemented by January 2002 (superseded recently by the "www.govt.nz" portal).

The Minister of State Services has advised public service chief executives that departments must explicitly incorporate e-Government[3] into their strategic business planning from 2001/2002 onwards. An e-procurement strategy and report has been provided to the Cabinet Economic Development Committee. E-procurement pilots have been undertaken by various agencies, and agencies' experience reviewed. An e-billing strategy report was prepared in early 2001 for the E-Government Advisory Board. It concluded that products in the market-place are not developed enough to recommend any particular approach.

Due to the limited market scope in New Zealand, the Ministry of Foreign Affairs and Trade[4] and Trade New Zealand[5] continue to work through New Zealand's overseas posts and offices to enhance market access opportunities using e-Commerce for New Zealand exporters and to promote New Zealand companies as innovative users of leading edge technology.

Building Capability

In line with the second role of the Government's strategy, different educational and motivational initiatives were established. The Government published the e-Commerce guide in November 2000 where more than 8,000 copies have been distributed to businesses all over New Zealand. In addition, more information has been made available through the ECAT website (e.g., multi-currency credit card services). The BIZInfo[6] programme through Industry NZ has developed an eight-module e-Commerce training programme aimed at SMEs. This programme is now available through the BIZ provider network. Trade New Zealand is well advanced in implementing its e-Commerce strategy including a revamped website, a client e-Commerce education programme, an online database to profile all New Zealand exporters, advice on digital market-places, and the incorporation of e-Commerce into its criteria for the export awards. Businesses with innovative e-Commerce and electronic business strategies can apply for the Enterprise Award Scheme administered by Industry NZ.

Enabling Regulatory Environment

There have been several developments on the third initiative. The Electronic Transactions Bill was approved by the parliament on October 10, 2002. It will enable statutory requirements for the writing, signature and retention and production of information to be met using electronic methods. This represents a significant development. Secure Electronic Environment[7] (S.E.E.) e-mail is now operational between different state agencies. The Crimes Amendment Bill (No.6) will address computer-related crime. It has been reported back from select committee and is awaiting parliament's consideration of the committee's report. The Telecommunications Bill is designed to create a more efficient and competitive telecommunications market in New Zealand for the benefit of both business and domestic consumers. Work on reform of evidence law, including electronic evidence, is at the policy approval stage. The Government has issued the New Zealand model code for consumer protection in e-Commerce to guide businesses to develop self-regulatory mechanisms and provide advice to business associations considering their own codes of practice. A national infrastructure protection strategy report was prepared and the Government has approved the establishment of a centre for critical infrastructure protection.

The Government has approved an initial pilot online service for immigration, visa and permit applications. New regulations have been promulgated. The New Zealand Immigration Service[8] (NZIS) has undertaken a migrant recruitment drive aimed at Indian ICT professionals. The current promotional activity is likely to be a pilot for a broader, global promotional campaign.

DISCUSSION

The Government has drawn on the wider framework to address e-Commerce adoption and diffusion in business in New Zealand and has advanced different initiatives aiming at bridging the gap between business and e-Commerce. It set the general guiding strategy and progressed admirably in achieving most of the impending issues that were highlighted in the strategy. The Government is acknowledging its leading role in empowering and driving e-Commerce in New Zealand; upgrading the capability of the business and setting the governing regulatory framework. At the heart of the Government's strategy is the joint leadership perspective between the Government and businesses in New Zealand. However, it is understood that choices about new technology and the exploitation of opportunities must be led by the private sector (individuals and business innovators).

The implication here is twofold. Initially, there is a need for more interdisciplinary e-Commerce research aiming at detecting the true progress and penetration of the Government's e-Commerce initiative into the business environment in New Zealand and, most importantly, how to develop accurate measures and benchmarks for e-Commerce success in businesses in general and in SMEs specifically. We need to identify the true impact of e-Commerce on market efficiency, the regions that are targeted and the regions that are progressing more than the others, the level of success and penetration of the strategy, the Government's priorities regarding e-Commerce diffusion, and the business perception of the strategy. In pursuing e-Commerce, the SMEs in that research were found not to be following any guidelines or measures set by the Government. The Government is addressing this and hence, focusing on this perspective with quality research could safeguard against any deviation or waste in targeting the most important issues that are of essence to the wide success of the e-Commerce strategy in business in general and in SMEs in New Zealand specifically.

Secondly, the guidelines in the strategy are set broadly and it could be agreed here that implementing the strategy will take many years and, indeed, looking at the progress occurring on the strategy, the Government is quite focused on achieving the e-Commerce strategy. However, although the Government has addressed the small sector in many places in the strategy, it should be emphasised here that focusing on the SMEs' perspective in greater detail could yield more effective and direct results. This research outlined some of the main features of the SMEs, which distinguish them from other businesses. The structure of the SMEs is too fragile to withstand any serious strategic investment on e-Commerce. Most of the research studies in this paper point to the wide adoption of the Internet, e-mail, and simple Web pages, but the utilisation of these technologies in business is not extensive. E-Commerce is more than businesses advertising. It is about undertaking business processes in a networked electronic environment, as envisioned by the Government (MOED, 2000). Accordingly, leaving the business to choose its own e-Commerce technology and to exploit it to the benefit of its own business has proven ineffective at least from the SMEs' perspective because SMEs lack the detailed knowledge about e-Commerce and business models in the first place. Waiting for the implementation of the whole e-Commerce strategy will take a long time and due to the rapid development in the e-Commerce technology, it is feared that many SMEs will always be in a position to miss taking the lead in e-Commerce. The Government acknowledges the threats from other businesses, which could influence the economic structure, drive prices down and undermine competitive positions of many businesses in New Zealand. There are many companies that have not formerly been seen as competitors that are addressing these challenges and exploiting new opportunities faster than New Zealand firms. E-Commerce also poses new risks as more agile competitors harness the power of the Internet and e-Commerce.

This research emphasised the importance of addressing four main issues: set the regulatory framework; increase the SMEs' awareness of e-Commerce; CEO's innovativeness; and address technology vendors performance in New Zealand. It is clear from the Government's strategy that it has addressed and achieved different steps toward the first two main issues. Issues like security, privacy, legal protection, lack of knowledge of e-Commerce and business models, and most importantly guiding the SMEs to the next level of e-Commerce (interactive initiatives where most of the benefits and risk fall!) is highlighted as the major deterrent. However, what is important alongside these initiatives is to promote these services effectively to the businesses community in general and to SMEs specifically in New Zealand. For instance, BizInfo provides free training on e-Commerce. However, BizInfo's chief executive says the support for e-Commerce is available but just not being used by businesses (Chapple, 2002)! This further highlights the need for more work to be done by the

Government in promoting its services to the business community in New Zealand. The training programmes need to be more "hands on" such as conducting workshops where the managers of the SMEs are exposed to real live situations and are encouraged to find solutions to such situations. Providing more case studies (success/failure stories) and analysing them could prove more insightful to the managers of the small business. Workshops aiming at guiding the SMEs to develop their e-Commerce initiatives starting with problem identification and analysis and ending with development (blueprint) are highly encouraged here. Allowing the SMEs to live the experience could remove many of the misperceptions that surround e-Commerce and could act as a motivator for adoption or joining a network.

As for the remaining two issues, this research emphasises the need for addressing and prioritising the CEO's innovativeness perspective in SMEs and the performance of technology vendors in New Zealand. Although the Government is acknowledging (MOED, 2000) the shortage of management, leadership, and entrepreneurial e-Commerce skills and the need to develop an innovation culture, this research emphasises that if the CEO's perspective is not addressed first, most of the Government's initiatives will not strike a bull's eye. The Government needs to reach out to the CEOs of the different SMEs in New Zealand and to target its messages to the managers of the different SMEs on a one-on-one basis in order to attract their attention. Perhaps creating a consistent marketing campaign could generate this momentum among the managers of the SMEs in New Zealand to adopt e-Commerce or to join a network. The ECAT role in this regard is apparent and highly commended. However, there is a tendency for businesses and financial institutions in New Zealand to be risk averse and many SMEs prefer debt rather than equity financing to avoid sharing ownership control and hence, a strong go-it-alone attitude prevails (MOED, 2000). This represents the greatest risk for initiating such networks among the SMEs in New Zealand, as they would perceive this call for clustering as interfering with their sovereignty. Promoting the entrepreneurial perspective and spirit (CEO's innovativeness) among the business owners in New Zealand is highly advised and targeted educational programmes and workshops could address this perspective.

Living in the global knowledge economy amidst rapid technological developments, this situation could lead to difficulties at the national level in New Zealand in the long run. On the other hand, latest reports by the media[9] about the resulting mergers between gigantic enterprises in the U.S. and Europe and the emergence of the European Union raises concerns in countries like New Zealand, which is dominated by smaller businesses. It seems the rapid deregulation and downsizing policies embraced by the New Zealand Government since the mid-eighties needs to be reviewed in the light of recent global economical changes and the online information age. The resulting merger between New Zealand's two largest dairy producers (Fonterra) in order to survive global competition is solid evidence for this change[10]. Assessing the structure of small business in New Zealand and hence, providing a framework for more collaborative, cooperative, integrative work could prove more useful to New Zealand SMEs. For instance, creating clusters of SMEs working in similar industries or dealing with similar products could put them in a better position to compete in the global marketplace. Building consolidations among suppliers, manufacturers, and buyers could prove effective to the SMEs. In the case of Fonterra, creating e-Commerce linkages between the parent company and the different farmers along the supply chains could introduce valuable efficiencies in the short run leading to a strategic advantage in the long run. It seems this call for clusters among the SMEs' community in New Zealand is more pressing now than ever. However, due to the limited market scope in New Zealand, prioritising and promoting these clusters in the direction of exporting could prove more effective and encourage SMEs reluctant to participate.

Other countries are doing the same. For instance, U.S. lawmakers approved an e-Commerce pilot programme[11] designed to help SME manufacturers (350,000) move their business online. The Korean Government is doing the same with domestic software companies, mostly SMEs, to streamline their distribution channels by establishing a software cyber-mall to link buyers and developers easily by bypassing lots of intermediaries along the selling/supplying chain (Turban et al., 2002). In Europe, there has been tremendous progress with respect to the economic significance of e-Commerce, the development of (self-) regulatory mechanisms and the creation of a modern policy framework (L'Hoest, 2001).

As for technology vendors in New Zealand, it should be emphasised here that like most of the developed countries, the Government's deregulation policy dictates that it could not intervene in how business owners should run their business. All it can do is generate the broad regulatory framework, which could govern relationships and interrelationships among businesses. However, what the Government can do is to provide a list of accredited technology vendors, who could deliver professional and economical advice and solutions. In this regard the Government could benefit from the business model of certificate authority and trusted-third-parties in cyberspace. This could encourage technology vendors registering for this service and meeting the requirements to increase their business stake in the SME sector.

CONCLUSION

This research reviews the Government's e-Commerce strategy in the light of recent e-Commerce research findings in New Zealand. The findings point to the significant role played by the New Zealand Government in creating and encouraging an atmosphere for the wide adoption and success of e-Commerce in New Zealand in the long term. The progress in implementing the strategy is significant. What this research stresses is to prioritise certain issues that are of significant importance to SMEs such as addressing the CEO's innovativeness and the performance of technology vendors in New Zealand. The call for clustering among New Zealand SMEs seems the only plausible solution to survive the rapid technological development and growing global competition.

This research represents an initial attempt in this policy direction to link e-Commerce research in SMEs with Government policy. Thus, expanding on the different issues highlighted in this research could contribute significantly to this policy, to SMEs and to researchers interested in this area. Monitoring the progress of the e-Commerce strategy alongside its different entities and stake-holders and creating accurate measures tracking its diffusion and success among the different businesses in general and the SMEs specifically in New Zealand is highly recommended here.

REFERENCES

Abell, W. & Black, S. (1997). *Business use of the Internet in New Zealand: A follow-up study.* Retrieved August 8, 2000 from the World Wide Web: http://www.scu.edu.au/ausweb96/business/abell/paper.htm.

Abell, W. & Lim, L. (1996). *Business use of the Internet in New Zealand: An exploratory study.* Retrieved August 8, 2000 from the World Wide Web: http://www.scu.edu.au/ausweb96/business/abell/paper.htm.

ACNielsen. (2001, July). *Electronic commerce in New Zealand: A survey of electronic traders.* New Zealand.

Adam, S. & Deans, K. (2000). *Online Business in Australia and New Zealand: Crossing a Chasm.* AusWeb2k-The Sixth Australian World Wide Web Conference, Rihga Colonial Club Resort, Cairns, 12-17 June 2000. Retrieved August 8, 2000 from the World Wide Web: http://ausweb.scu.edu.au/aw2k/papers/adam/paper.html.

Al-Qirim, N. (2003). The innovation theories in retrospect: The case of electronic commerce adoption in small business in New Zealand. In the *IFIP joint WG 8.2+9.4 Conference*, Athens, June 15-17, 2003. In Korpela, M., Montealegre, R. & Poulymenakou, A. (Eds.), *Organisational Information Systems in the Context of Globalisation* (pp. 117-137). Boston, Dordrecht, London: Kluwar Academia Publishers.

Al-Qirim, N. & Corbitt, B. (2002). An empirical investigation of an e-Commerce adoption model in small to medium-sized enterprises in New Zealand. *Proceedings of the 6th Pacific Asia Conference on Information Systems (PACIS 2002): The Next e-What? For Business and Communities.* Tokyo, Japan (September 2-4, pp. 343-362).

Chapple, I. (2002). Small firms drag feet with Internet. *The New Zealand Herald*. Retrieved August 14, 2002 from the World Wide Web: www.nzherald.co.nz/storyprint.cfm?stotyID=2347435.

Deloitte Touche Tohmatsu. (2000). *Deloitte e-Business survey: Insights and issues facing New Zealand business*. Retrieved August 8, 2000 from the World Wide Web: http://www.deloitte.co.nz/images/acrobat/survey.pdf.

E-Commerce Action Team (ECAT). (2001). *E-Commerce action team core group terms of reference, February 2001*. Retrieved August 14, 2002 from the World Wide Web: www.ecommerce.govt.nz/ecat.

Harper, D. (1992). *Entrepreneurship in New Zealand: Foundations for a Public Policy Framework*. NZIER: Wellington.

L'Hoest, R. (2001, January/February). The European dimension of the digital economy. *Intereconomics*, 44-50.

Ministry of Economic Development (MOED). (2000). *E-Commerce: Building the Strategy for New Zealand*. Wellington, New Zealand.

Ministry of Economic Development (MOED). (2000a, October). *Electronic commerce in New Zealand: A survey of business use of the Internet information technology*. Policy Group Competition and Enterprise branch. Retrieved May 16, 2001 from the World Wide Web: http://www.e-Commerce.govt.nz/ecat/resources/index.html.

Ministry of Economic Development (MOED). (2001). *E-Commerce: Building the Strategy for New Zealand, Progress Report, One Year On, November 2001*. Wellington, New Zealand.

Poon, S. (1999). Small business and Internet commerce: What are the lessons learned? In Sudweeks, F. & Romm, C. (Eds.), *Doing Business on the Internet: Opportunities and Pitfalls* (pp. 113-124). London: Springer-Verlag London Ltd.

Poon, S. (2000). Business environment and Internet commerce benefits – A small business perspective. *European Journal of Information Systems*, 9, 72-81.

Poon, S. & Swatman, P. (1997). Internet-based small business communication. *International Journal of Electronic Commerce*, 7(2), 5-21.

Poon, S. & Swatman, P. (1998). A combined-method study of small business Internet commerce. *International Journal of Electronic Commerce*, 2(3), 31-46.

Poon, S. & Swatman, P. (1999a). An exploratory study of small business Internet commerce issues. *Information & Management*, 35, 9-18.

Poon, S. & Swatman, P. (1999b). A longitudinal study of expectations in small business Internet commerce. *International Journal of Electronic Commerce*, 3(3), 21-33.

Premkumar, G. & Roberts, M. (1999). Adoption of new information technologies in rural small businesses. *International Journal of Management Science (OMEGA)*, 27, 467-484.

PWHC (Pricewaterhousecoopers). (1999). *SME Electronic Commerce Study* (TEL05/97T). Retrieved April 10, 2000 from the World Wide Web: http://apec.pwcglobal.com/sme.html.

Reid, A. (2002). North Shore City economy. Retrieved Thursday - July 18, 2002 4:39 PM from the email address (nabeel.alqirim@aut.ac.nz) (email letter sent to the author's email address by Alison Reid, research analyst in the North Shore City Council).

Thong, J., Yap, S. & Raman, K. (1994). Engagement of external expertise in information systems implementation. *Journal of Management Information Systems, 11*(2), 209.

Turban, E., King, D., Lee, J., Warkentin, M. & Chung, H. (2002). *Electronic Commerce: A Managerial Perspective 2002*. Upper Saddle River, NJ: Prentice Hall.

Walczuch, R., Braven, G. & Lundgren, H. (2000). Internet adoption: Barriers for small firms in The Netherlands. *European Management Journal, 18*(5), 561-572.

ENDNOTES

[1]   Indigenous people of New Zealand.

[2]   http://www.e-Commerce.govt.nz/ecat/

[3]   http://www.e-government.govt.nz/

[4]   http://www.mfat.govt.nz/

[5]   http://www.tradenz.govt.nz/

[6]   http://www.bizinfo.co.nz/

[7]   http://www.e-government.govt.nz/projects/see/index.html

[8]   http://www.immigration.govt.nz/

[9]   A news clip reported by TVNZ in 2002.

[10]   Retrieved 9 December, 2002 from the Web: http://www.fonterra.com/content/aboutfonterra/whoweare/default.jsp

[11]   Retrieved 23 August, 2002 from the Web: www.nist.gov

Chapter II

Building Infrastructure
for SME Adoption
of E-Business:
The Canadian Experience

Dawn N. Jutla, Saint Mary's University, Canada

ABSTRACT

Challenged to increase the country's productivity, the Canadian government issued a 10-year innovation strategy agenda in January 2001. Canada's innovation strategy identifies goals, targets, and government priorities in four key areas: knowledge performance, skills, innovation environment, and community clusters. Complementing the government's agenda, Porter (2002) similarly recommends that businesses in Canada: "(1) collaborate with competitors/government to create specialized infrastructure and education, (2) invest in cluster development, (3) serve sophisticated and global markets with demanding customers, and create unique products/ services, and (4) encourage local suppliers to meet global standards."

The Canadian government has explicitly stated that e-business is part of its innovation strategy (Innovation, 2001). Here we describe a model to guide governments in building infrastructure for a knowledge-based economy. Using specific Canadian initiatives, we will make an empirical case to illustrate the model that countries around the world can use to facilitate SME e-business adoption.

INFRASTRUCTURE MODEL FOR GOVERNMENT SUPPORT FOR E-BUSINESS READINESS

A major government role is the building and maintaining of infrastructure, be it for physical transportation, energy, waste and water, or information highways. Technological advances, and new emphases on particular values, have often made existing infrastructure inadequate. In some instances, connection of existing infrastructure components is a problem. In other cases, some core infrastructure pieces must be built from scratch. For the purpose of e-business enabling their SMEs, governments around the world must build support infrastructure. Since a significant percentage of economic growth in most countries comes from the small and medium-sized enterprise (SME) sector, it makes sense for governments to focus on creating relative advantage for these firms. In Canada, 60% of economic output comes from the SME sector, which is also responsible for 80% of national employment, and offers 85% of new jobs (INSEAD, 2002).

We need a working definition of the term infrastructure before we introduce the different areas of infrastructure that is essential to e-business. We adopted Slootweg and Verhoef's (1999) definition of infrastructure, and modified it to include assets such as workforce, and skills. In e-business, physical facilities include physical network backbones, databases, and hardware/software.

"An infrastructure is a large-scale technological system, consisting of physical facilities and knowledge assets, and delivering (an) essential public or private service(s) through the storage, conversion and/or transportation of certain commodities/ services. The infrastructure includes those parts and subsystems necessary for fulfilling the primary storage, transportation and/ or conversion function(s) as well as those supporting a proper execution of the primary function(s)."

A knowledge and innovation-based economy is the desired outcome of effectively building the following six components' infrastructures and processes. Each component has associated process inputs and outputs, as infrastructure is set up to support a particular flow (e.g., content, regulation, e-government service, communication, skill). We conceptualize dependencies in the model at a high-level in Figure 1. We refer the reader to Jutla et al. (2002) for details on the conceptual literature surrounding this model. We provide visibility in Canada's work in building each major infrastructure component, shown in the model in Figure 1, in the subsequent sections of this chapter.

1.   Communications and information systems infrastructure (A)
2.   Human infrastructure (B)
3.   Content infrastructure (C)
4.   Regulatory, trust, and financial infrastructure (D)
5.   e-Government infrastructure (E)
6.   Organizational infrastructure for knowledge and innovation (F)

    Some notes for reading and understanding the model shown in Figure 1:

a.   All infrastructure components (A, B, C, D, E, F) output (see broken lines) to the "create knowledge and innovation" process which then provides

Figure 1. A model for government support for e-business readiness in SMEs.

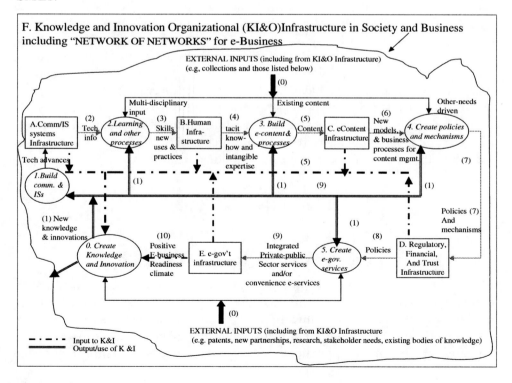

inputs (see double lines) to all other processes used to build the six infrastructure components.

b.   Each infrastructure component has complex processes inputting to it and accepting output from it. For simplicity, one aggregate process per infrastructure component is shown as input.

c.   The K&I organizational infrastructure (shown as the cloud) connects and "oils" the rest of the infrastructure components. Organizational and social science factors are often afterthoughts in technology diffusion processes. However, organizational infrastructure to support e-business diffusion needs to be built and woven into the fabric of society and business from the very beginning and governments can play an important role here.

d.   Information flows are labeled with numbers (1), (2), (3)…(10) in brackets.

e.   Processes are also numbered (0, 1, …5) without brackets.

   Common to all six models' infrastructure components are the profound effects that government policies and actions can have on each component in terms of creation and subsequently diffusion. Government efforts and programs that foster partnerships involving SMEs can help to ensure that this critical growth sector of the economy is not left behind in the digital economy.

   Although there appears to be a linear sequence among components in our proposed model, it is possible to have different orders and priorities of building infrastructure components; and it is recommended to build components in parallel whenever possible. The order we present in our model was the naturally occurring and logical ordering found in most government facilitation to date on e-business readiness. Indeed, organizational infrastructure often appeared quite late in most countries' e-government efforts, grafted on when change management in the workplace was identified as critical to success.

   For most countries, a model is useful to describe government's role in preparing SMEs to adopt e-business. A model can structure government efforts at developing an e-business readiness climate as well as efforts aimed at assessing the success of their concerted actions or initiatives.

INFORMATION AND COMMUNICATIONS INFRASTRUCTURE, CONNECTIVITY, AND USAGE

   Modern technologies and the access to those technologies in the areas of communications and information systems form the basis of all e-business readiness. Included in communications and information systems infrastructure are networking and computer hardware, underlying application software technologies for e-business applications, and the applications representing automated business processes. SMEs that create and commercialize evolutionary new technologies directly output innovations (see flow 1 shown as double lines).

Canada has made many advances in increasing the access of its citizens to communications and IT infrastructure. Indeed Canada's ICT sector's capital expenditures are dominated by the broadcasting and telecommunications services industry that include world-leading manufacturers of networking equipment, as well as deliverers of network services (Industry Canada, 2002). In the world connectedness index, Canada ranks second with respect to availability, third in price, and first in reach and use (Conference Board of Canada, 2002). According to the OECD (2001), the country is also second in the OECD in terms of broadband penetration. Com Score Metrix Canada and Nielsen Ratings report that approximately two-thirds of Internet home users in Canada are currently subscribing to broadband services in 2003. The Canadian figure is almost twice the broadband penetration of U.S. households. Current deployment of broadband infrastructure can support access from 80% of the population.

Results of the combined efforts of government and the private sector show that approximately 630,000 of Canada's one million businesses are now online. Small and medium enterprises employ six out of 10 working Canadians. The majority of Canadian businesses are very small. Ninety-seven percent (97%) of the one million Canadian businesses have less than 50 employees.

According to an electronic commerce and technology survey conducted in April 2002 (StatsCan, 2002), the informational and cultural industries have the largest usage (93%) and presence (65%) on the Internet while the retail sector shows the smallest uptake (65% access and 27% presence). Despite the low uptake in retail, the StatsCan survey found that the 2001 value of private sector e-commerce retail sales was ranked third at approximately $1.5 billion. Only manufacturing and wholesale trade outperformed the retail sector with $1.68 and $1.9 billion respectively. The ratio of B2B and B2C sales fell in line with the global 80-20 division. Approximately 55% of the SMEs answering the survey who did not engage in e-commerce said that their goods and services do not lend themselves to concluding transactions over the Internet. While uptake is good on email and informational marketing website applications, there is a marked lack of uptake on more sophisticated e-business applications such as customer relationship management and content management.

By March 1999, Canada had connected each school and public library to the Internet, under the SchoolNet (2002) and LibraryNet initiatives. Through the community access program (CAP, 2002), Canada connects 10,000 communities to the Internet. The VOLNet (2002) initiative connects an additional 10,000 voluntary organizations. Year 2001 data show that 65% of online Canadians use the Internet to search for information, 37% engage in e-commerce, while 29% use the Internet for work tasks (Industry Canada, 2002).

In 1998, Canada recognized that it may be creating a market dislocation problem in aggressively providing high connectivity to its citizens, and not simultaneously stimulating its private sector (Hull, 2000). This disparity led to more aggressive action on the part of the government to make SMEs aware of e-business potentials and practices. However, even after several years of government action, FF4 (2003) reports that more than a quarter (28%) of Canadians who engage in e-commerce do so in the USA. Perhaps, Canadian businesses still do not offer enough advantage to keep more citizens buying goods and services from them. The underlying sentiment is that great information and communications infrastructure is necessary but not sufficient for e-business success.

HUMAN INFRASTRUCTURE FOR SMEs

Knowledge skills in a workforce are an essential element to e-business readiness (Jutla et al., 2002; McConnell, 2001; International Development Center, 2001; EUScoreBoard, 2001). Despite the availability of electronic commerce services provision by Internet Service Providers (ISPs), many SMEs choose to develop and maintain web content in-house while the ISPs merely host the websites. FF4 (2003) reports that more than "20% of SMEs cannot find the skilled employees, they require to implement e-business." Specifically, there are not enough trained personnel with a hybridization of technical and business skills. Skills hybridization is important for SMEs to formulate sustainable e-business models, strategies, execution plans, and for successful implementations of the plans.

One of the more useful mechanisms for transferring knowledge and innovation to the SME sector is through distribution channels such as university business development centres and networks. These provide pertinent e-business development skills at very low cost to SMEs. Traditional services have included writing business plans, developing new products, and assisting with complex accounting and taxation issues. These centres and/or networks have existing client bases that they can directly influence and hence increase the rate of e-business adoption by SMEs.

The roles of associations extend to identifying exactly what labour skills are needed for the hosting country. For example, ITAC (the Information Technology Association of Canada), the Software Human Resource Council, and the Human Resource Development Corporation have identified a critical need for good labour market information. To further promote inclusion, IT associations often help place recent graduates from non-IT programs in internships in the IT industry.

Supporting Canada's 2001 Innovation Strategy is Industry Canada's Student Connections Program (SCP). Running out of provincial business service centers, community colleges, and university business centers, the SCP (http://www.scp-ebb.com) hires and trains post-secondary students and recent graduates from universities and community colleges as small business advisors. The SCP then matches the skills of these small business advisors with the requirements of individual Canadian employers from both SMEs and big business. Reportedly, since 1996, the SCP has trained more than 5,000 students to serve more than 132,000 clients. The SMEs benefit since they get work done for very small fees from these partially government-funded students. The students benefit by gaining job experience, and often their internships turn into full-time jobs at the employer SME. Although the Students Connection Program trains on a whole variety of business services, it has been responsive to the government's desire to e-business enable their SMEs, and currently offer face-to-face courses on Internet training, customized seniors Internet training, electronic commerce implementation, and electronic commerce strategy at beginner and advanced levels. Supplementary, free online course materials are also available. The SCP currently has six private and public sector sponsors, a telecommunications company (Bell Canada), a networking company (Cisco), an e-learning company (Vubiz), a wholly-owned bank of the Government of Canada (Business Development Bank of Canada — targeting specifically the SME market), the federal government electronic marketplace (SourceCan), and Industry Canada's ebizEnable site.

Another youth internship program is eCorps, dedicated to making smaller SMEs e-business ready. It differs from the SCP program in that interns earn fixed sums (Cdn. $9200.00) over a predetermined period (four months), working inside a host SME to complete an e-business project. The intern funding comes from Industry Canada. The SME contribute Cdn. $2500.00 towards program costs, and must have less than 80 employees to satisfy sizing criteria. To qualify for eCorps, the intern is between 19 and 30 years of age and a graduate who has earned a recent diploma or degree in an IT-related field. Interns create websites, deploy electronic accounting systems and databases, develop Intranets, implement transactional e-commerce capability, or implement security on transactional websites. The pilot eCorps program ran between Fall 2002 and Spring 2003 and placed 41 interns. Career Edge (www.careeredge.ca), the private-sector led, national not-for-profit company that manages the eCorps program reports that, "88% of the companies participating in eCorps improved their e-business capabilities by the by the end of the four month internships. Of the interns participating, 58% gained employment by the end of the pilot (Career Edge, 2003)."

Personnel in a majority of SMEs *learn* about — as opposed to creating — new technologies. They learn technologies and their impact to transform business processes, hybridize skill sets, and drive innovations (flow 3). In Figure 1, note that flow 3 goes to component B (human infrastructure) which then outputs to and acts as inputs (see broken arrows) to process 0 (create knowledge and innovation).

Larger SMEs have different skills requirements. According to FF4 (2003), "the skills gap in Canada is most severe in the core occupational disciplines of computer science, microelectronics design, photonics and wireless design, software design, and systems analysis." Thus, demand for skills is still high in overlaps of computer science (CS), management of information systems (MIS), and electronics and electrical engineering (EE) disciplines. Computer science and EE disciplines both offer courses on software design, microelectronics design, photonics, and wireless design. Systems analysis courses are taught in both computer science and management of information systems disciplines. These are the disciplines which tend to create skill sets to invent new technologies, techniques, and methods. Since teaching education is the mandate of provincial governments in Canada, provinces are being encouraged to provide extra support to these disciplines in community colleges and universities.

University research is mainly funded at the federal level through three councils, referred to as the Tri-Council. The Tri-Council is made up of the Natural Sciences and Engineering Research Council (NSERC), the Social Sciences and Humanities Research Council (SSHRC), and the Medical Research Council (MRC). Researchers apply to these three councils for individual, collaborative, and strategic research grants. The Canadian government has responded to the needs of larger SMEs by upping the budget of the NSERC body. Governments are supporting programs to create thousands of new spaces in college and university IT programs. Colleges and universities aid in skills development and extend the reach of certain skill development services through making them available through online learning and distance education. Online courses are rapidly becoming a commodity accessible to many employees of SMEs.

E-CONTENT

On increasing the sophistication of human infrastructure with the skills necessary to manage and execute new electronic processes, digitized content and processes to organize and manage the content becomes increasingly essential. SMEs require special mechanisms for content management. For example, what mechanism can be put in place to list an SME that sells Scottish kilts in the top three results of a web engine search? Data repositories, content for web pages, shop-fronts, and shopping cart icons are some examples of the output of process 2 (flow 5). Flow 5 in Figure 1 is simply labeled "content" but it includes new content, content models, and content management processes. Subsets of these content compilations are innovations in themselves, as are new patentable business and engineering processes (flow 5).

Digital collections for organized content focused on culture, science, geography, and so on can be found at http://collections.ic.gc.ca/. Most of the collections are created within a Youth Employment program where students aged 15-30 create the websites using content from Canadian museums, and other archives. Canada's original efforts at organizing content for SMEs are best found in the strategis (http://strategis.ic.gc.ca) website — a site that provides databases of information for trade, supply, export, legal research, business financing, patents, matches on private sector and university-based expertise to name just a few. These databases also power the www.CanadaInternational.ca site.

The March 2001 report (Ivis, 2001) from the SME e-Business Adoption Initiative sub-team streamed the top-level barriers inhibiting SME e-business adoption into four categories: information and education, costs and benefits, e-business resources, and security. According to the Ivis (2001), "SMEs not using the Internet cite ROI and cost as primary inhibitors, those using the Internet cite the lack of e-business strategy as the barrier, and those implementing transactional capability say that security is the barrier." Following a primary recommendation from this report, in October 2001, a "toolkit" was provided on the Canadian Strategis collection (EbizEnable, 2002). While the content on strategies is generic to all SMEs, a great deal of localization and syndication is still needed to enable the effectiveness of the toolkit throughout disparate regions in Canada. Toolkits are passive tools and their effectiveness is dubious. We next examine a far more active tool for e-business adoption in SMEs, that of the online marketplace.

A Model for SME Catalog Content

An online marketplace provides physical information technology infrastructure to support the buying and selling of goods online. The economies of scale from an online marketplace portal occur through amortization of infrastructure costs across all participants in the marketplace. Online marketplaces add value by facilitating the buy/sell transaction that includes the engage, order, and in some cases, the fulfill components of a typical customer interaction. In addition to support for online catalogs, secure transaction channels, multi-payment mechanisms, and multi-technology interfaces, an online marketplace can also support deployment of e-business applications such as customer relationship management (CRM) applications.

Online market facilitation of the buy/sell transaction takes two main forms: content aggregation and/or dynamic pricing support (Craig & Jutla, 2001). Content aggregation works for items with low cost but high purchase order transaction processing costs, for markets with many suppliers, and for items whose suppliers can be switched easily and cost-effectively. The creation of a common product catalog must be feasible. Support for SMEs in an online marketplace requires co-existence of business models. Some small business communities, such as FOB.com, are using reverse aggregation mechanisms that traditionally have favored buyers as opposed to sellers. First, the buying power of the small businesses is aggregated through the trading community which then makes one large buy from one or more distributors or suppliers. In this way, the small business benefits from distributor/supplier discounts for large volume purchases. Trading communities that use reverse auction mechanisms also favor the buyer, a particular need of small businesses. Examples of SME online marketplaces include allBusiness.com and BuyersZone.

The value of the online marketplace to government B2B e-procurement is well known. What has not been explored in the literature is the extension of the government's procurement infrastructure to provide a hands-on "model" for regional SMEs to learn and to get first-hand exposure to the e-business opportunities and applications. Such an extension can have a large impact on the e-business adoption in SMEs. Recall the barriers for SMEs to go online. Instead of the SME, the government would provide the secure channel over which e-business transactions could take place. The SME would not have to worry about crossing the security hurdle — the government portal would take care of that concern. The online marketplace incubator could provide a sandbox for SMEs plugged into the government's infrastructure to trade outside of the government, and garner experience before venturing out on their own. Calculations for return in investment for e-business applications would be more accurate due to the experience. Another benefit to the SME is its initial costs to go online are reduced.

SMEs will be encouraged to adopt e-business practices because the government online marketplace portal permits characteristics of innovation diffusion such as *observability, trialability, result demonstrability, and relative advantage* (Rogers, 1995). That is, the government could provide a "working" model of e-commerce applications to SMEs. The government may invite SME employees to attend hands-on demonstrations of the e-business technologies and applications in the marketplace. Thus, the SME employees would observe first-hand the infrastructure for going online. At the same time, the government may provide the SME the opportunity for a time-limited trial of using the government's infrastructure for the business' e-commerce transactions. The SMEs initial trial and costs will then exclude costs related to e-commerce technology infrastructure, such as technical infrastructure for online transactional capability.

We note that we are not minimizing the other costs the SME will incur in planning and executing online business process' automation, improvement, or reengineering. Also, we recognize the added SME costs in initial online catalog development, and human resources assigned to manage and service the online channel. However, we are stating that the government can provide a solution for increasing the important characteristics of innovation diffusion such as observability and trialability of the innovation. Result demonstrability may be shown by those SMEs who already are in the government's e-procurement marketplace. Further, relative advantage can be shown through statistics of the volume of transactions passing through the marketplace as well as through the network of SME managers represented in the marketplace.

A trial model of this magnitude is not without barriers and risk for the government. The first concern is, "can government really do this or will they be stepping on private sector toes?" Almost unanimously, the answer is the latter. However, the answer may be in the emphasis on the *incubator* piece of the proposed online marketplace concept. Governments have innovated through incubator means before. In Chile, government officials visited the most advanced aquaculture facilities around the world, brought back aquaculture technology to Chile, built a model of a working firm, and brought in businesses in aquaculture to see and learn for themselves. In a short time, the Chilean aquaculture industry was transformed and is known worldwide for its innovation. A more recent Chilean initiative develops an information system to support the integration of the Chilean aquaculture and fishery sector to the world market. It includes:

"(The technology platform) will allow a direct connection between suppliers, customers, service companies and R+D centers, so as to generate a virtual market in the aquaculture-fishery area. This market shall be promoted at the world level by a 'Portal web site' related to the area. The main characteristics of the platform are: to allow a direct communication between the different users through the multimedia, simulation of commercial processes in order to analyze the different scenarios, an interactive graphic interface between Platform and User, simplification of the commercial processes and standardization of processes and documents" (FONDEF, 2002).

Federal and provincial government initiatives currently fund many start-up business incubators in universities and business parks in Canadian provinces. As in the Chilean context, the Canadian government promotes partnerships with the private sector for economic development. The incubator model of the online marketplace for SMEs will be no different. However, in the current North American recession and investor disfavor in technology company stocks, some governments may take the driver's seat in economic development tied to information technology innovation, and find the appropriate private sector partners to increase e-business innovation uptake in SMEs.

Canada's Federal Online Marketplace

The Canadian government has initially chosen not to go the incubator route. In June 2001, the then Minister of Industry launched a service called SourceCAN billed as, "Canada's public and private sector e-marketplace, connecting Canadian businesses and their capabilities for the domestic and global e-marketplace and exposing opportunities through local and international e-business partnerships." Free access is provided to an up-to-date database of Canadian companies and their capabilities, business opportunities matching, posting, e-catalogues, and virtual trade shows. Five major feeds are input to the e-marketplace.

Federal and provincial government request for bids represent a major feed as the largest proportion of SME economic activity in Canada comes from servicing the government. The businesses that are marketplace members form another major feed into the e-market. Three major feeds come from the U.S. government. One feed provides general procurement information including sales of U.S. government property, procurement actions, and contract awards. Another U.S. feed is from the Trade Opportunity Program (TOP), a daily feed that lists all procurement opportunities with the U.S. government. The third U.S. feed is from the U.S. Department of Agriculture listing procurement opportunities in the U.S. agricultural sector.

Canadian businesses can display their catalogues free of charge in GE's Express Marketplace, a B2B digital marketplace that is administered by GE Global Exchange Services (GXS). However, SMEs do have to pay service charges to GE for selection, procurement, requirements, and transaction payment/billing (settling) services. According to a press release from GXS (2001), the Web-based GE Global eXchange Services' (GXS) Express Marketplace "supports SourceCAN by making supply chain services — such as reverse auctions, procurement workflow, purchase order status tracking, turning purchase orders into invoices, and tracking invoice payment status — available to SourceCAN member companies on a subscription and/or per-transaction basis." An online demonstration of the Express Marketplace can be found at https://www.gexmp.com/docs/en/demo1.html. Statistics on SME usage of SourceCan are not currently available.

One year after the SourceCAN release, in November 2002, the Canadian province of New Brunswick (NB) launched SourceNB — a syndicated, localized version of SourceCAN focusing on the Atlantic provinces (http://www.sourcenb.ca/E/press_nov20_02.cfm). With a higher profile than its parent, SourceNB lists requests for bids/tender from governments of several dozens of countries, including Australia, the Caribbean, Africa, Europe, Latin America, and Asia. Browsing the procurement requests, we find mainly postings from the U.S. and the smaller countries. Some countries post on these global lists when competition is required to depress the prices of high cost items. For example, the procurement listing for Trinidad and Tobago represents requests for proposals for ambulances, hearses, and prison vans — all highly customized, and high-priced items that are not easily available on the local Caribbean market.

REGULATORY, FINANCIAL, AND TRUST INFRASTRUCTURE

A positive e-business climate includes access to venture capital, incentivizing tax regimes, human performance rewards, and SME incentives for e-business practices. On a national level, SMEs are asking for leadership, consistency, and signs of commitment to policy, regardless of political party, from the local, provincial and federal governments who have a tendency to take different approaches to tax regulations, setting standards (e.g., security standards), and building infrastructure and systems.

E-business transactions that manipulate content (flow 6 in Figure 1) at first operated in the common regulatory framework of the day for business transactions. However, it is well known that the Internet, due to increased transparency, lack of borders, and enormous reach, creates a myriad of problems such as privacy, taxation, and jurisdictional conflicts. Thus, regulatory, trust, and financial infrastructure support for e-business is necessary for SMEs to break the online trust barriers to conduct e-business on any scale. Electronic processes, electronically stored data, and associated implications are examined by regulatory, financial, and trust bodies to create new policies or mechanisms (flow 7 in Figure 1) to facilitate SME conduct of e-business such as international trade.

Regulatory and Financial Infrastructure

Since the mid-nineties, the banking sector and third parties have responded to barrier issues such as expense of credit card processing fees and now offer inexpensive online credit card processing services to merchants. In 2003, the National Bank of Canada became the first bank to offer online recruitment assistance to SMEs. In partnership with Workopolis.com, and through its Internet Banking Solutions portal, National Bank gives its business customers job posting capability that is intended to reduce their SME customers cost-of-hire and time.

For many years, in comparison to its southern neighbor, the U.S., Canada's tax and regulatory structures were not as favorable for business. Comprehending the business and individual disadvantages to investing and staying in Canada, the government of Canada (GoC) created a five year Tax Reduction Plan in year 2000 which proposed the "largest tax cut in Canadian history". By mid-October 2000, the Canadian government had reduced the capital gains inclusion rate from 75% to 66% to 50%. The inclusion rate refers to that part of the capital gain that is subject to income tax. Recall that before the 2001 dot-com fallout, stock options were one of the largest incentives for e-business employees to join or stay with a company. The reduction in capital gains tax largely addressed making the Canadian business climate more competitive to retain talent. The lifetime limit for capital gains exemption was raised from quarter million to half a million for small business shares. There is no equivalent for this exemption in the U.S.

Other tax measures include average corporate tax to fall below the average U.S. corporate tax rate in 2003. In 2003, the previously 28% corporate tax rate has been cut to 25% and will fall to 21% in 2004. However, for small business, the reduced corporate tax rate at 21% was implemented almost immediately for income between Cdn. $200,000.00 and $300,000.00 in 2001. The 2003 tax year also brings reduction of the small business tax rate to 12%, applicable on the first $200,000.00 of qualifying income. The GoC proposes to increase the small business deduction limit from $200,000 to $300,000 over four years. The limit will be further increased in $25,000 increments over the next three years. By 2006 all qualifying income up to $300,000 is to be taxed at the 12% rate

In 2003, the Feds proposed a five-year phase out of the federal capital tax, mainly affecting larger corporations, starting in 2004. The GoC taxes the capital of all large corporations and financial institutions at federal and provincial levels. More than half of Canada's ten provinces levy a capital tax on financial and other corporations. Happily, for medium-sized businesses, the federal capital tax will be eliminated in a much shorter timeframe, entirely by 2004. Although Ontario leads the way in reducing provincial capital tax, many provinces still have to respond with similar legislation.

To encourage business to do research and development (R&D) and hence stimulate economic growth, tax legislation provides a 20% R&D tax credit in Canada for all R&D expenditures, not just incremental expenditures as currently existing in the U.S. For small Canadian-controlled business, an R&D refundable tax credit of 35% is available. Due to impending changes to regulations affecting limited partnerships and foreign investment, it will soon become more feasible for foreign institutional venture capitalists to invest directly in Canadian venture capital funds. The GoC is hoping to innovative SMEs that will then be able to attract more of the first, second, and third-round venture capital, often on their critical path to survival, by tapping into new funding sources.

Finally, intent on maintaining a "smart" and competitive regulatory environment in Canada, the GoC is not stopping at these tax measures. The 2003 Federal budget provides Cdn. $4 million to fund the work of the 2003 appointed chair of an External Advisory Committee on Smart Regulation. The Canadian federal plan is that, provided the U.S. tax legislation remains as is, by year 2006, Canadian corporate tax rate including capital taxes will be 5% lower than the U.S., and that the income tax rate will be 7.1% lower than in the U.S.

Regulatory and Trust Infrastructure for E-Business

Since 2001, Canada has used Entrust products (www.entrust.com) as part of its Secure Channel Initiative to provide security, specifically, public key infrastructure, for public services between government and SMEs, and government and individuals requiring secure information exchange such as tax filing, and checking employment records. More recently in 2003, other countries such as the UK government selected Entrust products to form the key infrastructure for its National Root certificate authority intended to support secure exchanges between government, citizens, and business. Canada also introduced an ePass certificate in late 2002 to allow users to communicate with various departments and agencies using a single authentication mechanism. Citizens that apply online for an ePass can currently use it to interact with the Canadian Customs and Revenue agency.

The Canadian government has been involved with other trust mechanisms for e-business. Evolving from the TrustInfo seal, the ChamberTrust B2B seal is a premier trust seal in use at the International Chambers of Commerce, the World Chamber of Commerce, the Paris Chamber of Commerce, and the British Columbia Chamber of Commerce in Canada. The seal is endorsed by the OECD, the government of Canada, SME chambers, and other key stakeholders in e-business among SMEs. The idea behind the security of the seal is the four-level check. In order for businesses to obtain the ChamberTrust seal, the business must be a member of a provincial government business registry, local chamber of commerce, a local bank, and must provide a contact person in the SME.

Canadian insurance companies are now designing insurance policies to cover e-business-related insurance concerns. SME coverage for "data and phone bandwidth interruption," and "data integrity insurance," and extended clauses on "good name" insurance to cater for website defamations and negative publicity from security attacks are being evaluated. Current progress can be viewed at http://www.insurance-canada.ca/ebusiness/ebusiness.php.

On the legislative front, Canada's Personal Information Protection and Electronic Documents Act (PIPEDA) came into effect in January 1, 2001. It recognizes the equivalence of electronic signatures and documents to their physical counterparts. It also legislates the privacy aspect of security for businesses and their customers. In 2001, the Act applied to only federally regulated organizations such as banks, airlines, broadcasting and telecommunications companies in all 10 provinces, yet applied to all businesses in Canada's three territories. In 2002, PIPEDA was extended to cover each individual's health information. By 2004, all Canadian businesses are expected to comply to PIPEDA or equivalent provincial regulations. Although Alberta and British Columbia have proposed equivalent privacy acts, they are not yet considered equivalent. Additionally, PIPEDA will govern all inter-provincial or international exchanges of PII in the course of a commercial activity.

In 2002, the European Union (EU) recognized Canadian privacy law equivalence to the EU 1995 Data Directive. The recognition allows the flow of PII between the EU and Canada. Canada's two privacy laws address the 4Ws: who can see individual PII, what process is the individual's PII undergoing, why is the PII being collected, and where is the PII being stored. Canadians have the right to access and correct their PII stored at any business and/or website. PIPEDA gives an individual some control over what information a website can collect from him/her and how his/her email address can be used, for instance. If an individual suspects that a business has used his/her PII inappropriately, a complaint can be lodged at the Office of the Privacy Commissioner.

The Office of the Privacy Commissioner was created in 1983 in Canada. That office investigates complaints but also comments on public policy or legislation that could impact individuals' rights to privacy. The Office provides a comprehensive website (www.privcom.gc.ca) that provides a guide to business responsibilities for consumers' privacy, a guide outlining individual privacy rights and what specifics are protected under PIPEDA, privacy rulings on privacy complaints that have come before the commission, links to significant privacy tools, opinions on current privacy issues, and annual reports with summary statistics on privacy issues since the Office's inception in 1983.

E-GOVERNMENT INFRASTRUCTURE

E-government services, similar to SME e-business services, build in parallel on the four preceding infrastructure components: (1) communication and information systems, (2) human, (3) content, and (4) regulatory, financial, and trust, and associated process flows. An example of flow 8 in Figure 1 would be a policy to avoid using cookies on a website.

The Canadian Government Online program which implement e-government services have a relatively small initial price tag of Cdn. 880 million dollars for years 2000-2005, augmented by individual departmental budgets. Clearly, this budget is in competent hands since in 2003, the private consulting firm, Accenture, ranked Canada's efforts in e-government as the best out of 23 leading countries because of maturity in service transformation. Accenture also ranked Canada as number 1 in two previous years studies. Canada has the largest percentage of citizen uptake of e-government services in the world, with continuing encouragement from their citizens for more online services. This statistic is very much unlike similar first-world countries such as the UK where citizen uptake is hovering in the single digit figures (Pinder, 2003).

Over and above providing specific e-government services, is the importance of the government's leadership role in creating model policy, business, and technical frameworks and processes, and in using Internet-based services effectively. Not only can SMEs and citizens view examples of best practices, but also they can leapfrog through their own innovative combinations of e-government services.

Leadership

Government plays a key leadership role in creating a networked society, giving e-business advantage to their SMEs, and providing a model with processes and procedures that can be adopted and adapted for use by many organizations, groups, communities, and individuals. Government is the largest employer in

Canada. Most of Canada's SMEs' commercial transactions are with government. In other words, governments will be leading exploiters and demonstrators of Internet-enabled opportunities.

SMEs can copy many of the best online practices from the Government Online program. For example, the Canadian government's Privacy Impact Assessments (PIAs) is a best practice policy where every government department and agency must do a detailed assessment of a service's potential impact on online privacy before the service can be offered online. The Office of the Privacy Commissioner receives the results of the PIA for approval. SMEs can similarly build privacy into their services from the ground up, and appoint an employee accountable for assurance.

Informational Services for SMEs and SME's Foreign Customers

Canada's Strategis website offers free access to a host of SME informational business resources from every government department across every tier of government. The Doing Business with Canada website provides foreign clients and potential investors with interactive tools to answer commonly asked questions related to trading with and investing in Canada. The site also is a marketing tool to promote Canada as a high-tech country, with a highly-trained technical workforce, and innovative e-businesses that offer real value and competitive advantage to foreign clients. This site integrates the services of ten federal departments (GoL, 2003). Another useful service for SMEs will be the Virtual Trade Commissioner intended to be a portal to international development business services. Services will be tailored to specific SME sectors and markets.

Provincial Online Services: Example from Nova Scotia

The online Business Registry is present in three of the 10 Canadian provinces: Nova Scotia, New Brunswick, and Ontario. The service is a joint federal (Customs Canada and Revenue Agency), provincial (Service Nova Scotia or Service New Brunswick, etc.), and external agency (Workers Compensation Board in the case of Nova Scotia) project. The business registry service allows business to renew annual registration, reserve a business name, register as a sole proprietor or partnership, register as a business name owned by a company, view and update general business and contact info, do a companies name search, register with the Workers Compensation Board, and do change of address with multiple departments online. An online registry of lobbyists is available. The Department of Motor Vehicle online services include paying for motor vehicle fines, parking tickets, and applying for special Move license for overweight/large vehicular loads. Businesses will apply, pay for, and renew licenses and permits from each provincial government department.

Nova Scotia's Online Property Registry (Property Online) provides graphical lot division, tagged with property assessment values in neighborhoods. There is even a service to provide historical and interesting information around place names. SMEs in the real estate sector can package these services for a more effective sales force.

Supporting the creation of human infrastructure, provincial departments of education are offering online student loan service and debt reduction of up to 40% on graduation. The statistics for Nova Scotia, an Atlantic province, show that 67% of student applicants used the online service (available at http://studentloans.ednet.ns.ca) in 2001, 85% in 2002, and to early July 2003, 90% of applicants were choosing the online route (NSGov, 2003). Advantages to students include no delays due to missing information, saves student personal information thus eliminating re-entering of information on future applications. According to NSGov (2003), the Nova Scotia's Department of Education receives approximately 21,000 applications each year.

Services for Business Integration to Produce Innovation

SMEs can incorporate e-government services to create new higher value aggregate services — a bouquet concept. A service example (see flow 9 in Figure 1) would be an SME travel company offering a seamless experience in providing the airline booking service, complete with fast online checks for the traveler's passport expiry dates, online application for new passports, and checks with the department of health for what vaccinations are required to travel to a particular country (Regio, 2002). Furthermore, it is imaginable that the travel company can go online and acquire appropriate licenses (e.g., hunting/fishing licenses), U-pick reservations for strawberry or cherry picking (from the Department of Agriculture and Fisheries), or book Bob's Harbour Cruise (from Tourism, Nova Scotia) months before its client ever leaves home. Weather forecasts and maritime advisory alerts, or tide and water-level predictions (from Fisheries and Oceans Canada) can be pushed to devices on pleasure craft vessels, or received by email a few days or at any specified time(s) before a trip. The SME travel agency could "wrap" these individual services from the government in a neat service bundle for the consumer.

Other imaginative services can be created on top of e-government offerings. According to GOL (2003), the GOL initiative will "include over 130 services from 30 federal departments and agencies by 2005." Many of these services will be integrated. It is up to the innovative SMEs to create aggregate services by incorporating them in their own unique products and services.

ORGANIZATIONAL INFRASTRUCTURE FOR KNOWLEDGE AND INNOVATION

Recognizing changing organizational structures, and needing to manage the modernization of jobs in the public service workforce as programs such as Government Online proceed, the Canadian government created an Organizational Readiness Office (ORO). The ORO is under the Chief Information Officer Branch of the Treasury Board of Canada Secretariat.   The ORO establishes governance structures to oversee support for information management, information technology, and service management communities. It also develops community work plans, and research and demographic-analysis capacity for knowledge sharing networks or communities of practice. According to the ORO's website (www.cio-dpi.gc.ca/oro-bgc/index_e.asp), "the ORO is also being recognized as a center of excellence in nurturing informal workplace learning and knowledge sharing networks."

The introduction of Internet technologies and e-business practices affects the organizational infrastructure of SMEs also in terms of job modernization and organization within the firm. But unlike government departments, which are used to interfacing with a large number of stakeholder networks, SMEs now must extend organizational structure to include interfacing with larger numbers of networks. Organizational infrastructure is depicted as component F in Figure 1.

Extending Organizational Structure in the SME

The internal organizational structure of SMEs is often inefficient, particularly in very small SMEs or micro-businesses which employ less than five employees. Many SME owners and their employees assume multiple roles. An SME employee can be all of marketer, salesperson, quality assurance manager, fundraiser, accountant, and technician in any given day. Many SME owners report being too busy trying to survive and deal with existing daily operations to find time to read about e-business opportunities and strategies. It is no wonder that SMEs tend to have little research capacity of their own. In such an environment, partnering to aggregate and align capabilities, capacities, and resources in many areas of business becomes important for commercial growth and sustainability. The latter is true for larger SMEs, as well, in terms of creating maximum value for shareholders and customers. Numerous research articles in Etzkowitz and Leydesdorf (1997) document the importance of the third role of universities (aside from teaching and research), that of industrial participation, for transfer of knowledge and innovation to SMEs.

Although strengthening linkages between university and industry will increase innovation transfer, interlocking and necessary factors for creation of innovation include shared vision, leadership, management skills, availability of funding, and a high degree of partnerships to name a few. Government has a role to play in creating the infrastructure (communication and human), often referred to as innovation networks, for such partnerships. Imaginably, the most complex innovation network would be a network of many existing networks. Conceptually such an innovation network could connect the SME association networks into government policy-making networks, public research sector networks, SME insurance brokers networks, technical developer networks, human resource networks, provincial and federal government agencies, law and computer science institutes, local boards of trade, government and university-managed business development centres, community colleges, private sector, individual SMEs, and so on. The EU programme entitled "innovation and participation of SMEs," launched in 1999, aims to "stimulate, disseminate, and exploit the results of research, in particular for the benefits of SMEs." It is under the umbrella of the Fifth Framework programme (coordinating body) and complements other specific 5th Framework programmes and coordinates schemes such as CRAFT, with its own distinctive initiatives. CRAFTis a program wherein SMEs can outsource co-operative research to university institutions. The overall aim is "to improve the economic and social impact of research, by ensuring better dissemination and exploitation of its results, and encouraging the transfer and dissemination of technologies" (CORDIS, 1998).

Furthermore, many researchers (e.g., Cohen & Levinthal, 1989; Fountain, 1998; Cossentino, 1996) show the importance of social capital to an SME's ability to innovate and to its eventual success. Social capital is created in a rich partnership model. Social capital involves tangible assets of goodwill, fellowship, sympathy, and social intercourse (Hanifan, 1920), and social relationships to promote or aid in the development of valued skills and characteristics (Loury, 1977).

Opening communication channels across partnership boundaries often causes acquisition of new skills by participating professionals. It also costs in terms of participating employees' time to manage and service the channels. According to Cooke (1999), "communicating across firm and cultural boundaries (as within a rich partnership network) is a profoundly social, interactive process where great care, attentiveness, and patience must be developed." It is an area where government and universities with a history of facilitation, partnership, and slow, careful decision-making have experience. SMEs can benefit from these and build their internal organizational structure with associated personnel responsibility and accountability for ensuring positive social capital in their networks.

In Canada, government strategies are pioneering a second generation of knowledge management infrastructure to support SMEs' economic goals. One example of the emphasis on KM is the Nova Scotian acquisition of a proprietary Google engine service, renamed "Ask Joe Howe," which was first deployed at a provincial level. This simple, yet highly effective, search service virtually created a provincial innovation network of easily located human contacts and connected previously unlinked data stores across the province of Nova Scotia. The technological service filled many structural holes in Nova Scotia's previously weakly-linked innovation networks. In addition, the Department of Services Nova Scotia and Municipal Relations (SNSMR) now possesses and uses the capability to customize government content, keywords, and to train the search engine based on questions that citizens type.

Following on the heels of the provincial success, the e-Director of SNSMR loaned personnel resources out to a rural municipality for a day to participate in the re-deployment of the proprietary Google search engine service at a local library in a rural community. That deployment supported the creation of a "Business Room" in the local library where local citizens could find many online and offline resources to business questions they may have. In mere hours, citizen search access over multiple municipal and localized business-related archives, as well as over provincial and federal business resources, such as the http://strategis.ic.gc.ca/ebizenable and www.businessgateway.ca sites, became feasible.

Behind the scenes, the Canadian government has enabled a network of government departments and agencies that service SMEs to coordinate and exchange research projects, experiences, and programs as an initiative under its "e-Business Growth Strategy." Outreach programs to the SME community are ongoing in the government's communications effort to get the message about e-business practices out. In 2000 and 2001, agencies of Industry Canada conducted dozens of workshops and seminars on e-commerce for the SMEs across Canada. To complement the public sector activities, a Canadian e-Business Opportunities Roundtable (eTeam, 2002) comprising of mainly private sector representatives was formed in mid-1999 to "accelerate Canada's leadership in the digital economy." Six subteams led by Roundtable members form the e-Team Canada umbrella. In 2002, the Roundtable disbanded and another public sector initiative called the Canadian e-Business Initiative was born (www.cebi.ca), with many of the same members from the previous Roundtable.

Impact of E-Business Technologies on Jobs

Coded in e-business applications today are best practices in non-core business processes. Noticeable in these applications is the split in functional service provision between the front and back office activities. Front office applications are mainly those related to customer touch points such as customer relationship management applications that encompass customer engagement, order, delivery, and service functions. Back office applications host service logic and data management tasks. Some examples of these applications are database managers, inventory managers, warehouse managers, and accounting reporters.

For efficiency purposes, the functional split between front and back office for service provision purposes requires re-assignment of job tasks among SME personnel.

Accompanying the introduction of new technologies are new processes designed for facilitating information and knowledge capture, and the subsequent dissemination, and use of the knowledge. Another requirement will be the training of employees on the organizational requirements of e-business applications. One example of such an organizational requirement is privacy. Many IT applications such as customer relationship management tailored for SMEs are not yet privacy-aware. SME employees must be aware. Identified in a May 2003 publication (FF4) is the statistic that more than 80% of SME owners did not know that their business must be compliant to the PIPEDA (Protection of Personal Information and Electronic Documents Act) by January 1, 2004.

Job re-organization highlights the opportunities for both internal and external collaboration between people and groups with technology. Technologies, such as knowledge-management software, easily make *information* and, not so easily, *knowledge* available. Collaborations profit since information is quickly accessible and available.

An issue for job redesign for external collaborative work is the management of partnering activities. For example, a joint project may require funding approvals from Partner A and from Partner B in order for the activity to proceed, or move into a specific phase of development. Partner businesses have the opportunity to combine the two approval processes since a simple electronic conversion of the requirement to have two approvals provides no efficiency gain. That is, it is not always the best practice to make old processes the same in an electronic context. This means that organizational relationships and structures sometimes change as a part of partner-integrated process redesign.

Job descriptions not only include task description, but employers are now writing in employees' requirements to use information technology to carry out tasks. A further change to job descriptions is that contract, project, and program management skills are being increasingly required of SMEs to maximize opportunities for government support when adopting e-business practices. Businesses in distressed communities often partner with regional development offices to articulate strategies and apply for funding to realize opportunities. Sharing ideas, planning, and writing proposals to get IT-innovation strategies funded are becoming *de rigueur*.

SUMMARY

Legacies of greatly improved delivery of services, positive economic development, and quality of life and the environment are among the key events for which we remember government leaders. Indeed, government's role in moving countries to the future knowledge-based economies has never been more significant (World Economic Forum, 2002; Jutla et al., 2002a). Collectively, government agencies are a country's largest providers of services, and can be either or both impediments or catalysts to innovation. For most countries, a model is useful in describing government's role and in structuring government's efforts in preparing SMEs to adopt e-business. The Canadian illustration of such a model, as presented in this chapter, highlights some of the catalysts as well as the problematic areas in building infrastructure for a knowledge and innovation-based economy.

ICT infrastructure is often the easiest to build although 100% rural broadband penetration and appropriate technology applications usage, even in first world countries, are not yet evident. In contrast, practitioners often cite *organizational infrastructure*, particularly the governance structure pieces, as the hardest infrastructure component to build. Not surprising since humans are far more complex than computers. It is far easier to make two or more computers talk to each other with appropriate protocols, than it is for two or more humans to interact seamlessly. Because of the complexities behind organizational infrastructure, it is the component that is often most underdeveloped. It is also often the infrastructure component responsible for the demise of much work on the other pieces of the infrastructure. Governments all over the world need to do much more work in building and prioritizing this component.

Most countries put large efforts into building human infrastructure but for many the challenges of mobility and brain-drain are ever present, thus retention mechanisms in terms of incentives such as environment and quality of life become important. In the future, governments need to take advantage of the mobility of an essential infrastructure element, and temporarily place skilled government workers in the communities that can most take advantage of their skills, at that snapshot of time, to advance knowledge and innovation agendas. Involvement of multiple communities in creating localized e-content with possibly thematic connections will become increasingly important. Regulatory, trust, and financial infrastructure will continue to morph as countries compete internationally to raise GDP.

Although our model may be applicable to many, countries must start from different places when creating strategies for e-business enabling their SMEs. For example, the European Union has millions of SMEs in an area far smaller than the size of Canada. In contrast, Canada hosts one million businesses in total, with well under 50,000 of those in the four provinces in Atlantic Canada. Thus, one reason that some countries' strategies will differ will be due to disparities in spatial and temporal scales. One size does not fit all. Certainly, maturation of infrastructure is a moving target. Accenture (2003) puts Canada's e-government efforts at the 60% maturation level. The maturation level of Canada's internal information and communications infrastructure is higher than that. Up to now, the maturation levels for the other infrastructure pieces have not been measured and benchmarked. However, we know that these pieces are important and instrumental to electronically networked societies. Moreover, we expect that different component infrastructures will mature at different rates and to different levels. What we have not come up with yet is the formula as to what extent each infrastructure piece must be built within any one country in order to for SMEs to achieve the economic potential of e-business. The way forward will include understanding the experiences of many diverse nations as these countries build infrastructure to support SME adoption of e-business, and absorbing the subsequent learning from best practices, models and frameworks that may evolve over time. Government visionaries will continue building their knowledge assets until success measures show a positive correlation between SME uptake of e-business and knowledge and innovation output.

REFERENCES

Accenture. (2001). Rhetoric vs. reality — closing the gap. *Second Annual Survey of e-government*. Retrieved February 2002 from the World Wide Web: http://www.accenture.com/xd/xd.asp?it=enWeb&xd=Industries%5CGovernment%5Cgove_study.xml.

Accenture. (2003, April). E-government leadership — realizing the vision. *The eGovernment Executive Series*. Retrieved July 2003 from the World Wide Web: www.accenture.com.

CAP. (2002). *Community access program: Connecting Canadians*. Retrieved January 2002 from the World Wide Web: http://cap.ic.gc.ca/english/5000.shtml.

Career Edge. (2003). *The eCorps program – backgrounder*. Media Release. Retrieved June 2003 from the World Wide Web: www.careeredge.ca.

Cohen, W. & Levinthal, D. (1999). Innovation and learning: The two faces of R&D. *The Economic Journal, 99*, 569-596.

Conference Board of Canada. (2002). *Pursuing excellence through connectedness: Canada's quest for global best,* June 2002. Retrieved July 2003 from the World Wide Web: http://www.conferenceboard.ca/pdfs/351-02Briefing.pdf.

Cooke P. (1999). Small firms, social capital, and the enhancement of business performance through innovation programs. *Small Business Economics*, 13(3), 219-234.

CORDIS. (1998). Introducing the "Innovation and participation of SMEs" programme—The key to making the most of the Fifth Framework Programme." *European CORDIS Database*, June 9, 1998.

Cossentino, F., Pyke, F. & Sengenberger, W. (1996). Local and Regional Response to Global Pressure: The Case Study of Italy and Its Industrial Districts. *International Institute for Labour Studies*.

Craig, J. & Jutla, D. (2001). *e-Business Readiness: A Customer Focused Framework*. Boston, MA: Addison Wesley.

EbizEnable. (2002). *SME e-business Information Toolkit*. Retrieved January 2002 from the World Wide Web: http://strategis.gc.ca/SSG/ee00240e.html and http://strategis.gc.ca/sc_indps/ebiz/engdoc/homepage.php.

ETeam. (2002). *Electronic commerce in Canada*. Retrieved January 2002 from the World Wide Web: http://e-com.ic.gc.ca/eteam/mission.html.

Etzkowitz, H. & Leydesdorf, L. (eds.). (1997). *Universities and the Global Knowledge Economy, A Triple Helix of University-Industry-government Relations*.

EUScoreboard. (2001). *The European innovation scoreboard:* October 2001. Retrieved December 2001 from the WWW: http://www.cordis.lu/innovation-smes/scoreboard/.

FF4. (2003). Fast Forward 4.0: Growing Canada's digital economy, A publication of the *Canadian e-Business Initiative*, May 2003, Retrieved July 2003 from the World Wide Web: http://www.cebi.ca/Public/Team1/Docs/ff4.pdf.

Fountain. (1998). Social capital: A key enabler of innovation. In L. Branscomb & J. Keller (Eds.), *Investing in Innovation*. (pp. 85-111). Cambridge, MA: MIT Press.

Germany. (2000). Benchmarking industry science relationships. A publication of the *Federal Ministry of Education and Research, and the OECD*, Berlin, October 16-17, 2000.

GoL. (2002). *Government on-line: Serving Canadians better*. Retrieved February 2002 from the World Wide Web: http://www.gol-ged.gc.ca/index_e.asp.

GoL. (2003). *Government on-line 2003*. Retrieved June 2003 from the World Wide Web: www.tbs-sct.gc.ca/report/gol-ged/2003/.

GXS. (2001). *GE Global eXchange Services Selected by SourceCAN to Provide Web-based Electronic Commerce Services*. Retrieved from the World Wide Web: http://www.gxs.com/gxs/press/release/20010627.

Hanifan, L. (1920). *The Community Center*. Boston, MA: Silver, Burdette.

Hosmer, L.T. (1995). Trust: The connecting link between organizational theory and philosophical ethics. *Academy of Management Review*, 20, 379-403.

Hull, D. (2000). Connecting Canadians: an agenda for the knowledge economy and society, *Information Highway Applications Branch of Industry Canada*. Presentation at the Distinguished Lecture Series, Dalhousie University, Halifax, Nova Scotia, February 24, 2000.

IEI. (2000). *Information economy initiative*. Retrieved February 2002 from the World Wide Web: www.gov.ns.ca/govt/accountability/tssaccrpt01.pdf.

IFIP84. (2002). *Call for papers - Seeking success in e-business: A multi-disciplinary approach*. Retrieved February 2002 from the World Wide Web: http://www.ifip2002.cbs.dk/.

Industry Canada. (2002, July). Key Indicators on ICT Infrastructure, Use and Content: July 2002. *Spectrum, Information Technologies and Telecom-*

munications Sector, Industry Canada. Retrieved January 2003 from the World Wide Web: http://sitt.ic.gc.ca.

INSEAD. (2002, November). *International e-Economy Benchmarking Report*.

International Development Center. (2001). *Harvard University: International Development Center e-readiness guide*. Retrieved January 2002 from the World Wide Web: http://www.readinessguide.org.

Ivis, M. (2002). Analysis of barriers impeding e-Business adoption among Canadian SMEs. *Canadian e-Business Opportunities Round Table Report*, March 2001.

Jutla, D. N, Bodorik P. & Dhaliwal, J. (2002). Supporting the e-business readiness of small and medium sized enterprises: Approaches & metrics. *Internet Research Journal: Electronic Networking Applications and Policy,* 12(2), 139-164.

Lefebvre, E. & Lefebvre, L.A. (2000). SMEs, exports, and job creation: A firm level analysis. *CIRANO and Polytechnique de Montreal,* December 15, 2000.

McConnell, (2001). *Ready? Net. Go! Partnerships leading the global economy,* May 2001. Retrieved on December 2001 from the World Wide Web: www.mcconellinternational.com.

Novakovic & Sturn (2000). *Start-up on campus – European models for the stimulation of academic spin-offs*. Retrieved June 2001 from the World Wide Web: http://www.tig.or.at/bilder/45.doc

NSGov. (2003). *Nova Scotians get the Fastest Online Student Loan Service*, Media Release, July 3, 2003. Retrieved July 2003 from the World Wide Web: http://www.gov.ns.ca/news/details.asp?id=20030704005.

OECD. (2001, October). The development of Broadband Access in OECD countries.

Pinder, A. (2003). Keynote address. *16th BLED International Conference on Electronic Commerce*, (June 9-12), Slovenia.

Porter, M. (2002). The Global competitiveness report 2001-2002. *World Economic Forum*, Oxford.

Regio, M. (2002). Government Virtual Services Network. e-Government Mini-track, *Hawaii 35th Annual International Conference on Systems Science*, Hawaii, (January 7-10, 9 pages).

SchoolNet. (2000). *SchoolNet's On-line Connectivity Survey: Final Report.* Retried May 2001 from the World Wide Web: http://www.schoolnet.ca/home/e/Research_Papers/Research/SchoolNet_Research/Final_Survey_Report_2000(English).htm.

Slootweg, J. & Verhoef, E. (1999). Infrastructure Definition. In *Interfaculty research center for design and management of infrastructures*, Delft University of Technology. Retrieved May 2003 from the World Wide Web: http://www.infrastructures.tudelft.nl/infradef.html.

StatsCan. (1996). Statistics Canada Labour Force Report, *1996 Census*. Retrieved January 2002 from the World Wide Web: http://www.statcan.ca/english/Pgdb/People/Labour/labour45a.htm.

VolNet. (2002). *Connecting voluntary organizations to the Internet*. Retrieved January 2002 from the World Wide Web: http://www.volnet.org/.

Chapter III

Helping SMEs to Engage in Electronic Commerce:
The Dutch Way

Maria-Eugenia Iacob, Telematica Instituut, The Netherlands

Piet Boekhoudt, Telematica Instituut, The Netherlands

Freek Ebeling, Telematica Instituut, The Netherlands

ABSTRACT

In this chapter we present an overview of the approach taken by the Dutch government regarding the development of the information society and in particular the diffusion of electronic commerce in small and medium organisations. Our analysis also includes an assessment of the current situation of SMEs with respect to the adoption of electronic commerce and their position with respect to the governmental policies. Furthermore, we refer to active policy implementation instruments ("iMPact" and "ASPect" projects). Finally, the last part of the chapter is devoted to a benchmarking of European e-business policies, so that meaningful comparison of the Dutch initiatives with other similar programs could be achieved.

INTRODUCTION

Dutch small and medium enterprises are one of The Netherlands main strengths and one of the most important sources of wealth creation and employment. No less than 99% of private enterprise in The Netherlands consists of medium and small-scale businesses. They provide employment for 2.3 million people (60% of the Dutch labour force) and account for 52% of the national income generated in the private sector (http://www.mkb.nl/mkbnederland/english.shtml).

SMEs are potentially in a position to grasp the opportunities offered by electronic commerce. In some cases this is not a matter of choice but a way of coping with competition. For many, electronic commerce is synonymous with having an online storefront. However, electronic commerce in its broadest form entails a whole chain of business processes (product presentation, ordering service, delivery payment, after-sales services), in which the integration between the front office (website) and the back office (internal business and production processes) plays an essential role. E-commerce can be very attractive for many SMEs not only because it facilitates potentially more commercial transactions, but also because it makes them more efficient and connected with the internal needs of the organisation, thus allowing significant decreases in costs. Yet, the SMEs seem to be reluctant in embracing it for several identifiable reasons. Among them are:

- the cost and access to expertise and technical skills,
- the concerns related to Internet security and legislation risks,
- the fear for an open competition with larger and more powerful companies,
- the cost of change and adaptation of the business processes, and
- the lack of awareness of the possible benefits from using the Internet as a base for business transactions.

These factors are the most significant perceived obstacles in the rapid and broad adoption of electronic marketplaces by the Dutch SMEs.

Today, the unused potential for SMEs not adopting electronic commerce is huge, although this varies by industry, size and segment of the diverse SMEs. Therefore, enabling the SMEs to engage in the digital economy is one of the key priorities of the Dutch government. This line of thinking is promoted through an important initiative: the "Nederland gaat digitaal" (The Netherlands go digital) program (http://www.nederlandgaatdigitaal.nl).

In this chapter we try to give, from a Dutch perspective, some answers to the main questions raised by this book. More precisely, the first section will provide the reader with information regarding the policies of the Dutch government for the development of the information society and in particular for the diffusion of electronic commerce in small and medium organisations.

The second section is devoted to SMEs. It presents their current situation with respect to the adoption of electronic commerce and their position with respect to the governmental policies.

In the third section we present the objectives, approach and outcomes of "iMPact" and "ASPect" projects (developed within Telematica Instituut[1]). As parts of the program "SME in the digital Delta," they are defined as active implementation instruments of the Dutch governmental policies. One of their main targets is to help branch organisations and their members to get a grasp on the use of electronic marketplaces and application service providing.

Finally, the last part of this chapter is concerned with a benchmarking of European e-business policies, so that meaningful comparison of the Dutch initiatives with other similar programs could be achieved.

PLACE OF SME IN THE ICT POLICY IN THE NETHERLANDS
Policies and Governmental Initiatives

"Nederland gaat digitaal" (The Netherlands go digital) is the central slogan of a broad campaign the Dutch government started in 2000 with the intention to modernise and change many aspects of the Dutch society. The idea of this campaign was to proactively stimulate the use of ICT in all the layers of the Dutch society: by the ordinary citizen, by the government, in education and healthcare or by companies. The main actors behind this large-scale, ambitious program were five ministries (Economic Affaires; Education, Culture and Sciences; Justice; Transport, Public Works and Water Management; and Interior Affairs). None of these ministries was accidentally participating in the program. Their coordinating and financing role was directed toward specific targets that fall in their areas of responsibility:

- The Ministry of Interior Affairs is taking care of the diffusion of ICT in the relationship between the citizen and the state, and in society in general. For instance, the city halls of the big cities receive support in opening digital offices and in providing services for citizens online, as well.
- The Ministry of Justice is coordinating the development of a legal frame-work that will regulate the use of the Internet for communication and business activities (including e-commerce).
- Plans were also made for the development of a solid electronic communication infrastructure under the supervision of the Ministry of Transport, Public Works and Water Management.
- The Ministry of Education, Culture and Sciences is coordinating the diffusion of ICT in the educational system.

- The Ministry of Economic Affairs has developed together with a number of organizations - ECP.NL — Electronic Commerce Platform Netherlands, Syntens[2], MKB[3] Nederland[4], and industrial branch organizations — its own SME campaign "Nederland gaat digitaal," aiming to enhance the involvement of SMEs in electronic commerce activities. At the time this program started almost half of the SMEs were not even connected to the Internet, and therefore they became the primary target of this campaign. The campaign was publicised via radio and television and advertised in the newspapers. Syntens offered workshops and free consultations to SMEs interested in finding out how they could benefit from the Internet and electronic commerce. Further on, MKB Nederland and Syntens have defined several separate "Nederland gaat digitaal" branch programs. These were meant to support the industrial branch organisations to develop strategies with respect to ICT, such that these, in turn, can inform and advise their members accordingly. Also various free informative brochures and booklets (and websites) were published and spread among SMEs. This campaign was planned to be finished by the end of 2001.

During 2001, the Ministry of Economic Affairs collected information from Syntens, MKB Nederland and other sources showing that there exists a great interest from small and medium organisation for more concrete support and for a continuation of the program. It has resulted in making 71% of the SMEs aware of the program and of its goals (see Ministerie van Economische Zaken, 2001). Consequently, the Ministry of Economic Affairs decided to step into the second phase of "Nederland gaat digitaal." This decision was supported by figures obtained from an NIPO survey (see Table 1) carried out in the first quarter of 2001 (see Ministerie van Economische Zaken, 2001 and NIPO, 2001):

The new program for 2002-2005 is called, "The SMEs in the Digital Delta" ("Het MKB in De Digitale Delta," see Ministerie van Economische Zaken, 2001). This time, the target group was clearly identified as being companies with less than 100 employees and the goals were very concrete: in the end of the

Table 1. NIPO half-way evaluation.

Category	4-th quarter 1999 (before the start of "Nederland gaat digitaal")	1-st quarter 2001 (half way evaluation)
Percentage of SMEs with internet connection	55%	68%
Percentage of SMEs that perform transactions online	18%	36%

program two-thirds of the SMEs should be present on the Internet with at least a "shop window" website and two-thirds of the SMEs should be doing business transactions via the Internet. Invested in this program were 22.7 million EUR. The plan (see Ministerie van Economische Zaken, 2001) identifies three obstacles that stand in the way to these targets: SMEs do not know what business opportunities the Internet can offer, they don't have in-house ICT expertise and knowledge, they don't trust the Internet (legally and technologically), and often they are not financially able to support innovation, and that includes ICT innovation. The approach taken by this new program is dealing only with the first two of the aforementioned problems and in short is the following:

1.   To increase the awareness of SMEs related to ICT opportunities and to provide them with tailored knowledge, an intensification of the former MKB campaign "Nederland gaat digitaal" is planned. Namely, supplementary founding is directed towards workshops, consultancy, information materials, training and support of branch organisations and of their members and development of pilot projects for a number of sectors. For this purpose several projects will be continued or started under the coordination of Syntens, MKB-Nederland and other organisations. A special emphasis is put on two projects, iMPact and ASPect, that are producing (tailored) knowledge, branch pilots and training concerning two areas: electronic marketplaces and application service providing.

2.   With respect to the enhancement of trust, the following activities were planned:

•   It was recognised by the program that the government must play an active role in the development of the legal framework for e-commerce. Therefore, a number of bills that implement European directives must be presented to and discussed in the Parliament (also with the contribution of the Ministry of Economic Affairs). Some of them are mentioned in the following paragraph.

•   ECP.NL and Syntens were appointed to supply an SME version of a Code of Conduct when transacting online. This document (also available as a website) is now available for SMEs (publication date September 27, 2002).

•   The reliability of the communication infrastructure falls into another national program (NACOTEL) coordinated by the Ministry of Transport, Public Works and Water Management.

•   The campaign "Internet and Security" will be initiated to inform the users about the risks and available solutions regarding the security of information exchange over the Internet.

Legal Support and Self-Regulation for Electronic Commerce in The Netherlands

One of the factors that have slowed down the expansion of electronic commerce is the lack of completely adequate national and international electronic commerce legislation. Many countries have recognised the need for such legislation and are striving to enact it as soon as possible. The Netherlands is no exception: efforts are being made for implementing the EU directives and thus for further strengthening the national legal framework. However, the Dutch legislation can support electronic transactions within acceptable limits. This has been confirmed also by The Ministry of Justice in 1998 in its white paper on "Legislation for the Electronic Highway" (see Lower House of Dutch Parliament, 1998). More precisely, several important regulations explicitly referring to the Internet and electronic commerce are already operational and a number of bills are currently being discussed in the Parliament. We will briefly summarise them in what follows:

- The European "Distance Selling Directive" (97/7/EC) was implemented in the Dutch legislation in the form of the Distance Sales Act (dated December 21, 2000, see Staatsblad, 2000, December).
- The new Personal Data Protection Act (dated July 6, 2000, Staatsblad, 2000, July) serves to implement the European Privacy Directives (95/46/EC and 97/66/EC).
- With respect to intellectual property rights, the Act Regarding the Legal Protection of Databanks, (dated July 8, 1999, Staatsblad, 1999) implements the EU Directive 96/9/EC.
- The Electronic Commerce Bill (Lower House of Dutch Parliament, 2001-2) is intended to implement the Electronic Commerce Directive 2000/31/EC.
- Bill with respect to Electronic Money (see Lower House of Dutch Parliament, 2001-1) is intended to implement the Directive 2000/46/EC on the pursuit of and prudential supervision of the business of electronic money institutions.
- Bill with respect to the Electronic Signature (see Lower House of Dutch Parliament (2000)) is intended to implement the Directive 1999/93/EC on a Community Framework for Electronic Signatures.

Apart from legislation, an important role in electronic commerce is reserved for self-regulation. The lack of a comprehensive national (as well as international) legislation on one hand, and the extremely dynamic evolution of electronic commerce on the other hand have created the need for an instrument that can be immediately used (without waiting for years of parliamentary debates) as a regulatory framework in business relationships over the Internet. Thus, self-regulation became a supplement to the existing legislation, and a temporary substitute where this is missing. Basically, self-regulation assumes that companies conducting business on the Internet adhere to and act according to a set of rules that form a Code of Conduct. The task of defining and disseminating such a Code of Conduct was carried out in The Netherlands by a non-profit organisation: The Electronic Commerce Platform Netherlands (ECP.NL). ECP.NL was founded in January 1998 with support of the Dutch Ministry of Economic Affairs and the Dutch employers Association, and brings together trade and industry, government, intermediary organizations, and education and research institutes. ECP.NL is also the representative of The Netherlands in international commissions of the UN, the EU and the OECD. The goal of ECP.NL is to create a centre of expertise that will contribute to the development of the Dutch digital economy, primarily on behalf of its participants. Therefore, different initiatives concerning electronic business are combined, developed and adopted within and disseminated via ECP.NL. We will mention here only two of the outstanding products that relate ECP.NL to the needs of SMEs:

1. The *"Model Code of Conduct for Electronic Business,"* version 4.0 (see ECP.NL, 2001) is a document stating clear rules of behaviour when conducting business activities online. This Dutch initiative was presented as a model by a number of relevant international organisations such as the OECD (Organisation for Economic Co-operation and Development), the United Nations and the European Commission.
2. *"Nederland gaat digitaal, netjes volgens het boekje"* (Netherlands go digital, by the book) (see ECP.NL, Syntens & EZ, 2002 and http://www.nederlandgaatdigitaal.nl/regels/) is a book written for SMEs. It offers practical guidance related to the relevant acts and regulations for electronic business, by means of questions, answers and practical examples. It also gives an overview flow diagram that can help companies understand which rules and acts apply in their particular situation.

OUTCOMES: WHAT SME'S HAVE TO SAY ABOUT POLICIES AND E-COMMERCE

Electronic Commerce in SMEs: The State of Affairs

In what follows we will present several statistics and figures that will shed some light on the current situation regarding not only the presence of e-commerce in SMEs, but also regarding the effects this has for their organisations.

Table 2. The use of the Internet by SMEs — 2002 (see CBS, 2002).

Category	5 to 20 employees (%)	20 to 100 employees (%)
With internet connection	78	88
With a Website	48	61
Doing Web surfing	69	81
Receiving and sending e-mail	74	87
Performing financial transactions (including electronic banking)	66	78
Ordering	34	44
Payments	16	19
Requesting payed information	17	21
Offering product information	47	59
Offering price information	25	23
Receiving orders online	33	37
Receiving payments online	10	10
Delivering digital products	9	10
Customer support	14	21

For this purpose we will use information from MKB Nederland et al. (2002) and CBS (2002).

The introduction of electronic commerce can theoretically lead to three types of improvements in an organisation: efficiency (doing things better), effectiveness (doing things differently) and innovation (doing other things).

Efficiency: From the SMEs, only 34% stated that using electronic commerce has lead to more efficient business processes, 32% state that they have a better marketing approach, and 25% state that they have realized savings by using e-commerce (see MKB Nederland et al., 2002).

Effectiveness: An enhancement of effectiveness due to the introduction of electronic commerce in a company almost always assumes a partial or total redesign of the business processes or even an entire new business model. From this point of view, there still is little progress for SMEs: only 22% of them announced that they have changed their business model and only 5% said that they use electronic commerce as a way to increase their revenues. These results are understandable if we consider the types of activities for which SMEs are using the Internet (see Table 2).

Innovation: One of the most significant novelties brought by e-commerce is that of providing a new transaction channel, which has made it possible to access new market segments. As a consequence, many companies have reconsidered their strategies with respect to marketing and procurement/sales, and even have developed new products/services to strengthen their position in the market. However, things are not moving very fast when it comes to SMEs. According to MKB Nederland et al. (2002), until now most Dutch SMEs see electronic commerce (in particular having a website) only as a cheaper alterna-

Table 3. Innovation and SMEs — 2002 (see MKB Nederland et al., 2002; CBS, 2002).

Category	%
New marketing/communication strategy	46
New products and services	36
New client targetgroups	35
New procurement processes	29
New production or business processes	28
Supply management	25
Distribution of products/services	19

tive for advertising themselves and their products. Table 3 gives more detailed information regarding the penetration of the different types of e-commerce innovations among the Dutch SMEs.

Conclusion

The survey completed by MKB Nederland (see MKB Nederland et al., 2002) has revealed that SMEs are *still* confronted with several "e-commerce-related" problems. Again, the most important one is the *insufficient expertise and lack of accurate information*: 37% of SMEs still believe that for them this is the biggest obstacle in the way of e-commerce. This is perceived as a big risk, since they are often not able to express clearly what they need from their ICT suppliers. Moreover, the opinion of SMEs is that the ICT market is not transparent because of a multitude of reasons:

- they cannot have any means to measure the quality of ICT products on the market, and therefore they cannot establish a relation between the price and quality or quantify them,
- they do not understand the ICT-jargon,
- there are too many and too many different ICT products/services,
- they do not know how to compare two IT products to see how they differ,
- ICT suppliers are thinking too much in terms of products and too little in terms of users of the products, and
- things are changing too fast and too often in ICT.

As an overall remark the majority (60%) of SMEs find that their ICT suppliers should consider more seriously specific branches and markets. With respect to their need for objective information, SMEs have expressed various requests: 20% need more information on ASPs, 22% on e-business, 25% on e-logistics, 34% on administration and 41% on CRM. However, not surprisingly, most of them need more information on prices and costs (54%) and on functionality of ICT products/services (66%).

A second perceived obstacle, which is related to the first one, is the *maintenance of information systems*: half of the SMEs administrate their ICT-infrastructure themselves, a quarter use the services of a person, who is either an acquaintance or a hardware supplier, and the rest occasionally hire a system-administrator. Although SMEs have declared that in general they are satisfied with the government approach in programs like "SME in the Digital Delta," they feel that more attention should also be paid to problems related to the internal administration of information systems. SMEs often do not have them completely under control, and if however they decide to transact on the Internet they are taking great risks.

Finally, SMEs consider that the program of *the government does not stimulate enough the effective implementation* of e-business and e-commerce. "Nederland gaat digitaal" succeeded to raise the SMEs interest in electronic commerce but a real investment in electronic commerce implementation is not part of it.

These findings are important not only because they reveal the status of e-commerce adoption, but also because they give important clues to policy implementers, such as iMPact and ASPect teams, about the problems they have to tackle and the language they have to speak with SMEs. The approach they took is explained in the next section.

TWO ROADS FROM POLICY TO REALITY: IMPACT AND ASPECT

Project Definition and Management

Providing the Dutch small and medium enterprises with tailored knowledge is the most direct way to help them to make informed decisions concerning the suitability of conducting business on line for their organisations, and to identify the opportunities this new business channel can offer to them. For this purpose, the program "SME in the Digital Delta" has (among others) selected two themes:

*   The *electronic marketplace model*, as a virtual intermediary between potential buyers and sellers. The government considers that electronic marketplaces can be very attractive for many SMEs not only because it facilitates potentially more commercial transactions, but also because it makes them more efficient, allowing in many ways significant decreases in costs.

- The *application service providing model*, as a relatively new solution for outsourcing applications and related services and making these applications remotely accessible via the Internet on a rental basis. Since SMEs are faced with a number of problems related to the availability of knowledge, money and people, which limit their ability to cope with ICT, the government considers that ASP might be an interesting solution to some of these problems.

The two research projects, namely iMPact and ASPect, developed around these themes, are to be carried out over two years (2002-2003), by Telematica Instituut and its partners: Syntens and the branch organisations. Their roles are explained below.

- Telematica Instituut covers the practical research work for the dissemination and introduction of e-marketplace and application service providing knowledge in the SME sector.
- Syntens is acting as an intermediary between Telematica Instituut and the SMEs. All iMPact and ASPect deliverables are transferred into Syntens hands, which in turn will disseminate them among SMEs, via its national SME consultancy network in the area of ICT.
- Branch organisations represent the interests of their SME members. On one hand, together with Syntens, they help SMEs to receive all necessary advice regarding electronic marketplaces and application service providing. On the other hand they are providing the project research teams with branch specific information. That will allow Telematica Instituut and Syntens to help them to define a branch strategy for electronic commerce by building pilots and examples, tailored to the constraints and needs of each branch.

Supporters of these projects are ECP.NL, MKB-Nederland, and VNO-NCW[5].

The work in iMPact and ASPect is carried out along three important directions:

1. *Knowledge management*: this direction is devoted to the development of organisational, legal, technological and business knowledge (the so-called knowledge base) about electronic marketplaces and application service providing, and of analysis and decision-support tools. The results of this direction are delivered through several channels (website, flyers, white papers, workshops, brochures, etc.). The type of information stored in the knowledge base is general, in the sense that it has no branch specificity.

However, efforts are made so that the information is communicated in a very structured and clear manner, and any unnecessary "ICT slang" is avoided.

2. *Education*: this direction is devoted to developing training materials and organising courses for Syntens advisors, and staff members of the branch organisations.

3. *Exploration and analysis of branches*: within this direction several industrial branches are surveyed. The aim is to define for each of them adequate adoption models for electronic marketplaces and application service providing. In order to successfully pursue the goals of this direction, the project teams are attempting to involve primarily large branches in the project activities.

From the way ASPect and iMPact have been defined it might appear that they are very similar. Indeed, they have a similar structure and they follow largely the same implementation mechanism, but their results are significantly different. The first important difference comes from the content specificity subsequent to the theme of each project. Then, each project has selected a different set of branches for the exploration and analysis line. Finally, each project has made its own choices related to the way they are presenting their deliverables to their target groups. These differences will become clear in the next paragraph.

Deliverables of the Projects

In this section we briefly present the main results of iMPact and ASPect that have been delivered so far. Since the projects are currently running (they started in April 2002 and will be finished in December 2003), some of these results are under development, and an important number of others are expected to be produced during the next year.

1. iMPact produced four white papers (in Dutch) on selected EMP themes:
• The "Organisation" white paper defines electronic marketplaces and several classification criteria of them. It also presents the main actors in a marketplace, the roles they play, the steps to follow from initiation to completion of a commercial transaction, and several price mechanisms and the functions and processes within a marketplace. The whole text emphasises what the implications of being connected to a marketplace are for the organisation and is accompanied with examples. The information presented in the white paper is based on several information sources (see Iacob & Smit, 2001; Poon & Swatman, 1999; Krammer, Browning, Rozwell & Shu 2001; Krammer, Hope-Ross & Spencer, 2001; Rooij & Vethman, 2001).

- The white paper "Legislation and trust" explains in simple terms the Dutch and European legislation that applies for electronic commerce and in particular for transactions in marketplaces. Among others, it deals with topics such as: taxation, conflicts, electronic contracts and their legal status, international trade, data protection and copyright, consumer protection and trust.

- The white paper "Technology and Trust" explains a number of technologies and standards currently in use in electronic marketplaces. The emphasis is on topics like XML, EDI, ebXML, authorisation, authentication, electronic payment and security, encryption, electronic signatures, etc.

- The white paper "Business" discusses topics such as: what types of costs and what kinds of financial benefits an SME should expect when transacting in electronic marketplaces, how to select the most appropriate marketplace, how to build a procurement or a marketing strategy, and analyses of several types of business models, etc.

Each white paper is also accompanied by a glossary for the technical terms.

2.   The ASPect project has produced a series of brochures (in Dutch) on selected application-service-providing themes. The themes are clustered in five main categories:

- ASP accents: Within this category, each theme emphasises one aspect of ASP (e.g., "ASP and Security," "The Social Side of ASPs," "ASP: The Technology," "ASP: Applications and Services," etc.);

- ASP applications: This category is devoted to examples of applications that can be outsourced via the ASP model: "ASP and the Payroll," "Webshop with ASP," "ASP and CRM," etc.;

- ASP lifecycle: This category contains a number of brochures that offers information in each phase of the ASP adoption process: from the orientation phase until the disposal of ASP (e.g., "ASP: Making a Choice," "ASP: Within the Company," "ASP: If the Roads Split," etc.).

- ASP innovation: This category is reserved for the newest developments in the area of ASP (e.g., "ASP and Mobile Access," "ASP and Web Services").

- ASP in the SME: The last category contains brochures presenting experiences of several SMEs with ASP. The SMEs are selected from the branch organisations participating in the project.

3.   Decision-support tools: The web-based eMA reasoning tool (still under development in iMPact) consists of two main parts. One part is an e-learning instrument that allows the user to browse into a collection of tree structures rooted in four main elements: Organisation, Legislation, Technology, and Financial and Business aspects. All the nodes in these trees

represents various aspects of electronic marketplaces and are accompanied by short explanatory texts and also associated to appropriate analysis instruments (such as questionnaires, checklists, models, examples, etc.). The second part is intended to become a decision-support tool. SMEs can use such an instrument in any migration situation of their organisation toward electronic commerce. The tool supports an analysis methodology developed previously in Iacob et al. (2002) (see also http://rsd.demo.telin.nl/analysis/), which is basically a step-guiding plan. The ASPect project also offers a decision support and analysis tool, which is based on the COPAFIJTH set of business aspects (see Bruin et al., 2000) and methodology (see BizzDesign, 2000).

4. Both projects have launched public websites: http://marktplaatsen.telin.nl and http://aspect.telin.nl, where the SMEs can find general information regarding the projects, demos and examples. They can also access the knowledge bases and the decision-support tools, and they can find out about the latest result of the projects.

5. Branch analysis reports and models: This part of the research is directed towards the investigation and development of customised electronic marketplace/application service providing introduction and adoption models for a number of different branches. The expected outcomes, per individual branch, encompass the introduction model, the assessment of opportunities, risks and perceived threats, and possibly implementation roadmaps and migration models. So far, work has been carried out with the assistance and involvement of four selected branch organisations:
   • the construction and metal-electro industries for iMPact, and
   • the car-body repairs and construction branch and metal branch for ASPect.

6. Course and training material: Both projects have given the first round of training to the Syntens advisors. The content presented included the white papers, brochures, several demos and the presentation of the website.

7. Dissemination and communication materials (e.g., CD, flyers, brochures).

BENCHMARKING E-BUSINESS POLICIES: PLACE OF DUTCH INITIATIVES IN EUROPEAN LANDSCAPE

Benchmarking different national e-business policies is a very difficult task. Each country has its own cultural legacy, and its own regulations concerning business practices. It is now clear that the new medium — the Internet — did not change them significantly. This is even more obvious if we are looking particularly to SMEs. Therefore, any national policy is confronted with very specific challenges, which makes them very different not only as approaches, but also in terms of objectives. In what follows we will present a short overview of several national framework policies, explicitly directed toward small and medium enterprises and somehow similar to the Dutch initiative. We will restrict ourselves only to European countries, since their efforts are intensively coordinated by the European Union, under the umbrella of a broad and ambitious program "eEurope go Digital."

We will use for our comparison three criteria that are also part of the model proposed by e-Business Policy Group (2002):

• the formulation of a clear *policy rationale* that will identify the problems and the target groups that are the subjects of the respective policy, based on solid evidence that an intervention is needed,
• the *definition of realistic and clear targets* that will allow the impact of the policy to be measured in order to identify its success or failure, and
• the *implementation* strategy that takes into consideration the mechanisms, and financial and human resources that will be needed for the implementation of the policy. Ideally, an implementation plan should be clearly defined from the very beginning of a program.

Most of the European governments have recognised the fact that e-business has drawn a clear separation line between large companies and SMEs. The costs of introducing and maintaining ICT in small companies is significant when compared with their turnover, and therefore they cannot afford experiments and expensive mistakes. Therefore, the *rationale* behind all the e-business policy programs was to help SMEs to avoid such mistakes and eventually to support them in making the right step towards e-business. Governments (e.g., UK, The Netherlands, Greece) have argued the need for such actions based on substantial surveys and large consultations of SMEs, SME (branch) associations, business and IT experts, and academia, which have also continued throughout the life of their programs. Hence, it is obvious why most of these programs have explicitly set a primary *target* to increase the awareness of businesses regarding the potential benefits of e-business and to provide advice and support for the adoption and use of ICT. Moreover, many specialised "awareness programs" have been started by several other member states (UK/Scotland - *First Steps Workshop Series,* Austria - *Ecaustria* ("Let's e-biz"), Sweden - *SVEA,* Germany - Lower Saxony - the *B-online project,* Spain - *Catalunya on the Net*). One can find other specific examples of measurable targets in the separate descriptions of some of these programs. In terms of ambitions, each national framework program strives to secure a leading position for that nation in the digital economy.

Significant differences between these programs appear in the selected *implementation* mechanisms. As one can see from the brief descriptions that follow, the implementation mechanisms take various forms: broad consultation forums, consulting, general training, web-based e-learning tools and toolboxes, tailored e-business strategies, or direct financial support for IT introduction.

In the area of framework policies, several member states provide good examples of solid practices (see e-Business Policy Group, 2002):

UK — *UK online for business.* The overall target for the programme is *to make the UK the best place in the world for e-commerce by 2004.* The extent to which such a goal can be achieved is assumed to be measured trough the cost of Internet access and the level of B2B and B2C electronic transactions. There are several important components of the programme, all having specific measurable targets, definition, and implementation: e-commerce showcase events, networks of business advisors, e-commerce awards scheme, web-based practical advice tools, e-commerce sector impact assessment, partnership programs, etc. The overall budget for this framework program for 2002-2003 is 55 millions euro. A recently released study (see Booz|Allen|Hamilton, 2002), has acknowledged this framework policy as being "the world's most effective," based upon an extensive benchmarking study in which the UK, Canada, Sweden, Germany, Italy, France, Japan, Australia and US were included.

Greece — the *e-Business Forum* is a framework policy that started from the idea to develop a continuous, broad consultation mechanism on e-business policies, involving the state, the business community and academia. The target of this policy is *to provide a mechanism for the exchange of opinions, ideas and expertise*, in order to better understand the real needs of SMEs, to identify market failures and to suggest concrete policy recommendations to resolve them. The total budget of the e-Business Forum is 1.3 million euro for 2001-2005. One of its main results is the initiation of the *Greek go Digital* program (100 millions euro budget), which is supposed to help 50,000 SMEs with up to ten employees to connect to the Internet. This should be accomplished via Go Digital Training, Digitisation of business Procedures, Promotion of creation of vertical e-marketplaces, and Development of Digital Content.

Norway — the *VeRDI programme* is a framework policy that has the overall aim *to strengthen SME competitiveness and profitability through increased awareness and use* of e-based systems and technologies. The target group of VeRDI are SMEs with less than 100 employees. The implementation instruments used by this policy are mechanisms for exchange of experience, use of independent advice and experts, promoting joint measures and infrastructure, dissemination of knowledge and support for professional development, special consultancy projects, and piloting tools (the "electronic toolbox") that will help SME to develop and execute e-strategies. The budget allocated to VeRDI for 2002 is 2.7 millions euro.

The Netherlands — *The Netherlands Go Digital* programme (as presented in the previous sections) offers a combination of support for the use of independent advisors and a variety of information channels ranging from individual business participation in workshops to encouraging sectoral participation via branch organisations. The broad aim is to push the Netherlands into a leading position in the digital economy. The concrete goal, as stated in the policy documents, is that two-thirds of all SMEs should have a web presence and should conduct transactions online by the end of the program. The Netherlands go Digital counts on reaching 15,000 SMEs and covering 150 sectors. The total budget of the program for 2002-2005 is 36 millions euro.

Finland — *eAskel* aims to enhance e-business all over Finland and increase SME management competencies in strategic e-business development and realise profitable e-business opportunities. The implementation of the program is in the hands of 15 Employment and Economic Development Centres, which appoint consultants to analyse (for two to five days) each of the participating companies and develop customised action plans. The target is to reach 500 companies every year, with a budget of 320000 euro.

CONCLUSION

Without any doubt the policies of the Dutch government are leading to important changes in way the branch organisations and subsequently the small and medium enterprises are looking at electronic commerce. This has been proven by the last national (and European) statistical surveys, some of which are referred to here. However, for SMEs there still is a way to go, and several milestones to leave behind. Some of them, such as expertise and skills can be improved through projects like iMPact and ASPect. For others, like standardisation and security technologies, the ICT forums and industry are striving to find better solutions. But there are obstacles that must be overcome by SMEs themselves. The government can help them, but they have to be determined to invest resources (financial and human) in electronic commerce.

REFERENCES

BizzDesign. (2000). *Handboek Testbed*, versie 6.1, juni 2000, Enschede (in Dutch).

Booz|Allen|Hamilton. (2002). *International e-Economy Benchmarking: The World's Most Effective Policies For The e-Economy*, London. Retrieved

19 November 2002 from the World Wide Web: http://www.e-envoy.gov.uk/
oee/oee.nsf/sections/esummit-benchmarking/$file/indexpage.htm.

Bruin, B. de, Verschut, A., & Wierstra, E. (2000). Systematic analysis of
business processes. *Journal of Knowledge and Process Management*,
7(2), 87-96.

CBS. (2002). *De digitale economie 2002*, Centraal Bureau voor de Statistiek,
Voorburg/Heerlen.

e-Business Policy Group. (2002). *Benchmarking National and Regional e-
Business policies for SMEs*, eEurope Go Digital, Final report. Retrieved
28 June 2002 from the World Wide Web: http://europa.eu.int/comm/
enterprise/ict/policy/benchmarking/final-report.pdf.

ECP.NL. (2001). *Model Code of Conduct for Electronic Business, version
4.0*. ECP.NL, Leidschendam.

ECP.NL, Syntens & EZ. (2002). *Nederland gaat digitaal, netjes volgens het
boekje, spelregels voor elektronisch zakendoen,* T. Wagemans & P.
Koudstaal (Eds.), (in Dutch).

Iacob, M.E. & Smit, A. (2001). *Electronic Markets*, TI/RS/2001/021, Telematica
Instituut.

Iacob, M.E., Boekhoudt, P., Fielt, E. & Faber, E. (2002). The BFIT electronic
business analysis methodology. *Proceedings of the Fifteenth Bled Electronic Commerce Conference,* (pp. 746-766).

Krammer, M., Browning, J., Rozwell, C. & Shu, L. (2001). *The SMB guide to
E-marketplaces*. Retrieved 7 September 2001 from the World Wide Web:
http://www3.gartner.com/Init.

Krammer, M., Hope-Ross, D. & Spencer, C. (2001). *Attention SMBs: E-
markets offer rewards and pitfalls,* Report, Gartner. Retrieved from the
World Wide Web: http://www4.gartner.com/Init.

Lower House of Dutch Parliament. (1998). *Wetgeving voor de Elektronische
Snelweg,* Parliamentary Documents 1997-1998, 25880, 1-2 (in Dutch).

Lower House of Dutch Parliament. (2000). *Elektronische handtekeningen,*
Parliamentary Documents 2001-2002, 27743, 1-2, 3, A, B (in Dutch).

Lower House of Dutch Parliament. (2001-1). *Elektronisch geld,* Parliamentary
Documents 2001-2002, 28189, 1-2, 3, A (in Dutch).

Lower House of Dutch Parliament. (2001-2). *Elektronisch handel,* Parliamentary Documents 2001-2002, 28197, 1-2, 3, A, B (in Dutch).

Ministerie van Economische Zaken. (2001). Het MKB in de Digitale Delta, Plan
van Aanpak van de toepassing van internet en electronic commerce door
het MKB's Gravenhage (in Dutch). Retrieved July 2001 from the World
Wide Web: http://www.ez.nl/upload/docs/Kamerbrieven/PDF-
Documenten/01033996-bijlage.pdf.

MKB Nederland, FHI, & Nederland-ICT. (2002). ICT voor productiviteitssprong
in mkb, Delft (in Dutch).

NIPO. (2001). *Nederland gaat digitaal, 1-meting*, Ministry of Economic Affairs. NIPO Business Monitor (in Dutch).

Poon, S. & Swatman, P. (1999). An exploratory study of SME Internet commerce issues. *Information & Management*, 35, 9-18.

Rooij, M.G.A. de & Vethman, A.J. (eds). (2001). *Elektronische marktplaatsen: Uw plaatsbewijs voor de nieuwe economie*. Cap Gemini Ernst & Young, Kluwer, Deventer (in Dutch).

Staatsblad. (1999). *Act Regarding the Legal Protection of Databanks*, Bulletin of Acts, Orders and Decrees 1999, 303 (in Dutch).

Staatsblad. (2000, December). *Distance Sales Act*, Bulletin of Acts, Orders and Decrees 2000, 617 (in Dutch).

Staatsblad. (2000, July). *Personal Data Protection Act*, Bulletin of Acts, Orders and Decrees 2000, 302 (in Dutch).

ENDNOTES

[1]   Telematica Instituut is a non-profit research institute managed and funded by top companies and the government. It is a partnership between the business community, research centres and government, to translate fundamental knowledge into market-oriented research, in the field of telematics (multimedia, electronic commerce, mobile communications, CSCW, knowledge management, etc.) for the public and private sectors.

[2]   Syntens is a national innovation network for SMEs, founded by the Dutch Ministry of Economic Affairs. It delivers expertise, consultancy and guidance in the area of technological innovation.

[3]   MKB is the Dutch abbreviation for SME.

[4]   The Royal Association MKB-Nederland is one of the largest employers' organisation in the Netherlands. MKB-Nederland promotes the interests of small and medium Dutch enterprises as an influential negotiating partner for local, national and European authorities.

[5]   VNO-NCW is the biggest Dutch employer association. It is somewhat similar to MKB-Nederland, but it is not exclusively intended for small and medium-sized organisations.

Chapter IV

E-Commerce as a Business Enabler for Small and Medium Size Enterprises:
Issues and Perspectives from Singapore

Leo Tan Wee Hin, Singapore National Academy of Science and National Institute of Education, Singapore

R. Subramaniam, Singapore National Academy of Science and National Institute of Education, Singapore

ABSTRACT

The new economy is posing challenges for countries to enhance their competitiveness through IP-based business initiatives. A key strategy is to get small and medium-size enterprises to be part of the e-commerce ecosystem. Singapore has put in place an advanced digital telecommunications network as well as the necessary regulatory and policy frameworks for the support of e-businesses. In this chapter, the status of e-commerce developments among small and medium size enterprises in Singapore is assessed. It is noted that, whilst these enterprises still have quite a way to go in terms of emulating e-business practices, market developments will force many of them to adopt e-commerce practices in due course. State intervention strategies are also especially imperative in getting promising enterprises as well as others in growth sectors to come on board the e-commerce platform.

INTRODUCTION

Small and medium-size enterprises (SMEs) play a very important role in the economies of all countries. They outnumber big corporations and are conspicuous by their ubiquity in all sectors of society. The contribution of SMEs to a country's Gross Domestic Product is high by virtue of the large number of people they employ and the diversity of services that they offer (Unctad, 2002). SMEs also offer a beginning platform for entrepreneurs to realize their dreams.

Traditionally, SMEs have pursued a domestic policy as they predominantly operate in local markets. A number of SMEs have, however, graduated into the Ivy League and gone on to become multinational corporations (MNCs). For example, Hewlett Packard started off as an SME in 1938 in the Silicon Valley before going on to become an MNC. An Asian example is that of Creative Technology, which started off as an SME in Singapore in 1981 before becoming an MNC. SMEs also constitute a critical node in the supply chains of big enterprises and multinational corporations in a country.

The impetus given to globalization in the 1990s and the advent of the Internet shortly thereafter has markedly transformed the world's economic landscape. Capital mobility and the connectivity provided by the Internet for business processes are reformatting the contours of international trade and giving rise to a global common market. In the process, traditional structures of businesses are starting to atrophy and new business models are beginning to emerge. All these are affecting the competitiveness of nations. Since these affect the employment of workers, they therefore impact on all business sectors, including SMEs. Those business outfits not able to compete in the emerging economic landscape face the possibility of being waylaid by the tsunamis unleashed by the forces of globalization and Internet-based business practices.

Globalized markets present a valuable opportunity for SMEs to address the challenges of the new economy (Hibbert, 1999). Enormous scope is afforded for re-engineering their operational and business practices as a way to reap efficiencies and reach out to new markets through geographical diversification. Failure to be market-responsive and competitive from an international standpoint can even be detrimental to the domestic survival of SMEs since they can be sidelined by e-commerce-enabled big businesses in a fast moving dynamic environment.

It has been estimated that in today's globalized markets, as many as 100 companies are involved at various stages in the making of a finished product (Fife and Pereira, 2001). The reason can be traced mainly to the absence of information about suppliers who can provide competitively priced, reliable components promptly for the manufacture of these products. As a result, 50% of the costs incurred in the manufacturing process is wasted (Bangkok Post, 2001). With Internet-based procurement solutions, cost savings of between 5-40% can be realized, with 15% being the norm. That means if profit margins are 20% of gross sales, a reduction in cost by US\$1 is equivalent to increasing sales by about US\$5 (Emiliani, 2000).

As a tiny island (600 sq km) with no natural resources, Singapore started its industrialization programme in the 1960s by encouraging the proliferation of SMEs in all sectors of the economy (Chia, 1997; Coe and Yeung, 1999). This strategy has played a useful role in promoting entrepreneurship in the country as well as providing gainful employment to many people. In parallel, Singapore also promoted foreign direct investment by encouraging multinational corporations to set up their operations here (Perry et al., 1997). Provision of a pro-business environment has been the cornerstone of this policy and is a key factor in the opening up of an export-driven economy which has allowed Singapore to achieve four decades of robust growth. Wong (1992, 1998, and 2001) has noted that the presence of MNCs in Singapore has been an important factor in promoting technology transfer and in molding the rise of competitive local industries, including SMEs. As MNCs are known to be very stringent about quality and price, they have thus played a useful role in stimulating best practices in SMEs which supply components and other services to them. Singapore's external economy is valued at thrice that of its domestic economy.

Singapore also places great emphasis on the judicious utilization of its available manpower (4 million), as well as the productive use of science and technology in various aspects of national endeavors to overcome constraints and other problems (Tan and Subramaniam, 1998, 1999 and 2000).

The challenges of the new economy have caused a re-look at many business practices in Singapore. An important consideration is to get SMEs to develop an e-business offshoot. This chapter assesses the role played by e-commerce in creating an enabling environment for SMEs in the digital economy. It also highlights the problems faced in the wider acceptance of e-business practices by SMEs.

SME STRUCTURE IN SINGAPORE

Whilst there is no general consensus in the literature on what constitutes an SME, various criteria are used in different countries. In Singapore, the following criteria is used to define an SME (http://www.singapore-sme.com):

- there must be local equity stake of at least 30% in the company,
- the net book value of the company's fixed assets, that is, factory building, machinery, and equipment, must not exceed S$15 million,
- the workforce must not exceed 200 for non-manufacturing enterprises.

That SMEs are a strong force to be reckoned with in the local economy, which is generally dominated by MNCs and government-linked companies (GLCs), can be seen from the following indicators (http://www.singapore-sme.com):

- over 100,000 businesses in Singapore are SMEs — this represents nine out of 10 business establishments,
- they employ over 50% of the workforce.

However SMEs generate only about 30% of the total value added to the economy. Most of the value-added comes from the 7,000+ MNCs, the GLCs, and other big enterprises.

Table 1 shows the industry mix of the SMEs. It can be seen that most of the SMEs are concentrated in the commercial, financial, business and manufacturing sectors. It has been estimated that 95% of the SMEs are in the brick-and-mortar business (http://www.comec.com/prs_171000.htm). In the year 2000, about 10% of the SMEs were using e-commerce for their businesses (http://www.singapore-sme.com).

By virtue of their large numbers, SMEs are potentially ideal targets for using e-commerce initiatives to increase their profit margins and market reach. The perceived advantages of e-business practices are manifold (Quayle, 2000):

- reduction in paper transactions, thus contributing to cost savings,
- speedy order cycle time and diminution in inventory stocks, as a result of prompt processing of purchase order related information,

Table 1. Make-up of small and medium size enterprises in Singapore in 1999.

Industry	Number of companies
Manufacturing	9,782
Construction	7,456
Commerce	42,129
Transport and communication	7,462
Financial and business services	33,911
Social and personal services	2,640
Others	1,082
TOTAL	104,462

Source: Yearbook of Statistics (2000)

- more opportunities to cement supplier/buyer relationships through business-to-business (B2B) communication networks,
- enhanced supply chain efficiency through availability of real time information on product stocks and shipment status.

INFRASTRUCTURE FOR SMEs
IN THE NEW ECONOMY

For SMEs to be able to compete in the digital economy, the necessary telecommunications, e-commerce and other infrastructures must first be put in place. A good infrastructure creates economic value for SMEs to ride on, as well as decreases their operating costs. It is generally recognized that a digital telecommunications network as well as appropriate regulatory and policy frameworks for e-commerce are imperative for businesses in the evolving digital economy.

These are elaborated upon in this section for Singapore.

Table 2. Evolution of broadband subscriber base in Singapore.

Year	Number of Cable Modem Subscribers	Number of ADSL subscribers
March 1999	NA	15,000
March 2000	NA	25,000
April 2000	8000	26,000
June 2000	16,500	NA
Sep 2000	22,000	34,000
Dec 2000	33,000	35,000
Jan 2001	40,000	NA
Feb 2001	43,000	37,000
March 2001	NA	40,000
April 2001	50,000	NA
June 2001	NA	40,000
August 2001	65,000	NA

Source: http://www.scv.com.sg and http:www.singtel.com.sg

Digital Telecommunications Network

A broadband telecommunications network leveraging on three platforms (Asymmetric Digital Subscriber Line, Hybrid Fibre Coaxial Cable Modem and Asynchronous Transfer Mode) has been in operation since 2000. The technical aspects of these services have been addressed in detail by Tan and Subramaniam (2000, 2001). Broadband penetration rates in Singapore are on the uptake, as can be seen from Table 2.

The maturation of the broadband market in Singapore can be seen from Table 3, which shows that Singapore is among the top ten broadband economies in the world.

Frameworks for Electronic Commerce

Singapore was among the early adopters of e-commerce in the world. A comprehensive range of initiatives and frameworks (http://www.ec.gov.sg) has been put in place to allow businesses to capitalize on the potential that e-commerce presents. Fine-tuning of the frameworks on the basis of accumulated experiences in the local market and cognizance of best practices in overseas countries has been done on an ongoing basis. Some of the more important initiatives are addressed in this section.

Alternative Payment Systems

It is recognized that for e-commerce to be entrenched in the business landscape, a variety of payment systems need to be made available. Four

Table 3. Top 10 economies by broadband penetration rates, as of June.

Country	Score	Rank
Republic of Korea	19.3	1
Hong Kong	12.1	2
Canada	9.7	3
Taiwan	7.2	4
Belgium	6.3	5
Sweden	5.4	6
Ireland	5.2	7
USA	5.0	8
Denmark	4.5	9
Singapore	4.4	10

Source: Asia Pacific Telecommunication Indicators (2002)

payment channels are in common use in Singapore, these being elaborated below:

- To service credit card purchases over the Internet, a Secure Electronic Transaction (SET) system was set up in 1997, this being a world-first.
- To service low value purchases (S$0.01-S$500.00), NETSCash, the digital equivalent of the cash card, is available. The anonymity feature that it incorporates has found a market among the online public who wish to purchase products and services from cyber merchants without the hassle of providing personal identification details.
- Debiting via Internet banking has been available since 1997, though this is currently limited to the big four local banks. Currently, there are over 300,000 users of Internet banking in Singapore.
- Electronic inter-bank payments, via NETS Financial Data Interchange.

Issuance of Digital Certificates

Assurance of the security of financial transactions on the Internet is imperative if businesses are to be encouraged to go online.

In this context, two government-linked Certification Authorities (CA) have been established and they have been empowered to issue digital certificates to businesses that require cross-checking of user credentials as well as assurance of high network security. The first CA was established in 1997 as joint venture between the then National Computer Board and the Network for Electronic Transactions, which has the distinction of being the first CA to be set up in South Asia. The second CA was set up in 1998 as a collaborative undertaking between Singapore Post and Cisco Computer Security.

On the certificate are digitally embedded details of the CA, the expiry date, encrypted information about the user's public key, and details of the account. When the certificate is issued to a party, an e-signature of the CA is stamped electronically. These security features preclude the signature from being replicated by a third party. Even if a party obtains fraudulent access to the certificate, the account details cannot be deciphered.

Digital certificates are issued on a variety of templates: either on smart cards or on validated tokens for high-value transactions, and on diskettes or hard disks for low-value transactions.

Application Service Providers

Application Service Providers (ASP) in the e-commerce industry provide a range of services. These include human resource management, sales and marketing, customer service, and even collaborative working arrangements with businesses. Their emergence has allowed companies to concentrate on their core competencies whilst auxillary functions are handled by these ASPs.

Currently, there are a good number of ASPs servicing online businesses. Their positioning as a key node in the e-commerce value chain has been among the factors that have helped to reduce business costs in Singapore.

The ASP Alliance Committee has also been formed. Comprised of a conglomerate of all the ASPs in Singapore, the Committee aims to position Singapore as an e-commerce hub in the Asia-Pacific region.

Business-to-Business Security Service Providers

For e-businesses that are hesitant to set up their own e-commerce infrastructure because of cost constraints and uncertainty of the business model, B2B service providers have emerged in the market. They provide this service through the provision of a secure e-commerce network between companies, thus saving these companies considerable manpower and infrastructure costs as well as recurrent expenses. It is recognized that without the emergence of these providers, who provide a suite of e-commerce applications at a fraction of the cost of setting up the necessary infrastructure, e-commerce development among businesses, especially among SMEs, would be stymied significantly. More importantly, the availability of a national Public Key Infrastructure since May 1997 has been an important factor in contributing to the rise in the number of B2B Security Service Providers who cater to the needs of businesses on a competitive basis.

Digital Rights Management

Digital Rights Management (DRM) is a service that offers content encryption for businesses wishing to protect their intellectual copyrights (Sinnreich et al., 1999). Its emergence was precipitated by the observation that duplication/ replication technologies have made it easier for the general public, knowingly or unknowingly, to violate copyright protection and for businesses to use copyright material for mass distribution on the Internet. This is especially pronounced in the music industry, where the file size of songs can be reduced tremendously by using compression technologies for free distribution over the Net without due compensation for the copyright owners.

DRM protects the works of copyright owners through any of the following means:

1. Digitally inserting a watermark in the copyright content so as to facilitate identification of the source of the content, regardless of the number of times a material has been replicated.
2. Encoding content via encryption algorithms so that access is permitted only for those with the authorized applications software.

3.   Use of permission sets to control distribution of online content, that is, via usage and business rules.
4.   Collating data from users for the purpose of charging.

Legal and Policy Frameworks

There is recognition that for the support of e-enterprises in the digital economy, government must take the lead in laying down the administrative frameworks relating to regulatory and legal issues. These frameworks must not only be transparent and pro-business, they must also be seen to not stymie the growth of enterprises or hamper innovation. Currently, the following frameworks are in place — they have benefited from fine-tuning on the basis of accumulated experiences and cognizance of best practices in more mature e-economies:

Intellectual Property Rights

Respect for intellectual property rights is very important in the Internet-driven economy. At the same time, there needs to be an appropriate balance between the rights of copyright owners and the rights of the online public for information access. Evolution of online enterprises as well as companies wishing to re-engineer aspects of their operations to tap the potential of the Internet will be affected if adequate safeguards are not in place in this regard.

Statutory amendments to the erstwhile Copyright Act have thus been made to ensure that the spirit of the Act prevails in the online environment as well. The amendments make clear the rights and obligations of the various stakeholders: copyright owners of intellectual property on the Internet, network providers, and online users.

Electronic Transactions Act

A legal basis for electronic contracts and electronic signatures has been formalized by this Act. Singapore was among the first few countries in the world to institute this Act as a means to promote e-commerce. Subsumed under the Act are the following:
1.   **Use of e-applications and e-licenses.** Applications and licenses can now be e-filed by businesses as a result of a legislative amendment that endows these with legal validity. This initiative was taken as a means for the public sector to be positioned as a key node in the e-commerce value chain.
2.   **Commerce code for e-commerce transactions.** The rights and obligations of businesses entering into e-commerce transactions are governed by this Code. In particular, laws relating to these transactions, sanctity of electronic signatures, procedures for the verification of transactions and defining of bounds of repudiation are addressed in detail.

3.   **Provision of Public Key Infrastructure.** Recognizing that PKI (Public Key Infrastructure) is the most secure platform for e-commerce transactions, the Act has provided for the appointment of a Controller of Certification Authority, who is entrusted with the framing of rules and regulations in relation to the licensing of certification authorities, cross-validation of foreign certification authorities, and other related matters.

4.   **Liability of service providers.** With content on the Internet growing exponentially, it is not possible for service providers, who simply provide online access, to vet content or be held accountable for objectionable material. A provision in the Act absolves these service providers from civil or criminal proceedings.

Computer Misuse Act

Instituted in August 1998, this Act mandates penalties for users who indulge in objectionable behavior when using the computer. Penalties for disruption of servers and revealing of access codes without authorization have also been included in this Act.

Evidence Act

The erstwhile Evidence Act has been amended to enable courts to accept electronic evidence as well.

Dispute Regulation

The Singapore IT Dispute Resolution Advisory Committee was established in 1997 to settle disputes in the Internet world amicably. The Committee also monitors issues related to intelligent enterprises and educates service providers and other players in the e-commerce market on best practices so that disputes can be averted.

Tax Issues

A clear and transparent tax regime is important in the online environment, where the tendency to avoid tax is greatest and difficult to detect. Clear rules are in place for the payment of two kinds of taxes in Singapore by online businesses: income tax and Goods & Services Tax.

Table 4 shows the timelines for important milestones in the development of e-commerce in Singapore.

E-GOVERNMENT

The pervasiveness of the Internet in the new economy is posing challenges for governments to be responsive to the needs of new businesses as well as those

Table 4. Timeline for e-commerce development in Singapore.

Year	Initiative
Aug 1996	Introduction of e-commerce Hotbed Programme
Jan 1997	Stock Trading on the Internet Formation of E-commerce Policy Committee
Apr 1997	First Secure VISA Card Payment over the Internet Internet website launched for Secure Electronic Commerce Project
Jul 1997	Netrust – South East Asia's first Certification Authority set up
Aug 1997	Singapore IT Dispute Resolution Advisory Committee set up
Oct 1997	Singapore Computer Emergency Response Team set up
Nov 1997	Canada and Singapore sign Information & Communication Technology Agreement S$50 million fund to boost innovation and multimedia content development in Singapore
Jun 1998	Canada and Singapore announce first cross certification of public key infrastructures Electronic Transactions Act introduced in Parliament Singapore, Canada and Pennsylvania sign education technology MOU using digital signatures Electronic Transactions Act passed in Parliament Computer Misuse (Amendment) Bill 1998 passed in Parliament
Jul 1998	E-commerce Co-ordination Committee formed
Sep 1998	Singapore acceded to the Berne Convention for the protection of literary and artistic works Singapore launches e-commerce Masterplan Government Shopfront offers government products and services over the Internet
Nov 1998	S$9 million Local Enterprise Electronic Commerce Programme launched
Feb 1999	Launch of the Regulations to the Electronic Transactions Act Australia and Singapore sign Information and Communication Technology Agreement
Apr 1999	e-Citizen Centre set up
Sep 1999	Berlin and Singapore sign a MOU to cooperate closely in Information and Communication Technology
Oct 1999	Helpdesk for businesses set up for enquires on e-commerce policies
Jan 2000	IASPs get guidelines on preventive security scanning Lifting of import control on cryptographic products
Jul 2000	First Infocomm Technology Roadmap – charting the future of technology in Singapore
Aug 2000	Singapore paves the way as a trusted e-commerce hub
Oct 2000	IDA and PSB announce S$30 million incentive scheme to spur e-business development and growth in Singapore

Source: http://www.ec.gov.sg

of its people. In Singapore, the answer has been the setting up by the government of a mirror site on the web (http://www.egov.sg).

After initiating the site in 1996, a further sum of S$1.5 billion was spent over the period from June 2000 to June 2003 to implement advanced digital infrastructure, including enabling the network for broadband access and migrating more offline content of its ministries and statutory boards online. Since December 2001 all government services that need to be accessed online by the public and businesses have been in operation — for example, e-filing of income taxes became operational in 1998. Through these initiatives, the government aims to provide the public and businesses more convenience and prompt services.

The heart of the e-government comprises GovII, an IT infrastructure of several layers that connects all ministries and statutory boards with external organizations and the public. A suite of applications are delivered over the network, and the more important of these include the Government Electronic Mail System, the government Intranet, and the Public Sector Smart Card.

A brief description of some of the key services deployed over e-government is given in the following:

e-Citizen Centre

Working on a 24/7 routine, the e-citizen Centre was launched in April 1999. By June 2000, about 130 public services were offered online. The Centre heralds a paradigm shift in the manner in which the public interacts with the government. All kinds of services that the citizen needs are available in this portal. It has been estimated that this portal alone saves the government about S$40 million a year.

Currently, over 200 online services are featured here, the most important of which are indicated below:

- Registering a business and applying for a patent.
- Allowing male citizens to register for national service, allowing them to apply for an exit permit when traveling overseas, and allowing reservists to book a date for their annual Individual Physical Proficiency Test.
- Searching for information on the more than 360 schools in Singapore, registering for the GCE "O" and "N" level examinations, and applying for government scholarships.
- Searching for jobs in the public sector, filing income tax returns, and checking balances in the employee's Central Provident Fund account.
- Applying for work permits for the employment of foreign maids and applying for birth extracts.

Government Internet Website

Operational since 1995 and honed over the years, this site is a repository of public-centric information.

A recent survey done by Andersen Consulting on the use of the Internet by governments ranked the Singapore government second, just below the U.S. government in terms of the number and variety of services offered online.

It has been found that the e-government serves as an important link in servicing businesses for their needs, especially in getting the necessary permits, licenses, approval, etc. Its efficiency in catering to the needs of online businesses has been acknowledged by the business community in Singapore.

DISCUSSION

The need for SMEs to be responsive to new economy paradigms is well established in the literature (Fife and Pereira, 2002). However, the penchant for SMEs in Singapore to warm toward the new economy has been slow for a number of reasons. In a study conducted by Saw (1999), a number of factors were identified as constraining the uptake of e-commerce by SMEs (Table 5).

We elaborate further on these and other factors.

High Cost of Setting Up E-Commerce Infrastructure

Even though the cost of doing business in Singapore through IP-based solutions has been brought down over the years, owing to government subsidies for telecommunications and other infrastructures, the cost of transacting online entails yet another solutions upgrade. It has been estimated that the cost of putting up a simple e-business initiative in Singapore in the form of a company website is in the region of S$25,000 (Koh, 2000). The cost increases by another S$75,000 if the website is to be enabled for e-commerce. This cost factor effectively excludes a large number of SMEs from embracing e-commerce initiatives. Also, initial cost overruns and high recurring expenses for software, hardware and maintenance are not uncommon.

New developments in technologies as well as the entry of more vendors in the market have, however, helped to decrease the cost of implementing e-business solutions. A recent report on the e-business applications market in Singapore by Frost and Sullivan (2003) has predicted that the next wave of e-commerce investments will be driven by SMEs which form the supply base of large enterprises. The report mentions that the e-commerce applications market in Singapore is growing rapidly — from US$15.5 million in 2002, a rise of 35% over 2001, to US$31.9 million for 2005. The report cites evidence to show that these investments in e-commerce are being driven mainly by application service providers.

Lack of Companies with Sufficient Annual Turnover

Over 90% of SMEs in Singapore have ten or fewer employees. This lean outfit has been a way of cutting business costs in an effort to stay competitive. With the majority of these companies operating in the brick-and-mortar business, it is not pragmatic to get them to embrace e-commerce initiatives. Their annual turnover is just not sufficient to get them to support full-fledged e-commerce initiatives. Even if they are capable, they need to be convinced about the return on investment, for otherwise their competitiveness can be eroded. Tables 6 and 7 summarize some recent feedback from companies on their attitude toward e-commerce.

Table 5. Constraints on the Uptake of EC by SMEs in Singapore.

Factor	Characteristics
Individual preference	Personal unfamiliarity with IT and electronic networks Personal preference for other forms of communication Personal concerns over reliability and security of electronic networks
Company culture	Resistance to change in dominant forms of communication Collective preference for more traditional forms of communication Continued preference for paper-based systems of communication
Awareness	Lack of awareness of different types of electronic networks Lack of awareness of potential uses of EC
Need	Business not deemed to require EC EC not used by competitors or customers
Social factors	Personal touch deemed crucial for business Face-to-face contact more important than electronic networks EC not seen to build trust in relationships
Cost	High cost of installing relevant hardware High cost of hiring qualified staff to maintain and update networks Widespread availability of cheaper alternative communications
Purpose	Perceived as only being useful for non-urgent functions Perceived as only being useful for large volumes of information Perceived as only being useful in long standing relations where trust has been established
Compatibility	Concerns over compatibility with customers and suppliers Concerns over compatibility with overseas parties

Source: Saw (1999)

Lack of Awareness of E-Commerce Capabilities

Many of the SMEs are not cognizant of the enabling dimension that can be conferred by e-commerce initiatives. This comes in their way of implementing IP-based solutions in their businesses. In many of these companies, the operations are more of a brick-and-mortar nature, which, again, are not conducive for e-commerce initiatives.

Lack of Suitable E-Business Models for SMEs

Adoption of e-commerce by big enterprises is not a problem in Singapore. There is, however, still no viable business model that SMEs can emulate, especially for those that do not have the necessary sales turnover. Such models need to be cost-effective, given the nature of the businesses many of the SMEs are in. In many cases, the business processes of many of the SMEs are not sophisticated or complex enough to ride on the web platform. A cost benefit analysis is necessary before SMEs can be persuaded to embrace e-commerce.

Skill Levels of SMEs

Many SMEs do not have a highly educated workforce to support e-commerce initiatives. This core structure comes in their way of moving up the IP-based value chain.

Sectoral Mix of SMEs

The make-up of the SME structure shows that many are brick-and-mortar companies (Table 1). Only a small percentage are technology-based or are big enough to embark upon web-based initiatives. This is a major impediment in promoting e-commerce among SMEs. The fact that many SMEs service the local market and do not have an export dimension is another factor.

City-State Structure

As a city-state, Singapore has the highest population density in the world. Retail stores and convenience outlets are often located within short traveling times. This stymies the penchant for online purchases by consumers, as it is normally done when large geographical distances are involved, like in the USA, where mail order companies are profitable. This is a factor which limits many SMEs from embarking on e-commerce initiatives catering to online purchases (Wong, 2001). Some recent developments in Singapore such as online music stores catering to diverse and wide-ranging interest groups, as well as online book stores providing cheaper access to magazines and books than those from overseas are, however, of significance.

Table 6. Internet and usage of business-to-business e-commerce by company size in Singapore.

Company size (employees)	Already trading on Internet	Interested	Not interested
More than 100	18	46	36
10 to 99	8	26	66
Less than 10	8	24	68

Source: Interpolated from data presented in Business-to-Business Electronic Commerce Survey 1999

Table 7.   Interest and usage of business-to-business commerce by industry in Singapore.

Company	Already trading on the Internet (%)	Interested (%)	Not interested (%)
Manufacture of electronic products	18	24	58
Freight forwarding	10	28	62
Publishing	8	32	60
Storage and warehousing	5	25	70
Chemicals and chemical products	3	25	72
Courier activities other than postal	2	40	58
Manufacture of aircraft and spacecraft	2	28	70

Source: Interpolated from data presented in Business-to-Business Electronic Commerce Survey 1999

Against the backdrop of the foregoing, there is official recognition that a targeted and focused approach on SMEs would have a better chance of success in encouraging more of them to embrace e-commerce. In this regard, a national plan to boost the capabilities of SMEs in the new economy was instituted in 2000. Called SME 21, the 10-year strategic plan aims to raise the status of SMEs in the emerging knowledge-based economy through the following means (http://www.singapore-sme.com):

1. **Developing productive sectors in the SME.** This plan aims to pivot SMEs up the value chain in the local economy through a process of re-structuring, revitalizing, and upgrading. The aim is to double the productivity of the retail sector from S$28,000 per worker to S$38,000 per worker.
2. **Groom innovative high growth SME.** This plan aims to triple the number of local SMEs with annual sales turnover of S$10 million and above from 2,000 to 6,000 companies. That is, it aims to ensure that one in 15 companies will go on to become large corporations.
3. **Institute a knowledge-based and pro-enterprise environment.** This plan aims to create conditions where appropriate mindsets for business are inculcated, technopreneurship and innovation are encouraged, and ob-stacles to growth removed. In this way, it is expected to quadruple the numbers of SMEs transacting online from 8,000 to 32,000 companies. That is, one third of local SMEs will be plugged into the global economy.

To accelerate the realization of the above targets, schemes to provide grants and subsidies to SMEs whose corporate focus is aligned with national objectives have been put in place. These include:

- E-strategic business programme, which helps override obstacles in the way of conducting Internet transactions by providing companies with a platform to develop or refine their e-business paradigms.
- Jumpstart, which aims to catalyse the adoption by companies of readily available e-commerce solutions packages for conducting Internet transactions.
- Local Electronic Commerce Programme, which provides a subsidy of S$20,000 for qualifying SMEs which cite budgetary constraints as a reason for not embracing e-commerce.
- Local Enterprise Finance Scheme, which provides loans at locked interest rates to SMEs so that they can upgrade and strengthen their operational efficiencies.

The government recognizes that in the context of Singapore's small domestic market, the need to groom more SMEs to be world players is a crucial aspect of safeguarding national competitiveness in the new economy.

The plus factors which have helped to pivot e-commerce among SMEs include:

Example Set by Government

It is recognized that for e-commerce to sink roots, a good example needs to be set by the state as this would set the pace for the thinking to percolate down to the business community. In this regard, the range of e-services transacted online with the various government ministries, for example, e-filing of business returns, e-filing of income tax, etc., have contributed to the mushrooming of more companies, including SMEs, transacting online.

That SMEs play a very important role in the national economy is underscored by the appointment of key national agencies such as the Trade Development Board, Economic Development Board, Spring Singapore, and Enterprise Promotions Centre to help SMEs embark on growth. The first two agencies are involved in the overall promotion of business and industry development. The latter two agencies provide consultancy support, certification, training, business planning and development, and also help to identify grants and subsidies for companies in their business promotion. Key aspects of these are e-commerce initiatives.

A scheme by the Economic Development Board funds up to 50% of fees incurred by SMEs when they engage consultants to map a business plan, conduct feasibility studies and initiate implementation of e-commerce for their businesses.

Of interest to note is the government's TradeNet initiative, which is an Internet-based system for processing 99% of all trade declarations made by businesses since 2002. This paperless processing system provides savings of about S$2.8 billion annually. Fisher (2000) has noted that enhancing business productivity through similar practices can boost GDPs of many Asian countries by 5-12% in the long run.

Recognizing that the logistics and transportation sectors contribute significantly (8%) to the GDP, a three-year plan costing S$12 million was rolled out by the government in 2000 to enable SMEs in these industries to use e-commerce.

The early adoption of e-business practices is seen as vital for SMEs to remain relevant in the global economy.

Good Network Infrastructure and E-Commerce Policy Frameworks

A good digital telecommunications network leveraging on a diversity of platforms is in place. Lack of access is not a problem in Singapore. The cost of access has been brought down through various initiatives — government investments on bandwidth so that telcos can pass on the savings to consumers and businesses, competition in the provision of Net access, etc. An efficient network infrastructure provides reliability, and also lowers the cost of doing business.

Tables 8-12 summarize some useful indicators. Clearly, the data shows that Singapore is an advanced ICT nation, and is networked effectively for the new economic order.

Importance of SMEs' Role in Supply Chains

By virtue of their being small and nimble, SMEs are in a position to respond to market developments more rapidly than established big businesses. With the growing emphasis on supply chain management theories, the trend towards outsourcing, subcontracting, licensing, downsizing of corporations, and just-in-time operations will become more pronounced in the digital economy. More SMEs have the potential to be part of these developments if they can e-enable their businesses.

It has been noted that about 80% of SMEs in Europe are involved in supply chains (Financial Times, 2001). A recent United Nations report has cautioned that B2B markets are perceived by SMEs as an instrument by big companies to put undue pressure on suppliers to lower costs (Unctad Secretariat, 2002). At the same time, the report suggests that SMEs see the need to embrace these practices, as they can be a conduit for their products. We may add that not entering the EC e-commerce mainstream may sideline SMEs. Where SMEs have been servicing large businesses in the traditional economy, when the former adopts IP-based business solutions, it becomes incumbent for SMEs to ensure that their operational methods, networks and business processes also conform accordingly. In a recent study of the SME sector in the UK, Quayle (2002) has warned that as purchasers reduce their supply base, the SME supplier is having to measure up to international standards of performance and this will expose fundamental structural and potentially terminal deficiencies at all points in the supply chain where SMEs are involved.

Many of the SMEs in Singapore are part of some supply chains. It is likely that market developments will force more of them to adopt e-commerce in due course.

Private Sector Efforts

Whilst the public sector has a role to play in laying the architecture and frameworks for e-commerce, private sector efforts to drive growth would also be effective. In this context, a number of SME portals have been set up by the private sector. For example, the site at http://www.singapore-business.com features FAQs on issues of interest to SMEs and facilitates access to cost-effective, IP-based business practices and e-marketplaces. Another portal at http://www.singapore-business.com professes the view that the key to getting SMEs to embrace e-commerce relies more on the comfort level of their senior management when dealing with consultants promoting IP-based solutions for their business projects. Besides providing consultancy support to SMEs, the portal encourages foreign and local SMEs to come together to explore synergistic business opportunities, and also helps local SMEs to obtain various types of funding from government agencies for their e-commerce initiatives. Another initiative is by a leading marketplace provider, Commerce Exchange, at http://

Table 8. Growth Competitiveness Index (GCI) rankings and 2001 comparison.

Country	Rank in 2002	GCI Score 2002	Rank in 2001
United States	1	5.93	2
Finland	2	5.74	1
Taiwan	3	5.50	7
Singapore	4	5.42	4
Sweden	5	5.40	9
Switzerland	6	5.38	15
Australia	7	5.36	5
Canada	8	5.27	3
Norway	9	5.24	6
Denmark	10	5.23	14

Source: Cornelius et al .(2002)

Table 9. Growth Competitiveness Index (GCI) component indices.

Country	Technology index	Public institutions index	Macroeconomic environment index
United States	1	16	2
Finland	3	1	14
Taiwan	2	27	6
Singapore	17	7	1
Sweden	4	15	34
Switzerland	6	8	5
Australia	9	5	4
Canada	8	9	12
Norway	10	12	7
Denmark	11	2	21

Source: Cornelius et al. (2002)

Table 10. Indicators of Internet infrastructure.

Country	Internet hosts per 1000 population in 1999[a]	Internet users per 1000 population in 1999[b]	Access cost for 40 hours during off-peak in US$[c]
Australia	57.58	316.84	33.85
China	0.06	7.03	na
Hong Kong	17.09	361.57	na
India	0.02	2.81	na
Indonesia	0.10	4.30	na
Japan	20.84	213.90	85.65
Korea	9.84	231.76	27.13
Malaysia	2.70	68.71	na
New Zealand	71.12	183.69	34.80
Philippines	0.17	6.72	na
Singapore	38.08	243.99	na
Taiwan	27.02	205.50	na
Thailand	0.66	13.15	na
USA	195.00	271.74	35.40

Source: Wong (2001)

Table 11. Indicators of e-commerce development in selected countries.

Country	Secure servers per 1,000,000 population in 1998[a]	Secure servers with strong encryption per 1,000,000 population in 1998[a]	Business-to-Business trade in US$M in 2000[b]	Business-to-Consumer trade in US$M in 2000[b]	% Internet users who purchased online in past month 2000[c]
Australia	33.70	16.87	5,160.55	394.09	10
China	0.01	0.00	954.37	72.88	na
Hong Kong	10.32	1.81	1,773.28	135.42	7
India	0.01	0.00	675.72	51.60	5
Indonesia	0.05	0.02	110.48	8.44	3
Japan	3.39	1.13	29,618.20	2,261.84	20
Korea	0.82	0.19	5,164.42	394.39	16
Malaysia	1.08	0.55	311.85	23.82	5
New Zealand	23.73	7.65	632.33	48.29	na
Philippines	0.04	0.01	111.70	8.53	2
Singapore	21.18	8.02	1,097.84	83.84	5
Taiwan	1.85	0.32	3,842.73	293.46	4
Thailand	0.10	0.05	432.15	33.00	1
USA	54.29	38.39	449,900,000	38,755.00	27

Source: Wong (2001)

Table 12. Networked readiness index for 2002/2003.

Country	Score	Rank
Finland	5.92	1
USA	5.79	2
Singapore	5.74	3
Iceland	5.51	5
Canada	5.44	6
United Kingdom	5.35	7
Denmark	5.33	8
Taiwan	5.31`	9
Germany	5.29	10

Source: Dutta and Jain (2002)

Table 13. Ownership of PCs in households in Singapore.

Year	Penetration %
1988	11.0
1990	19.1
1992	20.2
1996	35.8
1997	41.0
1999	58.9

Source: IT Household Survey (NCB)

www.comex.com. Its BecomeCo programme helps SMEs lower e-commerce costs through their innovative line of e-commerce packages ranging from S$2,300 to S$39,000.

Rising Internet Penetration Rates and PC Ownership

The rising rates for Internet penetration and PC ownership in families means that prospects for SMEs to cater to these segments are bright (Tables 13 and 14).

E-Business Hosting Centre

It is recognized that many SMEs may not want to invest initially in their own web architecture and ICT manpower or may not be in a position to invest in these services. Recognizing the tremendous business potential that this opportunity presents, IBM has been licensed to establish an e-business hosting centre in Singapore — its first in the Asia-Pacific region outside Japan (Nandy, 2000).

Run on IBM's proprietary system framework known as Universal Server Farm, the Centre offers a slew of web services and solutions to SMEs. A nominal package costing S$1300 provides a company with a web environment, replete with an Internet connection, firewall, server rack set-up, account management and a service portal. Other modularised packages are available at extra cost.

The intent behind the establishment of the Centre is to allow SMEs to focus on their core mission, whilst the tie-up will create a tributary for additional growth on the e-commerce platform.

Table 14. Internet access in households in Singapore.

Year	Percentage penetration
1996	8.6
1997	14.0
1999	42.1

Source: IT Household Survey (NCB)

Table 15. Business-to-business sales value in Singapore.

Year	Value (S$ million)
1998	5,671
1999	40,425
2000	92,701
2002	109,460

Source: Ho (2002)

More recently, the IBM Business Solutions Centre opened in Singapore to "tutor" SMEs on e-commerce practices. It offers SMEs a live demonstration on e-business versus traditional business solutions, as well as hands-on approaches for appreciating IP-based business solutions. Owners of SMEs are exposed to three packages: QuickBook for account management, ACT for contact management, and Shopfront for creating and maintaining Internet marketplaces.

Adoption of E-Commerce by Big Businesses

One way to increase the promotion of e-commerce practices by SMEs is to target large enterprises outside the SME fold. As they adopt e-commerce, SMEs by virtue of their linkages with these enterprises will be forced to adopt these practices in order to service them. For example, B2B turnover in Singapore is showing rapid growth (Tables 15 and 16), suggesting that many big businesses have entered the e-commerce ecosystem.

The slow adoption of e-commerce by SMEs is not unique to Singapore. In a survey commissioned by the Organization for Economic Cooperation and Development, slow adoption rates by SMEs in Europe have also been noted (OECD, 2000). The report attributes the reasons to inadequate access to capital and technology skills. It also indicates that SMEs:

> *"are too often busy employing scarce human and financial resources to make their initial business plans succeed and are reluctant to allocate resources in implementing a new EC strategy without a clearer understanding of the benefits and risk" (OECD, 2001).*

Given the nature of Singapore's export-driven economy and its enhanced linkages with global markets, e-commerce developments at the international level will affect it more than those countries which are insulated from e-economy developments. The strategy of the government taking the lead initiative in putting in place the necessary infrastructure as well as encouraging big businesses and SMEs with high turnovers to get hitched on to the e-commerce bandwagon is a step in the right direction. Singapore can ill afford to let the private sector take its time to warm toward e-commerce. Indeed, Wong (2001) has noted that the

Table 16. Cross-border electronic commerce.

Year	Domestic (S$ million)	Export (S$ million)
1998	1,758	3,913
1999	25,468	14,958
2000	52,840	39,862
2001	51,440	58,014

Source: Ho (2002)

presence of large numbers of manufacturers in Singapore catering to the export market positions Singapore as a strategic node in international production networks and the arising scope for leveraging on the Internet to streamline logistics and supply chain structures is very promising.

In summary, e-commerce initiatives in Singapore stand a very good chance of succeeding. The necessary infrastructure and policy frameworks are already in place for businesses, including SMEs, to ride on the opportunities that the emerging digital economy presents.

CONCLUSION

The telecommunications infrastructure as well as the regulatory and policy frameworks for the support of e-commerce in Singapore are of a high standard. Whilst there is still quite some way to go for SMEs to embrace e-commerce paradigms, the Singapore experience shows that state intermediation strategies to promote growth are very important. In many cases, market developments will also generate competitive pressures for SMEs to adopt e-commerce practices.

Getting SMEs to adopt e-commerce practices is crucial for their competitiveness, both locally as well as internationally in the digital economy. However, the focus must be on getting those growth enterprises in the country which have the potential to grow to be e-enabled for businesses.

REFERENCES

Asia Telecommunications Indicators. (2002). Retrieved April 10, 2003 from WWW: http://www.itu.int.

Bangkok Post. (2001). Business processes: Business urged to reduce waste. *Bangkok Post,* April 25.

Chia, S.Y. (1997). Singapore: Advanced production base and smart hub of the electronics industry. In W. Dobson and S.Y. Chia (Eds.), *Multinationals and East Asian Integration,* (pp. 31-61). Canada: IDRC.

Coe, N. and Yeung, H.W.C. (1999). Grounding global flows: Constructing an e-commerce hub in Singapore. *Conference on Global Networks, Innovation and Regional Development*, UC Santa Cruz, (November 11-13).

Commerce Exchange's BecomeCo Helps SMEs Lower E-commerce Costs. (Press Release, 17 October 2000). Retrieved April 11, 2003 from WWW: http://www.comex.com/prs_171000.htm.

Cornelius, P., Blanke, T. and Paua, F. (2001). The growth competitiveness index: recent economic developments and the prospects for a sustained recovery. In S. Dutta, B. Lonvin and P. Fiona (Eds.), *Global Information Technology Report 2002-2003* (pp. 3-21). London: Oxford University Press.

Dutta, S. and Jain, A. (2002). The networked readiness of nations. In S. Dutta, B. Lonvin and P. Fiona (Eds.), *Global Information Technology Report 2002-2003* (pp. 2-25). London: Oxford University Press.

Emiliani, M. (2000). Business-to-business online auctions: Key issues for purchasing process involvement. *Supply Chain Management, 5(4),* 176-186.

Euro News. (2002). Small and medium size enterprises take-up of e-commerce. Retrieved April 11, 2003 from WWW: http://www.waleseic.org.uk/euronews/0201a_main.htm.

Fife, E. and Pereira, F. (2002). Small-and medium-size enterprises and the e-economy: Challenges and prospects. *The E-Business*, 1-7.

Fisher, A. (2000). Race is on for supremacy. *Financial Times*, London, 22 September 2000, 27.

Frost and Sullivan. (2003). Report on Singapore e-business applications market (Excerpts). Retrieved April 21, 2003 from the WWW: http://www.telecomoutlook.com/pr_ebusiness.html.

Hibbert, E. (1999). The globalization of markets – How can SMEs compete? Retrieved April 11, 2003 from WWW: http://mubs.mdx.ac.uk/research/Discussion_Papers/Marketing/dpap_mkt_no10.pdf.

Ho, S. (2002). PKI towards building a secure e-business infrastructure. *Asia PKI Forum*, Beijing, China, July 4, 2002.

IBM uses ShopFactory to teach e-commerce. Retrieved April 11, 2003 from WWW: http://www.shopfactory.com/en-us/pg_98.htm.

Information and Communication Development Authority of Singapore. (1999). Business-to-Business Electronic Commerce Survey.

Koh, J. (2000, July). E-biz: Yet to touch small and medium size enterprises. *Business Times, 14.*

Nandy, A.M. (2002). *IBM targets SMEs with its first e-business hosting centre in Singapore.* Retrieved April 6, 2003 from WWW: http://wn.newscom-asia.com/oct1m20/wnl.html.

National Computer Board. (1999). IT household survey. Singapore.

National plan to boost small and medium enterprises. Retrieved April 11, 2003 from WWW: http:///www.singapore-sme.com.

OECD. (2000). Enhancing SME competitiveness. *OECD*, Paris, 2001, 158.

Perry, M., Kong, L. and Yeoh, B. (1997). *Singapore: A developmental city state.* London: John Wiley.

Quayle. M. (2001). E-commerce: The challenges for UK small and medium enterprises. *The 10ᵗʰ International Annual IPSERA Conference.*

Saw, T.C.A. (1999). *Wired Singapore? The impact of electronic networks on the geography of business linkages in Singapore.* Honours Thesis, Department of Geography, National University of Singapore, 86-87.

Singapore Department of Statistics. (2001). *Yearbook of Statistics 2000.* Department of Statistics: Singapore.

Sinnreich, A., Sacharow, A., Salisbury, J. and Johnson, M. (1999). *Copyright and Intellectual Property: Creating Business Models with Digital Rights Management.* New York: Jupital Communications.

Tan, W.H.L. and Subramaniam, R. (1998). Developing countries need to popularize science. *New Scientist*, 2139, 52.

Tan, W.H.L. and Subramaniam, R. (1999). Scientific societies build better nations. *Nature*, 399, 633.

Tan, W.H.L. and Subramaniam, R. (2000). Wiring up the island state. *Science*, 288, 621-623.

Tan, W.H.L. and Subramaniam, R. (2001). ADSL, HFC and ATM technologies for a nationwide broadband network. In N. Barr (Ed.), *Global Communications* (pp. 97-102). London: Hanson Cooke Publishers.

UNCTAD Secretariat. (2002). E-commerce and Development Report 2002. *United Nations Conference on Trade and Development.*

Wong, P.K. (1992). Technological development through subcontracting linkages: Evidence from Singapore. *Scandinavian International Business Review, 1(2),* 28-40.

Wong, P.K. (1998). Leveraging the global information revolution for economic development: Singapore's evolving information industry strategies. *Information Systems Research, 9(4).*

Wong, P.K. (2000). Information and communication industry development and differentiation in South-east Asia. *ASEAN roundtable 2000 on new development paradigms in South-east Asia: The challenges of information technology,* Institute of South-east Asian Studies, Singapore, October 12-13.

Wong, P.K. (2001). Globalization and E commerce: Growth and impacts in Singapore. Report for Centre for Research on Information Technology and Organizations, University of California. Retrieved April 11, 2003 from WWW: http://www.crito.uci.edu/git/publications/pdf/singaporeGEC.pdf.

Chapter V

An SME Experience of E-Commerce:
Some Considerations for Policy Formulation in Australia

Stephen B. Chau, University of Tasmania, Australia

Paul Turner, University of Tasmania, Australia

ABSTRACT

Previous research has identified that small business faces additional barriers to e-commerce adoption compared with large business. More recently it has emerged that the adoption of e-commerce technology has often not translated into the active utilisation and conduct of e-commerce by small business. The factors and problems that account for this apparent lack of benefit derived from e-commerce activity forms the focus of this chapter. This chapter identifies and critically analyses the range of factors impacting on small businesses conducting e-commerce. A framework is developed to explore potential problem areas for e-commerce implementation and utilisation. This framework is based upon a qualitative analysis of 34 Australian SMEs utilising e-commerce and from findings in a report conducted by Ernst & Young of an additional 34 Australian small businesses implementing e-commerce. The chapter endeavours to provide an outline of the issues that policymakers need to consider in developing e-commerce policy to motivate and support ongoing e-commerce initiatives among SMEs.

INTRODUCTION

The rate of e-commerce adoption by Australian SMEs is increasing (Small Business Index, 2001), however the rate of e-commerce integration lags significantly behind large organisations. The Australian government has acknowledged the importance of SMEs adopting e-commerce and has established several programs to encourage SMEs to uptake e-commerce. These programs include the formation of the National Office of the Information Economy (NOIE) promoting programs such as the Australian Electronic Business Network (AUSeNET), the Information Technology Online Grant program (ITOL) and the Tasmanian Electronic Commerce Centre (TECC).

Past IS researchers have identified numerous e-commerce benefits for SMEs including costs reduction, alternative sales and marketing channels and streamlined communication methods. To date there exists a vast amount of literature that has explored the adoption and uptake of e-commerce by SMEs. Equally there exists significant research into examining those factors that present barriers to the uptake of e-commerce by SMEs (Freel, 2000; Lawrence & Keen, 1997; MacGregor et al., 1998; Poon, 1997, 1998). Recent research also indicates that where SMEs have adopted e-commerce technologies, the actual utilisation and conduct of e-commerce does not necessarily lead to an active utilisation of e-commerce (NOIE, 2000; Wong & Turner, 2001).

Studies of those SMEs that are engaged in e-commerce suggest that the level of web-based e-commerce can be categorised into four phases of e-commerce utilisation Chau (2001a). These phases emerge as transitional states in the use of e-commerce where SMEs may establish themselves directly at any particular phase or migrate to or from other phases. The ability of SMEs to migrate between phases relates to the business environment in which they operate.

The analysis of a case study of 34 SMEs actively utilising e-commerce suggests that the potential to derive benefit from e-commerce activities increases where SMEs have been able to re-align business processes and structures (Chau & Turner, 2001b). The ability of SMEs to re-align business processes depends upon a number of factors. However, to date there has been little detailed investigation into the factors that impact on SME's ability to derive e-commerce benefits within any particular phase of e-commerce activity.

Research conducted by Chau and Turner (2002a) found that a combination of internal and external factors directly influence the ability of SMEs to conduct e-commerce and e-commerce business transformation. To some extent SMEs possess a limited ability to control many of their internal factors, however the external factors exerted on a business by government, industry and the online environment are often beyond the control of individual SMEs. Research is starting to emerge in the IS literature that explores the actual use of e-commerce by SMEs. However there exists little information about appropriate guidelines and policies to stimulate and encourage the use of e-commerce in SMEs.

This chapter endeavours to provide an outline of the issues that policymakers need to consider in developing e-commerce policy to motivate and support ongoing e-commerce initiatives among SMEs. The chapter reflects on an in-depth qualitative study of 34 Australian SMEs actively using e-commerce and the findings in a report commissioned by NOIE reviewing the activities of another 34 Australian SMEs implementing e-commerce. Similarities exist in the findings of both studies that indicate that the most significant problems associated with the use of e-commerce by SMEs relate to factors experienced externally by the organisation (Chau, 2002b). Policies aimed at encouraging the use of e-commerce by the government and industry sectors need to focus on creating an environment that promotes the adoption and use of e-commerce technologies while minimising the potential e-commerce problems faced by SMEs.

LITERATURE REVIEW

The evolution of the Internet and continued dramatic growth in web-based electronic commerce has irrevocably changed the global business environment. Numerous studies have illustrated the potential of electronic commerce to generate opportunities for leveraging competitive advantage. At all levels, electronic commerce has opened up possibilities for businesses to revolutionise internal and external operational and strategic business practices.

Despite these developments, many studies have illustrated the relative disparities that exist between large enterprises and small-to-medium-sized enterprises (SMEs) in the adoption and utilisation of e-commerce (Lowry et al., 1999; NOIE, 2000a; Poon & Swatman, 1998). While e-commerce clearly offers SMEs a range of potential benefits including global reach (Hughes, Ralf & Michels, 1998), equalising the business environment (Winston, Stahl & Choi, 1997), cost savings and increased productivity (Burgess, 1998) a relatively low adoption rate has continued.

In Australia, SMEs are a significant force in the economy, making up 95% of all enterprises and accounting for 50% of all private-sector employment. Previous research has extensively explored the range of factors inhibiting SME adoption of e-commerce in Australia (Cameron & Clarke, 1996; Corbitt et al., 1997; Freel, 2000). As increasing numbers of SMEs have become Internet enabled, it has emerged that even where SMEs have adopted e-commerce technologies this has often not converted directly into the active utilisation and conduct of e-commerce (Small Business Index, 1999; NOIE, 2000b). Research has highlighted that inhibitors to the active utilisation of e-commerce amongst SMEs include perceptions of the unsuitability of products and services for e-commerce; time and expense and a concern that e-commerce will lead to uncontrolled growth. In terms of B2B e-commerce, this survey also revealed many SMEs were reluctant to engage in B2B e-commerce because they feared uncertainty in the quality and availability of products, in delivery and supply arrangements and alienating existing intermediaries (Small Business Index, 2001).

From a theoretical perspective these insights resonate deeply with the view that small businesses are not the same as large businesses, and that the differences between them go beyond simple distinctions based on size, turnover and resources (Dandridge, 1979; Welsh & White, 1975). Clearly the complex processes involved in the adoption of e-commerce by SMEs require continued investigation. There is however, also a need for more research into the experiences of SMEs that do actively engage in e-commerce. Previous research by the authors has highlighted that the level and extent of web-based e-commerce activity amongst SMEs is far from homogenous and can be usefully categorised into four phases (Chau, 2001a). Building on the work of Venkatraman (1994), a recent extension of this model has explored the relationship between the level of SME organisational transformation and the potential benefits derived from e-commerce activities. From preliminary case study analysis it has emerged that the potential to benefit from e-commerce activities increases where SMEs have been able to re-align business processes and structures. Chau and Turner (2001b) revealed that SMEs adopt one of two distinct perspectives in relation to the use of e-commerce: experimental and strategic. This highlights that optimising benefits from e-commerce initiatives is linked to SMEs strategic decisions to re-align business structures (Chau & Turner, 2001b). To date, the range of internal factors that impact on SMEs' ability to engage in this type of e-commerce-related organisational transformation has been under-explored. Similarly there has been a lack of investigation into the influence of external factors on the ability of SMEs to acquire benefit from e-commerce initiatives at these different phases of e-commerce business transformation.

A REPORT BY ERNST & YOUNG

In 2001 Ernst & Young was commissioned by NOIE to explore the use of e-commerce amongst 34 Australian small businesses. The 34 cases are representative of a wide range of industries around Australia. The purpose of this report was to demonstrate the benefits acquired from e-commerce and to assist the small businesses to conduct their own cost benefit analysis of e-commerce. The report provided an overview of the experiences encountered by these small businesses which displayed different levels of e-commerce investment.

The report found that the businesses gained the most benefits from e-commerce in two ways. Firstly through efficiency savings and secondly by leveraging e-commerce as a source for additional revenue. In this report 55% of the businesses indicated that efficiency savings had been acquired through the introduction of e-commerce. It was found that the larger of the businesses gained the most efficiency savings. The ability to use e-commerce to expand communications, use a website for marketing purposes, conduct financial transactions online, facilitate online orders and integrate e-commerce within existing business processes all contributed to efficiency savings. The incentive to adopt e-commerce to improve the efficiency of business operations was reported by 62% of the businesses. Other benefits include the ability for businesses to generate additional revenue from e-commerce. In this study 45% of businesses signalled an increase in revenue received attributed from e-commerce.

The costs associated with conducting e-commerce varied depending on the type of e-commerce activity and the size of the business. The range of costs identified in the study included:

- website maintenance,
- telephony,
- ISP and website hosting,
- direct costs,
- responding to e-mail,
- advertising,
- licence fees,
- opportunity cost, and
- bank fees.

The three most significant costs for the businesses related to website maintenance, telephony and ISP charges. The costs of website maintenance was more substantial for medium and larger business than smaller business, however smaller businesses found the largest cost relating to the resources and the time required to respond to e-mail. Telephony was the next most significant cost especially where businesses needed to install extra telecommunications infrastructure to facilitate the use of e-commerce. The third highest cost related to the costs of maintaining their telecommunication access via Internet Service Providers (ISPs) and charges associated with website hosting. However, this cost was not as significant for those businesses with a large investment in e-commerce.

Problems encountered during the implementation of e-commerce were closely associated with three main areas:

- The development and support of e-commerce applications,
- Finding a cost-effective e-commerce infrastructure in terms of logistics, connectivity, and
- Finding a sufficient critical mass of suppliers and consumers actively using the Internet to conduct business.

The problems of gaining sufficient information about e-commerce to determine a value proposition and finding an appropriate person/business to develop and maintain the e-commerce application was a significant implementation obstacle.

Once the website was established, finding the resources to keep the website fresh and current proved timely and costly. Businesses in regional areas found the high costs of accessing ISPs prohibitive where connection rates were charged at long distance phone rates. The report also found that the major hurdle in implementing and conducting e-commerce relates to a lack of widespread use of the Internet amongst consumers and suppliers for business-related transactions.

METHODOLOGY

An interpretative research approach was considered the most appropriate means to capture information about the beliefs, actions, and experiences of SME actively using e-commerce within an organisation and the interactions between organisations. The interpretivist approach is based on an ontology in which reality is subjective, a social product constructed and interpreted by humans as social actors according to their beliefs and value systems (Darke et al., 1998). The research strategy and methods employed to collect information regarding the use of e-commerce relied upon the use of multiple case studies and qualitative research methods.

The application of a case study research strategy is considered a plausible and accepted research strategy in Information Systems research (Lee, 1989), where research and theory has been formulated at an early stage with little theoretical base (Galliers & Land, 1997; Galliers, 1992). Interpretative case studies have been widely used in the social sciences (Silverman, 1998), and are gaining wider acceptance in the Information Systems arena.

Conventional techniques were deployed to identify and select SMEs using e-commerce. Forty SMEs were formally approached and 34 agreed to participate in the study. Following a detailed review of existing literature relating to the use of IT by SMEs and SME e-commerce, a semi-structured question frame was developed to gather information about the utilisation of e-commerce within the organisations. The questions were formulated to encourage participants to discuss issues relating to the study without imposing limitations or constraints on how the questions may be answered (Doolin, 1996). The questions were arranged into four broad sections.

Section 1: Business Background: The aim of the first section of questions was to collect background information about the organisation. Questions were framed to determine the core product or services the organisation provide, the size of the organisation, customer market and an indication of the historical profile of the business.

Section 2: Current use of e-commerce: The questions in the second section focused specifically on the current use of e-commerce by the SME. For example, what were the drivers to use e-commerce and how is the organisation's website currently used? Further questions were also asked about other e-commerce technologies that may be in place, for example a discussion of electronic banking facilities and electronic payment systems.

Section 3: Impact of e-commerce: Section three questions were asked to explain the impact of e-commerce activities on business operations. Questions were posed to illicit the importance of e-commerce and the Internet to the organisation and to determine any changes in the business processes within the organisation and external to the organisation.

Section 4: Problems encountered using e-commerce: The section four questions were aimed at identifying problems that may have been encountered incorporating and using e-commerce. For example, problems may have appeared during the incorporation of e-commerce and problems may have appeared while conducting e-commerce activities. The final section also includes questions asking participants about the future of their e-commerce activities.

At the end of each interview the researcher checked through the major points of the interview with each participant. This was to ensure that the information was correct and to reduce the chance of misinterpretation. At the completion of the interview a transcript was constructed in preparation for data analysis. If any inconsistencies or ambiguities appeared during the preliminary data analysis, the researcher contacted the interviewees to clarify any points of confusion.

A combined approach to data analysis was used to examine the multiple case study data drawing on the principles of grounded theory and domain analysis. These methods utilise an inductive approach to theory generation whereby theories, concepts and models are derived directly from the data or grounded in the data. The inductive theory building process relies on an iterative cycle of reading and re-reading the qualitative data to detect emergent themes and constructs embedded or grounded in the data (Neuman, 2000).

The use of grounded theory and domain analysis provides a mechanism to reveal both the conceptual complexities in the data and the semantic relationships that exist within and between the data across the multiple cases. The combined approach leverages the strengths of ground theory and domain analysis. Grounded theory provides an essential device to condense the vast volume of data gathered for each case and the coding procedures intrinsic to grounded theory highlight the conceptual complexity within the data. Domain analysis complements and extends the initial data analysis by distinguishing the semantic nature and meaning of the inter-relationships, ensuring an enhanced insight into the relationships between codes, concepts, and themes. Significantly, domain analysis provides a method for a collective comparison of multiple cases while retaining a high degree of richness and meaning associated with concepts, themes, and relationships across all cases.

Characteristics of SMEs Included in the Study

The participant organisations were located in two states of Australia, Western Australia (WA) and Tasmania (TAS). The organisations involved in the study were representative of the small, medium and micro categories under the SME classification. Cases from both WA and TAS were included in each SME classification.

The breakdown of SMEs according to their size is summarised in the Table 1.

The classification of small, medium and large businesses used in the study were defined according to the definitions of micro, small and medium-sized businesses outlined by the Australian Bureau of Statistics classification of SMEs (Australian Bureau of Statistics, 1999).

The size of the businesses varied from husband-and-wife operators to medium-sized organisations employing more than 60 full-time staff. The businesses included in the SME classification encompassed organisations from traditional industry sectors that are deemed to be high users of technology. With reference to the ABS (1999) report on small business technology usage, SMEs were selected from the top 10 industries most likely to adopt e-commerce.

The businesses under study come from nine industry sectors that include

Table 1. Number of SMEs included in the study.

SME Categories	Tasmanian	Western Australia
Micro Business	6	11
Small Business	7	2
Medium Enterprise	5	3

Table 2. Tasmanian cases (18).

Case ID	Description	Industry	Age (years)	Size
A	Angus Stud Breeder	Agricultural	80	3
B	Scientific Software Supplier	Agriculture & Fishing	2	2
C	City Restaurant	Hospitality	2	3
D	Software Distributor	ICT	2	5
E	Distributor for Apparel and Work wear	Wholesale	15	19
F	Inner City Hotel	Hospitality	12	14
G	Fruit Tree Grower	Agricultural	1	4
H	Web Developer / Consultant	ICT	7	8
I	Mining Communications	Mining	11	27
J	Fishing Lure Manufacturer	Manufacture	9	9
K	Insurance Loss Adjuster	Finance	12	18
L	Computer Consultant	ICT	8	3
N	Essential Oil Wholesaler	Agriculture	3	8
O	Retail Bakery	Retail	14	26
P	Fish Farmer	Fishing	14	65
Q	Fruit & Vegetable Wholesaler	Wholesale	20	25
R	Credit Information Services	Finance	35	42
S	Wholesale Bakery	Manufacturer	45	49

Table 3. Western Australian cases (16).

Case ID	Description	Industry	Age (years)	Size
T	Flower Shop	Retail	4	1
U	Education Marking Services	Education	5	2
V	Craft Wholesaler / Retailer	Wholesale / Retail	15	1
W	Web Developer	ICT	2	4
X	Educational Products	Education	1	2
Y	Online Miscellaneous Retailer	Retailer	1	2
Z	Web Developer	ICT	3	12
AA	Online Stationery Retailer	Retailer	1	8
AC	Communication Product Distributor	Wholesale	7	45
AD	Web Developer	ICT	6	45
AE	Agricultural Information Provider	Agriculture	5	21
AG	Web Developer	ICT	2	4
AH	Online Bookshop	Retail	6	2
AI	Entertainment Retailer	Retail	10	2
AJ	Online Specialist Bookshop	Retail	4	4
AK	Web Developer	ICT	2	4

agriculture, education, finance, hospitality, ICT, manufacturing, mining, retailing, and wholesale trade. At the time of data collection these industries were considered to represent a substantial proportion of SMEs engaged in e-commerce activities. In Table 2 and Table 3, a summary of the organisations included in this research is presented.

Utilisation of E-Commerce by SMEs

The analysis of the case study data suggests that SMEs utilise e-commerce in at least six different ways; these include electronic banking, sales and marketing, communications, enhancing business processes, customer service and cost reduction. Table 4 provides a detailed summary of these e-commerce activities.

In the report by Ernst & Young (2001) the benefits received from the implementation of e-commerce correlate closely with the e-commerce activities outlined in Table 4. Specifically, the findings in the Ernst & Young Report identified gross benefits of e-commerce as a way to gain additional revenue and business efficiencies. Additional revenue was acquired from businesses engaged in selling products and services directly through their website. This coincides with the sales and marketing role of e-commerce described by participants in this study. The Ernst & Young (2001) report describe businesses as achieving business efficiencies through leveraging communications, using the website as a marketing tool and a way to conduct online financial transactions. The business efficiencies were gained by increasing their business growth without employing extra staff and using existing staff in a more productive manner. Table 5 outlines these business efficiencies across the businesses.

The report acknowledges other non-financial benefits that also concur with findings in this study. The non-financial benefits reported by Ernst & Young relate to improvements in:

Table 4. Summary of e-commerce usage by SMEs (Chau, 2002b).

Electronic Banking	Sales & Marketing
• EFTPOS • EFT • Payroll • Bill Payment	On-line store Electronic marketing Demonstrate products Electronic Publishing
Communications	**Enhance Business Processes**
• E-mail communications • Intranet • Extranet • Internet • Product transfer / electronic delivery • Electronic publishing • Quality Assurance • FTP	• Customer relationship management • Alternative order entry systems • Customer reporting / enquires processes • Internet access to central databases • Improve quality assurance systems • Internal communications – Intranets • Franchise management
Customer Service	**Reduced Costs**
• Provision of alternative communications • Customers able to self-serve • Acquire direct feedback from the end-consumers	• Operational / Production Costs • Publishing Costs • Marketing / Demo Costs • Communication / Reporting Costs • Product / service Delivery • Free up resources

Table 5. E-commerce efficiencies (percentage of total) (Ernst & Young, 2001:6).

	All	Small	Medium	Large
Staff productivity	45	3	22	51
Communication	33	39	43	31
Marketing	12	17	12	12
Transaction	10	41	23	6

- customer service,
- improved communications between customer and business,
- the ability to collect customer-specific information from their websites,
- the ability to link their website to key suppliers improving inter-organisational relationships, and
- increasing the business exposure through the use of the website.

The financial and non-financial benefits reported by Ernst & Young share similarities with the various e-commerce activities described in this study in terms of efficiency gains in sales and marketing, enhancing business processes, communication and cost reduction, electronic banking functions and improving the quality of customer service. The report reinforces the point that real benefit (financial and non-financial) can be achieved through incorporation of e-commerce, however there are factors that can promote or hinder the ability of SMEs to gain e-commerce benefit.

Four Phases of E-Commerce Utilisation

The analysis of 34 SMEs suggests that the use of e-commerce can be distinguished into at least four phases of e-commerce utilisation (Chau, 2001a). These phases can be described as:

- Phase 1: Having a static presence on the web,
- Phase 2: Using e-commerce as an adjunct to traditional business,
- Phase 3: Integration of e-commerce into existing business processes, and
- Phase 4: Creating a virtual business structure.

This research found that individual businesses could establish themselves at any one of the four phases without necessarily progressing through any prior phase. This finding differs from other advocates that perceive that the adoption of e-commerce occurs over a number of set stages (Poon & Swatman, 1997; KPMG, 1997; Grant, 1999).

Further it was found as an SME increases its level of e-commerce business transformation by integrating e-commerce into existing business processes, the potential benefits derived from e-commerce increase (Chau & Turner, 2001b).

Figure 1 depicts the relationship between the degree of organisational transformation and potential e-commerce benefit for each of the four phases of e-commerce utilisation. Phase (Po) acknowledges those conventional SMEs that conduct no web-based e-commerce. SMEs located in Phase 3 or Phase 4 have a greater potential to derive benefit from e-commerce than those businesses positioned in Phase 1 or Phase 2. It was found that SMEs categorised in Phase 3 and Phase 4 support a more strategic approach to the use of e-commerce while SMEs located in Phase 1 and Phase 2 instigate e-commerce with an experimental view. The most significant benefits from e-commerce can be attained where there is a seamless integration of e-commerce applications into information systems infrastructures. The ability of SMEs to gain a relative advantage or success from e-commerce is dependent on a range of factors that govern the environment in which these businesses operate. The analysis of the data suggest that factors internal and external to the business influence the ability for SMEs to conduct e-commerce business transformation and apply new forms of technology such as e-commerce. The distribution of cases across the four phases is presented in the tables.

Impact of Internal and External Factors

The motivation, support and organisational skills of management significantly affect the utilisation of e-commerce. The amount of technological and financial resources allocated to develop, implement and support e-commerce

Figure 1. Impact of internal and external forces on the potential e-commerce benefits across four phases (Chau & Turner, 2002).

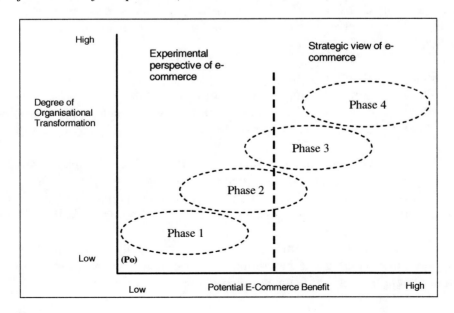

Table 6. Distribution of cases across the four phases.

Phase	Case	SME Type	Implications
Phase 1	Case C	Micro	• Product, business information
	Case A	Micro	• Static use of web
	Case F	Small	• Marketing, reduced publishing costs
	Case N	Small	
	Case P	Medium	
Phase 2	Case T	Micro	• Phase 2 e-commerce activities are focused at online sales systems and providing information about products and services.
	Case U	Micro	
	Case AE	Medium	
	Case AI	Micro	• No direct integration of e-commerce was found with established information systems.
	Case AJ	Micro	
	Case J	Small	
	Case Q	Medium	
	Case Y	Micro	
Phase 3	Case AC	Medium	• Integrated e-commerce system
	Case W	Micro	• E-commerce business transformation
	Case E	Medium	• Substantial benefit acquired from e-commerce
	Case Z	Small	• Use of e-commerce for customer information systems, supply chain management systems
	Case I	Medium	
	Case H	Small	• Increased workflow efficiencies
	Case AD	Medium	• Reduced production, communication, customer service and marketing costs
	Case L	Micro	
	Case K	Small	
	Case AG	Micro	
	Case O	Medium	
	Case R	Medium	
	Case S	Medium	
	Case AK	Micro	
Phase 4	Case B	Micro	• E-commerce application is central to their business
	Case D	Small	
	Case X	Micro	• Operate as a virtual enterprise
	Case V	Micro	• Online sales strategy
	Case AH	Micro	• Global client base
	Case G	Micro	
	Case AA	Small	

applications and the provision of suitable IT infrastructure to sustain e-commerce initiatives will determine the capacity of organisations to conduct e-commerce. In contrast, the influence of industry, external e-commerce service providers, government support and nature of the supply chain are all external factors which the organisation has little control of. The balance between those factors that can either positively influence the organisation or inhibit the ability of businesses to derive e-commerce benefit will ultimately determine the relative success of the business' capacity to effectively use e-commerce. If these factors impose a prohibitive or negative influence in the utilisation of e-commerce, potential problems can arise.

Potential Problems Associated with the Utilisation of E-Commerce

The most significant problems associated with the utilisation of e-commerce relates to those factors external to the business. In this study three types of external factors influenced the utilisation of e-commerce. The level of e-commerce services provided by ISPs and web developers, the critical mass of suppliers and consumers for e-commerce products and services, and the level of support from government and industry. The lack of appropriate services provided by ISPs and web developers and the lack of critical mass of suppliers and consumers were highlighted as collectively contributing to the ongoing problems associated with the utilisation of e-commerce in the SME business sector.

Lack of Services Provided by ISPs and Web Developers

The lack of regulation and standards for services and skills provided by the ICT industry have eventuated in numerous problems endured by the SMEs undertaking e-commerce. In this study 25% of the businesses experienced problems with the level of service and skills supplied by ISPs and web developers (Chau, 2002b).

ISPs emerged as important support structures for hosting websites and for providing input in their development. The problems reported by SMEs were associated to the poor level of service provided by ISPs and web developers who emerged as one of the largest external problem areas for SMEs utilising e-commerce.

> *Primarily, it (the ISP) evolved that they were not able to guarantee the level of access we required. They couldn't guarantee the number of connection hours. During peak time you may be online then you would be booted off. Which was hopeless. So that's basically why a succession of providers came and went. They did not provide the level of service that they claimed. (Case AI)*

This was particularly evident amongst SMEs with limited IT skills and experience.

> *I think the thing that a lot of us suffer from is a lack of well, we all suffer from a lack of knowledge apart from the guys who really are computer geeks but even then they suffer from a lack of commercial knowledge. They may have the technical knowledge but not the commercial knowledge and the problem, the main problem, is trying to find people who know what they're talking about and there is an awful lot of people out there offering all sorts of services and they haven't a bloody clue. (Case AJ)*

A lack of knowledge and experience by ISP/e-commerce developers was evident in three cases representing SMEs in different phases of e-commerce utilisation. From the case studies, businesses that developed e-commerce applications in-house had the least number of problems.

Critical Mass

Another significant e-commerce problem relates to the lack of a critical mass of suppliers and consumers that are e-commerce enabled and willing to conduct transaction online. The problem of critical mass was identified by many of the SMEs. Until a critical mass of suppliers actively using e-commerce eventuates across the supply chain, the potential for e-commerce benefits is limited.

> *The problem we have is that a lot of our customers have run small shops or small operations that don't have the technology so they can't sort of say we will put a PC in and email you an order. (Case S)*

Distributors and wholesalers included in the study expressed a desire to utilise more e-commerce in doing business with other resellers and participants but recognised these resellers were not at the time technologically capable. The critical mass of consumers is an important factor for those SMEs that primarily focus their e-commerce activities at the business-to-consumer side of the supply chain.

> *The problem is the customers. We discussed earlier on about the Internet situation as a hole open. When you start talking to teachers it's even worse. Firstly there's a huge range of teachers who are my age and not into computers. (Case X)*

The ability to reach a broader range of consumers located nationally and internationally has been a major driver in the use of e-commerce by many of the SMEs included in this study. However the relative success of the e-commerce systems is not only gauged by attracting clients to the site but converting the customer attraction into actual sales or active users of the services provided online. If the customers targeted by the business are not online or have access to the Internet the potential e-commerce benefit is significantly reduced.

> *I think being farmers they don't really have a lot to do with technology. Many farmers don't have the Internet available in some areas. So I can see coming from their angle they may say fine computers are good for what they do. But there is no huge benefit in having them. (Case AE)*

The SMEs that have previously established their business in the market-place are at a significant advantage. It is easier to trade to an established list of clients than it is to attract new clients and convert these into online sales or users of online services.

The Level of Support from Industry and Government

Analysis of the case studies indicated that the level of government assistance had been only a minor consideration in the adoption and utilisation of e-commerce among the cases studied. A number of government approaches were mentioned including: education and awareness programs for breaking down the barriers of misinformation and e-commerce adoption fears; direct financial assistance in terms of capital funds to subsidise e-commerce efforts helped a number of the small and micro enterprises. More generally the cases did reveal that other Government policies including tax and other initiatives were identified as potentially significant factors. These external factors affect the environment in which these SMEs operate. The SMEs indicated that the use of business champions showcasing the actual benefits derived from e-commerce as essential.

The problems discussed so far also coincide with findings in the Ernst & Young report listing the hurdles faced by the small businesses implementing e-commerce. The report by Ernst & Young (2001) found a series of implementation hurdles amongst their group of 34 small businesses using e-commerce. These included:

- Difficulty finding information about e-commerce and existing e-commerce applications.
- Difficulty finding an appropriate person or business that could develop their e-commerce application.
- Finding the time and resources to maintain and renovate their websites.
- Difficulty for regional businesses to gain access to ISPs at a cost-effective rate.
- Finding suitable logistic solutions for those businesses involved with exports.
- The lack of widespread use of e-commerce technologies by suppliers and customers.

Figure 2 illustrates the linkages between the various issues that may constrain the active utilisation of e-commerce by SMEs. The level of services provided by ISPs and web developers directly affects the ability of SMEs to design, develop, implement and maintain their e-commerce activities. Once the e-commerce applications have been established, the amount of suppliers and consumers willing to use e-commerce commercially directly influences the likely success of the business' e-commerce initiatives. Supporting all these agents is the government and respective industry bodies.

Figure 2. Confluence of potential problem areas that directly and indirectly affect the implementation and utilisation of SME e-commerce.

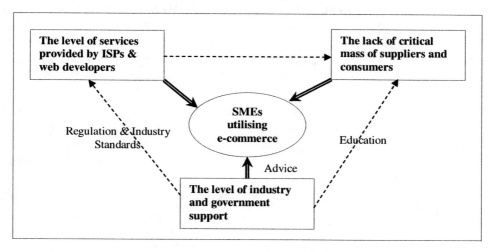

The government is in a prime position to directly support and regulate those businesses engaging in e-commerce but also the ICT industry plays an essential role providing services to SMEs requiring e-commerce skills and services. The influence of government and industry can have a profound influence on SMEs implementing and utilising e-commerce. The provision of financial aid and business advice can directly improve the relative success of e-commerce utilisation by SMEs. The level of service from the ICT industry sector responsible for providing e-commerce services to SMEs can be improved with government consultation with the ICT industry to develop a set of industry regulations and standards.

Similarly the government needs to promote and educate the value of e-commerce to those SMEs that are hesitant to incorporate e-commerce technologies within their business. An active educational and support service to encourage e-commerce participation may lead to attaining sufficient levels of critical mass of suppliers and consumers in industry sectors that are adverse to e-commerce participation.

CONCLUSION

This chapter has discussed the relative benefits available to SMEs contemplating the introduction of e-commerce. The level of potential e-commerce benefit depends upon a range of factors internal and external to the business. Internal factors can govern the ability of SMEs to engage in organisation transformation or integration of e-commerce into existing business processes.

However, it is the environment in which the business operates that can determine the ongoing success of the utilisation of e-commerce.

The report conducted by Ernst & Young (2001) investigating the relative benefits, costs and hurdles faced by a range of Australian small business implementing e-commerce supports many aspects of the research discussed in this chapter. It is of paramount importance that the government develops suitable public policy to encourage and support e-commerce participation by business and the community.

The government and industry associations have the power to formulate policies and guidelines to promote the participation of businesses to utilise e-commerce. The active use of government policy, regulations and industry support can encourage the effective use of e-commerce and indirectly address the issue of critical mass of e-commerce clients and suppliers and the regulation and of the ICT industry providing an acceptable standard of services to the business community.

SMEs are resource poor and have limited capital resources for technology innovation. SMEs can manage internal issues with limited resources but have little chance of controlling the business environment in which they operate. Through the effective use of government policies and regulations, governments can provide an essential mechanism to promote a business environment that encourages the active use of e-commerce among all SMEs.

REFERENCES

ABS. (1999). Australian Bureau of Statistics report. *Small Business in Australia*, No. 1321.0.

Burgess, S. (1998). *Information Technology in small business in Australia: A summary of recent studies.* Retrieved 10, 2002 from the World Wide Web: http://www.sbaer.uca.edu/docs.proceedingsII/98usa283.txt.

Cameron, J. & Clarke, R. (1996). Towards a theoretical framework for collaborative electronic commerce projects involving small and medium sized enterprises. *Proceedings of the Ninth International Conference EDI-IOS*, Bled Slovenia (June 10-12).

Chau, S. B. (2001a). Four phases of Ecommerce a small business perspective: An exploratory study of 23 Australian small businesses. *Proceedings of the Information Resource and Management Association Conference*, Toronto, Canada.

Chau, S. B. (2002b). *Developing a Four Phase Model: Thirty-Four Case Studies Exploring the Utilisation of Electronic Commerce in Australian Small and Medium Sized Enterprises.* Ph.D. Thesis, School of Information Systems, University of Tasmania.

Chau, S. B. & Turner, P. (2001b). A Four Phase Model of EC Business Transformation amongst Small to Medium Sized Enterprises: Preliminary Findings from 34 Australian Case Studies. *Proceedings of the 12th Australasian Conference on Information Systems,* Coffs Habour, (December 5-7).

Chau, S. B. & Turner, P. (2002a). A Framework for Analysing Factors Influencing Small to Medium Sized Enterprises (SMEs) Ability to Derive Benefit from the Conduct of Web-based Electronic Commerce (EC). *Proceedings of the Xth European Conference on Information Systems,* Gdansk, Poland (June 6-8).

Corbitt, B., Behrendorff, G. & Brown-Parker, J. (1997). SMEs and electronic commerce. *The Australian Institute of Management,* 14, 204-222.

Dandridge, T.C. (1979). 'Children are not little 'grown-ups': Small business needs its own organisational theory. *Journal of Small Business Management,* 17(2), 53-57.

Darke, P., Shanks, G. & Broadbent, M. (1998). Successfully completing case study research: combining rigour, relevance and pragmatism. *Information Systems Journal,* 8, 273-289.

Doolin, B. (1996). Alternative views of case research in information systems. *Australian Journal of Information Systems,* 3(2), 21-29.

Ernst & Young. (2001, September). *Advancing with e-commerce.* Commissioned by the National Office of Information Economy.

Freel, M. (2000). Barriers to product innovation in small manufacturing firms. *International Small Business Journal,* 18(2), 60.

Galliers, R. (1992). Choosing information systems research approach. In R. Galliers (Ed.), *Information Systems Research: Issues, Methods and Practical Guidelines.* Oxford: Blackwell Scientific Publications.

Galliers, R. D. & Land, F. F. (1997). Choosing appropriate information systems research methodologies. *Communications of the ACM,* 30, 900-902.

Grant, S. (1999). E-commerce for small business. *Proceedings of IeC99 2nd International Conference: Innovation through Electronic Commerce,* Manchester, UK (November 1-3, pp. 65-72).

Hughes, J., Ralf, M. & Michels, B. (1998). *Transform Your Supply Chain: Releasing Value in Business.* London: International Thomson Business Press.

KPMG. (1997). *Electronic Commerce Research Report 1997.* London.

Lawrence, K. L. & Keen, C. (1997). Factors inhibiting the utilisation of electronic commerce facilities in Tasmanian small- to medium-sized enterprises. *Proceedings of the 8th Australasian Conference on Information Systems.* Adelaide.

Lee, A.S. (1989, March). A scientific methodology for MIS case studies. *MIS Quarterly,* 13(1), 33-50.

Lowry, G., Singh, M. & Scollary, A. (1999). Electronic commerce initiatives in Australia: Identifying opportunity, meeting challenges and measuring success. *Proceedings of the 10th Australasian Conference on Information System,* Wellington, New Zealand (December 1-3, pp. 532-541).

MacGregor, R., Bunker, D. & Waugh, P. (1998). Electronic commerce and small/medium enterprises (SMEs) in Australia: An electronic data interchange (EDI) pilot study. *Eleventh International Bled Electronic Commerce Conference,* Bled, Slovenia (pp. 84-327).

Neuman, W. L. (2000). *Social Research Methods - Qualitative and Quantitative Approaches* (4th Edition). Allyn and Bacon.

NOIE. (2000a). National Office for the Information Economy, *Current State of Play-July 2000: Australia and the Information Economy,* Retrieved 1, 2001 from the World Wide Web: http://www.noie.gov.au/publications/index.htm.

NOIE. (2000b). National Office for the Information Economy, *Taking the Plunge - Sink or Swim: Attitudes and Experiences of SMEs to E-commerce.* Retrieved 1, 2001 from the World Wide Web: http://www.noie.gov.au/publications/index.htm.

Poon, S. & Swatman, P. (1998). Small business Internet commerce experiences: A longitudinal study. *Electronic Commerce in the Information Society, 11th International Bled Electronic Commerce Conference Bled.*

Poon, S. & Swatman, P.M.C. (1997). Emerging issues on small business use of the Internet: 23 Australian case studies. *Proceedings of the Fifth European Conference on Information Systems* (Vol. 2, pp. 882-895). Cork, Ireland.

Silverman, D. (1998). Qualitative research: Meanings or practices? *Information Systems Journal,* 8, 3-20.

Small Business Index. (1999, May). *Survey of computer technology and E-commerce in Australian Small and Medium Business,* Yellow Pages, Telstra Corporation Limited and National Office for the Information Economy.

Small Business Index. (2001, July). Survey of Computer Technology and E-Commerce in Australia Small and Medium Businesses. *Special Report: E-commerce and Computer Technology,* Telstra.

Venkatraman, N. (1994, Winter). IT-enabled business transformation: From automation to business scope redefinition. *Sloan Management Review,* 35(2), 73-87.

Welsh, J. & White, J. (1975). Cash flow forecasting: One solution to inadequate financing. *Journal of Small Business Management,* 13(1), 19-27.

Wong, M. & Turner, P. (2001, September). An Investigation of Drivers/Activators for the Adoption and utilisation of B2B Electronic Commerce amongst Small to Medium Sized Suppliers to the Tasmanian Pyrethrum Industry, *3rd Information Technology in Regional Areas Conference,* Central Queensland University, Rockhampton, Qld. 5-7.

Chapter VI

Obstacles to SMEs for E-Adoption in the Asia Pacific Region

Sushil K. Sharma, Ball State University, USA

Nilmini Wickramasinghe, Cleveland State University, USA

ABSTRACT

As electronic commerce (e-commerce) is becoming the way to trade, it is the large corporations that are exploiting their finances and technical expertise to jump into this abyss. Small and medium enterprises (SMEs) are finding too many obstacles to participate in e-commerce. SMEs in Asia Pacific in particular, face many obstacles and thus are still not comfortable with the concept of putting their business online, conducting transactions online or revamping entire business processes. This chapter describes the key factors that are hindering SMEs' participation in e-commerce and the obstacles to SMEs for e-adoption in Asia Pacific. Although this study is limited to the Asia Pacific region many of the findings do contribute significantly to the factors hindering all SMEs' e-adoption efforts.

INTRODUCTION

The fundamentals of competition are changing as a result of the growth of global markets, the increased speed of commoditization, the technological revolution and continued change in customer expectations. What is more the growth, integration, and sophistication of information and communication technologies (ICTs) is significantly impacting our society and economy. Today, computers and other electronic devices increasingly communicate and interact directly with other devices over a variety of networks, such as the Internet. Consumers and businesses have been particularly quick not only to recognize the potential but also to attempt to realize the benefits of adopting new computer-enabled networks. For instance, consumers now routinely use computer networks to identify sellers, evaluate products and services, compare prices, and buy and sell products and services. Businesses are using networks even more extensively to conduct and re-engineer production processes, streamline procurement processes, reach new customers, and manage internal operations. This is known as the electronic commerce (e-commerce) revolution.

The e-commerce revolution has affected all organizations but of particular interest is its effect on small and medium-sized enterprises (SMEs) since we can observe an interesting duality where these companies are most likely to benefit from the opportunities afforded by e-commerce (since through e-commerce it is possible to level the playing field) and yet they appear to be slowest in embracing many of these e-commerce possibilities. On several social and economic grounds, SMEs are of overwhelming importance in most of the Asia Pacific/Pacific Region. In fact, they comprise well over 90% of all enterprises in this region and provide employment for over half of the region's workforce (Wattanapruttipaisan, 2002; APEC, 2001). Typically, the SME sector accounts for upwards of 90% of all firms outside the agricultural sector of East and South-East Asia, and of Japan, as well (Alphonso, 2001; Regnier, 2000; Tambunan, 2000; Wattanapruttipaisan, 2002; A Report Prepared for Asia Pacific Foundation, 2002).

Given the importance of SMEs to this region, it becomes crucial to understand the obstacles they are facing and thus understand why e-commerce adoption has been slow, if at all, for these SMEs, and then, suggest changes to policy that may enable the alleviation of such obstacles and hence encourage the successful embracing of e-commerce for these SMEs. This chapter attempts to do just this by describing the key factors that are hindering SMEs' participation in e-commerce and the obstacles to SMEs for e-adoption in the Asia Pacific region based on qualitative findings from an on-going research study we are conducting that is focusing on SME adoption of e-commerce in the Asia Pacific region. Although the study is limited to Asia Pacific, we believe that the findings contribute significantly to our understanding of the hindering factors for all SMEs' e-adoption generally. The chapter is divided into three sections. The first section provides some background and then describes e-commerce for SMEs. The second section briefly discusses the research study and then presents the obstacles that are experienced by Asia Pacific SMEs for e-adoption that we found from the study and have confirmed and validated using the literature. The third section suggests the various measures and policy changes that are needed for encouraging SMEs to adopt e-commerce.

BACKGROUND

Electronic commerce (e-commerce) succinctly stated refers to any transaction completed over a computer-mediated network that involves the transfer of ownership or rights to use goods or services (Tambunan, 2000). E-commerce can be defined as the conduct of buying, selling and financial transactions by electronic means. E-commerce has been around for many years particularly in the form of EDI (electronic data interchange). However, it is the Internet that is bringing it to the fore (Afuah and Tucci, 2000) and the key aspect of e-commerce today, is doing business over the Internet. E-commerce levels the playing field and lets small organizations compete with large organizations. The concept of e-commerce is all about using the Internet to do business better and faster as well as shrinking traditional barriers of distance and time (ibid). It is about giving customers controlled access to your computer systems and letting people serve themselves. E-commerce is categorized into three categories: business to business or B2B (Cisco), business to consumer or B2C (Amazon), and consumer to consumer or C2C (eBay).

Despite the downturn in the Internet economy represented by the crash of many "dotcom" companies, several forecasts continue to predict huge potential in global e-commerce over the next several years (Turpin et al., 1998). For example, global business-to-business (B2B) e-commerce over the Internet is expected to reach between US$2 trillion to about US$10 trillion by 2004 (eMarketer Inc., 2002). With an estimated 188 million users at year-end 2002, the Asia Pacific-Pacific region constitutes the world's second largest Internet market as shown in Table 1, ahead of North America (eMarketer Inc., 2002), while Table 2 shows the number of Internet users for the main Asia Pacific/ Pacific countries.

South Korea, China, India, Singapore, Malaysia and Indonesia are leading in ICT proliferation and e-commerce offerings as compared to other countries (Hill, 1998). ICT use is related to general economic indicators, such as GDP, yet it is also affected by a wide range of other factors, including government policies, telecommunications costs, and social aspects (Beal, 2001; A Study Report on Thailand, 2001). Despite a sluggish economy in the Asia Pacific region, consumer demand for devices such as computers, mobile phones and personal digital assistants (PDAs) has remained consistent throughout the region, and

Table 1. Internet population.

Region	Number of Users (In Millions)
World Total	605.60
Africa	6.31
Asia Pacific/Pacific	187.24
Europe	190.91
Middle East	5.12
Canada and USA	182.67
Latin America	33.35

Source: eMarketer, Inc., NUA Survey www.nua.org

Table 2. Internet population in Asia Pacific.

Country	Internet Population in Millions	Percentage of Population %
Hong Kong	4.35	59.38
South Korea	25.6	53.8
Japan	56	44.1
Singapore	2.31	51.84
Malaysia	5.7	25.15
Indonesia	4.4	1.93
India	7	0.67
China	45.8	3.58

Source: eMarketer, Inc.

Internet usage is rising[1,2] (Debroy, 2002; UNCTAD, 2002; PriceWaterhouseCoopers, 1999), yet the adoption of e-commerce by SMEs has been notably slow.

Hong Kong leads the region in Internet penetration, as can be seen in Table 2. Proactive government support of Internet diffusion and an advanced communications and technology infrastructure have resulted in an Internet penetration rate of 59.38%. By contrast, the region's population giants like China, Indonesia and India suffer from relatively low Internet penetration rates (Liu, 1995). The variation in the Internet population is clearly affected by a number of complex factors, including size of the economy, both gross and per capita, telecommunications infrastructure, government policy, cultural preferences, and language (Beal, 2000; APEC, 1999).

As the usage of the Internet is growing, the e-commerce and e-business initiatives in Asia Pacific are growing at a very fast rate. eMarketer projects that business-to-business (B2B) e-commerce revenues will grow to exceed $300 billion in the Asia Pacific-Pacific region by 2004 (eMarketer, 2002, www. emarketer.com). Despite such a high growth of e-commerce in Asia Pacific-

Table 3. Revenues from e-commerce adoption.

Year	B2C E-commerce Revenues in the Asia Pacific-Pacific Region, 2000-2004 (in billions and as a % of revenues worldwide)
2000	$ 3.2 (5.3%)
2001	$ 8.2 (8.1%)
2002	$15.6 (9.3%)
2003	$ 26.4 (10.6%)
2004	Expected $ 38.0 (8.9%)

Source: eMarketer, Inc.

Pacific and other Asia Pacific countries, the percentage of revenues generated through business to consumers (B2C) e-commerce transactions are still very low as compared to developed countries (Beal, 2001) as can be evidenced in Table 3.

SMEs AND E-COMMERCE

E-commerce has been streamlining supply-chain activities, speeding inventory turnover and reducing cycle times, yet SMEs don't appear to be in the forefront of the e-commerce movement (Beale, 2000). SMEs have modernized and automated the way they do business and have been exploiting Internet technology to expand their reach and communication with their partners, suppliers and customers. However, their use of such ICT tools is limited to mostly administrative matters (ibid). SME use of information and communication technology (ICT) for e-commerce is still low. Many of the medium scale enterprises are focusing the Internet and ICT use only for office automation such as word-processing, spreadsheets, accounting, and payroll. SMEs in Asia Pacific have yet to take the actual plunge into e-commerce and are still skeptical of the e-commerce hype, and thus reluctant to embrace much of the required technology (A Report Prepared for Asia Pacific Foundation, 2002). E-commerce is still relatively a new playing field for these SMEs. Our study is looking at various factors affecting the SMEs' participation in e-commerce including but not limited to: the ICT infrastructure available to them, as well as many other factors at the macro and micro levels. SMEs account for approximately 70% of all business enterprises in the Asia Pacific region, and contribute about 25% of the gross national product (GNP), as well as provide jobs to about one-third of the total labor force in these countries (International Labor Organization, 2001). Given the important role that SMEs play in the generation of income and employment and the production of basic goods and services, it is imperative that SMEs embrace e-commerce to become more effective and efficient. In spite of this seemingly low penetration of SMEs in e-commerce, these indications do not mean that Asia Pacific is not yet e-ready. In fact, the proliferation of ICT and other technologies for e-commerce is increasing every year (Arunachalam, 1995; Sengenberger et al., 1990).

The adoption of e-commerce technologies is important for the ongoing survival of SMEs. The Internet can remove many of the competitive advantages of larger companies and provide opportunities for these smaller enterprises. It can also include a cost effective way for SMEs to market their business, launch new products, improve communications and information and identify potential partners (Sharma et al., 2003). Further, in the Internet-based economy, the large corporations would search for mergers and acquisitions, downsizing, relocation, and partnerships with SMEs to conduct business with efficiencies. SMEs have the advantage of their built-in flexibility, fast decision-making, low cost structure and 100% product and customer dedication. While electronic commerce technologies are important for SMEs, evidence reveals that growth in electronic commerce remains predominantly limited to more technically advanced companies (APCTT, 2000, 2001; Liedholm and Mead, 1998).

The most significant business benefits for SMEs from the use of electronic commerce are described below (Arunachalam, 1995; Sengenberger et al., 1990; Sharma et al., 2003; Afuah and Tucci, 2000).

- *Better service quality.* E-commerce can improve the quality of the marketing, sales, support and procurement process of SMEs by delivering more accurate, more timely and more complete information to the point of sale, point of decision or point of support. Service can also be delivered over a broader geographic and temporal base worldwide, or "any time, anywhere."
- *Reduced service costs.* The self-service Internet-based electronic commerce model is characterized by relatively low variable transaction costs, with increasing cost-effectiveness as the scale of activity increases. At higher volumes of activity Internet commerce channels for sales and support services are likely to be low-cost channels.
- *Increased revenue.* Extended geographic sales channels and improved service quality may lead directly to increased market share, improved competition among brands and greater revenue.
- *Reduced time to complete a business transaction.* By communicating electronically, the time required to place and confirm an order can be compressed by hours or, in some cases, days or weeks. This shortens the lead time for product delivery. As a result, it may be possible to reduce parts or finished goods inventories or receive critical products more rapidly to gain a competitive advantage.
- *Reduced administrative costs.* The cost of processing purchase requisitions, purchase orders and payments can be dramatically reduced, as can

invoice and bill presentation costs. The accuracy of business transactions is improved, increasing customer satisfaction, reducing transaction, auditing and administrative expenses, as well as reducing the costs of expedited manufacturing and/or shipping to correct erroneous or late orders.

- *Improved return on capital.* By shortening the "product turn" and payment cycles, enterprises can reduce the amount of material requirements and the time for which funds must be committed to pay for the production of inventory, materially lowering capital requirements.
- *Increased return on investment through better planning.* More timely planning and information allows more efficient acquisition and scheduling of capital equipment, reducing unit costs, increasing the return on investment, and ensuring a better match between manufacturing capacity, production and market demand.
- SMEs now can devote more time to their products and their customers and lose less time in unproductive administrative jobs; such as time savings associated with electronic purchasing and materials management.
- SMEs can enhance their local and international marketing efficiency through electronic catalogues and advertising through the Internet.
- SMEs can dramatically enhance their innovation capacity, i.e., technology watch, reverse and concurrent engineering, rapid prototyping and distance manufacturing.
- SMEs can bid on larger and international projects through networking with other partners worldwide and even with competitors.

Currently, there exist some studies that examine e-commerce adoption by SMEs in Asia Pacific (Beal, 2001; DRPAD, 1999; HSIAO, 2000; A Study Report on Thailand, 2001; Asia Pacific Foundation Report, 2002; OECD Report, 1998, 2002). All of these studies were reviewed before conducting our study. HSIAO (2000) presents a qualitative study of the barriers faced by SMEs to introduce business-to-business (B2B) e-commerce in Singapore. The investigation employs an interpretative approach that draws on the theory of "technological frames." The results of this study highlight four key factors that explain the adoption difficulties: lack of familiarity (with technology), risk aversion, lack of trust, and incongruent cultural practice. Similar to HSIAO, Dhawan and associates (Dhawan et al., 2000) performed a study examining the problems associated with building B2B e-marketplaces for SMEs. Both these studies were more focused on EDI aspects and B2B commerce rather than Business-to-Customers (B2C). However, all of these studies are relevant to understanding the adoption difficulties involved in e-commerce. Apart from these studies, we also examined studies not conducted in Asia Pacific (Allen et al., 2000; Arunachalam, 1995; Barrett, 1999; Barrett and Walsham, 1999; Kumar and Crook, 1999; Iacovou et al., 1995; Premkumar and Ramamurthy, 1995; Jones and Beatty, 1998; Pollalis, 2000). These studies suggest three groups of adoption barriers: technological, intra-organizational, and inter-organizational. Further, these studies mentioned various *technological barriers* such as network security, system integration, system migration, data conversion, and the compatibility of hardware and software, which includes problems related to the use of technology for EDI adoption (Jones and Beatty, 1998; Arunachalam, 1997; Bamfield, 1994; Curtis, 1996). Iacovou et al. (1995) examined *intra-organizational factors* such as lack of awareness of potential benefits and lack of appropriate training and education as adoption barriers for EDI and e-commerce. Few other researchers examined *inter-organizational factors* such as competitive pressure, power, trust and culture as adoption barriers (Reekers and Smithson, 1996; Premkumar, Ramamurthy and Crum, 1997). Given this extensive literature analysis we focused our study on examining the factors for e-commerce adoption by SMEs in the Asia Pacific region.

RESEARCH METHODOLOGY

The methodology adopted was based on a survey instrument and personal interactions and interviews with business executives of SMEs. For the purposes of our study, an SME was defined in accordance with the EU definition as firms with less than 250 full-time employees. Detailed structured and semi-structured interviews were conducted involving business executives. Two different kinds of data collected through structured questionnaires and interviews were analyzed. The sample consisted of 100 SMEs. E-mails along with structured questionnaires were sent to approximately 500 different SMEs in this region (i.e., South East Asia Pacific) through e-mail, but received only a one-fifth response rate. The selection was made from business reports and searching on the Internet. Clearly this would bias sample selection but in a positive fashion, i.e., we would be selecting, more likely than not, the most technology advanced SMEs and hence understanding the obstacles they faced in spite of comparative success would be a useful starting point in determining factors that affect e-adoption with respect to SMEs. The data was collected from Thailand (7), Singapore (31), Philippines (8), Malaysia (15), Cambodia (5), China (27) and Vietnam (7). Also, a request was made for in-depth interviews with key business executives. The chapter is based on only qualitative data the findings and not on quantitative analysis from this study. Hence, what follows is an identification of the obstacles and barriers we identified and how we believe changes in policy can alleviate some of these obstacles for SMEs. Our future quantitative analyses will provide rigorous mappings of differences within and between countries with respect to e-adoption by SMEs in the Asia Pacific region.

OBSTACLES OR BARRIERS TO THE ADOPTION OF E-COMMERCE

The potential opportunities and benefits of electronic commerce for SMEs include strengthening customer relationships, reaching new markets, optimizing business processes, reducing costs, improving business knowledge, attracting investment and creating new products and services (APEC, 1999). Specifically, e-commerce represents an opportunity for SMEs to compensate for their traditional weaknesses in areas such as access to new markets and gathering and diffusing information on a broad and international scale. E-commerce could enable SMEs to compete against larger, more established firms and in new and previously untapped markets. However, SMEs also have to be aware that Internet and e-commerce would also create more sophisticated and demanding customers with higher expectations, in terms of 24-hour access to company and product information and quicker response times to information requests. Asia Pacific governments are actively encouraging the diffusion of electronic commerce in SMEs as a way to improve their competitiveness and access to new markets. Many initiatives have been taken, such as raising awareness, establishing development centers, creating business access points, and providing education and training programs. Despite all these, the following are the various obstacles that are experienced by Asia Pacific SMEs for e-adoption that we have found through our study.

Lack of Awareness Among SMEs about E-Commerce

This first and basic obstacle for adoption of e-commerce usage among SMEs in Asia Pacific is the lack of awareness of e-commerce and the availability and access to telecom infrastructure at a reasonable cost. This finding was confirmed by the APEC Report (2002). Many SMEs are found to be unaware of the developments taking place and the role they could play in this new marketplace. At times, the persons involved in SMEs found e-commerce literature too technical and complicated. Unless governments or other agencies simplify technical information for them, SMEs find it difficult to get involved in e-commerce concepts and implementation. Many Asia Pacific countries also found the English language as a big barrier since the people involved conduct their business using local languages. The lack of awareness is closely linked to the fact that SMEs in Asia Pacific usually are slower in adopting new technologies given the often high investments necessary. Many of the Asia Pacific SMEs are also found to be less inclined to take risks and not ready to experiment (APEC, 1999; Hall, 2002).

Lack of Critical Mass of Customers, Suppliers and Business Partners

Another obstacle we found experienced by Asia Pacific SMEs is the lack of a critical mass among customers, suppliers, and business partners. The lack of a critical mass of these stakeholders is due to either ignorance or fears of a lack of security and privacy using electronic means. The e-commerce infrastructure is very poor in Asia Pacific countries and online shopping is not yet very popular among the masses. Due to low use of e-commerce, there is not enough of a mass of customers and suppliers for e-commerce and this acts as a discouraging factor for SMEs to jump in and join the e-commerce revolution. There are not very many marketplaces that could attract SMEs to take advantage (APEC, 1999). Until sufficient numbers of their main local customers or suppliers participate in online commerce activities, there is little incentive for individual SMEs to become engaged in electronic commerce themselves. In Asia Pacific countries, SMEs cited several factors contributing to low levels of customer electronic commerce use including: language barriers and low levels of English fluency, lack of comfort and familiarity with electronic commerce technologies, a cultural preference for more traditional trade practices involving face-to-face contact between buyer and seller, and continued preference for the use of cash in transactions. SMEs fear doing business with international marketplaces due to cultural backgrounds and a fear of getting deceived due to lack to knowledge of new technologies. These aspects are confirmed by many current reports (APEC, 1999; A Report Prepared for Asia Pacific Foundation, 2002; DRPAD, 1999; A Study Report on Thailand, 2001; Beal, 2000; Turpin, 2000; APCTT, 2000, 2001; Hall, 2002).

Recently, the governments have been offering citizens and businesses the opportunity to file tax return or customs declaration electronically. Electronic transactions between business partners are only just taking off. The possibility to hand in the tax return or customs declaration electronically has given a tremendous push in a few countries towards a stronger need for SMEs to get into e-commerce. There is a growing realization among few SMEs that if they do not keep up with the evolution of e-commerce, they are in danger of being left out in the international competition, particularly where larger corporations are pushing business that could be attractive for SMEs.

Trust and Confidence

Lack of trust and confidence in various aspects of the electronic marketplace was identified as another main obstacle to the growth of the electronic commerce market in general, and for SME engagement in e-commerce in particular. The security issue is perceived as very important across the Asia Pacific region, and the majority of SMEs have a fear of electronics. Security may not be a serious problem but due to low level of technology diffusion and awareness among SMEs, it is still a psychological barrier for SMEs as confirmed in various reports (APEC, 1999; A Report Prepared for Asia Pacific Foundation, 2002; DRPAD, 1999; Beal, 2000; Turpin, 2000; APCTT, 2000, 2001). Many of these SMEs do not have technical backgrounds, and are not convinced that technology standards such as encryption will protect them. Due to such perceived security fears, SMEs are not willing to use electronic payment systems. Credit cards and e-checks are naturally then a distant dream for many of them. Security, legal, and liability issues were frequently identified as very important concerns of participating SMEs in Asia Pacific. Asia Pacific SMEs don't trust electronic commerce or the technical infrastructure to support it. Trust and confidence in a sound legal framework and security standards are necessary to make e-commerce happen on a larger scale (APEC, 1999; Hall, 2002).

Confidence in Legal and Regulatory Framework

The lack of a comprehensive and acceptable legal and regulatory framework is an issue for Asia Pacific SMEs. Most of the responses indicate that SMEs want government interventions for developing an appropriate legal framework for protecting them against any frauds or disputes. Many of these Asia Pacific countries still do not have laws for electronic contracts, invoices and other types of documentation in place. E-commerce demands several legal and liability issues to be addressed before it is widely accepted by SMEs and others in the Asia Pacific. Conducting business through electronic networks raises numerous legal questions that include: the legal status and enforceability of electronic contracts; the legal jurisdiction of international e-commerce transactions; intellectual property rights and copyright protection for digital content; the privacy of personal data; and the validity of electronic "evidence" in legal disputes (APEC, 1999; Wade, 1990). All of these concerns about legal and liability issues are very important to participating SMEs. Most of the Asia Pacific countries still do not have a legal and regulatory infrastructure in place and have not addressed these issues. Unless these issues are addressed, Asia Pacific SMEs may not choose e-commerce as a medium for their business. Asia Pacific SMEs also have concerns about international legal protection such as global patent applicability, global taxation and consumer protection, as documented in many reports (APEC, 1999; A Report Prepared for Asia Pacific Foundation, 2002; DRPAD, 1999; A Study Report on Thailand, 2001; Beal, 2000; Turpin, 2000; APCTT, 2000, 2001).

Taxation

Asia Pacific SMEs are concerned about taxation issues. Taxation processes in these countries are not transparent and often subject to the discretion of evaluators. There are many malpractices to avoid taxes and they do not want to have other countries' tax laws, which they anticipate could be more stringent and tougher. SMEs also lack the guidance of lawyers since many of then cannot afford the high fees necessary for sound legal advice on these matters. The application of existing taxation on commerce conducted over the Internet should be consistent with the established principles of international taxation, should be neutral with respect to other forms of commerce, should avoid inconsistent national tax jurisdictions and double taxation, and should be simple to administer and easy to understand (Hall, 1995, 2000).

Lack of Knowledge of E-Commerce

Asia Pacific SMEs lack extensive knowledge of e-commerce technologies and that itself is one of the big obstacles for their participation and engagement in e-commerce. Due to a lack of knowledge of e-commerce technologies, there is an internal resistance to change and skepticism of the benefits of e-commerce among SMEs. E-commerce demands fundamental shifts in business strategies, operations and technologies. Many participating SMEs indicated that they have limited access to information about the business models and technologies that are the basis of e-commerce success. Lack of knowledgeable staff in SMEs is also responsible for non-adoption of e-commerce. An issue often cited by participating Asia Pacific SMEs was the general lack of success stories available to demonstrate that electronic commerce can be successfully implemented by firms that are similar in some way to their own. Asia Pacific SMEs do not have many success stories that could motivate other SMEs for e-commerce adoption.

Due to the dot.com bubble bust, it has created a significant discouraging factor in many of the SMEs' minds and a very conservative view to the adoption of e-commerce. Few early e-commerce adopters have not lived up to expectations and have experienced failures perhaps due to low customer use in domestic markets or lack of integration into firm business models. Many SMEs are not willing to engage in e-commerce because they fear that there will be many who will copy their ideas and approaches overnight if they disclose their tips on e-commerce.

Information Infrastructure Access, Quality, and Cost

Despite the cost reduction of Internet-based technology, implementing e-commerce solutions still represents a considerable and costly challenge for most SMEs in the Asia Pacific region. Large corporations with more funding, more attainable skills, and with strengths in building solid business strategies could afford e-commerce deployment. But most SMEs typically with less cash and a shortage of IT staff and necessary infrastructure are not able to afford to use e-commerce. Insufficient access to appropriate information infrastructure of suitable quality, at reasonable cost, is a fundamental barrier to SME adoption and use of electronic commerce in Asia Pacific (Hall, 1995). The information infrastructure required for electronic commerce involves reliable telecommunications links and Internet services being available to SMEs. The level of information infrastructure to support electronic commerce applications differs greatly among the Asia Pacific countries from very poor to moderate. E-commerce applications greatly cut enterprise procurement costs and bolster the efficiency of business operations. However, low-level computerization and inferior e-commerce infrastructure reduced Internet contributions to the majority of Asia Pacific SMEs. Our study shows that although 70% of SMEs have connected with the Internet, most of them simply opened a homepage and an e-mail address. E-commerce applications demand a good bandwidth both at the level of the firm and also in local and international telecommunications networks and many Asia Pacific countries do not have requisite infrastructure for the same (APEC, 1999; A Report Prepared for Asia Pacific Foundation, 2002; DRPAD, 1999; A Study Report on Thailand, 2001; Beal, 2000; Turpin, 2000; APCTT, 2000, 2001). The cost of telecommunication infrastructure for requisite bandwidth is also beyond the reach of many of the SMEs. Most of the Asia Pacific countries suffer poor infrastructure of electricity and energy. There are many parts where getting four to five hours electricity in a day itself is an issue, therefore, SMEs can not think of engaging themselves in e-commerce. Additionally, telecommunication access and usage costs are still prohibitively high in most Asia Pacific countries and are seen as a major obstacle to SMEs for e-adoption (APEC, 1999).

Payment and Delivery Systems

Although Asia Pacific's Internet players are rushing to promote e-commerce as a creative business mode for the new economy, few of them can break through the last-mile barriers against online purchasing. These barriers have been attributed to the lack of a standard credit system and an effective express network, two critical elements for the operation of online shopping and business transaction. Credit card and off-line payment, or a combination of the two, are by far the most used means of payment. Only very few SMEs — those that are technology developers themselves — support electronic cash, electronic checks and micro-payment. Asia Pacific SMEs do not have appropriate supporting payment and distribution systems in place for the adoption of electronic commerce. The majority of customers and suppliers do not use credit cards for their payments in Asia Pacific countries. Therefore, the development of electronic payment systems, including the use of credit cards, is limited. A relatively low credit card penetration among consumers acts as a domestic constraint to business-to-consumer e-commerce development. Also, in many cases it is the "mindset" which inhibits the adoption of online credit card payment. Credit card culture is not there in the society hence, both credit card companies and consumers shy away from using credit cards for transactions. The financial network of banks and other institutions do not have their databases integrated and available online (APEC, 1999; A Report Prepared for Asia Pacific Foundation, 2002; DRPAD, 1999; A Study Report on Thailand, 2001; Beal, 2000; Turpin, 2000; APCTT, 2000, 2001). Therefore, credit card companies are concerned about fraudulent transactions and their inability to track down suspicious transactions while consumers are concerned about illegal usage of their accounts by Internet hackers. These perceptions can also be attributed to a lack of awareness of current security technologies. Even for those SMEs who regularly use the Internet, business transactions continue to be completed via offline means (APEC, 1999).

Asia Pacific countries do not have a strong road, rail, and air network to support the e-commerce delivery system. Further, many postal systems are not as efficient as is found in developed countries. Due to the poor quality and limitations of postal delivery and other distribution channels, the speedy delivery of products and services is not possible. Thus consumers do not perceive the benefits of e-commerce for reducing costs and faster delivery (A Report Prepared for Asia Pacific Foundation, 2002; APCTT, 2001).

MEASURES AND CHANGES TO POLICY TO ENCOURAGE THE ADOPTION OF E-COMMERCE BY SMEs

The following measures could be undertaken by the Asia Pacific countries. In particular, the respective governments should address policy issues to encourage the adoption of e-commerce by SMEs.

Improve Information Infrastructure

Governments should promote an open and competitive telecommunications industry in the country. The lack of poor telecommunication infrastructure in the Asia Pacific region generally makes e-commerce a lot more difficult. The government should take special measures such as encouraging competition in the telecom industry, reducing ISP connection and communication costs, and developing and improving access to the Internet. The government should take measures toward improving and enhancing the development of the information highway and the supporting telecommunications infrastructure (Sugasawa and Liyanage, 1999). Since most of the Asia Pacific countries did not have electronic payment system infrastructure in place, government and financial institutions need to initiate the steps to increase credit card penetration among consumers and develop the legal framework to support the acceptance of credit card transactions (APEC, 1999; Wade, 1990; Liedholm and Mead, 1998).

Develop a Legal Framework

Measures to protect online customers from fraud, including e-commerce laws ensuring legality of online contracts and transactions, will be important in deepening e-commerce use. Changes to banking laws will be necessary in some countries to ensure that credit card transactions and foreign currency transactions are affordable and enforceable.

The development of a legal framework to support electronic commerce would be an important step towards building trust and confidence in the electronic marketplace. The government should create legal frameworks, appropriate laws and tax structures that provide the necessary protection for SMEs as they attempt to embrace e-commerce possibilities (A Report Prepared for Asia Pacific Foundation, 2002; A Study Report on Thailand, 2001; Beal, 2000; Turpin, 2000; APCTT, 2001).

Raise Business Awareness of Electronic Commerce

A key factor influencing the adoption and use of electronic commerce by SMEs is increasing the awareness and understanding of the benefits and opportunities that electronic commerce can offer SMEs. Measures to increase awareness of the relevance of e-commerce to the SMEs' businesses and of the capacity of electronic commerce to help increase customer service, competitiveness, productivity, and market access are thus important (Liedholm and Mead, 1998).

Improve Business Access to the Internet

Continued deregulation of the telecommunications industry will be important in lowering costs and increasing physical access to areas outside major cities. The government has to ensure that steps are taken to improve business access to the Internet. Most of the Asia Pacific countries have limited penetration of ISP hosts and Internet applications among SMEs, perhaps due to restrictions such as high cost of connection rates and limited access points. The government and other stakeholders have to promote and initiate awareness campaigns, program education and training among these SMEs, and convince them that greater opportunities exist for SMEs if more firms are engaged as a part of the larger e-commerce business network. There may be the need to establish development centers and pilot projects and creating business access centers and points of contact (APEC, 1999; A Report Prepared for Asia Pacific Foundation, 2002; DRPAD, 1999; A Study Report on Thailand, 2001; Beal, 2000; Turpin, 2000; APCTT, 2000, 2001).

Enhance Government E-Commerce Use and Services

The governments in these countries need to improve and offer government services on the Internet such as information products, advisory services, and business networking facilities to increase the adoption and use of electronic commerce (Hall, 1995; Wade, 1990).

Build Firm-Wide E-Commerce Capacities

Building firm-wide electronic commerce capacities through education, training and skills development is an important enabling condition for the diffusion of electronic commerce in SMEs. Training and skills development involves an important cost to SMEs, but builds awareness of electronic commerce and can facilitate the shift from awareness to implementation. The most important thing for the development of e-commerce within the SME population is the development of a track record of success stories (Beal, 2000; Turpin, 2000; APCTT, 2000, 2001; Liedholm and Mead, 1998).

How to Address Policy

From the findings of our study and the preceding discussion, we can categorize the obstacles faced by SMEs in the Asia Pacific region in terms of four broad dimensions: business infrastructure, regulatory or commerce infrastructure, user infrastructure and telecommunications infrastructure. Specifically, 1) the business infrastructure includes the areas discussed above such as the need to raise business awareness of electronic commerce and to improve business access to the Internet; 2) the regulatory infrastructure includes how to develop an appropriate legal framework; 3) the user infrastructure includes how to build firm-wide e-commerce capabilities; and 4) the telecommunications infrastructure includes but is not limited to the building, maintaining and support of phone lines, fiber trunks and submarine cables, T1, T3 and OC-xx, ISDN, DSL other high-speed services used by businesses as well as satellites, earth stations and teleports.

Using these four dimensions, we developed a strategic grid of e-business potential for SMEs as depicted in Figure 1. This gird serves at least two roles. First it enables SMEs to position their current state in terms of low or high with respect to these four key parameters and thereby identify the areas that they must address in order to achieve the desired state of high e-business potential. Of equal, if not greater importance, the grid facilitates government efforts to address policy changes. By looking at a plot of SMEs in a particular country, government officials and policy makers will be able to identify the key problem areas, for example regulatory or commerce infrastructure deficiencies, and then address these and effect new policies to provide the necessary support for the SMEs in this country.

Key considerations in maintaining and sustaining e-business potential is for government policies to focus on investments into R&D, attracting foreign investment and educating their population. Language, education and technical infrastructure are the three major reasons cited for a country or region lagging behind in the e-business race (Sprano and Zakak, 2000). Our strategic map and framework to assess e-business potential shows that there are other key considerations that must be taken into account. Furthermore, our framework shows that the key to developing a country's e-business potential rests with the development of a country's strategic polices and the role of government to facilitate, enable, support, and encourage all facets of e-business. As Kofi Annan notes in his forward to the e-commerce and development report (2002), "knowing that an instrument is powerful is not enough to ensure that it will be put to the best use. We need to understand how it works, and how and when it should be used ... and maximize its power." We are confident our framework will help to develop such an understanding by helping decision makers and policy makers have a robust and systematic tool to help them analyze the current state and then realize what is required with respect to policy to move from a low e-business potential reflected in our framework as 3 (refer to Figure 1) to a high e-business potential, reflected in our figure as position 1. Policy initiatives in this scenario

Figure 1. Strategic grid of e-business potential.

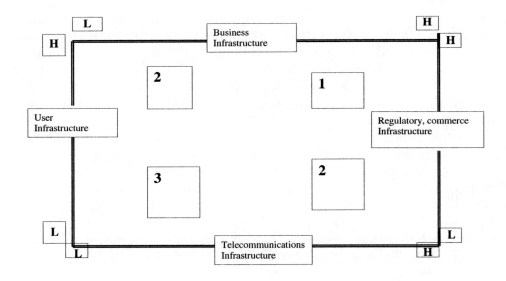

1   High e-business potential

2   Medium e-business potential

3   Low e-business potential

must focus on improving the key areas of user infrastructure, business infrastructure, telecommunications infrastructure as well as the regulatory, commerce infrastructure.

CONCLUSION AND SUGGESTIONS FOR FURTHER RESEARCH

Our study indicates that SMEs face many obstacles with respect to e-adoption. Furthermore, we note that governments have an important role to play in encouraging SMEs to embrace e-commerce in Asia Pacific countries. SMEs in Asia Pacific countries need to be made more competitive by promoting the development and use of electronic commerce. In particular, governments must address four key areas so that high e-business potential will ensue for these SMEs. Namely, they must address the areas of business infrastructure, regulatory or commerce infrastructure, user infrastructure, and telecommunications infrastructure. Measures should be taken to promote greater awareness of the opportunities and benefits of electronic commerce for SMEs, such as training and skills development programs and the distribution of best practices (Hall, 1995). In addition, governments should enhance the climate for investment to attract and retain venture capital and investment in SMEs with potential for rapid growth. Also measures are needed to ensure consumer and supplier access to the Internet and to appropriate electronic payment systems, the enhancement of consumer protection, and the maintenance of business ethics and good business practice in electronic commerce. There is also the need to strengthen the domestic legal framework, such as ensuring the validity and enforcement of contracts, intellectual property protection including copyright and trademark protection, and legal recourse mechanisms in disputes. It is only through the systematic efforts of government and policy makers to encourage e-commerce adoption by SMEs and at the same time ensuring that the appropriate safe guards and controls are in place will SMEs in the Asia Pacific region begin to embrace e-commerce. E-commerce is critical to the long-term success and sustainability of SMEs in this region and it is imperative that the full e-business potential that e-commerce affords can be utilized and maximized.

This chapter examined barriers or obstacles to adoption of electronic commerce by SMEs from all industry sectors in 15 Asia Pacific countries. Asia Pacific countries collectively or individually may undertake further studies to examine what specific policies and other action plans would be needed for e-commerce adoption by SMEs in their respective countries. An analysis of business models, business networks and communities of interest would provide SMEs with an understanding of the range of business models and e-commerce options that are available. Given the importance of SMEs to the Asia Pacific region we strongly urge for further research in this area.

REFERENCES

A Report Prepared for Asia Pacific Foundation. (2002). E-commerce and Asia Pacific, Castle Asia Pacific.

A Report by Development Research and Policy Analysis Division (DRPAD). (1999). Promotion of Trade and Investment through Electronic Commerce in Asia Pacific.

A Study Report on Thailand. (2001). SMEs and E-commerce, Asia Pacific Foundation.

Afuah, A. and Tucci, C. (2000). *Internet Business Models.* Boston, MA: McGraw-Hill Irwin.

APEC. (1999). *SME Electronic Commerce Study – Final Report.*

APEC. (2001). *The new economy and APEC.* Report to the Economic Committee of APEC. (Mimeographed).

Allen, D. K., Colligan, A. F. and Kern, T. (2000). Trust, Power and Inter-Organizational Information Systems: The Case of the Electronic Trading Community TranLease. *Information Systems Journal,* 10, 21-40.

Alphonso, O. M. and Co, M. R. (eds.). (2001). *Bridging the Gap – Philippine SMEs and Globalization.* Manila, Small Enterprises Research and Development Foundation.

Arunachalam, V. (1995). EDI: An Analysis of Adoption, Uses, Benefits and Barriers. *Journal of Systems Management,* 46(2), 60-65.

Bamfield, J. (1994). Learning by Doing: Electronic Data Interchange Adoption by Retailers. *Logistics Information Management,* 7(6), 32-40.

Barrett, M. and Walsham, G. (1999). Electronic Trading and Work Transformation in the London Insurance Market. *Information Systems Research,* 10(1), 1-22.

Barrett, M. I. (1999). Challenges of EDI Adoption for Electronic Trading in the London Insurance Market. *European Journal of Information Systems,* 8(1), 1-15.

Baskerville, R. and Smithson, S. (1995). Information Technology and New Organizational Forms: Choosing Chaos Over Panaceas. *European Journal of Information Systems,* 4(2), 66-73.

Beal, T. (2000). SMEs and the World Wide Web: Opportunities and Prospects. In A. M. Asri (Ed.), *Small And Medium Enterprises In Asia Pacific; Vol. III: Development Prospects.* Commack, NY: Nova Science Publishers.

Beal, T. (2001). Patterns of Internet development in the New Economy: Implications for Asia Pacific in SMEs. In A. M. Asri (Ed.), *Small and Medium Enterprises in the Information Age: Asia Pacific Perspectives.* Leeds: Wisdom House. (Forthcoming).

Chamarik, S. and Goonatilake, S. (1994). *Technological Independence: The Asia Pacific Experience.* Tokyo: United Nations University Press.

Charles, H. and Turpin, T. (1997). China's Market Reforms and Its New Forms of Scientific and Business Alliance. In C. A. Tisdell and J.C.H. Chai (Eds.), *China's Economic Growth and Transition.* New York: Nova Science.

Christerson, B. and Lever, T.C. (1996). *The third China? China's Rural Enterprises as Dependent Subcontractors or as Dynamic Autonomous Firms?* Paper presented to the Asia Pacific-Pacific Regional Conference of Sociology, Manilla, May 28-31.

Debroy, B. (2002). Information and communications technology and development: An Indian perspective. *Bulletin on Asia-Pacific Perspectives 2001/02* (Bangkok, ESCAP).

Dhawan, R. K., Mangaleswaran, R., Padhi, A., Sankhe, S., Schween, K. and Vaish, P. (2000). The Asia Pacificn Difference in B2B. *McKinsey Quarterly,* 4, 38-47.

eMarketer Inc. (n.d.). Retrieved from WWW: http://live.emarketer.com/

Hall, C. (1995). Investing in Intangibles: Improving the Effectiveness of Government SME Advisory Services in the APEC Region. *Report of APEC Symposium on HRD for SMEs,* APEC, China Productivity Centre, Chinese Taipei.

Hall, C. (2002). *Profile of SMEs and SME issues in APEC 1999-2000.* Final draft report, August. (Mimeographed).

HSIAO R. (2000). The Adoption Difficulty of B2B E-Commerce. In Asia Pacific, Department of Decision Sciences, NUS Business School, National University of Singapore, Singapore.

Hill, H. (1998). *Indonesia's Industrial Transformation.* Sydney: Allen and Unwin.

Hill, H. and Wie, T. K. (1998). *Indonesia's Technological Challenge.* Institute of Southeast Asia Pacificn Studies.

Iacovou, C. L., Benbasat, I. and Dexter, A.S. (1995). Electronic Data Interchange and Small Organizations: Adoption and Impact of Technology. *MIS Quarterly,* 19(4), 465-85.

International Labor Organization. (2001). *World Employment Report 2001, Life at work in the information economy.* Geneva.

Kumar, R. L. and Crook, C.W. (1999). A Multi-Disciplinary Framework of the Management of Inter-organizational Systems. *Database for Advances in Information Systems,* 30(1), 22-38.

Lallana, E.C., Pascual, P. and Andam, Z.R. (2002). *SMEs and e-commerce in three Philippine cities.* Prepared for the Asia Pacific Foundation.

Liedholm, C. and Mead, D. (1998). The dynamics of macro and small enterprises in developing countries. *World Development*, 26(1).

Liu, P. C. (1995). The Role of SMEs in Economic Development of Chinese Taipei. *Report of APEC Symposium on HRD for SMEs,* APEC, China Productivity Centre, Chinese Taipei.

NUA Internet Surveys. (n.d.). Retrieved from WWW: http://www.nua.ie/ surveys/

Organisation for Economic Co-operation and Development (OECD). (1998). Growth for electronic commerce: Present and Potential.

Organisation for Economic Co-operation and Development (OECD). (2002). *China in the World Economy – The Domestic Policy Challenges* (Paris, OECD Centre).

Pollalis, Y.A. (2000). *E-Commerce Opportunities for Small and Medium-sized Enterprises (SMEs): Analysis & Cases within the European Union.*

Premkumar, G. and Ramamurthy, K. (1995). The Role of Inter-organizational and Organizational Factors on the Decision Mode for Adoption of Inter-organizational Systems. *Decision Sciences,* 26(3), 303-337.

Premkumar, G., Ramamurthy, K., and Crum, M.R. (1997). Determinants of EDI Adoption in the Transportation Industry. *European Journal of Information Systems,* 6(2), 107-121.

PriceWaterhouseCoopers. (1999). *SME electronic commerce study.* Report to the APEC Telecommunications Working Group and Business Facilitation Steering Group. (Mimeographed).

Proceedings of the Regional Seminar on Electronic Commerce. (2001). Organized by the APT, Asia Pacific and Pacific Center for Transfer of Technology (APCTT) and Department of Telecommunication (DoT), Government of India, December 11-14.

Proceedings of the Seminar on Electronic Commerce Strategies for the Asia Pacific-Pacific. (2000). Organized by the APT and Asia Pacificn and Pacific Center for Technology Transfer of Technology (APCTT) and sponsored by Department of Telecommunications Services (DTS) and Department of Telecommunication (DoT), Government of India, August 8-10.

Ramsdell, G. (2000). The Real Business of B2B. *McKinsey Quarterly,* 3, 178-188.

Reekers, N. and Smithson, S. (1996). The Role of EDI in Inter-Organizational Coordination in the European Automotive Industry. *European Journal of Information Systems,* 5(2), 120-130.

Regnier, P. (2000). *Small and Medium Enterprises in Distress – Thailand, the East Asian Crisis and Beyond.* Aldershot: Gower Publishing.

Schive, C. (1995). Industrial Policies in a Maturing Taiwan Economy. *Journal of Industry Studies,* 2(1).

Sengenberger, W., Loveman, G. and Piore, G. (1990). *The Re-emergence of Small Enterprises: Industrial Restructuring in Industrial Countries.* International Institute of Labour Studies, Geneva.

Sharma, S.K., Wickramansinghe, N. and Gupta, J.N.D. (2003). *What Should SMEs Do To Succeed In Todays Knowledge-Based Economy.* (working paper).

Sprano, E. and Zakak, A. (2000). E-commerce capable: Competitive advantage for countries in the new world e-conomy. *Competitiveness Review,* 10(2), 114-131.

Sugasawa, Y. and Liyanage, S. (1999). Technology and Business Opportunities for small and medium enterprises in Japan: The role of research networks. *International Journal of Technology Management,* 18(3/4), 308-325.

Tambunan, T. T. H. (2000). *Development of Small-Scale Industries during the New Order Government in Indonesia.* Aldershot: Gower Publishing Limited.

Turpin, T. (2000). *SMEs and technology diffusion in Asia Pacific-Pacific economies: Indonesia a case-study.* Annual Conference of the Academy of International Business Southeast Asia Pacific Region, International Business Research Institute, University of Wollongong, Australia.

Turpin, T. and Xielin, L. (2000). Balanced Development: the Challenge for Science, Technology and Innovation Policy. In C. Harvie (Ed.), *Contemporary Development and Issues in China's Economic Transition.* Melbourne, Australia: Macmillan.

Turpin, T., Spence, H., Garrett, J.S. and Marsh, A. (1998). South-East Asia Pacific and the Pacific Rim. In H. J. Moore (Ed.), *World Science Report,* UNESCO (pp. 212-236). Paris: Publishing Elsevier.

UNCTAD. (2002). *Trade and Development Report 2002.* Geneva and New York: United Nations.

Urata, S. (2000). *Policy recommendations for SME promotion in Indonesia.* Report to the Coordination Ministry of Economy, Finance and Industry. (Mimeographed).

Wade, R. (1990). *Governing the Market: Economic Theory and the Role of Government in East Asia Pacificn Industrializations.* Princeton, NJ: Princeton University Press.

Wattanapruttipaisan, T. (2002). Promoting SMEs Development: Some Issues and Suggestions for Policy Consideration. *Bulletin on Asia-Pacific Perspectives 2002/03,* 57-67.

ENDNOTES

[1]   http://www.india-today.com/ctoday/20000901/telecom.html
[2]   http://www.atimes.com/atimes/China/EA18Ad06.htm

Chapter VII

Formulating Policy on E-Commerce and Trade for SMEs in the Asia Pacific Region:

An APEC Study

John Breen, Victoria University, Australia

Suzanne Bergin-Seers, Victoria University, Australia

Stephen Burgess, Victoria University, Australia

Gordon Campbell, Victoria University, Australia

Muhammad Mahmood, Victoria University, Australia

Robert Sims, Victoria University, Australia

ABSTRACT

This chapter examines the role that the Asia Pacific Economic Cooperation (APEC) has played in setting government policy to encourage increased trade by SMEs. A study of six "successful" micro and small businesses in APEC economies that was commissioned by APEC examines their attitudes towards trade and e-commerce. The case studies show that e-commerce can be a facilitator to trade for businesses with a propensity towards entrepreneurship and good management practices. To other businesses it may be seen as an inhibitor due to the lack of knowledge associated with its use and its benefits. The chapter shows how APEC used this study and some of its other initiatives to develop its IT and e-commerce policy for SMEs as part of its overall policy for SME development in the region.

INTRODUCTION

This chapter will examine the use of information technology in small business and the role that the Asia Pacific Economic Co-operation (APEC) has played in the setting of government policy to encourage increased trade by small and medium enterprises (SMEs). In particular, a study of six micro and small businesses in APEC economies that was commissioned by APEC examines their attitudes towards trade and e-commerce. Conclusions are drawn as to the role that information technology and e-commerce has to play in small business trade. The chapter concludes with the recommendations made to APEC by the study and a summary of the SME policy initiatives announced by APEC as a result of the study and other APEC activities.

BACKGROUND

The Asia-Pacific Economic Cooperation (APEC) treaty was established in 1989 in response to the growing inter-dependence among Asia-Pacific economies. It has since become a primary vehicle in the region for promoting open trade and economic cooperation. Its aim is to advance Asia-Pacific economic dynamism and sense of community (APEC, 2002a). One of the concerns of APEC is to set up an environment whereby all participating countries can be involved in free trade. When considering the use of information technology (IT) and e-commerce in small business, location is important. Why? The major answer to this is a combination of **resources** and **distance**. The further you are away from resources, the longer it takes and the more it costs to get them. This can particularly be the case with hardware and software purchases, training and support. Another reason for examining location is **culture**. Some countries, and even different regions within countries, have their own traditions and their own established ways of doing things. This can influence the behaviour of small businesses and the manner in which they use IT (refer next few sections).

Developing Countries

Small businesses make up a major portion of businesses in developing countries (in some countries the percentage is higher than in developed countries). Recognising their importance, many governments are providing support programs for small businesses (International Trade Forum, 1999).

One of the major barriers faced by small businesses in developing countries is access to information, especially information used in decision-making. Another problem is the lack of data sources from which to obtain the type of information required. Problems with the technological infrastructure of developing countries only exacerbate this (Sawyerr et al., 2000). As such, businesses in developing countries have difficulties in accessing trade information (Belisle and Czinkota, 1999).

New technologies (including information technologies) can provide these businesses with an opportunity to catch up with the rest of the world (Belisle and Czinkota, 1999; Mehta, 1999). To be able to access some of the benefits of e-commerce, such as faster service and shipments and precise transmittal of orders, it is necessary to have an efficient telecommunications structure, a problem area in many developing countries (Belisle and Czinkota, 1999). A starting point can be to increase the number of available telephone lines. After this, the quality of the transmission needs to be addressed as this has been cited as causing difficulties in the ability to obtain information from foreign sources and to effectively use the Internet (Sawyerr et al., 2000).

Today, the cost of installing a national telecommunications structure has fallen. When combined with reduced costs of international transport it is easier for small businesses in many developing countries to gain access to international markets (International Trade Forum, 1999). Uptake of the Internet in developing countries has been on the increase since 1996, the level of growth being hindered by the problems already identified with the telecommunications infrastructure (Gallagher, 1999). According to Belisle and Czinkota (1999), it is a matter of when, not if, such an infrastructure will be available in developing countries that desire it. There will, however, be vast areas of the world that will **not** have access to the Internet soon. For businesses in these areas, access to the Internet will remain secondary to other concerns, such as personal and business survival, secure food and water supplies and access to business institutions and credit (Mehta, 1999).

Rural Small Businesses

Some of the problems facing rural small businesses are similar to those facing small businesses in developing countries. Small businesses that are located away from major cities and towns face access issues similar to those already mentioned.

A study of small businesses in the rural areas of the United Kingdom (Management Services, 2001) indicated a wide and growing use of computers and the Internet, but a lack of ISDN or other broadband services had restricted access in some remote areas. It was felt that there was a lack of opportunity to develop familiarity with computers. It was thought that there could be a possibility of using local schools for acquiring these skills, but difficulties related to clashes with working time, distance, travel time and the relevance of the courses offered needed to be addressed.

One of the benefits that the Internet may provide is remote access to many desired IT resources, such as training.

E-Commerce in Small Businesses

Despite being widely regarded as a global phenomenon, almost three-quarters of all e-commerce by value is conducted within the USA. In addition, the USA accounts for 90% of all commercial websites (Iyer, Taube and Raquet, 2002). In some economies the level of e-commerce activity is restricted by the availability of suitable support infrastructure (mainly, access to reliable, cost-effective Internet connections). However, there is some evidence that there are emerging markets which can take advantage of the opportunities that e-commerce can provide (Iyer, Taube and Raquet, 2002).

E-commerce can provide global opportunities for businesses by facilitating the flow of ideas across national boundaries, improving the flow of information and linking increased numbers of buyers and sellers, thus providing opportunities for greater numbers of trading partners dealing in goods and increasingly in services (Iyer, Taube and Raquet, 2002).

Currently, the e-commerce adoption and usage patterns of small businesses tend to echo their usage of information technology in general; they lag behind their larger counterparts. Barriers to the use of e-commerce by small businesses include the cost of the technology, the availability of adequate infrastructure, the time needed to effectively plan, implement and maintain a website, the necessary information technology (IT) skills and the ability to understand and measure the benefits that e-commerce can provide (Burgess, 2002).

Despite these barriers, an increasing number of small businesses are connecting to the Internet and setting up websites. Leading the way are small businesses with the following characteristics (Burgess, 2002):

- Access to a suitable infrastructure that supports e-commerce.
- A culture of innovation.
- IT-skilled employees (or access to IT knowledge).
- Competitors who have already succeeded in using e-commerce.
- Pressure from supply chain partners to move onto the Internet.
- A long-term planning perspective.
- Awareness of the benefits that e-commerce can provide.

Increases in e-commerce activities will highlight a number of areas that need to be addressed by governments and traders. Traders will require an effective infrastructure to support reliable and cost-effective connections into the e-commerce environment (Burgess, 2002; Iyer, Taube and Raquet, 2002).

They will need to be aware of the cultural differences that exist in relation to website content (in terms of both language and sensitivity to content) and how business transactions are conducted in different areas (D'Amico, 2001).

Role of Government

If governments are keen to promote the benefits of e-commerce, they have a responsibility to ensure that businesses have access to the skills and knowledge required for successful implementation and are supported by suitable infrastructures. Evans (2002) has identified the conceptual linkages between e-commerce, governance and urban competitiveness. He has suggested that market factors (such as business environment, company characteristics and sectoral trends), combined with government factors (a sympathetic tax and regulatory framework, tackling market inefficiencies, addressing sustainability issues and taking a leading role by example) lead to the level of understanding of the benefits and "disbenefits" and the overall net effect on urban competitiveness.

Governments at all levels will need to determine how they will handle legal, taxation, infrastructure and other trade and regulatory issues in relation to e-commerce transactions (Iyer, Taube and Raquet, 2002; D'Amico, 2001; Lewis, 2001).

Asia Pacific Economic Co-Operation

APEC's priorities and goals are set annually at meetings of APEC Economic Leaders and Ministers. Member countries (economies) carry out projects to meet these goals, supported by the secretariat based in Singapore (APEC, 2002c). At the working level, APEC has a number of working groups, two of which are:

- Small and Medium Enterprises.
- Telecommunications and Information.

There are 21 participating economies in APEC. Each year, one country is chosen to host the ministerial, economic leaders and other meetings (in 2002 it was Mexico), including the APEC Small and Medium Enterprise Ministerial meeting, which was held in Acapulco in August 2002. In 2002, a focus of APEC was on the contribution of SMEs to APEC economies (APEC, 2002a).

THE STUDY

Given the focus of APEC for 2002, there was a decision made by APEC representatives to promote discussion and understanding of the barriers, enablers and needs of SMEs involved in intra-regional trade and investment, particularly in relation to technological (especially e-commerce), financial and regulatory factors.

A study of successful individual small and micro firms located in six APEC member economies was commissioned in early 2002 by the Asia Pacific Economic Cooperation to provide an overview of the contribution of small and medium enterprises (SMEs) to trade in the APEC region. The study, "Small Business and Trade in APEC," was tendered for and conducted by the Small Business Research Unit at Victoria University, Melbourne, Australia and was coordinated through the Australia Department of Foreign Affairs and Trade (DFAT)[1]. The purpose of the study was to promote discussion and understanding of the barriers, enablers and needs of SMEs involved in intra-regional trade and investment, particularly in relation to technological, financial and regulatory factors.

APEC indicated that they would like an even split between "micro" and "small" businesses across different countries in the region. The study involved in-depth case studies with six businesses — three "micro" businesses (from Australia, United States and Mexico) and three "small" businesses (from the Philippines, Japan and Malaysia). The number of cases (six) was determined by APEC. In addition, it was indicated by APEC that it was desirable that:

- Some of the case studies would have female owner/operators.
- They would be in different industries.
- There would be a range of e-commerce employed from basic to sophisticated.
- They would rely to varying extents on government support and/or external finance.

In other words, although it was virtually impossible to match all criteria, it was desired by APEC that a wide variety of small businesses would be interviewed and included in the study.

Through the authors, academic contacts in the participating countries were sent an interview "protocol," examining a range of drivers and barriers to trade. These contacts were drawn from associates of academics at Victoria University and from within APEC itself. The interview "protocol" was developed by the authors. The contacts then conducted the interviews with the results being emailed back to Melbourne. On most occasions, follow up questions were asked to clarify points of concern or to gain more information about the cases.

Some Contentious Issues
Issue of Business Size
The idea of an SME differs significantly from country to country within the APEC region, although most economies use a formal definition for statistical

purposes. A statistical definition of SMEs with fewer than 100 employees has become quite acceptable in the region (although most small businesses have fewer than 20 employees)[2]. For the purpose of this study, an enterprise employing between 20 and 100 staff is described as "medium," and one employing five to 19 persons is "small." A "micro" enterprise is one that has fewer than five employees. There were three micro businesses and three small businesses investigated in this study.

What Constitutes Success?

Much consideration was given to how to actually decide upon what constituted a business as being "successful." Many measures, such as profitability and longevity could be considered. In the final analysis, it was decided that if the business had been in existence for a number of years in the exporting industry then it would be regarded as successful. Therefore, the emphasis was intended to be on "successful" small businesses involved in export rather than small businesses that were successful in the use of e-commerce.

Findings

Micro Businesses

Australia: "Boots On Line"

Seven years ago, an Australian footwear retailer entered the export market by offering an Australian product, R M Williams boots, via the Internet. Today, export sales account for a large portion of the firm's annual turnover. The owner-manager is the only one of the five staff to possess IT skills. He has worked in the IT industry and also runs a small computer business. A combination of the potential he saw in the Internet and his search for "uniqueness" led him to the idea of offering Australian products overseas. The number of overseas customers that would visit the business, take a catalogue home, and place orders from overseas prompted this.

A number of factors can be identified as pivotal to the success of Boots On Line:

- The boots are a high quality product and are particularly popular in countries that share a cultural closeness with Australia.
- Prompt and efficient customer service. Delivery occurred within three to five days. All customer queries are answered within a day.
- It was easy to access the Internet with reliable support and acceptable levels of data security.
- In recent times, the declining value of the Australian dollar made purchases more attractive to overseas buyers.

The e-commerce section of the business is integrated with the rest of the business. The demand from overseas customers buffers the local shop from the seasonal variations in stock levels it had encountered in the past and allows it to carry the same level of stock year-round, thus benefiting domestic customers.

The owner-manager has identified a number of potential barriers to growth related to IT:

- The potential high freight costs for export sales over the Internet.
- The governments of overseas countries are beginning to show an interest in taxing Internet transactions and there are an increasing number of queries from customers related to this - which are most difficult to answer.
- The use of stolen credit cards. The owner estimates that about 20% of orders are made with stolen card details, which means that extreme vigilance is necessary (and time-consuming). The retailer must meet such losses, so the extra time is worth expending.
- The limited computer skills of the other four staff members. Further training of these employees and/or judicious recruitment of new employees will be required to reduce the Internet operation's reliance on the owner/manager.
- The owner/managers feels he is as concerned about to the level of security provided by the Internet Service Providers as other Internet traders, but feels that it is necessary to trust the level of security provided.

The business uses four computers, with one dedicated to the Internet site. The website currently accepts orders and provides customer service, and is partially linked with the overall business system. Payments, however, are still handled manually. A customer file is maintained for Internet business, but not for local customers. Although no separate cost/benefit analysis is carried out for the activities of the website the Internet sales can be easily identified if necessary.

In summary, the essential factors that have contributed to this SME's export success are product quality and customer service, reliable freight and IT infrastructures, and the vision and skills of the entrepreneur.

Mexico: "SPR Actopan"

The owner-managers of SPR Actopan in the east Mexican state of Vera Cruz established their business to distribute, process and promote fresh mangoes.

Although Actopan's growers produce mangoes which are among the finest varieties in the country, like many primary producers in developing economies, they face high freight costs, unreliable means of storing, preserving and processing their fruit and small powerful buyer blocs which control prices.

SPR Actopan now has five staff (four full-time and one part-time) and processes some of their fruit to sell to confectionery manufacturers. However, the bulk of their activity turns on the sale of fresh mangoes to small Mexico City supermarkets, to food processors and directly to retail customers. The region's small farmers produce all their incoming fruit.

The business has a number of strengths:

- The owners believe that the links they have established with local communities are the primary determinant of their success so far. Many growers see the business as a preferable alternative to informal product brokers.
- Valuable technical support in marketing provided by the firm's liaison with the country's leading agricultural science university.
- Their relative proximity to large markets (Mexico City and Puebla) is a favourable factor. Their high product quality and strong ties with growers ensures constant demand.

The firm has certainly not ignored the prospect of exporting their products, especially to nearby United States. However, severe price fluctuations and seasonality in production and the co-owners lack of experience and expertise on such matters as exchange rates, international freight costs and product hygiene standards set by importing nations are seen as barriers. As such, the company has **no** plans for any e-commerce involvement in the foreseeable future, citing network security, shortage of regional Internet providers and lack of staff skills as the major impediments to the achievement of full benefits from this technology. They perceive that e-commerce requires a technology-intensive effort that is not suited to small businesses. Certainly there is a much different attitude to e-commerce to that of the previous case.

USA: "The Fisherman's Wife"

The Fisherman's Wife was started in the year 2000. The business, run by two sisters, imports arts and crafts goods and clothing from a number of Latin-American countries and sells them in Texas, close to the Mexican border. The co-owners both also have full-time jobs.

The business employs a half-time salesperson at the primary shopfront, has a percent-of-sales arrangement with two other locations and is keenly pursuing opportunities to "on sell" its products around the US. Originally inspired by the entrepreneurial motivation of their mother, and the encouragement of other family members, the partners identify several factors as contributing to the successful growth of their venture:

- One owner's regular visits to a number of Latin American countries prompted her to establish links with two types of suppliers — indirect intermediaries, and direct producers or "cottage industry" families. Her ability to liaise closely and often with these suppliers and to cultivate trusting relationships has facilitated a steady flow of high-quality merchandise.

- Financial support. ACCION Texas, a non-government micro-lending organisation, provided seed capital which was used to purchase inventory stock. A Small Business Administration disaster loan, occasioned when the causeway between their original island location and the mainland was destroyed, enabled the partners to relocate their shopfront business.
- South Texas is a popular tourist destination for northern US residents and Mexican citizens, guaranteeing steady customer demand.
- Trading infrastructure. The Northern American Free Trade Agreement and strong trading links with Latin America encourage trade flows across the US-Mexican border.
- Family support. Various family members have contributed general assistance with business activities and specific professional expertise in legal, accounting and importing matters.

Both partners believe that few barriers have impeded the development of their business activities thus far, but identify a range of procedural and management concerns that will have to be addressed if they are to grow further:

- They need to regularise and consolidate more warehouse space for stock, some of which is currently kept in their homes.
- Cash flows with their retail customers need to be improved, especially with customer cheques that do not clear.
- Difficulties with the seemingly arbitrary nature of some customs inspection procedures need to be addressed.
- The partners wish to build their asset base, particularly by purchasing a commercial shopfront.
- The business needs to computerise its procedures. All computer operations are currently being carried out from home. There is an intention to computerise the inventory. The level of computer skills is described as being at the "secretarial" level.
- There are also plans to launch a website with the aim of marketing more widely and encouraging online product purchases. It is recognised by one of the partners that this would require extra skills on their part. One of the partners is considering a course on website design and operations, although they did indicate that they might have to work with a "web guy" if their limitations held them back. They acknowledge that such a transaction system would require a high degree of business computerisation and integration. There is a recognition of the potential for increased flexibility and growth in successful incorporation of a website.

In summary, the current success and continued growth of this enterprise depend on the range of knowledge and skills possessed by the owners (and their extended family), a supportive infrastructure (in terms of transport, communication and trading relationships), and a comprehensive adoption of Information (particularly Internet) Technology.

Discussion: Micro Enterprises

Strengths

A common theme found among the three micro enterprises studied is the entrepreneurial focus of the business operators. They are people with ideas and creative skills who discover an opportunity and then gather the resources to turn it into a reality. The entrepreneurs have been able to build a business opportunity out of their own skills or experiences. In one case the opportunity arises from their information technology skills, in another from their experiences resulting from visits to overseas destinations.

The cases suggest that you do not have to come up with a completely new concept or have great technical skills in order to develop a new business venture. Business opportunities are frequently identified as a result of personal life experiences — coming from involvement in recreational activities or a hobby, from a skill developed through education, from employment experiences or from simple, everyday personal interactions. Personal experiences can give the entrepreneur the confidence to take the next step and commence a business venture.

The successful entrepreneurs then bring other skills to the venture to complement their business idea. The operators among the micro enterprise case studies are very aware of their customers' needs and provide excellent customer service. They are also very skilled in developing relationships with their suppliers to ensure that inventory is available to meet their needs.

Barriers to be Overcome

As a general rule the smaller a business is in terms of the number of staff, then the less likely it will be to have access to a broad range of skills and expertise. Frequently operators have to provide the range of skills as best they can or access the skills and expertise from a range of sources, at minimum cost. Family members can often be one source of that low-cost expertise, while in some instances governments can provide specific support. This has certainly been shown to be the case here.

Several business operators mentioned the cost of transport, either to an overseas buyer or from an overseas supplier, as a concern. While transport costs are an unavoidable part of trade, they do need to be managed in a cost-effective way, to minimise their impact on business results. Additionally, lack of infrastructure in relation to distribution of products and lack of service providers for effective use of information technology impaired efficiency.

Level and Usage of IT

The micro enterprise case studies indicated that IT was important in the operation of their businesses. In two of the businesses, the owners used computers both at work and at home to support these operations. The general level of IT skills could be described as "adequate" across the businesses. In one business the owner was highly skilled and in another the expertise came from a family member outside the business. As was evident in the small business case studies, the general feeling came across that the businesses would benefit from their staff being further trained in the use of IT. The main activities that were computerised were accounting-related, with some inventory control.

Level and Usage of E-Commerce

There was a great deal of variation in the micro case studies in relation to their attitudes toward, and their use of, e-commerce. One of the businesses relied heavily on its website for overseas sales, which were used to expand the customer base of the business and to level out demand for its products over the calendar year. The website for this business was developed and maintained by the owner (described as the "highly skilled" owner in the previous section). No specific cost-benefit analysis for the website activities was carried out, but the owner was quite aware of the level of Internet sales at any time. In another case study the operators indicated a desire to set up a website to allow customers to view their products online, as a means of expanding their business. They recognised the need to develop their own skills and understanding of this area and the probable need to engage the services of an external consultant for assistance. A need was recognised within these two businesses for integration between the activities of the business and those on the website. The other business could see no immediate usage of e-commerce at all, citing barriers such as a lack of regional Internet service providers, security concerns and the low level of Internet-related skills within the business. The areas of security and e-commerce skills were mentioned by all micro case studies.

Small Businesses

Japan: "Unirex Kabushiki Gaisha"

Unirex Co. Ltd. commenced in 1996 in Sapporo. With a staff of 13, predominantly skilled in electrical engineering, sales and the English language, Unirex now has a flourishing export business. The company offers a range of products that have been developed through the reworking of existing technologies for new clients or industries. Several of these have worldwide patents, and are world best-practice technologies, including Bio Coal technology, Cadmium Removal technology and Electric Cold Food Smoking equipment.

The owner believes the company's success is based on several key elements:

- The combined experience and skills of the small workforce.
- Access to up-to-date technology. Unirex has established links with the research departments in several local universities.
- The company's focus on quality and customer-responsiveness.
- Opportunities to participate in large government Overseas Development Aid (ODA) projects in China and Indonesia.

The company sees a wide and growing customer base (currently nearly 100) as an important feature of its operations, but is also working with Mitsubishi Corporation on Bio Coal technology, an initiative which may well account for a large portion of all sales if it is successful. Overseas sales now account for nearly 20% of total turnover.

Most company employees are of a mature age and have limited IT experience. The management and staff are aware of the need to both improve staff computer skills and upgrade the IT facilities. Presently they have 11 computers, some of which are connected to a local area network and a rather slow network connection. They have a website that they use to accept orders for products and to provide online support. Their main use of the Internet at the moment, however, is as a tool to research the potential of e-commerce. As such, there is virtually no integration between their existing business and their "online" operations.

The most pressing current concerns relate to this need to further explore and eventually adopt an e-commerce capability, to lift the related skill level within the business, and to support export activities by recruiting someone with Chinese language skills and knowledge of Chinese legal, cultural and commercial matters, to man an office in China.

Malaysia: "Electrical Components"

Electrical Components (EC), in the state of Selangor, is a family-run Chinese small business, manufacturing AC capacitors for use in light fittings and electrical goods. Its founders ran the business on intuitive management principles and relatively informal arrangements with customers and suppliers, while a second generation of family managers have later introduced information technologies and more professional management techniques.

EC now has a staff of about 30, predominantly skilled and semi-skilled production workers and has been exporting for 10 years. The initial impulse to export was triggered by approaches from foreign manufacturers.

EC's owners cite a number of factors contributing to company growth:

- Internationally recognised quality certification on certain categories of its products has generated a competitive advantage over local competition, and it is hoped that present plans to attain ISO certification will similarly impress overseas customers.

- Low-interest, long-term government loans, incentives on export activities, exemption from customs duty on raw materials and equipment that are not available locally and government-sponsored seminars and trade fairs providing access to overseas contacts.
- Expertise, planning and networking which facilitate rapid delivery to overseas customers.
- Installation of business application software and adoption of Internet technology, which has increased productivity and efficiency.

One of EC's greatest problems is procuring and retaining skilled staff. The other major challenge is to build up a distinctive brand reputation for the company's capacitors.

The company's overseas business has declined from 10% to around 2% of its total turnover in recent years but it remains a key focus for management, because of the higher margins it generates and because of a general urge to expand the customer base. Strong and sustained communication with overseas clients, electronically or preferably face-to-face, is seen as a crucial platform for such business, and EC is even thinking of establishing local sales and service offices in selected overseas locations.

The company regards itself as a sophisticated user of computers and has thereby achieved efficiencies in the areas of accounting and inventory control, production planning and control, and general information management and communication. The business has a number of personal computers, modems, a fax machine and a digital camera. Management has supported their staff in the use of IT and the Internet by sending employees to related short courses. An interesting challenge for the business has been to convince shareholders that the investment in IT will deliver benefits — as the measures of return are intangible over the short term.

The establishment of a company website, carried out with the (free) assistance of friends in the IT industry, has improved communication with suppliers and customers, but as yet no transaction facility has been incorporated. Generally, the managers find that direct communication with customers is needed to verify orders, and the high costs of broadband connection represent another hindrance to the development of full e-commerce potential. Operating as it does on essentially a business-to-business model, EC sees e-commerce's viability as dependent upon their customers also becoming fully conversant with the technology. One of the barriers currently facing the business is that the broadband infrastructure in Malaysia is still being established and these services are expensive in comparison to dial-up services.

This company has fared well in resolving the conflicts inherent in the traditional family company that has been forced to embrace modern technology and management principles, invest more in staff development and take a longer-term, more quality-oriented view. Faced with a volatile world economy and ever-increasing demands for product quality, but aided by proactive government export incentives, they look positively to the future. The acquisition of international quality standard recognition is seen as something of a platform, from which a more strategic and sustained marketing campaign can be launched.

Philippines: "VJANDEP Pastel"

The owner of VJANDEP Pastel (VP) began baking her first Pastel products and hawking them around her neighbourhood in the remote Camiguin Island province in 1990. Today the business employs 39 staff. The owner and her husband are proud of the hard work and strong spiritual beliefs that underpin the success of their business, but also pay tribute to the external support which has contributed to its growth:

- A series of loans that has funded the purchase of baking utensils and equipment, and the expansion of the business to the regional capital of Cagayan de Oro.
- Various government-sponsored training programs (in entrepreneurship, business management and good manufacturing practices).
- Government-sponsored trade fairs and exhibits, which have generated requests (which are still being evaluated) for distributorship of VP's Pastel products in other regions.

VP's owners have pursued any potential government assistance and have taken the red tape and bureaucratic requirements, which intimidate many other SME's, in their stride. Their commitment to staff development has prompted them to occasionally close their baking operations for several days to take advantage of the available training programs. VP's staff turnover is significantly lower than industry standards, which they attribute in part to their strong training culture and a policy of delegating authority.

The two partners also ascribe their success to a number of other factors:

- A focus on customers, product quality and ethical practices. Quality (of ingredients, packaging, transport and customer service) is repeatedly stressed. Only fresh, natural ingredients are used, no potentially harmful preservatives, and unused materials or equipment are donated to social and civic organizations.
- Inventory management and cash-flow management are seen as vital elements of successful management, and are very carefully monitored.
- The owner-managers' belief that risk-taking and growth should be carefully planned.

VJANDEP Pastel faces several challenges as they contemplate the further growth, which clearly beckons. Only recently have they begun to computerise their financial and supplies/materials inventory data, yet this is still handled by their accountant whose office is 285 km from Cagayan de Oro. The partners' eldest son, who manages their third branch in Cagayan de Oro, has established a website for the business, which they are still trying to link with an integrated website for Northern Mindanao businesses initiated by the Department of Science and Technology. However, the prospect of e-commerce is a daunting one, as their present production capacity could not cope with any significant expansion in demand and they are concerned about the perishability of their main product. Given the owner-managers' philosophical objections to the addition of preservatives to their products, the shelf life of five to six days remains an effective barrier to any market expansion beyond the immediate region. Another barrier is the reluctance of the partners to divulge the secrets of their products to potential international partners. One possibility that is being investigated is the use of some type of vacuum packaging to preserve the product longer. Expansion, particularly into the export market, is an attractive proposition, but finance, distribution, technology and export knowledge and skills would all need to be improved.

Discussion: Small Businesses
Strengths

The three case studies support the notion that being genuinely **entrepreneurial** is an important part of success in small business. The entrepreneurs are able to identify an opportunity and can draw together the resources required to get the business started. They usually have a vision for their business and want the business to grow in the future.

The business operators are very conscious of their customers and their needs, and they work hard to deliver a service that creates repeat business. The small firms generally operate in niche markets and their unique products/services are seen as a strength. The cases also indicate that product quality is important, as is the provision of a consistent product that meets the needs of the buyer.

The operators place great importance on the development of the skills of their staff in order to deliver good customer service and quality products. They see the skill base of their workers as important in taking their business to the next level of turnover.

These firms were able to capitalise on the operators' networks of contacts in generating sales opportunities and in accessing valuable information and support from government.

Their ability to overcome barriers is largely due to good management, in the broadest sense of the word.

Barriers to Overcome

The barriers to success that were identified tended to be firm specific and depended both on local issues and more regional concerns as well as the reasons why they exported. Some appear to have an intuitive understanding of exporting issues while others lack confidence, skill and knowledge in this area. The local issues included the costs of transporting goods to customers and the difficulties in accessing transport infrastructure. Others were concerned with gaining quality accreditation. At the regional level there was a need for skill development in dealing with customers in export markets. This involved language and cultural understanding as well as developing knowledge about some of the legal issues involved in trade.

Most of the cases indicated a need to improve their understanding of e-commerce matters.

Trade and E-Commerce

The case studies indicated various degrees of IT utilisation, from virtually none at all to a system of PCs linked by a network. Use and success of e-commerce was dependent on the product or service offered. The firm with the most sophisticated IT usage specifically identified IT as being important to the business and had a number of employees possessing reasonable IT skills. The other small businesses had limited IT expertise, but did indicate a desire to increase the level of IT know-how within the business. The most common business activities that were computerised were accounting, and in some cases inventory control. The major concern is the level of IT expertise within the case study businesses.

Level and Usage of E-Commerce

The case studies varied in the level of e-commerce that they had adopted. The most basic website provided details about the business. The other case studies had websites that provided business details and other features. One business used the Internet to facilitate communication with suppliers and customers and the other was experimenting with (but had not implemented) online sales. Each business was looking to expand its e-commerce activities in the future. The website was developed internally in one of the case studies, and by a family member in another. In each case, website activities were not specifically linked to the overall business. A separate cost-benefit analysis of Internet activities had not been carried out. Major concerns relate to the security of credit card transactions, infrastructure, Internet-related skills and understanding of the potential benefits of e-commerce.

Export Orientation

The case studies indicate that there is no one set track to export success. It is possible for some businesses to be "born global" and focus on their overseas markets from the start of their business operations. Some see export markets as a way of increasing turnover and sometimes providing improved margins. Others only contemplate export when confronted by a customer from another country seeking to access a particular product. It is important for governments to recognise that there are different tracks to export success and develop a range of initiatives to support the firms as they begin to assess export opportunities.

Summary

One indication from the case studies is that exporters do not have to be large businesses. The case-study businesses were characterised by:

- An entrepreneurial owner-manager.
- A niche product or service.
- Good management practices.

Those businesses involved in trade also demonstrably utilised:

- Adequate IT skills.
- Networking with overseas contacts.
- Access to information/knowledge about trade.

Firms that have the right fundamental characteristics for business success and are able to harness IT and networking to proactively develop their knowledge about trade have achieved export success.

Inhibitors to trade included:

- Lack of infrastructure with respect to transport and IT and communications.
- Lack of access to the right mix of skills.

Firms not yet at the export stage indicated the need for skill development in relation to IT, networking and information gathering. These firms were observed to have some of the necessary attitudes and characteristics for export success, but still required some skill development in accordance with the learning stage of the model.

In summary, the case studies support the notion that e-commerce can be a facilitator to trade for businesses with a propensity towards entrepreneurship and good management practices. To other businesses it may be seen as an inhibitor due to the lack of knowledge associated with its use and the benefits it can provide.

RECOMMENDATIONS TO APEC

It is difficult to claim overall generalisable results from this study as conducted under the auspices of APEC and the guidelines that were set up. It is possible, however, to say the study certainly highlighted a number of common issues related to e-commerce and trade that were identified in the earlier literature review. These common issues could be used to inform APEC of the challenges facing small businesses that are considering this path. This section discusses how APEC subsequently formulated their policy in this area.

A major finding of the six case studies was that for all of the businesses it was not enough to concentrate upon e-commerce issues alone as a way of involving more SMEs in trade. E-commerce needs to be considered alongside a number of other important areas.

This study finds that while small business faces competitive pressure as a consequence of open markets, its inherent characteristics do not preclude it from greater participation in international trade. Indeed open markets may provide it with increased opportunities.

A primary task for governments in assisting further participation of small business in international trade is to reduce barriers to trade beyond tariffs. While further reducing tariffs, APEC's new agenda now also focuses on a range of issues, ... (APEC, 2002b).

One of the "new agenda" issues listed was a commitment to e-commerce and increasing access to the Internet.

This is of great importance for small business, which struggle to keep pace with larger firms already enjoying such success. (APEC, 2002b)

As a result of the study, a number of recommendations were made to APEC:

1.   APEC needs to continue, and if possible intensify, its core work on trade and investment liberalisation and facilitation.
2.   APEC efforts to cooperate on capacity building are particularly important for small business.
3.   APEC needs to share experience and expertise to build the policy environment for the creation and promotion of small businesses.
4.   APEC needs to ensure small businesses also have access to key drivers of growth: infrastructure, technology, information, finance and skills and training.
5.   APEC needs to identify and address trade and non-trade barriers affecting the growth and development of small businesses.

Note that the fourth recommendation concerning infrastructure, technology and information is linked with finance and training as key drivers of small business growth.

Promoting entrepreneurship — the basic driver of small business — and other key small business drivers is particularly important in enabling developing economies to contribute more fully to, and enjoy the benefits of, economic growth in the Asia Pacific region by the year 2020. (APEC, 2002b)

NEW POLICY INITIATIVES ANNOUNCED BY APEC

A joint ministerial statement was released at the APEC Small and Medium Enterprise Ministerial Meeting held in August 2002: "Expanding the Benefits of Cooperation for SMEs" (APEC, 2002d). At this meeting a discussion ensued as to how APEC SMEs could contribute to economic growth in the region and respond to new challenges. A number of areas, such as financing, human capacity building, access to information and markets, a transparent legal and regulatory environment, and access to information and communications technologies were targetted. A set of action plans for the SME working group was endorsed to implement the "E-APEC" strategy, including (APEC, 2002d):

- Improved access to information for SMEs through IT.
- Consolidation of infrastructure for IT applications.
- E-commerce.
- E-learning.
- Application of IT to business management.

In 2003, APEC also updated its Integrated Plan of Action for SME Development (SPAN). SPAN provides guidelines for domestic SME policy, a framework for economic cooperation within APEC and a means for addressing submissions from the business community. From an IT point of view, this year's proposed enhancement to SPAN (APEC, 2002e) addresses issues such as skill enhancement, improved telecommunications infrastructure and access to it, and increased awareness of the benefits of IT and e-commerce leading to improved decision-making. SPAN is important because it also addresses the need to have clear policies and programs for SMEs and a means by which to evaluate their success (in this instance efficiency criteria, relevance to priorities and objectives and cost effectiveness have been identified).

Some examples of practical projects initiated by APEC this year include the introduction of the APEC Training and Certification Program for Small Business Counsellors, a portal dedicated to SMEs in the APEC region (www.bizapec.com/main.html) and some new funding initiatives to encourage capacity building in the APEC region.

In addition to this, the theme of the 2003 APEC annual meeting, hosted by Thailand, is "A World of Difference: Partnership for the Future," in which work carried out in 2002 is being extended. Two important keys topics relevant to this chapter for 2003 are participation in the knowledge-based economy and support for small, medium and micro-enterprise development.

CONCLUSION

This chapter has examined the role that the Asia Pacific Economic Co-operation has played in the setting of government policy to encourage increased trade by small and medium enterprises (SMEs). In particular, a study of six "successful" micro and small businesses in APEC economies that was commissioned by APEC examined their attitudes toward trade and e-commerce. The study showed that it is not enough to concentrate upon e-commerce issues alone as a way of involving more SMEs in trade. E-commerce needs to be considered alongside a number of other important areas. Entrepreneurship and good management practices need to be supported by a suitable e-commerce infrastructure, an environment where SMEs can determine the advantages and disadvantages of e-commerce and access to the skills necessary to achieve this. This is in addition to the focus on other areas that are needed to support trade, such as access to finance and markets. This chapter has shown how APEC used this study and other initiatives to develop its IT and e-commerce policy for SMEs as part of its overall policy for SME development in the region.

REFERENCES

APEC. (2002a). *Asia-Pacific Economic Cooperation.* Retrieved December 15, 2002 from the World Wide Web: http://www.apecsec.org.sg/.

APEC. (2002b). *Small Business and Trade in APEC.* Department of Foreign Affairs and Trade, Canberra.

APEC. (2002c). *APEC: Outcomes and Outlook.* Retrieved January 6, 2003 from the World Wide Web: http://www.apecsec.org.sg/ download/pubs/ 2002OutcomesNOutlook.pdf.

APEC. (2002d). *Expanding the Benefits of Cooperation for SMEs.* APEC Small and Medium Enterprise Ministerial Meeting, Acapulco, Mexico, August 24-25. Retrieved January 8, 2003 from the World Wide Web: http://www.apecsec.org.sg.

APEC. (2002e). *Proposal for Enhancing the Integrated Plan of Action for SME Development (SPAN).* APEC Small and Medium Enterprise Ministerial Meeting, Acapulco, Mexico, August 24-25. Retrieved January 9, 2003 from the World Wide Web: http://www.apecsec.org.sg.

Austrade. (2002). *Knowing and Growing the Exporter Community: A Report from the Australian Trade Commission.* Canberra, Australia.

Belisle, J., Dennis and Czinkota, M. (1999) Trade must extend to poorer countries. *International Trade Forum,* Geneva, 3, 11-13.

Burgess, S. (ed.). (2002). *Managing Information Technology in Small Business: Challenges and Solutions.* Hershey, PA: Idea Group Publishing.

D'Amico, E. (2001, September). Global e-commerce. *Chemical Week,* 163(36), 24-29.

Department of Foreign Affairs and Trade (DFAT). (2001). *The APEC Region Trade and Investment 2001,* Canberra, Australia.

Evans, R. (2002, May). E-commerce, competitiveness and local and regional governance in Greater Manchester and Merseyside: A preliminary assessment. *Urban Studies,* 39(5/6), 947-975.

Gallagher, P. (1999). E-commerce trends. *International Trade Forum,* Geneva, 2, 16-18.

Hall, C. (2001). *Profile of SMEs and SME Issues in APEC 1990-2000,* 2nd draft report, Canberra.

International Trade Forum. (1999). Export Strategies for Small Firms, Geneva, 1, 9-12.

Iyer, Lakshmi, S., Taube, L. and Raquet, J. (2002). Global e-commerce: Rationale, Digital Divide, and strategies to bridge the Divide. *Journal of Global Information Technology Management,* 5(1), 43-68.

Lewis, J. (2001, November/December). Weaving electronic commerce into global business and financial management. *AFP Exchange,* Bethesda, 21(6), 14-17.

Mehta, L. (1999, October). From darkness to light? Critical reflections on the World Development Report 1998/99. *The Journal of Development Studies,* 36(1), 151-161.

Sawyerr, O., Edbrahimi, B. and Thibodeaux, M. (2000, June). Executive environmental scanning, information source utilisation, and firm performance: The case of Nigeria. *Journal of Applied Management Studies,* 9(1), 95-115.

ENDNOTES

[1]   The final report of the study, Small Business and Trade in APEC, is available from the Australian Department of Foreign Affairs and trade (www.dfat.gov.au). Refer to the references for details.

[2]   This information was provided to the authors by DFAT.

Chapter VIII

EU E-Commerce Policies:
Enhancing the Competitiveness of SMEs Through Innovation

Anne Wiggins, London School of Economics and Political Science, UK

ABSTRACT

This chapter not only presents an overview of the theoretical awareness and understanding of innovation, but also identifies and discusses existing EU innovation policy initiatives for SMEs, deliberating on the impact such policy initiatives have on their specific considerations. This chapter examines the strategic implications of the adoption and implementation of e-commerce by two successful start-up SMEs in the UK presented against a backdrop of relevant EU policy initiatives. SMEs, and start-ups particularly, find themselves having to operate without role models and tested business plans within an increasingly complex and competitive environment.

INTRODUCTION

This chapter will present an overview of the theoretical awareness and understanding of innovation and develop an outline of existing European Union (EU) innovation policy initiatives for entrepreneurs and small and medium-sized enterprises (SMEs). Entrepreneurial attributes such as creativity, flexibility and dynamism are frequently associated with the SME sector, and an understanding of the nature of these attributes and what generates them is essential in order to develop appropriate policy instruments.

The point of departure of this policy-oriented study is that innovation is a good thing (both on regional and organisational levels) and that there is a call for public intervention in order to provide more of it. Drawing from the literature, this study builds on these basic assumptions. The motivation for this research arises from a practical problem: SMEs need suitable opportunities to assist them in adopting and implementing electronic commerce (e-commerce), not least because of the way that e-commerce enables companies of *all* sizes to compete with and out-manoeuvre market dominants and facilitates the radical transformation of both technical and business operations.

Experiences from SMEs' adoption of e-commerce show that small businesses have typically been reactive rather than proactive, usually doing just enough to meet their customers' requirements (Chen and Williams, 1998). Those SMEs that understand the relevance of e-commerce in relation to their operations, however, and employ strategies in order to harness the opportunities it presents, can successfully adopt and implement e-commerce.

A significant number of EU projects and policy initiatives have been introduced in recent years to motivate e-commerce adoption and implementation by SMEs. However, uncertainty as to how to address the challenges e-commerce presents remains a major impediment to its widespread adoption by SMEs. The practical impact of EU policy initiatives on SMEs who have successfully managed the adoption and implementation of e-commerce in the UK will be examined, with a view to instruct feasible changes, and with the implication that future policy initiatives may become more relevant, accessible and coherent to SMEs.

Through two in-depth, qualitative case studies this chapter seeks to answer the following questions: How do SMEs cope with starting and managing a company based on the adoption and implementation of e-commerce? And how relevant, accessible and coherent to UK SMEs are EU policies and projects initiated for that purpose?

RESEARCH METHODOLOGY

The research undertaken enabled discussion to take place about the requirements of SMEs within the context of their organisational and cultural situation so that relevant notions of the strategic implications could emerge. Information was obtained through semi-structured interviews with the principals of the case studies. Although the researcher pre-established a set of questions to direct the interviews (see Appendix A), the interviewees were able to express their views on any and all aspects they considered to be important and/or relevant.

These interviews were supplemented with observations, which enabled the researcher to not only witness connections and relationships, and record the phenomenon under study in its real context, but also to collect data from different sources to corroborate, elaborate, or illuminate the research (Yin, 1994; Silva and Backhouse, 1997).

SME DEFINITIONS

There is no single definition of an SME. However, schemes that are targeted at small firms adopt a variety of working definitions depending on their particular objectives. In February 1996, the European Commission adopted a communication setting out a single definition of SMEs to be applied to programmes and proposals dated from December 31, 1997. The communication includes a (non-binding) recommendation to Member States, the European Investment Bank and the European Investment Fund encouraging them to adopt the same definitions for their programmes.

Firm size has been directly associated with technological success. SMEs face different challenges than larger organisations, and by no means emulate their ability and willingness to adopt, utilise and manage technology.

It is crucial to appreciate the nature and context of SMEs. SMEs cannot compete with large companies head on, as their advantages stem from different business characteristics. A number of unique internal elements influence the SME environment and provide them with a different set of priorities and initiatives. These include: small teams, owner influence, centralised power and control, informal and often inadequate planning and control systems, multi-functional management, and a lack of specialist staff. The SME environment is also affected by external elements, which include: a limited product range, a limited customer base, and a lack of control over the business environment.

A large company can take advantage of economies of scale, spreading out fixed costs through the product line using its sheer size. An SME, while unable to do this, is usually more flexible and controllable, and able to react faster than large companies. SMEs are able to take advantage of niche markets, but they

Table 1. Official EU SME definitions.

Criterion	Micro	Small	Medium
Max. number of employees	9	49	249
Max. annual turnover	-	7 million euros	40 million euros
Max. annual balance sheet total	-	5 million euros	27 million euros
Max. % owned by one, or jointly by several, enterprise(s) not satisfying the same criteria	-	25%	25%

operate with limited resources, and usually cannot afford disasters or failure (Nunes and Cunha, 2000).

Despite early predictions (Auger and Gallaugher, 1997) that SMEs would benefit most readily from e-commerce adoption and implementation, recent studies have shown that larger businesses have more readily benefited, and that many of the tangible benefits of adopting e-commerce (such as reduced lead time, administration and production costs, and increased sales) are marginal (Roberts and Wood, 2002; Barry and Milner, 2002). Perceived benefits, such as improvement in the quality of information, control of the business, and relations with business partners or customers, were considered to be of far greater value (Abell and Limm, 1996; Poon and Swatman, 1997; Trappey and Trappey, 2001; Quayle, 2002).

Electronic commerce adoption can radically alter commercial relationships as well as expose a given business to external risks (Stauber, 2000; Raymond, 2001). SMEs that have developed a strategy can realistically expect an increase in efficiency. However, for those that have not, flexibility can be reduced (Tetteh and Burn, 2001; Lee, 2001).

DEFINING INNOVATION

Innovation would seem to be an important engine of long-term competitiveness, growth and employment. The OECD estimates that between 1970 and 1995 more than half of the total growth in output of the developed world resulted from innovation, and that this proportion is increasing as economies become more knowledge-intensive (Irwin, 2000). However, a comprehensive definition or description of innovation is difficult to articulate. As a result, innovative businesses cannot be neatly classified.

Definitions of innovation have evolved from linear models to multi-dimensional systems dynamics. This is an apparent trend both in academic research and in policy development. Nauwelaers and Wintjes (2000) note a shift in policy statements reflecting the view that innovation is an interactive rather than linear process in their SMEPOL research, a comparative study of policies aiming at supporting SME innovation at the EU regional level. Gemuenden (1999) describes innovation as being a "multiple activities" process. Amidon (1993) defines innovation as being "the creation, exchange, evolution and application of new ideas into marketable goods and services," while Demarco (1999) describes innovation as being "the utilisation of the creative act to result in a quantifiable gain." But while innovation encompasses creativity, organisations must also be open to outside sources of knowledge, and have the capacity to integrate them (Tidd, Bessant and Pavitt, 1997; Olave and Neto, 2001).

Drucker (1974) has stated that innovation is the establishment of a new or altogether different product or procedure, of which invention is an integral part.

Drucker (1998) further claims that innovation arises most often from "the systematic pursuit" of opportunities, and that engaging in disciplined work is fundamental to the generation of innovation. Drucker (1998) is adamant that innovators "consciously and purposefully" seek "focused solutions" and share a commitment to the "disciplined and systematic" search for imaginative and useful ideas to improve a business's potential. Irwin (2000) advocates a complementary view, of innovation being "opportunity spotting," while Schrage (1999) claims that creative improvisation and collaborative interactions ("serious play") lead to innovation.

WHAT CAUSES INNOVATION?

But what spurs an organisation to innovate? In some cases it is triggered by new knowledge, in others by the opportunity to fulfil a market need (Mahdjoubi, 1997). According to Schien (1997), organisations tend to develop stable routines and cultures, and change does not occur without the motivation to do so. Such motivation is usually provided when "assumptions, attitudes, or behavioural routines" no longer work or are out of date. This "disconfirmation" is usually triggered or brought about by a champion spearheading change who is responsible for the performance of the organisation. The innovation champion can consciously manage or adjust value systems and environments (Land and Jarman, 1992; Wheatley, 1992; Quinn, 1996).

Collective knowledge and activities become embedded within all organisations (Dacin, Ventresca and Beal, 1999) and can be a productive facility of competitive advantage (Saviotti, 1996; Teece, Pisano and Schuen, 1997). But for lasting change to occur, new behaviours must be learned so that "perceptions, attitudes, and feelings" are replaced (Boland, 1987; Senge, 1990). There are multiple forces for maintaining the status quo, such as: group performance norms, fear of change, member complacency, and lack of skills (Stoner and Freeman, 1989; Bergquist, 1993). Failure to adopt innovation, however, can lead to "irrelevance, stagnation, and eventual demise" (Mason and Rohner, 2002).

The personalities, attributes, interests and training of management play an important role in determining the speed with which a firm introduces innovation (Kelly and Kranzberg, 1975). While the implementation of innovative ideas is an organisational change process (Hoffer, George and Valacich, 1996), lasting competitive change takes application, time, and involves individual and organisational learning and adaptation. An organisation must possess (and be willing to commit) the resources needed to implement a new technology for innovation adoption and implementation to be successful (Ginzberg, 1981a, 1981b; Mohr, 1982; Amidon and Mahdjoubi, 1999). Risk, however, doesn't have to be the cost of innovation (Plotkin, 2002). A balance between partitioning and integration, and performance and growth, can be achieved while remaining accountable to the core business by implementing human resources policies with structure and processes (Smallbone, North, Vickers and McCarthy, 2000; Day, Mang, Richter and Roberts, 2001).

As innovation adoption and implementation success would seem to be dependent on investing in resources and the capabilities to manage them (Tidd, Bessant and Pavitt, 1997), the thrust of policy approaches could therefore be to increase the availability of external resources for innovating organisations whilst simultaneously developing internal and learning capacities to reflect the key role of human capital.

Knowledge as a resource has the following characteristics: extraordinary leverage and increasing returns, a tendency towards fragmentation and leakage, a need for refreshment, and uncertainty with regard to value creation and value sharing (Drucker, 1998). As a result, the need to manage knowledge more effectively is both a primary driver of, and a practical constraint on, disaggregation. As knowledge-based innovation is often market dependent (Davenport, 1992; Cobbenhagen and Nauwelares, 1999), an organisation with a knowledge challenge could be blindsided by competitors exploiting opportunities of which it is not even aware.

The operating climate is increasingly competitive, turbulent and uncertain (Bekker and Staude, 1988; Goldman, Nagel and Preiss, 1995), and e-commerce is a resource that is rapidly innovating not only traditional business processes but also the very nature of competition, enabling market fragmentation, the information capacity to treat mass clients as individuals, convergence between products and services, global production networks, and simultaneous cooperation and competition between firms.

INNOVATION AND SMEs

There can be no doubt that SMEs are drivers of innovation, of economic growth, and of employment, and that they play a vital role as developers of new ideas and as adopters of new technology. Indeed, SMEs have the potential to act as a vehicle for the industrial and economic change of regions (Oakey, 1985).

SMEs benefit from organisational strengths (such as speedy decision-making and a high degree of employee commitment) that often eliminate the need for formal strategies to ensure communication and co-ordination (Tidd, Bessant and Pavitt, 1997). SMEs share the advantages of having the flexibility to react quickly to the market place, an absence of bureaucracy, and informal and efficient communication systems (Oakey, 1985; Olave and Nato, 2001). However, SMEs tend to lack the internal resources and the external networks necessary for ready access to the knowledge, skills, technologies and finance on which innovation depends. The difficulty of identifying and obtaining appropriate

sources of finance and technical skills, especially, affects small firms dispropor-
tionately. Thong et al. (1993) label this "resource poverty."

Along with achieving growth and maintaining performance, SME owner/
managers are responsible for detecting new possibilities and ideas, for combining
them with other resources and ideas, and for giving them appropriate organisational
form. This concentration of power can lead directly to challenges that impede
innovation: a lack of information or skills, organisational rigidities, and a conservative attitude towards risk and change. In some cases, new ideas are
suppressed too quickly, while in others, projects are promoted before their true
potential has been assessed. Many SMEs cannot afford the financial needs or
risk to innovate and develop new products, processes and systems in spite of
latent capabilities, as they do not have resources in reserve after meeting day-
to-day requirements. Customers, organisational structures, and prejudices
dispose them to stick with the familiar.

The EU-sponsored SISMEs Report (1996) identified three main business
drivers that propel SMEs to innovate: customer orientation, increasing competition and time-to-market. As the vast majority of SMEs are founded and run by
entrepreneurs, and as entrepreneurs are subjectively acting individuals, it is a
major challenge to arrange effective support programmes for the provision of
information and financial means, as the needs that exist among all firms are
heterogenous (Kirzner, 1973; Lachmann, 1986; Curran and Blackburn, 1994;
Johannisson and Monsted, 1997; Boter, Hjalmarsson and Lundstrom, 1999).

INNOVATION POLICY DEVELOPMENT

The importance of stimulating the establishment of new enterprises by
creating an environment rich with opportunities through the support of entrepreneurial characteristics cannot be overstressed. The capacity to innovate
relies not only on possessing the skills to recognise and harness potential, but also
on conditions that permit, encourage and sustain entrepreneurs. Policy initiatives
can create the infrastructure and environment in which organisations are able to
recognise, realise and maximise potential competitive advantage. Governments
can create an economic, fiscal and regulatory framework within which innovation and entrepreneurship can flourish by raising awareness of the benefits of
innovation and of adopting good management, financial and environmental
practices, and by providing financial resources for business support services.

Relevant innovation policy depends on an understanding of what "really"
drives innovation, the external barriers that prevent or delay it, and its impacts
on competitiveness and employment. Incentive schemes and policies intended
to lead to the sustained growth of the SME sector need, therefore, to take into
account the culture, performance, and networking abilities of SMEs.

While an evolution towards more interactive support is visible, there is a high degree of heterogeneity in policy instruments aiming at fostering innovation in SMEs in the EU. At one extreme, reactive policies raise the stock of given resources in firms and regions, aiming to increase innovation capacity by making resource inputs available. At the other, proactive instruments focus on learning, attempting to change behavioural aspects such as the organisational culture, innovation strategies, management, mentality and awareness.

The adoption of a comprehensive innovation support infra-structure would provide SMEs with assistance through mentoring, alliances and networks, as well as increase the availability of, and enable access to, specific skills and tools (Jeal and Wroe, 1999; Leo and Booth, 2001). SMEs tend to be cautious about alliances and networks, however, despite the potential advantages (Sengenberger, Loveman and Piore, 1990). Acting as collective systems, smaller firms are often able to perform better than large integrated firms, in terms of their responsiveness to customer needs, flexibility, ability to identify and exploit opportunities, and adopt new technologies (Jeal and Wroe, 1990). Alliances and networks could give individual SMEs ready access to the skills, capabilities, and capacity needed to compete globally, yet allow them to retain their culture and ownership characteristics.

While commercial relationships constitute the dominant form of interaction between firms, formal and informal collaboration between companies operating in the same industry and between suppliers and customers along supply chains is becoming increasingly common in the EU. Around a quarter of EU innovative firms have been estimated to have been recently involved in collaborative arrangements, but the rate of collaboration among innovating organisations increases with their size (CIS, 2001).

EU INNOVATION POLICY INITIATIVES

Throughout Europe, hundreds of policy measures and support schemes and programmes aimed at improving innovation have been recently implemented, some of the most influential of which are outlined in this section. Many of these policies, schemes and programmes are interlinked. For example, the EU's *Regional Technology Plan* (RTP) contributed to the *Green Paper on Innovation* (introduced in 1995 and revised in 1996), which was introduced to develop "a genuine European strategy for the promotion of innovation."

The *Action Plan for Innovation in Europe*, 1996, paved the way for a common European analytical and political framework for innovation policy. Building on this, the *Trend Chart on Innovation in Europe* was introduced as a tool for policy makers. Formulated along the lines of the Community Innovation Survey (CIS), which is jointly implemented by Eurostat and DG Enterprise under the aegis of the European Innovation Monitory System (EIMS), the *Trend Chart* updates and analyses information on innovation policies at the national and community level, and provides a forum for benchmarking and the exchange of "good practices" in innovation policy development.

The European Council Summit in Lisbon, 2000, announced the goal of making the EU the "most competitive and dynamic knowledge-based economy in the world" by 2010. This objective necessitated the creation of additional innovation policy initiatives at EU national and regional levels, many of which were still being framed in early 2003. The summit called for a series of benchmarking exercises to monitor progress by Member States towards the implementation of effective policies in support of innovation. *Innovation in a knowledge-driven economy, 2001*, describes the Commission's intention to develop a framework for dialogue on innovation policy-making and policy co-ordination, to improve the availability of innovation statistics, and to identify "best practices" in innovation policy development.

Building an Innovation Economy in Europe, 2001, the first in a series of Innovation Policy Studies undertaken for the European Commission's Enterprise Directorate-General, summarises 12 reports, nine of which examine the trends and impacts of European innovation policy. The other three assess: specific actions addressing the financing of innovation; the promotion of innovation management techniques among SMEs; and the development of regional innovation strategies. Collectively, the reports aim to improve understanding of the dynamics of European innovation in order to reinforce the ability of policy-makers to develop effective and appropriately targeted initiatives.

SME-SPECIFIC EU INNOVATION POLICY INITIATIVES

That the SME sector is crucial to European innovation development (Mulhern, 1995) is confirmed by this consistent introduction of a series of EU policies formulated to facilitate the creation of a business environment in which SMEs can innovate and flourish. The capacity for e-commerce adoption and implementation by SMEs relies not only on their possessing the skills to recognise and harness, but also on conditions that permit, encourage and sustain, the motivation to innovate.

The *Innovation and SME Programme* supports European SMEs to participate in the *Fifth Framework Programme* (FP5) and to optimise their advantages from such participation. The programme encompasses a set of interrelated projects: the *Regional Innovation Strategy* (RIS), the *Regional Innovation and Technology Transfer Infrastructures and Strategies* (RITTS) and the *Regional Technology Transfer Projects* (RTT). Twenty-eight European regions have been participating in RIS and RITTS since they were launched in 1994, and an additional 40 regions have enlisted for similar initiatives. This calculates to approximately one region in four across the EU participating in projects concentrating on enhancing local innovation capabilities, providing the most comprehensive structure for the development of regional systems of innovation in the world, by far.

The RIS project aims to establish a clear strategic framework for regional innovation, to create networks that promote inter- and intra-regional co-operation, to identify and prepare innovation projects, to strengthen regional research and technology adoption and development, and to orient the design of new programmes to promote innovation. The complementary RITTS projects support local and regional governments and organisations to analyse and develop an innovation and technology transfer infrastructure to assess, enhance and optimise regional innovation capabilities, with the objective of specifically meeting the needs of SMEs.

The Integrated Programme for SMEs: A General Framework for All Community Actions in Favour of SMEs was adopted in 1996 to contribute to the development of SMEs in the EU. That same year, the *Third Multiannual Programme for SMEs in the European Union* was also adopted as the cornerstone of the community's actions aimed at improving the conditions in which SMEs operate.

The Bologna Charter on SME Policies, 2000, the first Conference of EU Ministers responsible specifically for SMEs, recognised the importance of entrepreneurship and of "a dynamic SME sector," and acknowledged that the "vital" contribution of innovation to SME competitiveness and to the central role SMEs play in national systems would be improved by increasing access to information, financing and networking. Recognising that e-commerce creates opportunities and challenges for SMEs, the Charter recommended that full account be taken of SME perspectives in the drafting of guidelines, rules and regulatory initiatives and instruments related to e-commerce, and that greater awareness of the benefits to SMEs of adopting e-commerce and of integrating it into their business strategies be encouraged. Accordingly, the participating ministers agreed to work to improve the compatibility of initiatives to foster SME partnerships and to enhance the availability of instruments to promote SME development.

UK INNOVATION POLICY INITIATIVES

The UK Government (HM Treasury, 2001) has stated that it aims to create an innovative environment and framework. In accordance with this objective, the UK has introduced its lowest ever corporation rates for small companies, and the lowest starting rate for a major industrialised country, in addition to comparatively generous R&D tax credits.

According to the UK's Small Business Service (SBS), there were an estimated 3.7 million businesses registered in the UK at the start of 2000. Ninety-nine percent (99%) of these had less than 50 employees, but provided 45% of the UK non-government employment and 38% of the economy's turnover. The SME sector is, therefore, an extremely important source of income and employment for the UK. The SBS provides a network of Business Link Partnerships, through the sharing and exploiting of knowledge, through providing access to finance, through access to focused advice and support, and through providing incubators and managed workspace.

The Economic and Social Science Research Council (ESRC) responded to the 1995 White Paper on innovation, *Realising our Potential*, by investing £10m to establish three research centres and a programme of innovation management research projects carried out with researchers working alongside business. Such programmes can have a real, if limited, impact. For example, a UK-based EU-funded study on 20 SMEs initiating e-commerce was conducted in 1999 (O'Neill, 2000). The participating companies were predominantly micro-businesses. Most of the companies began the study with a very low level of ICT skills. Whilst 52% of the companies saw themselves as innovative, 92% wanted to expand, and 42% were keen to increase profits. They all anticipated that benefits would be gained from e-commerce, including: access to more customers (92%), improved communications with customers (92%), increased profits (83%), increased status (75%), faster communications (67%), global presence (58%), improved communications with suppliers (58%), reductions in marketing costs (42%), and reduced transaction costs (17%).

The project saw each of the companies launching information-point only websites. Six months after launch, 86% were exchanging emails with their customers, and 43% with their suppliers. Forty-three percent (43%) of the companies thought that they had increased access to customers, while 14% thought that they had experienced faster communications to customers and suppliers, in addition to increasing their status. The majority of the participating companies were positive about the developments they anticipated in the near future: 86% expected access to more customers, while 57% expected a reduction in marketing costs, and 86% expected improved communications with suppliers and customers.

E-COMMERCE ADOPTION AND IMPLEMENTATION FACTORS

Several early studies attempted to identify the organisational differences between large and small companies and the effects of these differences on IT adoption and implementation (Ein-Dor and Segev, 1978; Cheny et al., 1986; Raymond, 1990). The findings were consistent with results published in the 1999

KITE project's *Analysis of e-commerce practice in SMEs* (based on 89 examples of SMEs practicing e-commerce across 17 European countries) which showed that SMEs typically have more difficulty in achieving e-commerce success because of characteristic SME attributes.

In line with the fact that most of the e-commerce activities are experimental add-ons to existing businesses, many of the surveyed SMEs had low expectations of the cost-benefits to be gained from e-commerce. They were very interested, however, in quality benefits such as access to new markets. This suggests, as do this chapter's two featured case studies, that some SMEs engaging in e-commerce are also prepared to take on new challenges, such as learning how to service these new markets, and to develop ways of dealing with expansion in their customer base (e.g., use of e-commerce to streamline internal and supplier-facing processes, or setting up virtual relationships with business partners).

From the results of the KITE questionnaire, SME e-commerce adoption and implementation success would appear to depend on a number of factors including:

- Having an original idea and/or targeting a unique market niche
- Developing a business case for e-commerce adoption and implementation
- Finding sufficient funding to carry out e-commerce properly
- Finding the right business and technology/promotional partners
- Ensuring the right fit between the company's product or service and the demographics of the Internet
- Being flexible enough to be able to innovate
- Being able to manage and scale growth.

OVERVIEW OF CASES

- **Davis and Co. <www.davisco.net>:** Since 1993, this London law firm has pioneered a business model utilising teleworking, lean management and contingent working.
- **Lobster <www.lobster.co.uk>:** Established in 1993, Lobster, essentially an online delicatessen, strives to transform the way people buy gourmet foods.

Davis & Co. <www.davisco.net>
Introduction

Flexible working utilizing the Internet and mobile technologies can radically transform the way companies operate, providing more freedom and greater job satisfaction among staff, reducing overheads, and boosting individual and company performance. Christopher Davis is a leading exponent of this type of work practice. In 1995 he established Davis & Co., a London law firm specializing in mergers and acquisitions with an international client base, built entirely around flexible working. The firm leases a Regus office in the City for central calls and meetings, but the company's "virtual" network of 40 lawyers and support staff all operate remotely.

Davis & Co. has won numerous awards, including the 1997 BT Work Smarter Award (a national award for the best use of IT in business) and the 1998 Hifal/Lawyer Awards Bronze Award (Best Use of IT). The firm was a finalist in the 1998 Legal Business Awards (Most Entrepreneurial Law Firm) and the 1997 Hifal/Lawyer Awards (Best Use of IT).

Business Model

Strategic planning is not formally structured or presented in Davis & Co., and profit is shared on a case-by-case basis. Colleagues who bring in a job receive 10% of the fee, while all those working a given case typically receive a share of 65% of the time charged. The firm receives the remaining 25%, which means the profit margin is 75%.

Consultants at Davis & Co. necessarily rely heavily on technology to share information, using a database of all the documents and developments of a major case that all parties can access. The firm's members and clients are linked by a secure email system, audio and conferencing facilities, fax, and voicemail and phone.

Flexible working with Internet and mobile technologies has enabled Davis & Co.'s network members to work from any location while remaining in touch with customers and colleagues via technology, such as WAP, messaging services, voice-over IP and Internet-enabled call centres, or a laptop and mobile phone.

Benefits to the firm have included lower overheads and increased productivity. The firm provides an excellent example of how flexible working should be introduced in a systematic and culturally sensitive way in order to be effective.

Innovation Factors and Processes

Forming a "virtual" company was a way of achieving a "full-service" law firm without outlaying a large capital expenditure. Consequently, Christopher Davis founded the firm on the concept of developing relationships with specialist lawyers who were working either on their own or in very small practices. Originally, he built a team to work on deals from the clients he was advising on credit risk insurance, but increasingly encouraged consultants to bring their own cases and clients, for which the firm attends to the bureaucratic regulatory requirements, such as professional indemnity and accounting.

Development and Operational Issues

Relevant EU e-commerce policy initiatives "did not register on the radar" at the time Davis founded the company, and he claims to remain "oblivious" to current policies and initiatives. Davis believes that quality control is "all in the recruitment," but without any central performance review, it is not always easy to monitor the quality of work being performed by colleagues, and it can also be difficult to develop institutional loyalty.

Conclusion

The greatest disadvantage for the firm appears to be that its clients do not yet take full advantage of the cost-saving uses of technology. Nonetheless, Davis & Co. is able to successfully draw together teams to collaborate (almost exclusively) virtually on clients' cases. And Davis is confident that in the future his colleagues will take instructions and payments online, in addition to having all information and documents needed to close a transaction or document litigation made accessible through online client deal and case "rooms."

Lobster <www.lobster.co.uk>

Introduction

Lobster aims to transform the way people shop for fine foods and wines. Essentially, it is an up-market online delicatessen, targeting customers with discerning tastes. Launched in December 1999, Lobster is privately owned, has annual revenue "in the mid-six figures" and employs three full-time and four part-time staff. Lobster's founder and Managing Director, Alex Fitzgibbons, insists that the company provides its customers with "better personal service" than they could ever expect to experience in a shop. Lobster will search for specifically requested products on behalf of its customers, and offers same-day delivery in London, with next-day delivery throughout the rest of the United Kingdom.

Business Model

Because it sells high-quality foodstuffs that customers cannot see, smell or examine, Lobster is presented with disadvantages that other online retailers are not subject to. However, it has an advantage over offline gourmet delicatessens, as the company is able to order stock daily to fulfill orders.

All aspects of the website, and many other aspects of the company's operations, such as its distribution and delivery systems, are outsourced. This has proved to be considerably cheaper than having the infrastructure for the staff and facilities on retainer. However, the aspects of Lobster's business that will "never" be outsourced are the selection, the storage and the packaging of the products it sells - the very aspects other companies tend most to outsource! But the product is "so key" that it is "inconceivable" to Fitzgibbons that others should handle it.

Lobster became cash flow positive in December 2000 — a notable achievement for an online company at a time when many were floundering, if still in operation. Although it is a very small company, there is a formal, disciplined structure of accountability and corporate governance at Lobster, due to the requirements laid down by the investor, Rocco Forte. Clear monthly, quarterly and annual budgets are developed, as are five-year financial forecasts, but strategic planning is "informal and organic."

The key business drivers, according to Fitzgibbons, are "the products, the IT, and the fulfilment procedure." The IT must work, so that orders can successfully be taken, and the products — the food — must be of the highest quality, well packaged and delivered on time.

Innovation Factors and Processes

Lobster launched in early December 1999. From the outset there was a clear business proposition, a single private investor, and — initially — a small group of suppliers. Lobster was a "100% business-driven" idea. Fitzgibbons' interest in gourmet food, in combination with how ineffectively more traditional and long-established gourmet food competitors (such as Harrod's and Fortnum and Mason's) were handling online retailing meant that Lobster was able to easily execute his vision.

Development and Operational Issues

As an Internet pure-player start-up, adopting e-commerce was a given. Despite this, most of the development and implementation of Lobster's website and IT development and operations has been outsourced. New features are added as the company's range of products and services grows, and products, recipes, menus and ready-to-go dinners are regularly updated.

Conclusion

Fitzgibbons' advice for firms launching operations is to treat online busi-nesses as being "essentially the same" as any other retail business, to approach selling "from an e-tail point of view" and to keep costs within a "comfortable" margin, all the while considering "time and access" to be the "great calls to purchase."

DISCUSSION

The literature has stressed the need for businesses of all sizes to fully develop market strategies before adopting e-commerce (Giaglis et al., 1998; Pollard and Hayne, 1998). The findings arising from these two case studies show that e-commerce can be successfully adopted and implemented by SMEs to develop new markets when a strategy is in place.

Hawkins et al. (1995) and Hyland and Matlay (1997) found that SMEs with fewer than ten employees were less likely to adopt e-commerce than larger small businesses. These findings are contradicted by findings from the two case companies. However, the fact that the case companies are both pure-player start-ups has inevitably and fundamentally affected their propensity towards e-commerce adoption, in line with the findings of Donckels and Lambrecht (1997), who offered "market focus" as a primary motivator for SME adoption of e-commerce.

Poon and Swatman (1997) have suggested that SMEs adopt e-commerce to reach new markets. The current data from these case companies supports this view. However, confirmation of this issue would require further investigation with a broader variety of case companies. Certainly, these two cases provide excellent examples of how online business models can be used in tandem with offline activities, and their e-commerce activities appear to have been driven primarily by a combination of tactical objectives with emergent business/IT strategy models.

The principals of the participating case studies, Davis & Co. and Lobster, recognized the potential strategic e-commerce opportunities offered by embracing e-commerce, and sought to realize these opportunities. Both companies have identified and retained their most profitable customer base, found their most valuable customer segments, and understood their customers' specific needs.

Other than the need to adhere to legalities (such as tax and VAT requirements) neither company was aware, or indeed a conscious beneficiary, of projects or policy initiatives intended specifically to encourage them, which strongly indicates that such measures should, at the very least, be better targeted and advertised towards a broader SME audience.

On the basis of the experiences communicated by the principals of these case study companies, it would seem that the following attributes are crucial to the successful adoption of e-commerce by UK SME start-up pure players:

- Recognition of and support for the strategic implications of e-commerce.
- Recognizing, analysing and employing effective strategies to launch, adapt and maintain e-commerce operations.
- Comprehensive integration of the Internet into the companies' core activities.

The founders of these case companies felt that their companies were, in addition to utilizing existing technology, tactically looking to achieve the following:

- To provide additional channels to market.
- To increase responsiveness, and the ability to react to changing market conditions, which would in turn increase competitive advantage and market share.
- To increase efficiencies and reduce overhead and costs per transaction.

The firms profiled illustrate successful implementations of e-commerce, which presents the opportunity for strikingly different business ventures as well as radically new ways to run existing businesses. New technologies may be harnessed by organizations to help them to achieve competitive advantage; to transform relationships with customers, suppliers and business partners; and to redesign their industries through innovating their organizations. In short, e-commerce can result in fundamental changes to current business practice for SMEs.

CONCLUSION

While a single definition of innovation may be difficult to articulate, an examination of the literature enables us to reach a broad consensus. As a response, throughout Europe, hundreds of policy measures and support schemes aiming at innovation have been recently implemented or are under preparation. But what is the relevance of all these policy initiatives? Do they tackle "real" needs? Comprehensive answers to such questions are beyond the scope of this chapter, but will shape the direction of the author's future research.

There are a number of limitations that must be considered from this study. Firstly, the generalizability of these results across SMEs in other industries and cultures needs to be carefully considered. Secondly, reliance on the perceptions of one key informant from the two case companies, who was the instigator of e-commerce adoption may imply cognitive biases. Raymond (2001), however, has demonstrated that this methodology can draw valid conclusions.

The data presented in this chapter has attempted to examine the adoption, implementation and management of e-commerce by these UK-based SMEs case companies concerning the relevance and direction of EU policy initiatives introduced for that purpose. It can be considered, from the data presented by the principals of the case companies, that a significant number of EU projects and policies initiated to motivate SMEs to adopt and implement e-commerce were and are neither relevant, accessible nor coherent to start-up SMEs in the UK, and as a result, offer little practical guidance for them.

In conclusion, the most desirable outcomes for entrepreneurs and SMEs in successfully adopting and implementing innovation will be achieved only if appropriate public policies are introduced. It is the design, implementation and evolution of these policies that is the real challenge facing policy-makers. Clearly, further research needs to be undertaken on the issues raised.

REFERENCES

Abell, W. & Limm, L. (1996). *Business Use of the Internet in New Zealand: An Exploratory Study.* Retrieved from the World Wide Web: http//www.scu.edu.au/sponsored/ausweb96.

Amidon, D. (1993, Fall). Knowledge innovation: The common language. *Journal of Technology Studies*, Epsilon Pi Tau.

Amidon, D. M. & Mahdjoubi, D. (1999). Atlas of Knowledge Innovation: Beyond Business Planning. *Year 2000 Handbook of Business Strategy: A Comprehensive Resource Guide to Strategic Management*, Faulkner & Gray. Retrieved from the World Wide Web: http://www.entovation.com/whatsnew/atlas1.htm.

Auger, P. & Gallaugher, J.M. (1997). Factors Affecting Adoption of an Internet-based Sales Presence for Small Businesses. *The Information Society,* 13(1), 55-74.

Barry, H. & Milner, B. (2002). SMEs and E-business: A Departure from the Traditional Prioritisation of Training? *Journal of European Industrial Training,* 25(7), 316-326.

Bekker, F. & Staude, G. (1988). *Starting and Managing A Small Business.* Juta & Co.

Bergquist, W. (1993). *The Postmodern Organization.* San Francisco, CA: Jossey-Bass.

Boland, R.J. (1987). The In-formation of Information Systems. In R.J. Boland & R. Hirschheim (Eds.), *Critical Issues in Information Systems Research* (pp. 363-379). Chichester, UK: Wiley.

The Bologna Charter on SME Policies. (2000). Retrieved from the World Wide Web: http://www.mimmc.ro/bcsme/bologna/bologna_charter.htm.

Boter, H., Hjalmarsson, D. & Lundstrom, A. (1999). *Outline of a Contemporary Small Business Policy.* Swedish Foundation for Small Business Research.

Chappell, C. & Feindt, S. (1999). *Analysis of E-commerce practice in SMEs.* Esprit KITE project (Knowledge and Information Transfer on Electronic Commerce). Retrieved from the World Wide Web: http://kite.tsa.de.

Chen, J.C. & Williams, B. C. (1998, October). The Impact of EDI on SMEs: Summary of Eight British Case Studies. *Journal of Small Business Management*, 36(4), 68-72.

Cheney, P.H., Mann, R.I. & Amoroso, D.L. (1986). Organisational Factors Affecting the Success of End-User Computing. *Journal of Management Information Systems,* 3(1), 65-80.

Cobbenhagen, J. & Nauwelares, C. (1996). *Building Regional Innovation Strategies*, MERIT (Mastricht Economic Research Institute on Innovation and Technology), The Netherlands.

Community Innovation Survey. (2001). CORDIS. Promotion of Innovation and Encouragement of SME Participation. Retrieved from the World Wide Web: http://www.cordis.lu/innovation-smes/src/cis2.htm.

Competitiveness through Partnerships with People. (1997). DTI. Retrieved from the World Wide Web: http://www.dti.gov.uk/mbp/bpgt/m9m000002/m9m0000021.html.

Curran, J. & Blackburn, R. A. (1994). *Small Firms and Local Economic Networks.* Paul Chapman Publishing.

Dacin, M. T., Ventresca, M. J. & Beal, B. D. (1999). The embeddedness of organizations: Dialogue and directions. *Journal of Management*, 25, 317-356.

Davenport, T. H. (1992). *Process Innovation: Reengineering Work Through Information Technology.* Cambridge, MA: Harvard Business School Press.

Day, J. D., Mang, P. Y., Richter, A. & Roberts, J. (2001). The Innovative Organisation. *The McKinsey Quarterly*, 2.

DeMarco, D. (1999, March). *Innovative Management Network*, 6(23).

Department of Trade and Industry. (2000). Business in the Information Age. *Business Benchmarking Study.*

Donckels, R. & Lambrecht, J. (1997). The Network Position of Small Businesses: An Explanatory Model. *Journal of Small Business Management*, 35(2), 13-28.

Drakopoulou-Dodd, S., Jack, S. & Anderson, A.R. (2002). Scottish Entrepreneurial Networks in the International Context. *International Small Business Journal*, 20(2), 213-219.

Drucker, P. (1974). *Management: Tasks, Responsibilities, Practices.* New York: Harper & Row.

Drucker, P. F. (1998, November-December). The Discipline of Innovation. *Harvard Business Review*, 3480.

Ein-Dor, P. & Segev, E. (1978). Organisational Context and the Success of Management Information Systems. *Management Science*, 24(10), 1064-1077.

European Commission. (1993). *White Paper on Growth, Competitiveness and Employment*, EC, Luxembourg.

European Commission. (1994). *Regional Technology Plan Guide Book*, EC DGXIII/DG XVI, Luxembourg.

European Commission. (1994). *Regional Technology Plan Guide Book*, EC DGXIII/DG XVI, Luxembourg.

European Commission. (1995). *Green Paper on Innovation*, EC, Luxembourg.

European Commission. (1996). *Action Plan for Innovation in Europe*, European Community.

European Commission. (1996). *Green Paper on Innovation*, EC, Luxembourg.

European Commission. (1996). *RITTS & RIS Guide Book*, EC DG XVI, Luxembourg.

European Commission. (1996). *Systems Engineering in Software-Intensive SMEs (SISMEs) Final Report*. DGIII Industry Programme for Research and Technology Development in Information Technologies (1994-1998).

European Commission. (2000). *Italian Proposal for the International Network for SMEs* (INSME), DSTI/IND(2000)6.

European Commission. (2000). *Statistics on innovation in Europe*, 2000 Edition. Retrieved from the World Wide Web: http://www.cordis.lu/innovation-policy/studies/gen_study5.htm.

European Commission. (2001). *Building an Innovation Economy in Europe: A review of 12 studies of innovation policy and practice in today's Europe*. Retrieved from the World Wide Web: http://www.cordis.lu/innovation-policy/studies/ca_study1.htm#download.

European Commission. (2001). *The Commission Innovation in a knowledge-driven economy*. Adopted in September 2000 (COM(2000)567).

European Commission. (2001). *Commission Staff Working Paper, 2001 Innovation Scoreboard, Brussels*, 14(9), 1414.

Fifth framework programme of the European Community for research, technological development and demonstration activities (1998-2002). Retrieved from the World Wide Web: http://europa.eu.int/comm/research/fp5.html.

Fourth Multiannual Programme for SMEs 2001-2004. Retrieved from the World Wide Web: http://europa.eu.int/comm/enterprise_policy/mult_entr_programme/4th-programme.htm.

Gemuenden, H. G. (1999, March). *Innovative Management Network,* 6(21).

Giaglas, G., Klein, S. & O'Keefe, R. (1999). Disintermediation, Reintermediation, or Cybermediation? The Future of Intermediaries in Electronic Marketplaces. *12th Bled E-business Conference*.

Ginzberg, M.J. (1981a, June). Key Recurrent Issues in the MIS Implementation Process. *MIS Quarterly*, 47-59.

Ginzberg, M.J. (1981b). Early diagnosis of MIS implementation failure: Promising results and unanswered questions. *Management Science*, 27(4), 459-478.

Goldman, S., Nagel, R. & Preiss, K. (1995). *Agile Competitors and Virtual Organizations*. Oxford: John Wiley & Sons.

Hargadon, A. & Sutton, R. I. (2000). Building an Innovation Factory. *Harvard Business Review,* (May/June).

Hawkins, P., Winter, J. & Hunter, J. (1995). *Skills for Graduates in the 21ˢᵗ Century*. Report Commissioned from the Whiteway Research, University of Cambridge, Association of Graduate Recruiters, Cambridge.

HM Treasury, Inland Revenue. (2001). *Designs for Innovation: A consultative note*. Retrieved from the World Wide Web: http://www.ht-treasury.gov.uk/mediastore/otherfiles/ACF525.pdf.

Hoffer J.A., George, J.F. & Valacich, J.S. (1996). *Modern Systems Analysis and Design* (2ⁿᵈ ed.). Benjamin/Cummings.

Hyland, T. & Matlay, H. (1997). Small Businesses, Training needs and VET Provisions. *Journal of Education and Work,* 10(2).

Innovation and SME Programme. Retrieved from the World Wide Web: http://www.cordis.lu/innovation-smes/home.html.

The Integrated Programme for SMEs: A General Framework for all Community Actions in Favour of SMEs. Retrieved from the World Wide Web: http://europa.eu.int/ISPO/ecommerce/sme/policy.html.

Irwin, D. (2000). OECD. *Enhancing the competitiveness of small businesses in the global economy: Enhancing the competitiveness of small businesses through innovation.* Retrieved from the World Wide Web: http://www.sbs.gov.uk/content/pdf/oecd.pdf.

Jeal, B. & Wroe, J. (1999). *Innovation and Industry: The SME Standpoint. Australian Department of Industry, Tourism and Resources.* Retrieved from the World Wide Web: http://isr.gov.au/industry/summit/reference/submissions/73-JealWroe.pdf.

Johannisson, B. & Monsted, M. (1997). Contextualising Entrepreneurial Networking – The case of Scandinavia. *International Studies of Management Organisation,* 27(3), 109-136.

Kelly, P. & Kransberg, M. (1975). *Technological Innovation: A Critical Review of Current Knowledge.* Atlanta: Advanced Technology and Science Studies Group, Georgia Institute of Technology.

Kirzner, I.M. (1973). *Competition and Entrepreneurship.* Chicago, IL: University of Chicago Press.

Lachman, L. M. (1986). *The Market as Economic Process.* Oxford: Blackwell.

Land, G. & Jarman, B. (1992). *Breakpoint and Beyond: Mastering the Future Today.* New York: HarperCollins.

Lee, C.S. (2001). An analytical Framework for Evaluating E-commerce Business Models and Strategies. *Internet Research: Electronic Network Applications and Policy,* 11(4), 349-359.

Leo, H. & Booth, G. (2001). *European Trend Chart on Innovation. Country Report: Principality of Liechtenstein.* Covering period January 2001-June 2001. European Commission Enterprise Directorate-General Innovation/SMEs Programme. Retrieved from the World Wide Web: http://trendchart.cordis.lu/reports/documents/liechtenstein_cr_june.2001.pdf.

Mahdjoubi, D. (1997). *Regional Innovation Strategies in the European Community.* Retrieved from the World Wide Web: http://www.gslis. utexas.edu/~darius/ris_ec/ris_ec.html.

Mason, H. & Rohner, T. (2002). *The Venture Imperative: A New Model for Corporate Innovation.* Cambridge, MA: Harvard Business School Press.

Mohr, L.B. (1982). *Explaining Organisational Behaviour: The Limits and Possibilities of Theory and Research.* San Francisco, CA: Jossey-Bass.

Mulhern, A. (1995, July). The SME Sector in Europe: A Broad Perspective. *Journal of Small Business Management,* 3, 83-87.

Nauwelaers, C. & Wintjes, R. (2000). *SME Policy and the Regional Dimension of Innovation: Towards a New Paradigm for Innovation Policy?* (SMEPOL). MERIT Research Memorandum, no. 00-23. MERIT, University of Maastricht. Retrieved from the World Wide Web: http://www.edocs.unimaas.nl/files/mer0023.pdf.

Nunes, N. & Cunha, J. (2000). Wisdom: A Software Engineering Method for Small Software Development Companies. *IEEE Software,* 17(5), 113-119.

O'Neill, J. (2000). Innovation through e-Commerce: Implementing e-Commerce Solutions in SMEs. Paper presented at *Innovation through e-Commerce Third International Conference,* UMIST, November, 2000. Retrieved from the World Wide Web: http://www.staffs.ac.uk/CEBS/conference.doc.

Oakey, R. (1985). Innovation and regional growth in small high technology firms: evidence from Britain and the USA. In D.J. Storey (Ed.), *Small Firms in Regional Economic Development: Britain, Ireland and the United States.* Cambridge: Cambridge University Press.

Olave, M.E.L. & Neto, J. A. (2001, March). Managing Innovation: The Point of View of SME's Networks in Brazilian Electronic Industry. *Proceedings of the Twelfth Annual Conference of the Production and Operations of Management Society,* POM-2001.

Plotkin, H. (2002). Is Risk the Cost of Innovation? *Harvard Management Communication Letter,* 4/1/02.

Pollard C.E. & Hayne, S.C. (1988). The Changing Faces of Information Systems Issues in Small Firms. *International Small Business Journal,* 16(3), 70-87.

Poon, S. & Swatman, P. (1997). The Internet for Small Businesses: An Enabling Infrastructure. *Fifth Internet Society Conference,* 221-231.

Quayle, M. (2002). E-commerce: The Challenge for UK SMEs in the Twenty-First Century. *International Journal of Operations and Production Management,* 22(10), 1148-1161.

Quinn, J. B. (1996). *Innovation and Corporate Strategy: Managed Chaos.* In C. Marshall & G. Rossman (Eds.), *Technology in the Modern Corporation: A Strategic Perspective.* New York: Pergamon Press.

Raymond, L. (1990). End-user Computing in the Small Business Context: Foundations and Directions for Research. *DATA BASE*, 20(4), 20-26.

Raymond, L. (2001). Determinants of Web Site Implementation in Small Business. *Internet Research: Electronic Network Applications and Policy,* 11(5), 411-422.

Roberts, M. & Wood, M. (2002). The Strategic Use of Computerised Information Systems by a Micro Enterprise. *Logistics Information Management,* 15(2), 115-125.

Saviotti, P.P. (1996). *Technological Evolution, Variety and the Economy.* London: Edward Elgar.

Schein, E. (1997). Organization Development and the Organization of the Future. *Organization Development Journal,* 15(2), 11-19.

Schrage, M. (1999). *Serious Play: How the World's Best Companies Simulate to Innovate.* Cambridge, MA: Harvard Business School Press.

Senge, P.M. (1990, Fall). The Leader's New Work: Building Learning Organizations. *Sloan Managemen Review,* 32(1) 7-23.

Sengenberger, W., Loveman, G. & Piore, M. (1990). *The Re-emergence of Small Enterprises: Industrial Restructuring in Industrial Countries.* Geneva: International Institute of Labour Studies.

Silva, L. & Backhouse, J. (1997). Becoming Part of the Furniture: The Institutionalisation of Information Systems. In A.S. Lee, J. Liebenau, & J.I. DeGross (Eds.), *Information Systems and Qualitative Research* (pp. 389-414). London: Chapman & Hall.

Small Business Statistics – Frequently Asked Questions. Small Business Services. Retrieved from the World Wide Web: http://www.sbs.gov.uk/statistics/statisticsfaqs.asp.

Smallbone, D., North, D., Vickers, I. and McCarthy, I. (2000). Policy Support for R&D in SMEs: The UK Government's Smart Award Scheme. In W. During, R. Oakey & S. Mukhtar (Eds.), *New Technology-Based Firms at the Turn of the Century.* Vol. VII. Pergamon, (pp. 143-159).

Stauber, A. (2000). *A Survey of the Incorporation of e-business in Tasmanian Small and Medium Sized Enterprises.* Tasmanian e-business Centre, 37.

Stoner, J. A. & Freeman, R. E. (1989). *Management.* Englewood Cliffs, NJ: Prentice-Hall.

Teece, D.J., Pisano, G. & Schuen, A. (1997). Dynamic capabilities and strategies. *Strategic Management Journal,* 18(7), 509-533.

Tetteh, E. & Burn, J. (2001). Global Strategies for SME-business: Applying the SMALL Framework. *Logistics Information Management,* 14, 171–180.

Third Multiannual Programme for SMEs 1997-2000. Retrieved from the World Wide Web: http://europa.eu.int/comm/enterprise_policy/mult_entr_programme/3rd-programme.htm.

Thong, J.Y.L., Yap, C.S. & Raman, K.S. (1993). *Environments for Information Systems Implementation in Small Businesses.* Working Paper, National University of Singapore.

Tidd, J., Bessant, J. & Pavitt, K. (1997). *Managing Innovation: Integrating Technological, Organzational & Market Change.* John Wiley & Sons.

Trappey, C.V. & Trappey, A.J.C. (2001). e-business in Greater China. *Industrial Management and Data Systems,* 105(5).

Wheatley, M. J. (1992). *Leadership and the New Science.* San Francisco, CA: Berrett-Koehler.

White Paper Realising Our Potential: A Strategy for Science, Engineering and Technology. (1993). DTI.

Yin, R.K. (1994). *Case Study Research: Design and Methods,* 2nd edition. Thousand Oaks, CA: Sage.

APPENDIX A — INTERVIEW QUESTIONNAIRE

Case Study Interview Questions

1.   Background Details

1.1   What is the name of your company?

1.2   When was your company founded?

1.3   Where was your company founded?

1.4   What is your company's major market?

1.5   What do you see your company's major market being in five years time?

1.6   Is your company private or publicly owned?

1.7   How many staff does your company employ?

1.8   Approximately, what is your company's annual revenue?

1.9   Has your company's growth over the past five years exceeded your expectations? To what extent is this due to the adoption and implementation of e-business?

1.10 How many locations/branches does your firm have, and where are they located?

1.11 What is your company's reporting structure for IT?

2.   *Industry & Business Environment*

2.1   To what business sector does your company belong?
2.2   What do you see as being the major differences between this and other business sectors?
2.3   Is e-business usage different in your sector to others? If so, how?
2.4   What is the rate at which products/services become obsolete in your business sector?
2.5   How predictable are the actions of your company's competitors?
2.6   How different are your company's products/services compared with those of your competitors?
2.7   Do you monitor your competitor's activities? How?
2.8   How severe a threat does price competition present?
2.9   How severe a threat does quality competition present?
2.10 How severe a threat does declining demand present?
2.11 What do you consider to be the greatest threat facing your company/ industry?
2.12 How predictable are the demands and tastes of your company's customers?
2.13 At what rate has technology changed in your company's industry?
2.14 How often must your company change marketing practices in response to competition?
2.15 What are your company's key business drivers?

3.   *Overview of e-Business Adoption and Implementation*

3.1   How did the company's e-business adoption arise?
3.2   Was a formal decision made, or did the situation arise organically?
3.3   Were subsequent decision-making processes formal and informal?
3.4   Was adoption primarily driven by business or technology motivations? If by both, please elaborate as to the combination.
3.5   Who made the decision to innovate?
3.6   What were the five most important factors that led to e-business adoption?
3.7   What were the major obstacles or barriers that had to be overcome for your company's adoption, implementation and operation of e-business to be a success?
3.8   What were the processes of adoption?
3.9   Was adoption in direct alignment with the strategic business plan (formal or informal) or direction of the company at that time?
3.10 Were there any concerns?
3.11 What mobile technologies does your company employ?

3.12 Were there any mobile technologies introduced that were subsequently abolished?

3.13 What Internet applications does your company employ?

3.14 Were there any Internet applications introduced that were subsequently abolished?

3.15 Was there any internal resistance to adoption at any stage? If so, how did this manifest?

4.   *Strategic Business Planning*

4.1   Does your company undertake strategic business planning?

4.2   Is it formal or informal planning?

4.3   How often does planning take place?

4.4   Who are the participants in this process?

4.5   Is a formal strategic business plan produced? If so, who receives a copy?

5.   *The Development and Implementation of e-Business*

5.1   What aspects of the overall e-business operation has your company developed in-house? What aspects have been outsourced? What aspects have been purchased "off-the-shelf"? How satisfactory was each aspect?

5.2   How do you determine the level of satisfaction?

5.3   From the decision to adopt e-business to the first live e-business application, and how long did it take?

5.4   Were there any difficulties with e-business implementation generally, or adopting specific individual aspects of either the initial project, subsequent projects, or technology generally?

5.5   Was each e-business technological aspect implemented according to a schedule?

5.6   Were there operational problems (i.e., Equipment failure, integration problems, and procedural inadequacies)? Also, at what stage did they occur? And how were they resolved?

5.7   How many subsequent versions of each e-business aspect have been implemented and were subsequent experiences similar to or different from the initial experiences? How?

5.8   To what extent are the current e-business operations integrated with other IT systems (e.g., sales, inventory, ordering, accounting, etc.) and business processes?

5.9   Has implementation of e-business improved or inhibited relationships with your suppliers and/or clients? How?

5.10 Has e-business implementation brought your company additional clients or revenues?

5.11 Do you consider that e-business has been a success for your company?

5.12 How is success determined?

5.13 Has the introduction of e-business influenced and reshaped your company's agenda?

5.14 Has e-business altered the way your company operates?

5.15 Has the adoption of e-business affected your relationship with your customers?

5.16 Has the adoption of e-business affected your relationship with your peers?

5.17 As e-business affected collaboration in any way amongst those in your industry?

5.18 Has e-business made your business dealings more transparent to your suppliers or clients?

6.   *Policy Initiatives in the EU and UK*

6.1   Do you think e-business, with a particular focus on Internet and mobile technologies, is redefining business processes and functions in your industry in the UK in the light of EU policy initiatives?

6.2   How aware are you/have you been of those policy initiatives, and if so, through what means?

6.3   How relevant, accessible and coherent are these policy initiatives to your industry?

6.4   Did you consider these initiatives before adopting e-business?

6.5   Did you consider EU policy initiatives for SMEs embracing e-business to be relevant, accessible and coherent?

6.6   What factor did these initiatives play in adoption and/or implementation?

6.7   What policy initiatives would have been better facilitated awareness and procedures of your company's adoption of e-business?

6.8   Through what means could these have been effectively communicated?

6.9   What policy initiatives would have facilitated awareness and procedures of your company's implementation of e-business?

6.10 What policy initiatives would more effectively facilitate your company's e-business operations?

7.   *The Future*

7.1   What do you consider to be the major challenges to companies generally in future use of e-business as a revenue channel?

7.2   What do you consider to be the major challenges to your industry in future use of e-business as a revenue channel?

7.3   What do you consider to be the major challenges to companies in future use of e-business as a method of streamlining the supply-chain?

7.4   What future changes of your company's e-business operations do you anticipate?

7.5   If your company was facing the same e-business decisions today, would anything be done differently?

7.6   Do you have any advice for other companies seeking to adopt and implement e-business operations?

7.7   Do you have any further comments?

Section II:

Policy Implication for Networked SMEs in Supply Chain

Chapter IX

B2B E-Commerce Infrastructure Success Factors for Small Companies in Developing Economies

Murray E. Jennex, San Diego State University, USA

Don Amoroso, San Diego State University, USA

Olayele Adelakun, DePaul University, USA

ABSTRACT

This chapter looks into the key infrastructure factors affecting the success of small companies in developing economies that are establishing B2B e-commerce ventures by aggregating critical success factors from general e-commerce studies and studies from e-commerce in developing countries. The factors were identified through a literature review and case studies of two organizations. The results of the pilot study and literature review reveal five groups of success factors that contribute to the success of B2B e-commerce. These factors were later assessed for importance using a survey. The outcome of our analysis reveals a reduced list of key critical success factors that SMEs should emphasize as well as a couple of key policy implications for governments in developing countries.

INTRODUCTION

Information and Communication Technology (ICT) can provide a small enterprise an opportunity to conduct business anywhere. Use of the Internet allows small businesses to project virtual storefronts to the world as well as conduct business with other organizations. Heeks and Duncombe (2001) discuss how IT can be used in developing countries to build businesses. Domaracki (2001) discusses how the technology gap between small and large businesses is closing and evening the playing field, making B2B and B2C e-commerce available to any business with access to computers, web browsers, and telecommunication links. This chapter discusses how small start-up companies can use ICT to establish e-commerce applications within developing economies where the infrastructure is not classified as "high-technology".

E-commerce is the process of buying, selling, or exchanging products, services, and information using computer networks including the Internet (Turban et al., 2002). Kalakota and Whinston (1997) define e-commerce using the perspectives of network communications, automated business processes, automated services, and online buying and selling. Turban et al. (2002) add perspectives on collaboration and community. Deise et al. (2000) describe the E-selling process as enabling customers through E-Browsing (catalogues, what we have), E-Buying (ordering, processing, invoicing, cost determination, etc.), and E-Customer Service (contact, etc.). Partial e-commerce occurs when the process is not totally using networks. B2C e-commerce is the electronic sale of goods, services, and content to individuals, Noyce (2002), Turban et al. (2002). B2B e-commerce is a transaction conducted electronically between businesses over the Internet, extranets, intranets, or private networks. Such transactions may be conducted between a business and its supply chain members, as well as between a business and any other business. A business refers to any organization, public or private, for profit or nonprofit (Turban et al., 2002, p. 217; Noyce, 2002; Palvia and Vemuri, 2002). Initially, B2B was used almost exclusively by large organizations to buy and sell industrial outputs and/or inputs. More recently B2B has expanded to small and medium sized enterprises, SMEs, who can buy and/or sell products/services directly, Mayer-Guell (2001). B2B transactions tend to be larger in value, more complex, and longer term when compared to B2C transactions with the average B2B transaction being worth $75,000.00 while the average B2C transaction is worth $75.00 (Freeman, 2001). Typical B2B transactions involve order management, credit management and the establishment of trade terms, product delivery and billing, invoice approval, payment, and the management of information for the entire process, Domaracki (2001). Noyce (2002) discusses collaboration as the underlying principle for B2B. The companies chosen as mini-cases for this study meet the basic definition of B2B with their e-commerce ventures as both are selling services over the Internet to other business organizations. Additionally, both provide quotes and the ability to negotiate pricing over the Internet and both are attempting to establish relationships with their buyers.

This chapter proposes a set of five infrastructure success factor groups for SMEs that are starting e-commerce ventures. Tetteh and Burn's (2002) define SMEs as firms with less than 500 employees. This is further broken down into micro companies, those with less than five employees, small companies, those with from five to 20 employees, and medium companies, and those between 20 and 500 employees. Infrastructure is the underlying foundation of networks, hardware, software, skills, processes, and resources that must exist before an organization can build e-commerce applications. Infrastructure may be internal and/or external to the organization.

Success factors were determined through a review of the literature. Inhibitors and obstacles to success are used to identify what is needed for infrastructure to support successful implementation of e-commerce ventures. Literature pertaining to developing countries was used to ensure the infrastructure success factors are relevant to conditions in those countries. Finally, surveys of B2B e-commerce participants were used to rate the importance of the success factors.

The chapter first presents the literature review used to build the research model. The model is then presented followed by the methodology. This is followed by the results of the survey used to determine the importance of the success factors. The chapter concludes with discussions on conclusions, limitations on the research, and future areas of research.

LITERATURE REVIEW
Success Factors for E-Commerce

Several studies have been done looking at success factors, issues, and requirements for e-commerce. Palvia and Vemuri (2002) discuss obstacles and critical success factors for global e-commerce. Obstacles include e-tailers not shipping overseas due to complexities and issues with customs, tariffs, currency exchange, and shipping. Other key obstacles include a lack of trust between transacting parties, lack of access to computers and the Internet, and limited electronic payment capability. They list as critical success factors the ability to maintain a personal touch while using a Web site for business; localizing the Web site to fit local customer requirements including recognizing culture, local regulations, pricing constraints, and language; keeping automated processes simple and fast due to low attention spans of customers and less reliable connections in developing countries; foster trusting relationships between customers or organizations involved in a B2B relationship; focus on processes that improve convenience, information, intermediation, and pricing; have the site found near the top of the search engine results; evolve the site as technology changes and capabilities expand, and plan for mobile connectivity. Sairamesh et al. (2002) also discusses the importance of search and navigation but focuses on these features within the e-commerce site.

Gattiker et al. (2000) discusses the importance of economic and cultural factors. Global economic factors include the cost of connecting and having disposable income for shopping online. Global cultural factors include differences in work habits and language. It has been found that simply translating documents does not ensure the translation will contain the same cultural meaning as the original. Hall (2002) expands on cultural issues by discussing the importance of localization. Kang and Corbitt (2001) discuss cultural issues with respect to the use of graphics and graphical components. Finally, Mayer-Guell (2001) discusses the importance of organizational culture of the organization implementing an e-commerce strategy and finds that e-commerce initiatives will not reach their full potential if the organization's workers cannot adapt to the changes in processes caused by e-commerce.

Sairamesh et al. (2002) discusses the importance of contracts. Freeman (2001) discusses contract and other legal risks including intellectual property protection, conflict and dispute resolution, fulfillment of contracts, use of patented business processes, and trademark and copyright issues. The success factor from these risks is having legal consultation available for review of documents, processes, and contracts.

Castelluccio (2000) lists fourteen critical success factors. These are having adequate business processes, maintaining account information and a relationship profile, good site navigation, good use of graphics, providing decision support and communications, using shopping cart technology, monitoring post purchase delivery, acquiring and retaining customers, providing gift services, maintaining site content and continuity, providing international services and multi-channel integration. Additionally, Castelluccio (2000) found several issues that detracted from success. These included dead links on sites, inaccessible call/help centers, deceptive post-purchase spam, sites not living up to promise, and lack of convenience for potential customers who do not yet have an account.

Developing strategies to adopt and market e-business technologies and services requires an organization to make significant investments. Deciding to make the initial and ongoing investments is contingent on the organization's perception that the future benefits will outweigh the costs involved. Mitra and Chaya (1996) propose that there is a need to quantify the benefits from the investments in e-business systems and that building quality e-business systems will require solid evidence of value-add to customers. The added value for customers will result in additional profit for the organization, as they are able to maintain current customer relationships and develop new ones based on the attractive offerings a new e-business presence affords.

E-Business for Small Companies

Developing an e-business niche will allow an SME to provide the best possible deliverable to the customer, even if this means passing part of the deal to a competitor who specializes in another aspect of the e-business system. Bakos (1991), found that ultimately all e-business systems reduce buyers' search costs and increase the efficiency of e-commerce transactions, and therefore create numerous possibilities for the strategic uses of these systems. Operating within an e-business framework offers a more cost-effective model, with feasible elimination of several steps of the traditional sales process. Powell and Dent-Micallef (1995) identified an emerging trend from single-source sales channels to electronic markets, lowering coordination costs for producers and retailers and resulting in fewer distribution costs. Smaller businesses ultimately benefit from lowered sales costs and gain access to larger markets. Executives are "sold" on technology spending based upon the strategic value-add nature of the opportunities. Given an adequate availability of talent for development of e-business systems, as reported later in this chapter, we feel that it is imperative for e-business applications to have strong consideration in SMEs.

Amoroso and Sutton (2002) found that small organizations need to focus on providing their customers with a set of Web applications that best serve the customer, rather than using a hit-and-miss approach. They found evidence to support that the greater the degree of clarity of e-business service offerings, the more the need to have these Web-based applications developed by partner firms. The decision to outsource e-business applications is crucial to building a quality Internet presence, especially important in smaller organizations. Organizations that focus on key online applications will have a greater degree of success. These applications will need to be planned in advance in order to yield bottom-line value added results. The e-business applications found to have the greatest impact on small organization success are presented in Table 1. With the many e-business applications available to development and the careful discretion of resource allocation, these applications were found to be the most beneficial for generating downstream revenues and cost reduction for small businesses. Due to the span of components in an e-business system, many organizations find difficulty in fulfilling all customers' needs; therefore a focused strategic planning session around value-add will yield IT investment successes (Brynjolfsson and Hitt, 1996). There is a strong degree of focus on e-business e-catalogs, workflow systems, and online customer services, given the data presented in Table 1.

The authors examined the factors that would lead to the success of small organization's e-business applications. Clearly, several mega-categories of e-business success factors emerged including: (1) understanding the customer base needs, (2) support of substantial e-business initiatives in an ongoing basis, (3) developing e-business applications using a proven development methodology, (4) branding the Web sites for competitive advantage, and (5) reshaping the organization's corporate culture (Amoroso, 2001). How the organization manages the knowledge gathering process for their customer base will have strong impacts on their ability to meet their needs and their needs for specific Web site features, such as multi-lingual support, click-through capabilities, and customer profiling. The degree of Internet application maturity will determine the way that customers interact with the Web sites and how integrated the applications will support customer-side requests. The development of small organization applications will depend upon acquiring development methodologies that extent the company's technical talent and enable the company to successfully manage the e-business projects. Having a set of strong e-business applications to deliver to company customers via the Web will not be successful if they are not accessible to the customer base, thus facilitating the need for strong product branding efforts. Finally, the corporate culture will need to support conducting business in a new way given new e-business initiatives and ultimately new corporate processes for promoting and delivering products and services.

Amoroso (2001) found a set of corporate performance factors that small organizations need to consider and eventually quantify with respect to e-business initiatives. E-business initiatives, like other corporate investments, will need to provide the needed payback to the organizational bottom-line. Clearly, e-business applications have been found to have a greater emphasis on speed-to-market than traditional IT applications found Hart and Saunders (1998). Corporate performance factors found in previous research found: (1) customer-focused factors, (2) corporate-financial factors, and (3) business process factors.

Corporate-focused factors include those attributes of success that enhance a customer's attraction to conduct e-business with the organization, a customer's retention to conduct business in the future, and a customer's satisfaction with current e-business products and services. Corporate-financial factors include those factors related to the incremental revenue growth provided by e-business applications, lower cost of sales to conduct business on the Internet, a tighter degree of cost control, and potentially increased market share due to e-business. Business process factors are related to streamlining organizational processes and decreased cycle time (Amoroso, 2001).

Table 1. Value-added e-business applications/services.

Applications	Percent	Services	Percent
Electronic catalogs	71.4	E-Database integration	57.1
Workflow systems	71.4	Web monitoring	57.1
Online customer service	71.4	Supply chain automation	42.9
Order management	57.1	Online communities	42.9
Electronic billing systems	42.9	Sales force automation	42.9
Online auctions	28.6	Electronic marketplaces	28.6
B2B exchanges	28.6	XML solutions	28.6

Turban et al. (2002) discuss critical success factors for SMEs. Included in their SME Critical Success Factors are: providing niche or specialty or information products; focusing on localized markets, having a low capital investment; maintaining little to no inventory; using secure electronic payments (when using electronic payments) and flexible payment methods; having quick and reliable logistics services; submitting the Web site to directory-based search engines like Yahoo!; and, having a membership in an online service or mall such as AOL or ViaWeb's Viamall.   Also, the Web site should follow basic good design principles, market properly, understand customers and their buying habits, price correctly, anticipate cash flow, monitor competition/technology/marketplace changes, keep growth slow and steady, delegate, develop good internal communications.

Infrastructure for E-Commerce in Developing Countries

Several studies have been done looking at what basic infrastructure requirements for e-commerce in developing countries. Mukti (2000) found that problems restricting the expansion of e-commerce in Malaysia include security concerns, payment issues, Internet access issues, and technical skills of workers. Sachs et al. (2001) developed a tool for countries to assess their readiness for the networked world. They look at 19 factors distributed between network access, networked learning, networked society, networked economy, and networked policy as areas of concern. Users of the tool rate their economies and infrastructure to one of four stages. Stage 4 is fully ready for e-commerce while stage 1 needs a lot of development. The tool is designed to aid governments in planning for moving their economy to stage 4.

The Electronic Commerce Steering Group, Asia Pacific Economic Cooperation (APEC) (2000), have published the E-commerce Readiness Assessment Guide. This guide is designed to aid governments in developing policies that will support e-commerce. The guide looks at the areas of basic infrastructure and technology, technology and commercial services, current Internet usage, standards committees, people skills, and government policies and regulation.

Cloete and Courtney (2002) discussed SME acceptance and adoption of e-commerce in South Africa. They found that e-commerce adoption is heavily influenced by factors within the organization. Lack of access to computers, software, other hardware, and telecommunications at a reasonable cost; low e-commerce use by competitors and supply chain partners; concerns with security and legal issues; low knowledge level of management and employees; and unclear benefits from e-commerce were all found to inhibit adoption.

Dedrick and Kraemer (2001) discussed e-commerce in China. They found that although there is considerable interest in e-commerce, there are also significant barriers to establishing e-commerce ventures. Limited diffusion of computers, high cost of Internet access, and a lack of online payment processes directly inhibit e-commerce. Inadequate transportation and delivery networks, limited availability of banking services, and uncertain taxation rules indirectly inhibit e-commerce. Government policies promoting IT and e-commerce and attacking software and intellectual property piracy are encouraging e-commerce. Regulation in the areas of international contracts, foreign participation, and digital signatures and encryption is needed to continue encouraging e-commerce. Additionally, growing computer manufacturing and IT services industries are creating a technical base for supporting e-commerce.

Chepaitis (2002) looked at the information environment in Russia and found that the information environment can be an impediment to the development of e-commerce in emerging economies. Many developing countries do not have a culture of sharing data. The ability to pool data for statistical analyses is necessary for many business processes and organizations. The absence of shared data can result in a lack of effective information systems due to the lack of reliable and consolidated marketing, customer, and economic data. This also usually results in low data quality and trust in the data that is available. Twelve factors were identified that affect the information environment in an emerging economy. The factors focus on the business culture of the economy and will limit the emergence and scope of e-commerce in these economies. The factors include unsuccessful/intrusive government planning and regulation; formal barriers to entry and dictated pricing in distribution and supply; informal entrepreneurship such as black markets and barter; ineffective methods for managerial accounting; political fear and widespread avoidance of information sharing; unstable currency, nascent financial regulations, and a dearth of financial services; a reluctance to divulge information without compensation or reciprocity; proprietary attitudes towards data ownership; rigid, hierarchical management styles with a reluctance to share information or empower employees; communication behaviors that rely on oral tradition or more than one language; and an emphasis on price and availability to the exclusion of quality.

The Electronic Commerce Infrastructure Info-Communications Development Authority of Singapore (IDA) (Staff, 2002) describes the e-commerce infrastructure in Singapore. Key components of this infrastructure include infrastructure services; a legal and regulatory framework, a set of open standards for technical services such as security, network protocols, email, and information exchange; and an incentive system of investment and tax breaks designed to encourage e-commerce development and investment. Infrastructure services include network services for linking online businesses, directory services for search and retrieval, security services for secure identification and communication, secure payment services, and solution providers for creating e-commerce systems.

Sukovskis (2002) describes the IT sector in Latvia. Factors supporting e-commerce in Latvia include government support for regulation encouraging e-commerce, a fairly well developed telecommunications infrastructure available for a price, and a growing cadre of IT professionals. Inhibitors to e-commerce are a relatively low use of the Internet and computers by Latvian companies, only 26.4% of companies used the Internet and 46.5% used computers in 2001; modern hardware and software is available but expensive; limited availability of investment capital; and the small number of available IT professionals (the demand for IT professionals is greater than the supply).

Jennex et al. (2004) and Jennex and Amoroso (2002) performed case studies on two micro-sized B2B e-commerce organizations, IT Business Solutions, ITBS, and International Business Solutions, IBS. ITBS was in Italy and IBS was in Ukraine. Key critical success factors identified as contributing to success or failure include pricing of services, telecommunications infrastructure, availability of current hardware and software, technical skills of workers, project management and controls, business organization and processes, client interface, legal representation, tax and other regulations, and payment processes. Some interesting findings with respect to B2B e-commerce follow.

Jennex and Amoroso (2002) analyzed the Web sites used by IBS as distinctive, sophisticated, interactive sites. They provide audio and image information as well as text information. They work best with high-speed connections and higher end personal computers. Technically the sites are very good. They appear easy to use and navigate, although this is the authors' impression and not verified through any usability testing. However, some issues that were identified included the sites constantly playing music, excessive scrolling, lack of e-business applications, long site load time, and poor site branding. Ultimately the value of the site is in the business it generates. By IBS' own admission, the sites have generated many inquiries but little to no business.

Jennex et al. (2003) found that ITBS uses B2B e-commerce to communicate with clients. They do not have a site of their own and rely on sites they have created for advertising. The main e-commerce applications used by ITBS are email and remote monitoring and maintenance of the applications ITBS maintains for their clients. This is inadequate for a long-term B2B enterprise. ITBS needs to, as a minimum, establish a web presence that advertises its business and allows for potential client contact. Additional processes that should be considered are an electronic payment system and links to the sites they've built and maintained for use as an online catalog of capabilities.

E-BUSINESS RESEARCH MODEL

To organize the research conducted for this study, a model was developed from the literature identifying infrastructure success factors for companies establishing e-commerce ventures. There are five main success factor groups: People factors, Technical Infrastructure, Client Interface, Business Infrastructure, and Regulatory Interface. Each group has several success factors that were evaluated for importance using a survey discussed later in this chapter. Figure 1 provides a model of how these factors affect the relationship between a client and provider.

The E-commerce Infrastructure Success Factor Model shows the relationships between the five main factors and the participants in a B2B e-commerce transaction. The model shows that both participants operate within a regulatory environment. This environment provides the legal framework in which both entities must operate. The environment can hinder the ability of the participants to perform the transaction, or it may encourage it. India is an example of a regulatory environment that encourages business while Ukraine is an example of one that does not. Participants also operate within an external technical infrastructure comprised of the telecommunications and electrical systems of

Figure 1. E-commerce Infrastructure Success Factor Model.

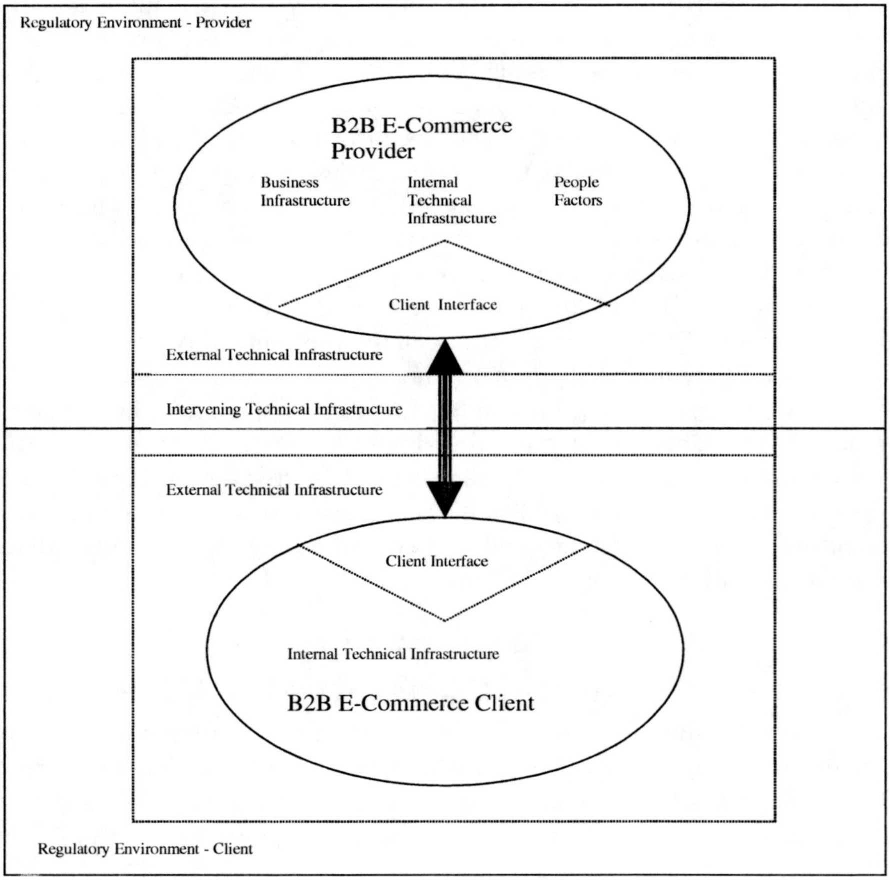

each of the participants' countries as well as any country geographically between the participants. The reliability and availability of these infrastructure components directly impact the ability of the participants to implement e-commerce.

Internal to the participants are the client interface, internal technical infrastructure, business infrastructure, and people factors. The client interface is the defined communications process between the participants. This directly impacts the transference of requirements and knowledge and guides the participants in the resolution of conflicts. The business processes of the e-commerce provider determine the likelihood that the provider will remain viable for an extended partnership. The internal technical infrastructure ensures the provider has the ability to implement e-commerce initiatives. People factors ensure the provider has the ability to understand the context in which the client operates.

METHODOLOGY

The literature review discussed previously was used to generate a list of success factors for each factor in the E-commerce Infrastructure Success Model, Figure 1. Table 2 maps the success factors to their source. An exploratory study was then done to determine the importance of these critical success factors and to identify the key critical success factors that SMEs in developing countries should emphasize. To do this study a survey was generated based on the list of critical success factors. To validate the survey, the survey was given to the graduate classes of one of the authors. These students were selected because they: 1) were familiar with IT and e-commerce principles, 2) usually had previous business experience, and 3) were mixed international and US in origin. Results of the pilot survey were used to create the final form of the survey.

The survey was then administered to personnel from B2B providers and companies that were B2B clients. Distribution of the survey was through meetings, personal contacts of the authors, and email solicitation. Approximately 225 surveys were distributed with 181 surveys returned and 175 surveys usable for an approximate 78% usable return rate. One hundred and eleven surveys were from B2B providers, 56 from US and 55 from non-US organizations. Of the 55 non-US surveys 25 were from Asia (India, Thailand, Malaysia, Vietnam, Pakistan, Philippines, Peoples Republic of China, and Taiwan), thirteen from Europe (Ukraine, Italy, United Kingdom, Russian Federation, Latvia, Finland, and Germany), eight from Australia, New Zealand, or Japan, four from the Middle East (Turkey and Israel), two from Africa (Nigeria and Kenya), one from South America (Brazil), and two from Canada. Additionally, 100 of the 111 B2B provider respondents fit Tetteh and Burn's (2002) definition of SMEs (micro is

Table 2. Map of attributes to literature review and case study findings.

CSF Group	Success Factor	Source
People Factors	General Knowledge Skills of Workers	Cloete & Courtney (2002), Jennex et al. (2004), Mayer-Guell (2001), Sukovskis (2002)
	Language Skills of Workers	Chepaitis (2002), Gattiker (2000), Jennex, et al. (2004), Palvia & Vemuri (2002)
	Cultural Awareness of Workers	Amoroso (2001), Chepaitis (2002), Gattiker (2000), Hall (2002), Jennex & Amoroso (2002), Kang & Corbitt (2001), Mayer-Guell (2001), Palvia & Vemuri (2002)
	Project Management People Skills	Chepaitis (2002), Cloete & Courtney (2002), Gattiker (2000), Hall (2002), Jennex et al. (2004), Kang & Corbitt (2001), Palvia & Vemuri (2002)
Technical Infrastructure	Reliable and Cost Effective Telecommunications Infrastructure	Cloete & Courtney (2002), Dedrick & Kraemer (2001), Domaracki (2001), Gattiker (2000), Jennex & Amoroso (2002), Palvia & Vemuri (2002), Mukti (2000), Staff (2002), Sukovskis (2002)
	Up to date PCs, Other Computer Hardware and Software are Available	Amoroso (2001), Cloete & Courtney (2002), Dedrick & Kraemer (2001), Jennex & Amoroso (2002), Palvia & Vemuri (2002), Sukovskis (2002)
	Technical Skills of Workers	Amoroso (2001), Cloete & Courtney (2002), Dedrick & Kraemer (2001), Mukti (2000), Palvia & Vemuri (2002), Sairamesh et al. (2002), Sukovskis (2002), Staff (2002), Turban et al. (2002).
Client Interface	Knowledgeable Client Contact Point	Amoroso (2001), Jennex et al. (2004)
	Trust Between Client and Provider	Molla & Licker (2001), Palvia & Vemuri (2002)
	Client Contact Can Communicate in a Language the Provider Understands	Chepaitis (2002), Gattiker (2000), Jennex et al. (2004), Palvia & Vemuri (2002)
	Problem Resolution Process in Place	Freeman (2001), Jennex et al. (2004)
Business Infrastructure	Business Plan in Place	Jennex et al. (2004)
	Business Organization in Place	Amoroso (2001), Jennex et al. (2004), Mayer-Guell (2001)
	Business Process in Place	Amoroso (2001), Castelluccio (2000), Jennex et al. (2004), Palvia & Vemuri (2002),
	Cash Control Processes Exist	Castelluccio (2000), Dedrick & Kraemer (2001), Jennex et al. (2004), Turban et al. (2002)
	Advertising Is In	Amoroso (2001), Jennex et al. (2004), Palvia and Vemuri (2002), Turban et al. (2002)
	Effective Client Contact Methods	Castelluccio (2000), Jennex et al. (2004), Staff (2002)
	Payment Processes Are In Place	Dedrick & Kraemer (2001), Jennex et al. (2004), Mukti (2000), Palvia & Vemuri (2002), Staff (2002), Turban et al. (2002)
	Legal Representation/Support is Available	Cloete & Courtney (2002), Dedrick & Kraemer (2001), Freeman (2001), Jennex et al. (2004), Sairamesh et al. (2002), Staff (2002)
	Cost Advantage Exists	Palvia & Vemuri (2002), Turban et al. (2002)
Regulatory Environment	Intellectual Property Protection	Dedrick & Kraemer (2001), Freeman (2001), Jennex et al. (2004)
	Tax Laws Favor E-Commerce	Dedrick & Kraemer (2001), Jennex & Amoroso (2002), Palvia & Vemuri, Staff (2002), Sukovskis (2002)
	Bank Laws Support E-Commerce	Dedrick & Kraemer (2001), Jennex & Amoroso (2002)
	Customs/Import/Export Laws Support E-Commerce	Dedrick & Kraemer (2001), Jennex & Amoroso (2002), Palvia & Vemuri (2002), Staff (2002), Sukovskis (2002)
	Exchange Rules/Rates Favorable	Palvia & Vemuri (2002)
	Telecom Regulations favor E-Commerce	Dedrick & Kraemer (2001), Jennex et al. (2004), Palvia & Vemuri (2002), Staff (2002)

less than five employees, small is five to 20 employees, medium is 20 to 500 employees) (Note that B2B clients were predominately large companies, this is considered acceptable.) Surveys were analyzed with respect to the origin of the respondent and as a B2B provider or a client. Means and standard deviations were calculated with critical success factors that scored less than 2.0 determined to be the most critical success factors. The selection of 2.0 as the basis for key critical success factors is selected based on the scale used to rate importance, 1 was critical, 2 was very important, 3 was important, 4 was somewhat important, and 5 was not important; and is somewhat arbitrary. Only descriptive statistics are used to analyze the data, no tests were done to determine if the importance scores were significantly below 2.0 as this threshold is arbitrary and all items were considered critical success factors.

RESULTS

The finding of this study is a list of infrastructure success factors for companies establishing B2B e-commerce ventures. There are five main success factors: People factors, Technical Infrastructure, Client Interface, Business Infrastructure, and Regulatory Interface. Each factor has several attributes. These attributes were assessed for importance using a survey. The survey was distributed to both clients and providers. Provider respondents were asked to rate the importance of the attribute with respect to success of their organization. Client respondents were asked to assume they were evaluating potential partner organizations and were to rate the attributes with respect to importance of selecting a partner. The scale used for the survey was 1 – Critical, 2 – Very Important, 3 – Important, 4 – Useful, and 5 – Not Important. Respondents were given the option to add attributes, however, none were added. The following tables list the factors and their attributes, and importance means with standard deviations.

People Factors

People factors ensure the provider organization has adequate human resources to meet the demands of its clients. This involves having knowledgeable workers that understand the culture and language of the client. Worker knowledge skills are considered the most important by all groups of respondents. Project Management skills were considered second most important by all but non-US providers. Language skills were considered the second most important by non-US providers, who probably speak English as a second language, but was considered less important by the US respondents, providers and clients alike. All respondents considered cultural Awareness the least important critical success factor of this group.

Technical Infrastructure

The Technical Infrastructure group of critical success factors ensures that the underlying networks, hardware/software, and technical skills exist so that organizations can create the applications and Web sites necessary for organizations to implement and sustain e-commerce ventures. Technical infrastructure exists for clients and providers and for the geographical areas between them.

Table 3. Importance of people factors attributes.

Critical Success Factors	Total		Providers						Clients	
			Total		US		Non-US			
	Mean	SDev	Mean	SDev	Mean	SDev	Mean	SDev	Mean	SDev
Knowledge Skills of Workers	1.66	0.70	1.59	0.67	1.55	0.66	1.62	0.68	1.80	0.74
Language Skills of Workers	2.20	0.96	2.23	0.95	2.21	1.00	2.24	0.90	2.16	0.98
Cultural Awareness of Workers	2.57	1.05	2.53	1.05	2.66	1.10	2.40	0.99	2.64	1.06
Project Management People Skills	2.01	0.89	1.96	0.84	2.04	0.83	1.89	0.85	2.08	0.98

Table 4. Importance of technical infrastructure attributes.

Critical Success Factors	Total		Providers						Clients	
			Total		US		Non-US			
	Mean	SDev	Mean	SDev	Mean	SDev	Mean	SDev	Mean	SDev
Telecom infrastructure	1.88	0.87	1.86	0.88	1.61	0.76	2.13	0.92	1.91	0.87
Up to date PCs, other computer HW/SW	2.19	0.93	2.14	0.95	1.88	0.90	2.44	0.88	2.27	0.95
Technical Skills of Workers	1.81	0.80	1.85	0.80	1.71	0.76	1.98	0.83	1.75	0.80

Worker technical skills attribute was considered the most important critical success factor. Telecommunication infrastructure was the second most important critical success factor. This is considered indicative that organizations recognize that e-commerce requires technical ability and solutions.

Client Interface

The Client Interface critical success factor group establishes and maintains the relationship between participants in B2B e-commerce. This factor has three highly rated critical success factors and is judged the most critical of the five critical success factor groups. Trust in the relationship and a knowledgeable client contact were rated most important of this group with contacts that can speak the provider's language being the next most important critical success factor. Note that all three of these factors are considered key.

Business Infrastructure

The Business Infrastructure success factor group ensures the viability of the B2B provider and allows for the establishment of long-term business relationships. These critical success factors ensures that business and payment processes are in place, that legal advice is available for contracts and other

Table 5. Importance of client interface attributes.

Critical Success Factors	Total		Providers						Clients	
			Total		US		Non-US			
	Mean	SDev	Mean	SDev	Mean	SDev	Mean	SDev	Mean	SDev
Client contact is knowledgeable	1.70	0.85	1.67	0.83	1.52	0.69	1.82	0.94	1.77	0.89
Trust between client and provider	1.70	0.83	1.62	0.78	1.55	0.76	1.69	0.79	1.83	0.92
Client contact can communicate in a language the provider company understands	1.99	0.96	2.06	0.96	1.95	0.82	2.18	1.07	1.88	0.95
Problem resolution process is in place	2.14	0.84	2.05	0.79	1.95	0.82	2.15	0.76	2.31	0.91

needs, that communication and advertising is available and effective, and that sufficient funds are available to support the B2B provider. Potential client contact methods were considered the most important critical success factor of this group. An interesting observation is that cost was not the most important critical success factor of this group. This is a very important finding as it indicates that providers and clients recognize that there is more to a B2B relationship than just cost.

Regulatory Environment

The Regulatory Environment critical success factor group sets the rules for how e-commerce will be conducted. In a global marketplace differences between regulatory environments can make or break e-commerce ventures. India and Singapore are examples of countries encouraging global e-commerce, Ukraine is a country that does not. Intellectual Property Protection is considered the most important critical success factor by all respondents, providers and clients alike.

Table 6. Importance of business infrastructure attributes.

Critical Success Factors	Total		Providers						Clients	
			Total		US		Non-US			
	Mean	SDev	Mean	SDev	Mean	SDev	Mean	SDev	Mean	SDev
Business Plan	2.27	0.91	2.27	0.90	2.13	0.92	2.42	0.88	2.28	0.93
Business Organization	2.43	0.94	2.38	0.92	2.29	1.06	2.47	0.77	2.52	0.98
Business Processes	2.35	0.94	2.33	0.95	2.09	0.92	2.58	0.92	2.39	0.94
Cash Control Processes	2.45	1.01	2.37	1.04	2.18	0.97	2.56	1.07	2.58	0.97
Advertising is effective	2.98	1.01	2.89	0.96	2.80	0.94	2.98	0.97	3.13	1.08
Client contact methods are effective	2.10	0.89	2.05	0.82	2.05	0.84	2.05	0.80	2.17	1.02
Effective Payment Processes	2.37	0.95	2.35	0.98	2.36	1.12	2.35	0.82	2.41	0.90
Legal Support available	2.51	1.01	2.48	1.00	2.46	1.11	2.49	0.88	2.56	1.04
Product costs competitive advantage	2.54	0.86	2.54	0.88	2.52	0.93	2.56	0.83	2.55	0.83

Table 7. Importance of regulatory interface attributes.

Critical Success Factors	Total		Providers						Clients	
			Total		US		Non-US			
	Mean	SDev	Mean	SDev	Mean	SDev	Mean	SDev	Mean	SDev
Intellectual Property Protection	2.02	1.06	2.03	1.09	1.82	0.99	2.24	1.15	2.02	1.02
Tax laws encourage B2B/E-Commerce	2.43	1.04	2.38	1.04	2.46	1.14	2.29	0.94	2.53	1.04
Banking/Wire Transfer laws support overseas/ electronic payments	2.49	1.02	2.42	1.02	2.55	1.16	2.29	0.85	2.59	1.02
Customs Laws support global E-commerce	2.46	1.10	2.42	1.07	2.57	1.19	2.27	0.91	2.53	1.17
Exchange Rules/Rates favorable	2.71	1.07	2.64	1.09	2.77	1.19	2.51	0.96	2.84	1.04
Telecom Regulations favor business	2.47	1.00	2.36	1.03	2.46	1.08	2.31	0.92	2.63	0.98

DISCUSSION

The list of e-commerce infrastructure critical success factors presented in this chapter are an aggregate of critical success factors for general B2B e-commerce and B2B e-commerce in developing countries; and are a reasonable indicator of potential success for startup B2B e-commerce ventures in a developing economy when used to measure the readiness of that country's infrastructure to support B2B e-commerce. The list of critical success factors is considered to be reasonably independent of regional or country biases. Companies from Eastern and Western Europe were looked at while studies from several developing economies were used. The strength of these success factors is their incorporation of published studies, action research with actual B2B e-commerce ventures, and validation by a mix of US/Non-US and client/provider respondents. The only potentially missing attribute is security. The original companies did not mention security during interviews nor did any of the respondents. However, security is built into some of the attributes, being able to accept payments, up to date technical skills, trust, and reliable telecommunications all assumed a base level of security. It is concluded that the list of attributes as is has security implied.

However, there are 25 critical success factors spread across five success factor groups. SMEs will find it difficult to focus on all 25 critical success factors due to limited resources and capabilities. Additionally, governments in developing countries also need to know what to focus their efforts on in order to effectively support a budding outsourcing industry. To assist SMEs and governments in determining what factors to focus on, Table 8 lists those critical success factors with importance ratings of 2.0 or less, these are considered by the survey respondents to be the most important to B2B e-commerce success.

Table 8. Key critical success factors.

Critical Success Factor	US B2B Provider	Non-US B2B Provider	B2B Clients
Knowledge Skills of workers	X	X	X
Technical Skills of workers	X	X	X
Client contact is knowledgeable	X	X	X
Trust between client and provider	X	X	X
Project Management People Skills	X	X	
Telecom infrastructure	X		X
Client contact can communicate in a language the provider company understands	X		X
Problem resolution process is in place	X		
Up to date PCs, other computer HW/SW	X		
Intellectual Property Protection	X		

There are ten key critical success factors; four have been identified by all three respondent groups, one by just B2B providers, two by US B2B providers and B2B clients, and three by just US B2B providers. SMEs should focus on ensuring their personnel are well trained and educated, that their processes create and maintain trust between them and their clients, and that they have the best telecommunications connections and hardware/software that they can obtain. Governments in developing countries need to focus on providing educational and technical infrastructure, incentives for the educated to remain, and intellectual property protection.

CONCLUSION

This chapter has discussed critical success factors for e-commerce by SMEs in developing countries through a literature review, case studies, and an exploratory survey. It was found that SME B2B start-up companies need to focus on providing B2B applications that create and maintain trust with their clients. This involves creating secure systems and having clear and honest business processes and practices. To do this SMEs need employees with good technical skills that understand business processes and their clients' business. Governments in developing countries need to focus on providing an e-commerce infrastructure. This includes telecommunication infrastructure, access to current hardware and software, and intellectual property protection.

A mild surprise was the relatively low importance rating for cost by all three respondent groups. This is indicative of e-commerce participants recognizing that there are other more important critical success factors to establishing an e-commerce relationship as discussed in the preceding paragraph.

Limitations

The main limitation to this research is the relatively small sample size for the survey and the selection process for choosing respondents. However, given that the respondents are all involved in e-commerce, are predominantly from SMEs, and represent many different countries and organizations and were selected because of their attendance at conferences or other academic functions, the selection threat is considered acceptable. The small size of the sample has limited the statistical analysis of the data but is adequate for looking at means.

Implications for Future Research

Future research should focus on continuing to gather data from providers and clients, inside and outside of the US. After a larger sample has been collected the results can be statistically analyzed for differences between groups and significance of critical success factors.

REFERENCES

Amoroso, D. (2001). *e-Business Success Factors.* Working Paper, San Diego State University.

Amoroso, D. (2002). *Successful Business Models for e-Business: An Exploratory Case Analysis of Two Organizations.* Working Paper, San Diego State University.

Amoroso, D. & Sutton, H. (2002). Identifying e-Business Readiness Factors Contributing to IT Distribution Channel Reseller Success: A Case Study Analysis of Two Organizations. *35th Hawaii International Conference on System Sciences, IEEE Computer Society.*

Bakos, J. (1991). A Strategic Analysis of Electronic Marketplaces. *Management Information Systems Quarterly*, 15(3), 295-310.

Bakos, J. (1997). Reducing Buyer Search Costs: Implications for Electronic Marketplaces. *Management Science,* 43(12), 1613-1630.

Brynjolfsson, E. & Hitt, L. (1996). Paradox Lost? Firm-level Evidence on the Returns to Information Systems Spending. *Management Science*, 42(4), 541-558.

Carmel, E. & Agarwal, R. (2002). The Maturation of Offshore Sourcing of Information Technology Work. *MIS Quarterly Executive*, 1(2), 65-77.

Castelluccio, M. (2000). So, How'm I Doin'? *Strategic Finance*, 82(4), 85-86.

Chepaitis, E.V. (2002). E-Commerce and the Information Environment in an Emerging Economy: Russia at the Turn of the Century. In P.C. Palvia, S.C.J. Palvia, & E.M. Roche (Eds), *Global Information Technology and Electronic Commerce: Issues for the New Millennium*, (pp. 53-72). Ivy League Publishing.

Cloete, E., Courtney, S. & Fintz, J. (2002). Small Businesses' Acceptance and Adoption of e-Commerce in the Western-Cape Province of South-Africa. *Electronic Journal on Information Systems in Developing Countries*, http://www.ejisdc.org, 10(4), 1-13.

Dedrick, J. & Kraemer, K.L. (2001). China IT Report. *Electronic Journal on Information Systems in Developing Countries*, http://www.ejisdc.org, 6(2), 1-10.

Deise, M.V., Nowikow, C. King, P. & Wright, A. (2000). *Executive's Guide to E-Business, From Tactics to Strategy.* John Wiley & Sons.

DeLone, W.H. & McLean, E.R. (1992). Information Systems Success: The Quest for the Dependent Variable. *Information Systems Research*, 3, 60-95.

Domaracki, G.S. (2001). The Dynamics of B2B e-Commerce. *AFP Exchange*, 21(4), 50-57.

Electronic Commerce Steering Group (2000). Asia Pacific Economic Cooperation (APEC). *E-Commerce Readiness Assessment Guide*, www.ecommerce.gov/apec. Accessed September 2002.

Freeman, E.Q. (2001). B2B's Operational and Risk Implications. *Financial Executive,* 17(3), B14-B16.

Gattiker, U.E., Perlusz, S., & Bohmann, K. (2000). Using the Internet for B2B Activities: A Review and Future Directions for Research. *Internet Research,* 10(2), 126-140.

Hall, P.A.V. (2002). Bridging the Digital Divide, the Future of Localisation. *Electronic Journal on Information Systems in Developing Countries*, http://www.ejisdc.org, 8(1), 1-9.

Hart, P. & Saunders, C. (1997). Power and Trust: Critical Factors in the Adoption and Use of Electronic Data Interchange. *Organization Science,* 8(1), 23-42.

Heeks, R. & Duncombe, R. (2001). *Information, Technology and Small Enterprise: A Handbook for Enterprise Support Agencies in Developing Countries.* Institute for Development Policy and Management, University of Manchester.

Heeks, R. & Duncombe, R. (2001). *Information, Technology and Small Enterprise: A Handbook for Entrepreneurs in Developing Countries.* Institute for Development Policy and Management, University of Manchester.

Jennex, M.E. & Amoroso, D.L. (2002). e-Business and Technology Issues for Developing Economies: A Ukraine Case Study. *Electronic Journal on Information Systems in Developing Countries*, 10(5), 1-14.

Jennex, M.E., Amoroso, D.L., & Adelakun, O. (2004). E-Commerce Infrastructure Success Factors For Small Companies In Developing Economies. Forthcoming in *Electronic Commerce Research*, 4(3/4).

Kalakota, R. & Whinston, A.B. (1997). *Electronic Commerce: A Manager's Guide*. Reading, MA: Addison-Wesley.

Kang, K.-S. & Corbitt, B. (2001). Effectiveness of Graphical Components in Web Site E-commerce Application-A Cultural Perspective. *Electronic*

Journal on Information Systems in Developing Countries, http://www.ejisdc.org, 7(2), 1-6.

Mayer-Guell, A.M. (2001). Business-to-Business Electronic Commerce. *Management Communication Quarterly*, 14(4), 644-652.

Mitra, S. & Chaya, A. (1996). Analyzing Cost-effectiveness of Organizations: The Impact of Information Technology Spending. *Journal of Management Information Systems*, 13(2), 29-57.

Molla, A. & Licker, P.S. (2001). E-Commerce Systems Success: An Attempt to Extend and Respecify the DeLone and McLean Model of IS Success. *Journal of Electronic Commerce Research*, 2(4).

Mukti, N.A. (2000). Barriers to Putting Businesses on the Internet in Malaysia. *Electronic Journal of IS in Developing Countries*, http://www.ejisdc.org, 2(6), 1-6.

Noyce, D. (2002). eB2B: Analysis of Business-to-Business E-commerce and how Research Can Adapt to Meet Future Challenges. *International Journal of Market Research*, 44(1), 71-95.

Palvia, S.C.J. & Vemuri, V.K. (2002). Global e-Commerce: An Examination of Issues Related to Advertising and Intermediation. In P.C. Palvia, S.C.J. Palvia, & E.M. Roche (Eds), *Global Information Technology and Electronic Commerce: Issues for the New Millennium*, (pp. 215-254). Ivy League Publishing.

Powell, T. & Micallef, A.D. (1997). Information Technology as Competitive Advantage: The Role of Human, Business, and Technology Resources. Strategic Management Journal, 18(5), 375-405.

Sachs, J. D. & Staff (2001). Readiness for the Networked World: A Guide for Developing Countries. *Information Technologies Group, Center for International Development at Harvard University*, http://www.readinessguide.org/guide.pdf, accessed January, 2002.

Sairamesh, J., Mohan, R., Kumar, M., Hasson, T., & Bender, C. (2002). A Platform for Business-to Business Sell-Side, Private Exchanges and Marketplaces. *IBM Systems Journal*, 41(2), 242-252.

Smetannikov, M. (2002), The New Russian Revolution. *Inter@ctive Week*, June 4, 8(22).

Staff (2002). *Electronic Commerce Infrastructure in Singapore*. Electronic Commerce Infrastructure Info-Communications Development Authority of Singapore (IDA). Found at http://www.ec.gov.sg/resources/internal/ECFramework6x.html. Accessed September, 2002.

Sukovskis, U. (2002). *IT Sector Development in Latvia*. Presented at the IS Development Conference 2002, Riga, Latvia, September 12, 2002.

Tetteh, E.O. & J.M. Burn (2002). A Framework for the Management of Global e-Business in Small and Medium-Sized Enterprises. In P.C. Palvia, S.C.J. Palvia, & E.M. Roche (Eds.), *Global Information Technology and*

Electronic Commerce: Issues for the New Millennium, (pp. 215-254). Ivy League Publishing.

Turban, E., King, D., Lee, J., Warkentin, M., & Chung, H.M. (2002). *Electronic Commerce 2002: A Managerial Perspective.* Prentice Hall.

Chapter X

Comparison of Factors Pertaining to the Adoption and Non-Adoption of Electronic Commerce in Formally Networked and Non-Networked Regional SMEs:

A Study of Swedish Small Businesses

Robert MacGregor, University of Wollongong, Australia

Lejla Vrazalic, University of Wollongong, Australia

Deborah Bunker, University of New South Wales, Australia

Sten Carlsson, Karlstad University, Sweden

Monika Magnusson, Karlstad University, Sweden

ABSTRACT

This chapter examines the adoption and non-adoption of electronic commerce (EC) by formally networked and non-networked small to medium enterprises (SMEs) using the findings from a study of 339 Swedish SMEs. The results of the study indicate that there are no considerable differences between formally networked and non-networked SMEs in terms of EC adoption. This raises a number of questions concerning the nature and role of formal networks in the small business arena, and how these impinge upon the perception of the benefits, usefulness and problems of adopting and using EC.

INTRODUCTION

The adoption and diffusion of electronic commerce (EC) in small to medium enterprises (SMEs) remains a critical area of investigation in the information systems (IS) literature. Studies pointing to a technologically uncertain and globally focused economy have examined both the adoption of EC by SMEs as well as perceived barriers preventing adoption. A number of studies (Miles et al., 1999; Overby & Min, 2001) have suggested that in order to accommodate these changes brought on by EC, many small businesses are turning towards some form of strategic alliance or network where the locus of the impact of change is inter-organisational rather than organisational. These authors suggest that through involvement in formal networks (alliances that have a defined set of shared values, roles, responsibilities and governance) SMEs not only find a ready source of technical and marketing expertise, but that the very nature of the network "buffers" the impact of global market turbulence.

Despite the view of these studies that formal networking is vital to the successful adoption of EC, a number of authors have found that many SMEs avoid such arrangements, opting instead to remain self-directed where EC use is concerned. A number of reasons are suggested in the literature. Drakopoulou-Dodd et al. (2002) found that in studies of European SMEs more than 50% reported that they derived their technical support, financial advice and business know how from family and friends. Gimeno et al. (1997, cited in Dennis, 2000) found that many SME owners negatively affect potential networks by withholding necessary information to their network partners. McBer & Company (1986, cited in Dennis, 2000) found that SME owners refuse to trust or cooperate with similar business owners in the same industry. Added to this are the findings of a number of studies that have shown that factors such as size of the business, age of the business, market focus and business sector impinge both on EC adoption as well as formal network membership.

This chapter will begin by briefly examining the special circumstances of SMEs. It will then examine the nature and role of formal networks in the small business arena. The chapter will then present data gathered from 339 regional small businesses in Sweden, which profiles those SMEs that are part of a SME network and those that have decided to remain independent (in terms of number of years in business, number of employees, type of business, market focus, gender of the CEO and the educational level of the CEO). Finally, the chapter will present a set of comparisons between formally networked and non-networked SMEs that have adopted or not adopted EC technology. These comparisons will focus on the criteria for adoption, perceived benefits of EC and perceived disadvantages of EC adoption for those SMEs that have adopted the technology; and the perceived barriers for those that have decided against EC adoption.

SPECIAL CIRCUMSTANCES OF SMEs

There are many studies in the literature showing that the SME sector in general exhibits characteristics that differ from their larger counterparts. These include management style (Murphy, 1996), lack of technical expertise (Barry & Milner, 2002), lack of adequate capital (Gaskill et al., 1993; Raymond, 2001), inadequate planning (Tetteh & Burn, 2001; Miller & Besser, 2000), and limited product and service range (Reynolds et al., 1994). For brevity, these are summarised in Table 1. For the purposes of this study it is assumed that the characteristics below are applicable to Swedish SMEs as well.

Perhaps central to the characteristics distinguishing SMEs from their larger counterparts are the views of Westhead and Storey (1996) and Hill and Stewart (2000) who suggest that uncertainty is the key difference between small and large businesses. They suggest that while "internal" uncertainty is more a characteristic of large business, it is "external" uncertainty that characterises smaller organisations. While some of this external uncertainty may be attributable to those factors cited in Table 1, Hill and Stewart (2000) suggest that the major reason for external uncertainty is the lack of influence over the market environment. In order to cope with the changing market place small businesses are often obliged to operate in a regime that is far more short term.

In recent years, governments around the world have funded projects that assist small businesses in their adoption of EC technologies. These projects have ranged from and include: simple Internet commerce adoption, virtual business networks, societal issues and technology diffusion (see Smith et al., 2002; Damanpour, 2001; Dahlstrand, 1999; Papazafeiropoulou et al., 2002; Jeffcoate et al., 2002). Not only have these projects provided a variety of approaches to EC adoption by SMEs but there has been a growing realisation that many approaches that were successful with larger businesses may not be appropriate with smaller organisations. Despite early predictions (Auger & Gallaugher, 1997; Cyber Dialogue, 1998) that small business would benefit from EC adoption, recent studies (Riquelme, 2002; Roberts & Wood, 2002; Barry & Milner, 2002) have shown that it is larger businesses that have more readily adopted electronic commerce. A number of reasons have been forthcoming including poor security, high costs, and lack of requisite skill, however some researchers have begun to examine the processes by which SMEs make their decisions and have begun to question those processes.

Table 1. Features unique to the SME sector.

SME Characteristics	Literature
SME orientation	• Reynolds et al. (1994) o Small business product-oriented, large business customer-oriented

Decisions are intuitive	• Bunker & MacGregor (2000)
	  o IT decisions are not based on detailed planning
	• Reynolds et al. (1994)
	  o Decision making does not entail exhaustive study

Strong Owner influence	• Bunker & MacGregor (2000)
	  o IT decisions are usually made by the owner
	• Reynolds et al. (1994)
	  o Little use of consultants in decision making

More risky than big business	• Walker (1975) and Brigham & Smith (1967) o SMEs fail more easily than large businesses
Difficulties obtaining finance	• Gaskill & Gibbs (1994) • Reynolds et al. (1994)

Informal and inadequate planning	• Tetteh & Burn (2001)
	  o IT decisions are not based on detailed planning
	• Miller & Besser (2000)
	  o Decisions are often made with community in mind rather than business
	• Reynolds et al. (1994)
	  o Decision making does not entail exhaustive study

Poor record keeping	• Markland (1974)
Reluctance to take risks	• Walczuch et al. (2000) and Dennis (2000) o SMEs are more reluctant to spend on technology

Intrusion of family values	• Dennis (2000)
	  o Family often used in place of consultants
	• Bunker & MacGregor (2000)
	  o Family often used in place of consultants, particularly with EC and IT decisions
	• Reynolds et al. (1994)
	  o SMEs are very often family concerns

Strong desire for independence	• Dennis (2000)
	  o Owners often withhold details from colleagues
	• Reynolds et al. (1994)
	  o SMEs tend to avoid joint business ventures if it impinges on independence

Small centralised management	• Bunker & MacGregor (2000)

Lack of technical staff	• Martin & Matlay (2001) and Bunker & MacGregor (2000)
	  o Lack of IT expertise
	• Reynolds et al. (1994)
	  o Lack of specialist staff

EC ADOPTION IN SMEs

A number of studies have begun to look at the criteria used by small businesses in their decisions to adopt EC technology. While some studies have found that the "government-imposed" criteria are oversimplified (Kai-Uwe Brock, 2000; Martin & Matlay, 2001), others have shown that the unique features of small business operation (refer to Table 1) impinge upon the decision-

Table 1. Features unique to the SME sector.(continued)

SME Characteristics	Literature

Lack of control over environment	• Hill & Stewart (2000)
	  o Uncertainty about environment
	• Westhead & Storey (1996)
	  o Small business externally uncertain

Limited use of technology	• Poon & Swatman (1997) • MacGregor & Bunker (1996) • Abell & Limm (1996)

Limited market share	• Quayle (2002) and Hadjimonolis (1999)
	  o SMEs often move towards niche markets
	• Lawrence (1997)
	  o Small businesses can't compete with their larger counterparts

Heavy reliance on few customers	• Reynolds et al. (1994)
Narrow product/ service range	• Bunker & MacGregor (2000) • Reynolds et al. (1994)

Education/ experience/skill practical but narrow	• Bunker & MacGregor (2000)
	  o Little IT skill or training
	• Reynolds et al. (1994)
	  o Little training provided for staff

making processes where EC adoption is concerned. The studies surrounding the criteria for EC adoption are presented in Table 2.

Benefits and Disadvantages of EC Adoption by SMEs

Unlike previous technological initiatives EC is a "disruptive" innovation that is radically changing the way firms do business. Where previous innovations have sought to minimise dependency on other organisations, allowing the business to dictate production, marketing etc., EC has forced organisations to reassess their boundaries and to focus their attention inter-organisationally rather than organisationally. Not only has the focus shifted but also the nature of that focus has altered. Where in the past technology tended to be applied to production and adaptation to the technology was predictable, sequential and measurable, the advent of EC has turned the focus of technology towards the marketplace. As such, adaptation to the technology has become unpredictable and non-sequential in nature.

For small businesses these changes have produced both positive and negative effects. Studies by Raymond (2001) and Ritchie and Brindley (2000) found that while EC adoption has eroded trading barriers for SMEs this has often come at the price of altering or eliminating commercial relationships and exposing the business to external risks. Lawrence (1997), Tetteh and Burn (2001) and Lee (2001) contend that EC adoption fundamentally alters the internal procedures within SMEs. Indeed, Lee (2001) adds that the biggest challenge to

Table 2. Summary of research on criteria used by SMEs in the decisions to adopt and use EC.

Criteria	Literature
Demand/Pressure from customers	• Power & Sohal (2002) • Reimenschneider & Mykytyn (2000) • PriceWaterhouse Coopers (1999)
Pressure of competition	• Raisch (2001) • Poon & Strom (1997)
Pressure from suppliers	• Raymond (2001) • Reimenschneider & Mykytyn (2000) • Lawrence (1997) • MacGregor & Bunker (1996)
Reduction of costs	• Raisch (2001) • Auger & Gallaugher (1997) • Abell & Limm (1996)
Improvement to customer service	• Power & Sohal (2002) • Auger & Gallaugher (1997) • Abell & Limm (1996) • Senn (1996)
Improvement in lead time	• Power & Sohal (2002) • Reimenschneider & Mykytyn (2000) • Abell & Limm (1996)
Increased sales	• Lee (2001) • Phan (2001) • Abell & Limm (1996)
Improvement to internal efficiency	• Porter (2001)
Strengthen relations with business partners	• Raymond (2001) • Evans & Wurster (1997) • Poon & Swatman (1997)
Reach new customers/markets	• Power & Sohal (2002) • Reimenschneider & Mykytyn (2000) • Poon & Swatman (1997) • Lawrence (1997)
Improve competitiveness	• Raymond (2001) • Turban et al. (2000) • Reimenschneider & Mykytyn (2000)
External technical support	• Abell & Limm (1996)
Improve marketing	• Power & Sohal (2002) • Reimenschneider & Mykytyn (2000) • Poon & Swatman (1997) • Lawrence (1997)
Improve control and follow-up	• Domke-Damonte & Levsen (2002) • Poon & Joseph (2001) • Reimenschneider & Mykytyn (2000) • Auger & Gallaugher (1997)

SMEs is not to find the best EC model but to change the mindset of the organisation itself. For those that have developed an organisational-wide strategy these changes can lead to an increase in efficiency in the firm. For those who have not developed this strategy, this can reduce the flexibility of the business (Tetteh & Burn, 2001) and often lead to a duplication of the work effort (MacGregor et al., 1998).

A number of studies have examined both the tangible and intangible benefits achieved by SMEs from the adoption of EC. Studies by Abell and Limm (1996), Poon and Swatman (1997) and Quayle (2002) found that the tangible benefits (such as reduced administration costs, reduced production costs, reduced lead-time, increased sales) derived from EC were marginal in terms of direct earnings. These same studies found that the intangible benefits (such as improvement in the quality of information, improved internal control of the business, improved relations with business partners) were of far greater value to SMEs. Studies by Poon and Strom (1997) and Abell and Limm (1996) also found that SMEs benefited in their ability to reach new customers and new markets through the use of EC. This has been supported in more recent studies (Vescovi, 2000; Sparkes & Thomas, 2001).

A number of studies have provided conflicting results. Raymond (2001), in a study of the effect of EC on travel agents, found that very often EC replaced previously held business partners. He suggested that EC removed the need for intermediaries in many small business dealings. Stauber (2000) also noted the negative effect of EC on SMEs. Specifically he found that many firms felt that there was a decline in contact with customers, in some cases managers felt that this had led to a loss of revenue. By comparison, a study by Poon and Swatman (1997) found that EC had led to an improved relationship with customers, but not with suppliers. In their study they found that small business operators complained that EC failed to meet expectations concerning marketing or sales, nor had they experienced any savings in terms of communications costs. A number of studies (MacGregor et al., 1998; Sparkes & Thomas, 2001) have also suggested that indirect drawbacks of EC use in SMEs include dependence on the technology and the high cost of maintenance of the technology itself.

It is interesting to note that various authors (Poon & Swatman, 1997; Abell & Limm, 1996; Trappey & Trappey, 2001; Martin & Matlay, 2001) all suggest that tangible benefits are marginal in the short term, contrary to the expectations of small business operators, and that at best these may be more fruitful in the longer term. This is supported in a recent article by Vrazalic et al. (2002). For summary purposes, benefits and disadvantages of EC adoption are listed in Tables 3 and 4 respectively.

Not only do SMEs differ from their larger counterparts in both day-to-day activities as well as management style, but their perceptions of advantages and disadvantages of EC adoption have been found to differ as well. As such, recent findings have shown that there are perceived barriers to EC adoption that are unique to small businesses. For brevity, these studies are presented in Table 5.

As already stated, many SMEs are turning towards formal networking arrangements as a mechanism to overcome perceived difficulties with the adoption of electronic commerce. It is appropriate that we now examine the nature and role of formal networking in the small business environment.

Table 3. Benefits found by SMEs in their use of EC technology.

Benefits	Literature
Lower administration costs	• Quayle (2002) • Poon & Swatman (1997) • Abell & Limm (1996)
Lower production costs	• Quayle (2002) • Poon & Swatman (1997) • Abell & Limm (1996)
Reduced lead time	• Quayle (2002) • Poon & Swatman (1997) • Abell & Limm (1996)
Reduced Stock	• Quayle (2002)
Increased Sales	• Abell & Limm (1996)
Increased internal efficiency	• Tetteh & Burn (2001) • MacGregor et al. (1998)
Improved relations with business partners	• Poon & Swatman (1997)
New customers and markets	• Quayle (2002) • Ritchie & Brindley (2001) • Raymond (2001) • Sparkes & Thomas (2001) • Vescovi (2000)
Improved competitiveness	• Vescovi (2000)
Improved marketing	• Sparkes & Thomas (2001) • Vescovi (2000) • Quayle (2002)
Improved quality of information	• Quayle (2002) • Poon & Swatman (1997) • Abell & Limm (1996)

Table 4. Disadvantages found by SMEs in their use of EC technology.

Disadvantages	Literature
Deterioration of relations with business partners	• Raymond (2001) • Stauber (2000)
Higher costs	• Stauber (2000)
Computer maintenance	• MacGregor et al. (1998)
Doubling of work	• MacGregor et al. (1998)
Reduced flexibility of work	• Lee (2001) • MacGregor et al. (1998) • Lawrence (1997)
Security issues	• Ritchie & Brindley (2001)
Dependence on EC	• Sparkes & Thomas (2001)

Table 5. Barriers to EC adoption by SMEs.

Barrier	Literature
EC doesn't fit with the SMEs products/services	• Eid et al. (2002) • Kendall et al. (2001) • Tambini (1999) • Abell & Limm (1996)
EC doesn't fit with the way the SME does business	• Sawhney & Zabin (2001) • Mehrtens et al. (2001) • Bakos & Brynjolfsson (2000) • Farhoomand et al. (2000) • Poon & Swatman (1999) • Abell & Limm (1996) • Iacovou et al. (1995)
EC doesn't fit the way the SME's customers work	• Kulmala et al. (2002) • Bakos & Brynjolfsson (2000) • Abell & Limm (1996)
SMEs don't see the advantages of using EC	• Lee & Runge (2001) • Chau & Hui (2001) • Purao & Campbell (1998)
Lack of technical know how	• Mirchandani & Motwani (2001) • Farhoomand et al. (2000) • Purao & Campbell (1998)
Security risks	• Oxley & Yeung (2001) • Reimenschneider & McKinney (2001) • Purao & Campbell (1998) • Aldridge et al. (1997)
Cost too high	• Reimenschneider & McKinney (2001) • Ratnasingam (2000) • Purao & Campbell (1998)
SMEs unsure what to choose	• Farhoomand et al. (2000) • Purao & Campbell (1998)

ROLE OF NETWORKS IN SMES

It could be argued that by the very nature of business, all organisations relate to others and are thus part of some form of network arrangement. On the surface these relationships may appear to be nothing more than exchanges of goods and payments but relationships with customers, suppliers, competitors can never be simply described in terms of financial transactions. Dennis (2000) suggests that any dealing with other organisations must impinge on the decision-making process even if these decisions only involve the strengthening or relaxing of the relationships themselves. Nalebuff and Brandenburg (1996) state that for a relationship to be truly a network it must be conscious, interdependent and cooperating towards a predetermined set of goals.

Viewed then as "self designing" partnerships Eccles and Crane (1998, cited in Dennis, 2000) suggest that networks are a dynamic arrangement evolving and adjusting to accommodate changes in the business environment. Achrol and Kotler (1999) take this a step further by stating the following:

"Networks are more adaptable and flexible because of loose coupling and openness to information. Environmental disturbances transfer imperfectly through loose coupled networks and tend to dissipate in intensity as they spread through the system."

Thus member organisations have interconnected linkages that allow more efficient movement towards predetermined objectives than would be the case if they operated as a single separate entity. By developing and organising functional components networks provide a better mechanism to learn and adapt to changes in their environment. In addition to providing much needed information networks often provide legitimacy to their members. For businesses that provide a service and whose products are intangible, company image and reputation becomes crucial since customers can rarely test or inspect the service before purchase. Cropper (1996) suggests that network membership very often supplies this image to potential customers. Properly utilised, formal networks can also provide a number of advantages over stand-alone organisations. These include the sharing of financial risk (Jorde & Teece, 1989), technical knowledge (Marchewka & Towell, 2000), market penetration (Achrol & Kotler, 1999) and internal efficiency.

The advent of EC technology has given rise to a "new wave" of research examining the role of networking, particularly in SMEs. Much of this research has been prompted by the realisation that old hierarchical forms of company organisation produced relationships which are too tightly coupled (Marchewka & Towell, 2000) and do not fit an often turbulent marketplace (Overby & Min, 2000; Tikkanen, 1998).

There are many definitions of networks in the literature. Dennis (2000) suggests that:

"...networks are dynamic arrangement(sic) that are constantly evolving and adjusting in order to accommodate changes in the business environment. Member companies have interconnected linkages that allow them to move more efficiently towards set objectives than those operating as a separate entity."

She adds that while all companies form relationships with suppliers, customers, etc., it is the extent of the closeness, interdependence and consciousness of these relationships that determines whether they are truly part of a network. This definition implies that only those inter-organisational links that have formal governance can be termed networks. By comparison, Yeung (1994) defines a network as:

> *"an integrated and coordinated set of ongoing economic and non-economic relations embedded within, among and outside business firms."*

Thus for Yeung (1994) a network is not only a structure but embodies processes between organisations. These processes may be formal economic processes or may be informal cooperative relationships, sharing expertise and know how. Indeed, Dahlstrand (1999) suggests that informal links may be conscious or unconscious mechanisms. While recent studies (Keeble et al., 1999; O'Donnell et al., 2001; Overby & Min, 2001) stress the importance of informal inter-organisational links, the definition of these links in small business varies widely. As this study has as its focus SME networks with some form of governance (be they organisationally linked small businesses or firms which have made use of small business associations), the definition of formal networks provided by Achrol and Kotler (1999) will be adopted, viz:

> *"an independent coalition of task or skill-specialised economic entities (independent firms or autonomous organisational units) that operates without hierarchical control but is embedded by dense lateral connections, mutuality, and reciprocity, in a shared value system that defines 'membership' roles and responsibilities."*

NETWORK TAXONOMIES

As with the origin and definition of networks, there are a number of differing taxonomies of networks in the literature. These taxonomies are normally based on structure, process or power. It is appropriate to consider each of these styles of classification.

Structure

Veradarajan and Cunningham (1995) suggest that networks can be subdivided into four groups:

- Functional networks link functional aspects of organisations that result in joint manufacturing, marketing or product development. These networks tend to share knowledge, information and resources.
- Intra-inter-organisational networks focus on developing relationships either nationally or internationally. These networks share information.
- Intra-inter-industry networks aim to build relationships through resource pooling. These networks share resources.
- Motivational networks share marketing and technological know how. These networks tend only to share knowledge.

This is similar to the subdivisions suggested by O'Donnell et al. (2002) who termed their subdivisions vertical, horizontal, industrial and social.

Process

Whereas Veradarajan and Cunningham (1995) subdivided networks in terms of structure, Johannisson et al. (2002) suggest that networks can be subdivided into four groups based on process. The four groups are:

- Resource-based where each firm controls their own unique resources which are combined to strategic advantage;
- Industrial organisation where firms act as autonomous entities establishing their own unique market position;
- Virtual organisation where independent yet interdependent organisations strive for joint variety using advanced technology;
- Industrial district where small firms, characterised by production type, are organised for internal cooperation and external competition.

Achrol and Kotler (1999) also suggested that networks can be subdivided in terms of process. They provide four types:

- Internal networks designed to reduce hierarchy and open firms to the environment;
- Vertical networks that maximise the productivity of serially dependent functions by creating partnerships among independent skill-specialised firms;
- Intermarket networks that seek to leverage horizontal synergies across industries;
- Opportunity networks that are organised around customer needs and market opportunities and are designed to seek the best solutions to them.

Power

Dennis (2000) considers power to be the most important factor upon which to classify networks. She provides two classifications:

- Dominated networks where a group of smaller companies dominated by a single larger company; and
- Equal partner networks where there is no governing partner and each relationship is based on reciprocal, preferential, mutually supportive actions.

An obvious bi-product of network taxonomies is the analysis of organisations which form the various network types. Golden and Dollinger (1993) in an exploration of business relationships concluded that:

> *"differences in strategic postures are associated with differences in the quality and type of intra-organisational relationships."*

This is particularly apparent in smaller organisations. Jarratt (1998) suggests that particular strategic postures lead organisations to adopt particular network alliance forms. She suggested that there were four distinct categories of strategic posture, termed as follows:

- Defenders, those which were more likely to select conjugate relationships;
- Prospectors, those which were more likely to select confederate relationships;
- Analysers, those which were more likely to select agglomerate relationships;
- Reactors, those whose business relationships were unpredictable.

SME NETWORKS

Early studies of SME networks (Gibb, 1993; Ozcan, 1995) concentrated on formal networks. Indeed, Golden and Dollinger (1993), in a study of small manufacturing firms concluded that few small firms were able to function without some form of inter-organisational relationship having been established. They added that these inter-organisational relationships were associated with successful strategic adaptation by small businesses. Dean et al. (1997) suggested that formal networks were used by SMEs to:

> *"pool resources and talents together to reap results which would not be possible (due to cost constraints and economies of scale) if the enterprise operated in isolation."*

In the 1990s many SME networks took a more semi-formal approach. Local or government agencies such as small business associations and chambers of commerce provided a formal umbrella in the form of advisory services that assisted in legal, financial, training or technical advice. Individual members operated formally with the umbrella organisation but could interact informally with fellow members.

While researchers, government agencies and practitioners have continued to examine and refine both formal and semi-formal networks, recent literature (Rosenfeld, 1996; Premaratne, 2001) suggests that informal or social linkages may provide a higher and more stable flow of information and resources in the small business environment. Thorelli (1986) states that central to the concept of formal networking is the distribution of power which he defines as the ability to influence the decision of others. The five factors he cites as the potential sources of power for members are: economic base, technology, expertise, trust and legitimacy. Miles et al. (1999) suggest that for SMEs the decision to network comes from a perception of goals by the individual organisation. If the organisation sees itself as strong in its own right, a network may be seen as an option to increase that strength. The distribution of power moves in favour of the strong organisation allowing it to capitalise and influence weaker members without losing its own identity.

If, on the other hand, the organisation sees itself as weak, a network may be a necessity in order to survive and compete in the larger marketplace. For these organisations the distribution of power works away from them leaving them in a weak position in exchange relationships. This of course varies from network to network. In a small network (few participating organisations) there is more likely to be an asymmetric relationship between partners. As the size of the network increases there are a greater number of potential partners, providing a greater chance to benefit for all members. If as suggested in the literature, many small businesses are moving towards some type of formal networking arrangement through which EC adoption may be possible, it is appropriate that we now consider both EC adopters as well as non-adopters and compare those that are formally networked and those that remain self directed.

SURVEY INSTRUMENT

A questionnaire was developed for SME managers. The current study was part of a larger study examining EC adoption and use by SME in Sweden. For the purposes of brevity, the description of the survey instrument and responses will be confined to the benefits and disadvantages found by using EC in SMEs and the differences between formal networking and non-networked small businesses. A subset of the questionnaire, containing the questions relevant to this study is provided in Appendix A. A total of 1,170 questionnaires were distributed to SMEs around four regional areas of Sweden: Karlstad, Filipstad, Saffle and Arvika.

Respondents were asked whether their firm was part of a network of small businesses or an organisation for small businesses. In line with the findings of Donckels and Lambrecht (1997), respondents were asked the size of the business in terms of number of employees (single owner operator, one to nine employees, 10-19 employees, 20-49 employees, 50-199 employees, >200 employees), the sector of the business (industrial, service, retail, finance, other), the number of years the firm had been in business (<1 year, one to two years, three to five years, six to 10 years, 11-20 years, >20 years), and whether the CEO had a university qualification. Based on the findings of Blackburn and Athayde (2000) respondents were asked their market focus (local, regional, national, European Union, international). In line with the findings of Mazzarol et al. (1999) respondents were also asked the gender of the CEO.

Respondents were asked whether they had adopted electronic commerce in their business. Those respondents who indicated that they had adopted electronic commerce were asked to rate each of the criteria in Table 2 across a 5-point Likert scale (1 being very unimportant in the decision-making process and 5 being extremely important in the decision-making process). Those respondents who indicated that they had not adopted EC were asked to rate each of the barriers (see Table 5) across a 5-point Likert scale (1 being very unimportant to my situation and 5 being extremely important to my situation).

ANALYSIS OF RESPONSES

Responses were obtained from 339 SME organisations giving a response rate of 28.9%. Of the 339 responses, 148 indicated that they belonged to a network of small businesses or an organisation for small businesses. These have been termed **formally networked respondents**. One hundred and ninety one respondents indicated that they were not part of such an arrangement. These have been termed **non-networked respondents**. Table 6 provides a description of the respondents.

Table 6. Description of respondent group.

Networking	Formally networked respondents			Non-networked respondents		
Respondents	148			191		

Number of years in business	<1 year	1-2 years	3-5 years	6-10 years	11-20 years	> 20 years
Respondents	5	14	45	61	83	131

Sectors	Industrial	Service	Retail	Finance	Other	
Respondents	84	118	63	9	54	

Market	Local	Regional	National	European	International	
Respondents	174	30	96	16	23	

Number of suppliers	1 to 5	6 to 10	11 to 20	21 to 40	More than 40	
Respondents	68	57	72	59	69	

Homepage	Organisation has a homepage		Organisation has no homepage		Unsure	
Respondents	185		102		52	

E-commerce	Organisation is engaged in EC		Organisation is not engaged in EC		Unsure	
Respondents	176		125		38	

Table 7. Comparison of formally networked and non-networked SMEs and their decisions to adopt electronic commerce.

	Existence of Network	
Have Adopted EC	**Networked SMEs**	**Non-Networked SMEs**
Yes	61	115
No	63	62
Unsure = 38		

Significance Level .004

The data was analysed using a chi-square analysis to determine whether the decision to adopt EC was associated with the firm being part of a formal networking arrangement or not. Table 7 shows the results of the chi-square analysis. The data was then divided into two distinct groups, those who indicated that they were part of a networking arrangement and those who did not. Within each group a series of chi square tests were carried out to determine which factors were associated with the decision to adopt electronic commerce. Table 8 provides data for those SMEs in a networking arrangement, while Table 9 provides the data for those who were not. For brevity, only significant data is shown.

For respondents that had adopted EC, a comparison of the means of the rating of each of the adoption criteria (see Table 2) was carried out using a two-tailed t-test. Table 10 provides the means and the t-values. A comparison of means of the ratings of benefits and disadvantages (networked group versus non-networked group) was also carried out using a two-tailed t-test. Table 11 provides the means and the t-values. An examination of Tables 3 and 4 indicates that certain factors (costs, value of information, internal efficiency and customer relationships) appear both as benefits as well as disadvantages. A series of t-tests, comparing the rating of benefits to disadvantages in these areas was carried out. Table 12 provides the results of these. Finally, a comparison of means of the ratings of the barriers to EC was carried out using a two-tailed t-test. Table 13 provides the means and t-values. This data was broken down into business sector and market focus and a series of two-tailed t-tests were carried out to determine whether there was any significant difference between the formally networked and non-networked SMEs. For brevity, only the significant data is shown in Table 14.

DISCUSSION

Before examining the data in detail it is interesting to note that of the 339 respondents only 148 (43.7%) indicated that they considered that their business was part of a formal network. There are two possibilities for this lower than expected result:

Table 8. Factors associated with decisions to adopt EC — formally networked SMEs.

	EC Adoption	
	Have adopted EC	Have not adopted EC
No of Employees		
1 to 9	8	17
10 to 19	32	35
20 to 49	5	8
50 to 199	9	1
More than 200	7	1

Significance Level   .001

Market Focus	**Have adopted EC**	**Have not adopted EC**
Local	23	40
Regional	3	5
National	23	14
European Union	3	1
International	9	3

Significance Level   .002

Business Sector	**Have adopted EC**	**Have not adopted EC**
Industrial	20	7
Service	17	29
Retail	11	14
Finance	4	0
Other	6	10

Significance Level   .002

CEO has university qualification	**Have adopted EC**	**Have not adopted EC**
Yes	27	19
No	34	44

Significance Level   .002

Factor	**Most likely to adopt EC**	**Least likely to adopt EC**
Employees	50 to 199	1 to 9
Market focus	EU & international	Local
Business Sector	Industrial & finance	Service
CEO has university qualification	Yes	No

1.   While many respondents may have dealt with other businesses, these interactions were informal rather than under some form of enforced governance. This is supported by the findings of Premaratne (2001).

2.   As the study was conducted on regional SMEs the ability to form and maintain any form of network was more difficult than it might have been for city-based SMEs. This is supported by the findings of Dahlstrand (1999) who suggests that geographic proximity is essential for the development and maintenance of networks particularly in small business arena.

Table 9. Factors associated with decisions to adopt EC — non-networked SMEs.

No of Employees	EC Adoption	
	Have adopted EC	Have not adopted EC
1 to 9	7	8
10 to 19	40	32
20 to 49		
50 to 199	21	8
More than 200	18	2

Significance Level   .000

Major customer base	Have adopted EC	Have not adopted EC
Retail	19	14
Private business	40	28
Public organisations	3	3
Individuals	22	17

Significance Level   .000

Number of suppliers	Have adopted EC	Have not adopted EC
1 to 5	1	0
6 to 10	8	12
11 to 20	19	7
21 to 40	22	19
More than 40	22	11

Significance Level   .003

CEO has university qualification	Have adopted EC	Have not adopted EC
Yes	62	27
No	53	35

Significance Level   .014

Factor	Most likely to adopt EC	Least likely to adopt EC
Employees	More than 200	1 to 9
Major customer base	Private business	Individuals
Number of suppliers	More than 40	Less than 10
CEO has university qualification	Yes	No

Factors Associated with EC Adoption in Formally Networked and Non-Networked SMEs

Table 7 compares the adoption of EC with the decision by the SME to formally network. Recent studies (Papazafeiropoulou et al., 2002; Riquelme, 2002; Tetteh & Burn, 2001) have concluded that adoption of EC is best carried out in a formal networking environment. The data shown in Table 7 does not appear to support this view. While 64.9% of the non-networked respondents

Table 10. A comparison of means of ratings of criteria for adoption of electronic commerce for networked and non-networked SMEs.

Criteria	Formally networked SMEs		Non-networked SMEs		t-value
	Mean	Sd	Mean	Sd	
Demand/pressure from customers	1.82	1.40	2.10	1.41	1.259
Pressure of competition	2.10	1.69	2.34	1.39	0.951
Pressure from suppliers	1.61	1.33	1.71	1.26	0.483
Reduction of costs	3.03	1.76	3.00	1.26	-0.111
Improvement to customer service	3.64	1.79	3.64	1.58	0
Improvement in lead time	2.44	1.77	2.59	1.68	0.544
Increased sales	2.70	1.86	2.98	1.59	0.988
Improvements to internal efficiency	3.38	1.71	3.71	1.40	1.294
Strengthen relations with business partners	2.69	1.72	2.98	1.52	1.107
Reach new customers/ markets	2.84	1.85	2.91	1.64	0.248
Improve competitiveness	2.97	1.89	3.42	1.59	1.586
External technical support	1.16	0.9	1.42	1.09	1.692*
Improve marketing	2.72	1.85	3.01	1.72	1.014
Improve control and follow-up	2.25	1.68	2.72	1.55	1.814*

* significant at .05 level

have adopted electronic commerce, those respondents that indicated they are part of some form of formal networking structure are, at best, equivocal where EC adoption is concerned.

A number of authors (Hawkins et al., 1995; Hyland & Matlay, 1997) have noted that the adoption of EC appears to be significantly linked with the size of the firm. SMEs with fewer than 10 employees were less likely to adopt EC than larger small businesses. More recently, Fallon and Moran (2000) and Smith et al. (2002) have suggested that in order to get round this problem, smaller SMEs were more likely to engage in some type of formal network. If we compare those businesses who had between 10 and 50 employees in Tables 8 and 9, we can see that the non-networked SMEs are far more likely to adopt electronic commerce than those who are part of a formal networking arrangement. Thus while small SMEs (less than 10 employees) might gravitate to some form of network, this is not borne out in their patterns of adopting electronic commerce.

A number of authors (Donckels & Lambrecht, 1997; Keeble et al., 1999; Schindehutte & Morris, 2001) have offered market focus as an indicator to SME adoption of EC. An examination of the data in Tables 8 and 9 pertaining to market focus shows that it only appears to be a significant factor for EC adoption with those organisations that operate within a formal network structure. No significant association was found for those who have stayed outside such an arrangement.

Studies by Keeble et al. (1999) and Schindehutte and Morris (2001) have concluded that very often links with customers and suppliers may replace the need to formally network by providing much needed technical and marketing

Table 11. Comparison of means of benefits and disadvantages following the adoption of electronic commerce in networked and non-networked SMEs.

	Formally networked SMEs	Non-networked SMEs	t-value
Benefits	Mean	Mean	
Lower administration costs	2.85	2.76	-0.349
Lower production costs	2.64	2.80	0.372
Reduced lead time	2.82	2.75	-0.265
Reduced stock	1.85	2.06	0.897
Increased sales	2.51	2.43	-0.321
Increased internal efficiency	2.57	2.87	1.204
Improved relations with business partners	2.56	2.50	-0.231
New customers and markets	2.67	2.95	1.085
Improved competitiveness	2.00	1.97	-0.128
Improved marketing	2.82	2.82	0
Improved quality of information	2.66	2.85	0.733
Disadvantages			
Deterioration of relations with business partners	1.16	1.29	0.912
Higher costs	1.59	1.98	1.923*
Computer maintenance	1.89	2.24	1.728*
Doubling of work	1.44	1.83	2.146*
Reduced flexibility of work	1.05	1.25	1.650*
Security	1.13	1.50	2.642**
Dependence on EC	1.44	1.64	1.110

* significant at .05 level; ** significant at .01 level

Table 12. Comparison of means of benefits and disadvantages following the adoption of electronic commerce in networked and non-networked SMEs.

Formally Networked Respondents		
Benefit	**Disadvantage**	**t-value**
Lower administration costs Mean 2.85	Higher costs Mean 1.59	4.667***
Lower production cost Mean 2.64	Higher costs Mean 1.59	4.056***
Improved relations with business partners Mean 2.57	Deterioration of relation with business partners Mean 1.16	6.527***
Improved quality of information Mean 2.82	Reduced flexibility of work Mean 1.13	8.922***
Increased internal efficiency Mean 2.57	Doubling work Mean 1.05	8.373***

Non-Networked Respondents		
Benefit	**Disadvantage**	**t-value**
Lower administration costs Mean 2.76	Higher costs Mean 1.98	4.907***
Lower production cost Mean 2.80	Higher costs Mean 1.98	2.118*
Improved relations with business partners Mean 2.87	Deterioration of relation with business partners Mean 1.29	12.218***
Improved quality of information Mean 2.82	Reduced flexibility of work Mean 1.50	9.513***
Increased internal efficiency Mean 2.87	Doubling work Mean 1.25	12.453***

* significant at .05 level; ** significant at .01 level; *** significant at .001 level

know how. A comparison of the data pertaining to numbers of suppliers in Tables 8 and 9 provides a number of interesting findings. Firstly, where EC adoption is concerned, only those SMEs outside a networking arrangement showed any significant association between the number of suppliers and decisions to acquire and use electronic commerce (see Table 9). There was no significant association for the formally networked respondents (see Table 8). Furthermore, Table 9 shows that those SMEs who had less than 10 suppliers were less likely to adopt electronic commerce than those with more than 10.

As already mentioned, Keeble et al. (1999), in a study of SMEs in the Cambridge area found that customers often provide know how and technical advice to SMEs replacing the need to network. Studies of business-to-business interactions (BarNir & Smith, 2002; Tikkanen 1998; Auger & Gallaugher, 1997) have concluded that dealings with other SMEs in a formal manner often gives rise to informal flows of information and advice. Responses were examined to determine whether the type of customer (individual, retail, private business,

Table 13. Comparison of means of barriers to adoption of electronic commerce in formally networked and non-networked SMEs.

Barriers	Formally networked SMEs Mean	Non-networked SMEs Mean	t-value
EC doesn't fit with the SMEs products/ services	3.14	2.27	-2.597**
EC doesn't fit with the way the SME does business	2.92	2.27	-1.949*
EC doesn't fit the way the SME's customers work	2.65	2.47	-0.542
SMEs don't see the advantages of using EC	2.86	1.81	- 3.408***
Lack of technical know how	2.84	2.21	-1.937*
Security risks	2.29	1.84	-1.541
Cost too high	2.33	2.52	0.557
SMEs unsure what to choose	2.41	2.11	-0.907

* significant at .05 level; ** significant at .01 level; *** significant at .001 level

public business) was associated with the adoption of EC. Results (see Tables 8 and 9) show that it was only the non-networked group that showed any significance between customer base and EC adoption. The data shows that those firms that dealt with retailers or private companies were more likely to have adopted EC than those that dealt with individual companies or public businesses.

Comparison of Means

Before examining the data in Table 10 in detail, it is interesting to note that the mean for almost all the criteria was below the median value of 3. This would suggest that most of the criteria are not particularly important in the decision-making process. Of those criteria with a mean above 3, the most important in the decision-making process are improvement to internal efficiency, improvement to customer service and improved competitiveness. Thus despite the "media hype" suggesting electronic commerce should be adopted to develop new markets, increase sales and strengthen relations with business partners, little evidence of their importance is shown in the findings.

Only two criteria showed significant difference between the two groups of respondents. These were the importance of external support and the importance of control and follow-up in business. While still below the median point, both were rated significantly higher in the non-networked group than by their formal networking counterparts. One possible explanation for this is that sufficient

Table 14. Comparison of means of barriers to adoption of electronic commerce in formally networked and non-networked SMEs subdivided by business sector and market focus.

	Formally networked SMEs	Non-networked SMEs	t-value
Barriers by Business Sector	Mean	Mean	
Service			
SMEs don't see the advantages of using EC	2.90	1.78	-2.146*
Retail			
EC doesn't fit with the SMEs products/services	3.00	1.40	-2.553*
EC doesn't fit with the way the SME does business	3.14	1.20	-3.510**
SMEs don't see the advantages of using EC	3.29	1.20	-3.715***
Lack of technical know how	3.93	2.90	-2.772**
Security risks	3.14	1.60	-2.218*
Barriers by Market Focus	Mean	Mean	t-value
Local			
EC doesn't fit with the SMEs products/services	3.35	2.33	-2.311*
EC doesn't fit with the way the SME does business	3.03	2.03	-2.282*
SMEs don't see the advantages of using EC	3.03	1.61	-3.624***
Lack of technical know how	2.90	1.88	-2.397*

* significant at .05 level; ** significant at .01 level; *** significant at .001 level

technical support and business know how existed within the formal network arrangement to satisfy its members. This expertise may not have been available to the individual non-networked businesses. This would tend to support the views of Overby and Min (2000), Keeble et al. (1999), and Foy (1994, cited in Dennis 2000) who suggest that many SMEs seek out a network to acquire these skill that are absent in their own organisation.

Perhaps of greatest interest is the lack of any significant difference between the formally networked and non-networked groups. This may be explained by the low means on the criteria tested. An alternative explanation may be that the decision to enter into a formal networking arrangement may not be prompted by the desire to adopt electronic commerce or move towards some form of global marketing. This would tend to bring into question the views of authors such as Dennis (2000) who suggests that a prime motivation for small businesses to network is the desire to extend their market coverage through EC adoption.

An examination of the data in Table 10 provides a number of interesting findings. Firstly, as opposed to the views of Achrol and Kotler (1999) and Marchewka and Towell (2000), there were no significant differences, in terms of benefits between the formally networked and non-networked respondents. One possible explanation is that in both the formally networked and non-networked SMEs, respondents expected greater benefits from EC adoption than was apparent. If we examine the disadvantages, five of these (higher costs, computer maintenance, doubling of work, reduced flexibility of work and security) showed a significant difference between the formally networked and non-networked respondents. In all cases the non-networked group found a higher level of disadvantage from these factors than did the networked group. This would tend to support the views of Overby and Min (2000) and Achrol and Kotler (1999) that difficulties dissipate through a network more readily than they might in a single stand-alone unit.

Finally Table 12 presents a comparison of those factors that appeared both as potential benefits as well as potential disadvantages. Four factors (cost, relationships with business partners, internal efficiency and quality of information) were considered to be both possible benefits or possible disadvantages. An examination of Table 12 shows that in both the formally networked and non-networked group, the ratings of benefits in each of these four categories was significantly higher than the rating of possible disadvantage. Thus, while the ratings of both benefits and disadvantages fall well below the median value (3), the respondent groups reported a significantly greater benefit in terms of cost, relationships with business partners, internal efficiency and quality of information than perceived disadvantages. This would tend to support the many advocates for EC adoption in SMEs (Fuller, 2000; Mirchandani & Motwani, 2001; Mouggayer, 1998; Turban et al., 2000; Violino, 2000).

Barriers to EC Adoption

An examination of the data in Table 13 shows that most of the barriers to EC were rated below the median value of 3. This implies that across the respondent population none of the barriers are particularly applicable as reasons for non-adoption of EC technology. Secondly, with the exception of cost, all ratings of barriers are higher in the formally networked group. There are several possible explanations. Miles et al. (1999) suggested that SMEs often join a network because they perceive their own weaknesses when confronted with new marketing techniques or new technology. If this is the case with the formally networked respondents, we would expect them to rate barriers higher than those SMEs who felt more confident with EC. A second possibility is that through network connections, the respondents may have greater insight into problems with electronic commerce than the self-directed small businesses have.

An examination of the data in more detail shows that four of the barriers (EC doesn't fit with products/services, EC doesn't fit with the way the SME does business, SMEs don't see the advantage of using EC, lack of technical know how) show a significant difference between the formally networked and non-networked respondents. A number of authors (Miles et al., 1999; Marchewka & Towell, 2000; Dennis, 2000) have suggested that formal networks provide a number of advantages over self-directed SMEs. These advantages include technical knowledge, assistance in product/service adjustment to suit a larger market, and assistance in business methods to suit EC techniques. An examination of the data, however, shows that these factors are significantly less of a barrier to the stand-alone group than they are to the networked SMEs, apparently in contradiction to the findings of Miles et al. (1999), Marchewka and Towell (2000) and Dennis (2000).

Table 14 presents the differences of means of barriers (in formally networked and non-networked SMEs) further subdivided by business sector and market focus. Before examining the data in detail, it is interesting to note that neither the industrial nor the financial groups showed any significant differences between formally networked and non-networked respondents. Also of interest is the fact that it is only those businesses that have a local focus, which showed any significant difference (formally networked/non-networked). A number of authors (Poon & Swatman, 1997; Lawrence, 1997; Reimenschneider & Mykytyn, 2000; Power & Sohal, 2002) have suggested that SMEs adopt EC to reach new markets. These authors have also suggested that one of the many mechanisms small businesses use to achieve this is the development of formal networks. While the current data neither supports nor refutes this view, it is interesting to note that membership of a formal network does not significantly alter perceptions of barriers for those businesses seeking larger market share.

Several authors (Marchewka & Towell, 2000; Achrol & Kotler, 1999; Dennis, 2000) suggest that formal networks "soften" barriers to new market penetration and technology acquisition by providing expertise and know how to member businesses. An examination of the data in Table 14 suggests that for the service and retail groups, this "softening" is not apparent. The data shows that while the non-networked respondents find barriers (EC doesn't fit with products/services, EC doesn't fit with the way the SME does business, SMEs don't see the advantage of using EC, lack of technical know how and security risks) of little applicability to their situation, the formally networked respondents rate these as far more applicable barriers to EC adoption. In particular, the formally networked retail respondents not only appear to have had difficulty in adjusting their businesses to EC adoption, but have also ranked their lack of technical expertise in EC technology highly (3.93).

As stated, the data was subdivided to examine whether particular market focus groups varied (formally networked/non-networked). Table 14 shows that it is only those business trading locally that show a significant difference between the formally networked and non-networked respondents. One immediate argument might be that many local businesses rely on face-to-face customer dealings rather than some form of computer-based transaction. This, however, raises the question as to why the non-networked respondents rated barriers (EC doesn't fit with products/services, EC doesn't fit with the way the SME does business, SMEs don't see the advantage of using EC) significantly lower than their formally networked counterparts. It also raises the question as to whether those local respondents that are part of a formal network have done so for reasons other than EC adoption or increased market focus. This question would need further investigation to establish.

CONCLUSION

There are a number of limitations that must be considered from this study. Firstly, as already stated, the membership/non-membership of some type of formal network may be biased either by the lack of geographic proximity to other SMEs needed to form and maintain some type of viable network. It may also be biased by the perception of the respondent as to what constitutes a network. Secondly, the generalizability of these results across SMEs in other cultures needs to be carefully considered. Finally, reliance on the perceptions of one key informant, the owner or CEO of the small business may imply cognitive biases. However, previous empirical studies (Raymond, 2001) have demonstrated this methodology to be valid.

Unlike previous studies that have focussed on formal networking and adoption of EC technology, the data presented in this chapter has attempted to examine both the adoption as well as the non-adoption of electronic commerce by formally networked and non-networked SMEs. The results raise a number of questions concerning the nature and role of formal networks in the small business arena and how these impinge upon the decision making and perception of the benefits, usefulness and problems of adopting and using EC. The implications are significant because the results raise doubts about the validity and usefulness of government initiatives to promote formal networks between SMEs as a means of leading SMEs towards successful EC adoption. The study shows that there are no considerable differences between formally networked and non-networked SMEs in terms of EC adoption. It appears, therefore, that government initiatives in the networking arena may not necessarily lead to any substantial outcomes. However, more research needs to be done to determine how formal network membership, or non-membership impacts on the decision-making processes surrounding EC use.

REFERENCES

Abell, W. & Limm, L. (1996). *Business Use of the Internet in New Zealand: An Exploratory Study*. Retrieved from the World Wide Web: http//www.scu.edu.au/sponsored/ausweb96.

Achrol, R. S. & Kotler, P. (1999). Marketing in the Network Economy. *Journal of Marketing*, 63, 146-163.

Aldridge, A., White, M. & Forcht, K. (1997). Security Considerations of Doing Business Via the Internet: Cautions to be Considered. *Internet Research-Electronic Networking Applications and Policy*, 7(1), 9-15.

Auger, P. & Gallaugher, J. M. (1997). Factors Affecting Adoption of an Internet-based Sales Presence for Small Businesses. *The Information Society*, 13(1), 55-74.

Bakos, Y. & Brynjolfsson, E. (2000). Bundling and Competition on the Internet. *Marketing Science*, 19(1), 63-82.

BarNir, A. & Smith, K. A. (2002). Interfirm Alliances in the Small Business: The Role of Social Networks. *Journal of Small Business Management*, 40(3), 219-232.

Barry, H. & Milner, B. (2002). SMEs and Electronic Commerce: A Departure from the Traditional Prioritisation of Training? *Journal of European Industrial Training*, 25(7), 316-326.

Blackburn, R. & Athayde, R. (2000). Making the Connection: The Effectiveness of Internet Training in Small Businesses. *Education and Training*, 42(4/5), 289-298.

Brigham, E. F. & Smith, K. V. (1967). The Cost of Capital to the Small Firm. *The Engineering Economist*, 13(1), 1-26.

Bunker, D. J. & MacGregor, R. C. (2000). Successful Generation of Information Technology (IT) Requirements for Small/Medium Enterprises (SMEs) – Cases from Regional Australia. *Proceedings of SMEs in a Global Economy, Wollongong, Australia*, (pp. 72-84).

Chau, P. Y. K. & Hui K. L (2001). Determinants of Small Business EDI Adoption: An Empirical Investigation. *Journal of Organisational Computing and Electronic Commerce*, 11(4), 229-252.

Cropper, S. (1996). Collaborative Working and the Issue of Sustainability. In C. Huxham (Ed.), *Creating Collaborative Advantage*. London: Sage.

Cyber Dialogue. (1998). *Small Business Survey*. Retrieved from the World Wide Web: www.cyberdialogue.com.

Dahlstrand, A. L. (1999). Technology-based SMEs in the Goteborg Region: Their Origin and Interaction with Universities and Large Firms. *Regional Studies*, 33(4), 379-389.

Damanpour, F. (2001). E-Business E-Commerce Evolution: Perspective and Strategy. *Managerial Finance*, 27(7), 16-33.

Dean, J., Holmes, S. & Smith, S. (1997). Understanding Business Networks: Evidence from Manufacturing and Service Sectors in Australia. *Journal of Small Business Management*, 35(1), 79-84.

Dennis, C. (2000). Networking for Marketing Advantage. *Management Decision,* 38(4), 287-292.

Domke-Damonte, D. & Levsen, V. B. (2002, Summer). The Effect of Internet Usage on Cooperation and Performance in Small Hotels. *SAM Advanced Management Journal,* 31-38.

Donckels, R. & Lambrecht, J. (1997). The Network Position of Small Businesses: An Explanatory Model. *Journal of Small Business Management*, 35(2), 13-28.

Drakopoulou-Dodd, S., Jack, S. & Anderson, A. R. (2002). Scottish Entrepreneurial Networks in the International Context. *International Small Business Journal,* 20(2), 213-219.

Eid, R., Trueman, M. & Ahmed, A.M. (2002). A Cross-Industry Review of B2B Critical Success Factors. *Internet Research: Electronic Networking Applications and Policy*, 12(2), 110-123.

Evans, P. B. & Wurster, T. S. (1997, Sept-Oct). Strategy and the New Economics of Information. *Harvard Business Review,* 70-82.

Fallon, M. & Moran, P. (2000). Information Communications Technology (ICT) and manufacturing SMEs. *Proceedings of the 2000 Small Business and Enterprise Development Conference, University of Manchester*, (pp. 100-109).

Farhoomand, A. F., Tuunainen, V. K. & Yee, L. W. (2000). Barriers to Global Electronic Commerce: A Cross-Country Study of Hong Kong and Finland. *Journal of Organisational Computing and Electronic Commerce*, 10(1), 23-48.

Fuller, T. (2000). The Small Business Guide to the Internet: A Practical Approach to Going Online. *International Small Business Journal*, 19(1), 105-107.

Gaskill, L. R. & Gibbs, R. M. (1994). Going Away to College and Wider Urban Job Opportunities Take Highly Educated Youth Away from Rural Areas. *Rural Development Perspectives,* 10(3), 35-44.

Gaskill, L. R., Van Auken, H. E. & Kim, H. (1993). The Impact of Operational Planning on Small Business Retail Performance. *Journal of Small Business Strategy*, 5(1), 21-35.

Gibb, A. (1993). Small Business Development in Central and Eastern Europe – Opportunity for a Rethink. *Journal of Business Venturing*, 8, 461-486.

Golden, P. A. & Dollinger, M. (1993, Summer). Cooperative Alliances and Competitive Strategies in Small Manufacturing Firms. *Entrepreneurship Theory and Practice,* 43-56.

Hawkins, P., Winter, J. & Hunter, J. (1995). *Skills for Graduates in the 21ˢᵗ Century.* Report Commissioned from the Whiteway Research, University of Cambridge, Association of Graduate Recruiters, Cambridge.

Hill, R. & Stewart, J. (2000). Human Resource Development in Small Organisations. *Journal of European Industrial Training*, 24(2/3/4), 105-117.

Hyland, T. & Matlay, H. (1997). Small Businesses, Training needs and VET Provisions. *Journal of Education and Work*, 10(2).

Iacovou, C. L., Benbasat, I. & Dexter, A. S. (1995). Electronic Data Interchange and Small Organisations: Adoption and Impact of Technology. *MIS Quarterly*, 19(4), 465-485.

Jarratt, D. G. (1998). A Strategic Classifiaction of Business Alliances: A Qualitative Perspective Built from a Study of Small and Medium-sized Enterprises. *Qualitative Market Research: An International Journal*, 1(1), 39-49.

Jeffcoate, J., Chappell, C. & Feindt, S. (2002). Best Practice in SME Adoption of E-Commerce. *Benchmarking: An International Journal*, 9(2), 122-132.

Johannisson, B., Ramirez-Pasillas, M. & Karlsson, G. (2002). The institutional embeddedness of local inter-firm networks: a leverage for business creation. *Entrepreneurship & Regional Development*, 14(4), 297-315.

Jorde, T. & Teece, D. (1989). Competition and Cooperation: Striking the Right Balance. *Californian Management Review*, 31, 25-38.

Kai-Uwe Brock, J. (2000). Information and Technology in the Small Firm. In S. Carter & D. Jones-Evans (Eds.), *Enterprise and Small Business. Prentice Hall*, 384-408.

Keeble, D., Lawson, C., Moore, B & Wilkinson, F. (1999). Collective Learning Processes, Networking and 'Institutional Thickness' in the Cambridge Region. *Regional Studies*, 33(4), 319-332.

Kendall, J. D., Tung, L. L., Chua, K. H., Hong, C., Ng, D. & Tan, S. M. (2001). Receptivity of Singapore's SMEs to Electronic Commerce Adoption. *Journal of Strategic Information Systems*, 10(3), 223-242.

Kulmala, H. I., Paranko, J. & Uusi-Rauva, E. (2002). The Role of Cost Management in Network Relationships. *International Journal of Production Economics*, 79(1), 33-43.

Lawrence, K. L. (1997). Factors Inhibiting the Utilisation of Electronic Commerce Facilities in Tasmanian Small-to-Medium Sized Enterprises. *Proceedings of the 8ᵗʰ Australasian Conference on Information Systems*, (pp. 587-597).

Lee, C. S. (2001). An analytical Framework for Evaluating E-commerce Business Models and Strategies. *Internet Research: Electronic Network Applications and Policy*, 11(4), 349-359.

Lee, J. & Runge, J. (2001). Adoption of Information Technology in Small Business: Testing Drivers of Adoption for Entrepreneurs. *Journal of Computer Information Systems,* 42(1), 44-57.

MacGregor, R. C. & Bunker, D. J. (1996). The Effects of Priorities Introduced During Computer Acquisition on Continuing Success with IT in Small Business Environments. *Proceedings of the Information Resource Management Association International Conference,* Washington, (pp. 271-277).

MacGregor, R. C., Bunker, D. J. & Waugh, P. (1998). Electronic Commerce and Small/Medium Enterprises (SMEs) in Australia: An Electronic Data Interchange (EDI) Pilot Study. *Proceedings of the 11th International Bled Electronic Commerce Conference.*

Marchewka, J. T. & Towell, E. R. (2000). A Comparison of Structure and Strategy in Electronic Commerce. *Information Technology and People,* 13(2), 137-149.

Markland, R. E. (1974). The Role of the Computer in Small Business Management. *Journal of Small Business Management,* 12(1), 21-26.

Martin, L. M.. & Matlay, H. (2001). "Blanket" Approaches to Promoting ICT in Small Firms: Some Lessons from the DTI Ladder Adoption Model in the UK. *Internet Research: Electronic Networking Applications and Policy,* 11(5), 399-410.

Mazzarol, T., Volery, T., Doss, N. & Thein, V. (1999). Factors Influencing Small Business Start-ups. *International Journal of Entrepreneurial Behaviour and Research,* 5(2), 48-63.

Mehrtens, J., Cragg, P. B. & Mills, A. M. (2001). A Model of Internet Adoption by SMEs. *Information and Management,* 39, 165-176.

Miles, G., Preece, S. & Baetz, M. C. (1999). Dangers of Dependence: The Impact of Strategic Alliance Use by Small Technology Based Firms. *Journal of Small Business Management,* 20-29.

Miller, N. L. & Besser, T. L. (2000). The Importance of Community Values in Small Business Strategy Formation: Evidence from Rural Iowa. *Journal of Small Business Management,* 38(1), 68-85.

Mirchandani, D. A. & Motwani, J. (2001). Understanding Small Business Electronic Commerce Adoption: An Empirical Analysis. *Journal of Computer Information Systems,* 41(3), 70-73.

Mouggayer, W. (1998). *Opening Digital Markets.* New York: McGraw Hill.

Murphy, J. (1996). *Small Business Management.* London: Pitman.

Nalebuff, B. J. & Brandenburg, A. M. (1996). *Co-operation.* Philadelphia: Harper Collins Business.

O'Donnell, A., Gilmore, A., Cummins, D. & Carson, D. (2001). The Network Construct in Entrepreneurship Research: A Review and Critique. *Management Decision,* 39(9), 749-760.

Overby, J. W. & Min, S. (2001). International Supply Chain Management in an Internet Environment: A Network-oriented Approach to Internationalisation. *International Marketing Review*, 18(4), 392-420.

Oxley, J. E. & Yeung, B. (2001). E-Commerce Readiness: Institutional Environment and International Competitiveness. *Journal of International Business Studies*, 32(4), 705-723.

Ozcan, G. (1995). Small Business Networks and Local Ties in Turkey. *Entrepreneurship and Regional Development,* 7, 265-282.

Papazafeiropoulou, A., Pouloudi, A. & Doukidis, G. (2002). A Framework for Best Practices in Electronic Commerce Awareness Creation. *Business Process Management Journal*, 8(3), 233-244.

Phan, D. D. (2001, Fall). E-business Management Strategies: A Business-to-Business Case Study. *Information Systems Management,* 61-69.

Poon, S. & Joseph, M. (2001). A Preliminary Study of Product Nature and Electronic Commerce. *Marketing Intelligence & Planning*, 19(7), 493-499.

Poon, S. & Strom, J. (1997). Small Business Use of the Internet: Some Realities. *Proceedings of the Association for Information Systems Americas Conference,* Indianapolis.

Poon, S. & Swatman, P. (1997). The Internet for Small Businesses: An Enabling Infrastructure. *Proceedings of the Fifth Internet Society Conference,* (pp. 221-231).

Porter, M. (2001, March). Strategy and the Internet. *Harvard Business Review,* 63-78.

Power, D. J. & Sohal, A. S. (2002). Implementation and Usage of Electronic Commerce in Managing the Supply Chain: A Comparative Study of Ten Australian Companies. *Benchmarking: An International Journal*, 9(2), 190-208.

Premaratne, S. P. (2001). Networks, Resources and Small Business Growth: The Experience in Sri Lanka. *Journal of Small Business Management*, 39(4), 363-371.

PriceWaterhouseCoopers. (1999). *SME Electronic Commerce Study Final Report*, 37pp.

Purao, S. & Campbell, B. (1998). Critical Concerns for Small Business Electronic Commerce: Some Reflections Based on Interviews of Small Business Owners. *Proceedings of the Association for Information Systems Americas Conference*, Baltimore, (August 14-16, pp. 325-327).

Quayle, M. (2002). E-commerce: The Challenge for UK SMEs in the Twenty-First Century. *International Journal of Operations and Production Management,* 22(10), 1148-1161.

Raisch, W. D. (2001). *The E-marketplace: Strategies for Success in B2B.* New York: McGraw-Hill.

Ratnasingam, P. (2000). The Influence of Power on Trading Partners in Electronic Commerce. *Internet Research,* 10(1), 56-62.

Raymond, L. (2001). Determinants of Web Site Implementation in Small Business. *Internet Research: Electronic Network Applications and Policy*, 11(5), 411-422.

Reimenschneider, C. K. & Mykytyn, Jr.,P. P. (2000). What Small Business Executives Have Learned about Managing Information Technology. *Information & Management,* 37, 257-267.

Reynolds, W., Savage, W. & Williams, A. (1994). Your Own Business: A Practical Guide to Success. *ITP.*

Riquelme, H. (2002). Commercial Internet Adoption in China: Comparing the Experience of Small, Medium and Large Business. *Internet Research: Electronic Networking Applications and Policy*, 12(3), 276-286.

Ritchie, R. & Brindley, C. (2000). Disintermediation, Disintegration and Risk in the SME Global Supply Chain. *Management Decision*, 38(8), 575-583.

Roberts, M. & Wood, M. (2002). The Strategic Use of Computerised Information Systems by a Micro Enterprise. *Logistics Information Management,* 15(2), 115-125.

Rosenfeld, S. (1996). Does Cooperation Enhance Competitiveness? Assessing the Impacts of Inter-firm Collaboration. *Research Policy,* 25(2), 247-263.

Sawhney, M. & Zabin, J. (2001). The Seven Steps for Nirvana. McGraw-Hill.

Schindehutte, M. & Morris, M. H. (2001). Understanding Strategic Adaption in Small Firms. *International Journal of Entrepreneurial Behaviour and Research,* 7(3), 84-107.

Senn, J. A. (1996, Summer). Capitalisation on Electronic Commerce. *Information Systems Management.*

Smith, A. J., Boocock, G., Loan-Clarke, J. & Whittaker, J. (2002). IIP and SMEs: Awareness, Benefits and Barriers. *Personnel Review*, 31(1), 62-85.

Sparkes, A. & Thomas, B. (2001). The Use of the Internet as a Critical Success Factor for the Marketing of Welsh Agri-food SMEs in the Twenty First Century. *British Food Journal,* 103(4), 331-347.

Stauber, A. (2000). *A Survey of the Incorporation of Electronic Commerce in Tasmanian Small and Medium Sized Enterprises.* Tasmanian Electronic Commerce Centre.

Tambini, A.M. (1999). E-Shoppers Demand E-Service. *Discount Store News,* 11(38).

Tetteh, E. & Burn, J. (2001). Global Strategies for SME-business: Applying the SMALL Framework. *Logistics Information Management,* 14(1/2), 171-180.

Thorelli, H. B. (1986). Networks: Between Markets and Hierarchies. *Strategic Management Journal,* 7, 37-51.

Tikkanen, H. (1998). The Network Approach in Analysing International market-
    ing and Purchasing Operations: A Case Study of a European SMEs focal
    net 1992-95. *Journal of Business and Industrial Marketing,* 13(2), 109-
    131.
Trappey, C. V. & Trappey, A. J. C. (2001). Electronic Commerce in Greater
    China. *Industrial Management and Data Systems*, 105(5).
Turban, E., Lee, J., King, D. & Chung, H. (2000). *Electronic Commerce: A
    Managerial Perspective.* NJ: Prentice Hall.
Veradarajan, P. R. & Cunningham, M. (1995). Strategic Alliances: A Synthesis
    of Conceptual Foundations. *Journal of the Academy of Marketing
    Science*, 23(4), 282-296.
Vescovi, T. (2000). Internet Communication: The Italian SME Case. *Corporate
    Communications: An International Journal,* 5(2), 107-112.
Violino, B (2000). Payback Time for E Business. *Internetweek*, Special Issue
    811.
Vrazalic, L., Bunker, D. J., MacGregor, R. C., Carlsson, S. & Magnusson, M.
    (2002). Electronic Commerce and Market Focus: Some Findings froma
    Study of Swedish Small to Medium Enterprises. *Australian Journal of
    Information Systems*, 10(1), 110-119.
Walczuch, R., Van Braven, G. & Lundgren, H. (2000). Internet Adoption
    Barriers for Small Firms in the Netherlands. *European Management
    Journal,* 18(5), 561-572.
Walker, E. W. (1975). Investment and Capital Structure Decision Making. In E.
    W. Walker (Ed.), *The Dynamic Small Firm: Selected Readings.* Texas:
    Austin Press.
Westhead, P. & Storey, D. J. (1996). Management Training and Small Firm
    Performance: Why is the Link so Weak? *International Small Business
    Journal,* 14(4), 13-24.
Yeung, H. W. (1994). Critical Reviews of Geographical Perspectives on
    Business Organisations and the organisation of production: Towards a
    Network Approach. *Progressive Human Geography*, 18(4), 460-490.

APPENDIX A
SUBSET OF QUESTIONS FROM SURVEY

How long has your organisation been in business?
1.   Less than a year
2.   1-2 years
3.   3-5 years
4.   6-10 years

5.   11-20 years
6.   More than 20 years

How many employees does your organisation have?
1.   0
2.   1-9
3.   10-19
4.   20-49
5.   50-199
6.   More than 200

Which is your branch of business?
1.   Industry
2.   Service
3.   Trading/Retail
4.   Finance
5.   Other

Where is your main market located?
1.   Local
2.   Regional
3.   National
4.   EU
5.   International

How many suppliers does your organisation have?
1.   0
2.   1-5
3.   6-10
4.   11-20
5.   21-40
6.   More than 40

Is your company part of any network or organisation for companies?
1.   No
2.   Yes

Does your CEO have a university degree?
1.   No
2.   Yes

What is the gender of your CEO?
1.   Male
2.   Female

Does your company use any type of e-commerce?
1.   Yes
2.   No

Next is a list of driving forces that may have affected your organisation's decision to adopt e-commerce. Rate each driving force on a scale of 1 to 5, with 1 being very unimportant and 5 being extremely important to your decision making process.

1.   Demand/ Pressure from customers
      1   2   3   4   5

2.   The pressure of competition
      1   2   3   4   5

3.   Pressure from the suppliers
      1   2   3   4   5

4.   Cost reduction
      1   2   3   4   5

5.   Improvements to customer-service
      1   2   3   4   5

6.   Reduction of lead time
      1   2   3   4   5

7.   Increase in sales
      1   2   3   4   5

8.   Improvements to internal efficiency
      1   2   3   4   5

9.   Strengthening relations with business partners
      1   2   3   4   5

10. Possibility of reaching new customers/markets
      1   2   3   4   5

11. Improvements to competitiveness
     1   2   3   4   5

12. We were offered technical support
     1   2   3   4   5

13. Improvements to our marketing

     1   2   3   4   5

14. Improvements to control and follow-up
     1   2   3   4   5

Below is a list of benefits that your organisation may have experienced after adopting e-commerce. Rate each benefit on a scale of 1 to 5, with 1 being very unimportant and 5 being extremely important to your situation.

1. Lower administration costs
    1   2   3   4   5

2. Lower production costs
    1   2   3   4   5

3. Reduced lead time
    1   2   3   4   5

4. Reduced stock levels
    1   2   3   4   5

5. Increased sales
    1   2   3   4   5

6. Increased internal efficiency
    1   2   3   4   5

7. Improved relations with business partners
    1   2   3   4   5

8. New customers/markets
    1   2   3   4   5

9.   Improved competitiveness
         1   2   3   4   5

10. Improved marketing
         1   2   3   4   5

11. Improved quality of information
         1   2   3   4   5

Next is a list of disadvantages that your organisation may have experienced after
     adopting e-commerce. Rate each disadvantage on a scale of 1 to 5, with 1
     being very unimportant and 5 being extremely important to your situation.

1.   Deterioration of relations with business partners
         1   2   3   4   5

2.   Higher costs
         1   2   3   4   5

3.   Computer maintenance
         1   2   3   4   5

4.   Being forced to double the work
         1   2   3   4   5

5.   Reduced flexibility in work
         1   2   3   4   5

6.   Reduced security
         1   2   3   4   5

7.   Dependence on EC
         1   2   3   4   5

Below is a list of reasons why your organisation may not have adopted e-
     commerce. Rate each reason on a scale of 1 to 5, with 1 being very
     unimportant and 5 being extremely important to your situation.

1.   It doesn't fit with our products/services
         1   2   3   4   5

2.   It doesn't fit with our way of working
     1   2   3   4   5

3.   It doesn't fit with our customers' way of working
     1   2   3   4   5

4.   We don't find any advantages
     1   2   3   4   5

5.   Lack of technical know how
     1   2   3   4   5

6.   The security seems doubtful
     1   2   3   4   5

7.   The investment amount is too high
     1   2   3   4   5

8.   Not sure what to choose
     1   2   3   4   5

Chapter XI

Bridging B2B E-Commerce Gaps for Taiwanese SMEs: Issues of Government Support and Policies

Yu Chung William Wang,
Yuan-Pei University of Science and Technology, Taiwan

Michael S.H. Heng, University of South Australia, Australia

ABSTRACT

Many Small and Medium Enterprises (SMEs) have been under pressures from large firms to implement Business-to-Business e-commerce (B2B e-commerce) information systems. However, these SMEs have faced various challenges to do so in the supply chain. This chapter explains the role of Taiwanese government in supporting SMEs in implementing e-commerce by analysing the interactions of government teams with current projects, and challenges of Taiwanese SMEs. Discussions and analyses focus on the government help in setting up infrastructure, B2B e-commerce implementation, and interfirm interactions among SMEs and larger firms. The Taiwanese government has been promoting its global logistic strategy for economic development which stresses supply chain integration by bridging information flows among overseas enterprises, domestic large firms, and local SMEs. Government projects related to this strategy are intended to anchor SMEs' growing needs in linking B2B e-commerce with large firms. Our analyses and proposal dwell on how government can further bridge the gaps between the intrinsic barriers of SMEs and the interactions with larger firms in B2B e-commerce implementation.

INTRODUCTION

In January 2002, Taiwan joined the World Trade Organisation (WTO) as a formal member. This has increased the visibility and opportunities for Taiwanese industries in international business environment, while also forcing them to face direct competitions from overseas. Taiwanese Small and Medium Enterprises (SMEs) (Appendix 1), which represent 98% of the total numbers of firms, have played a significant role in the Taiwanese economy (Appendix 2). Economic development in Taiwan depends heavily upon exports, as in the past. Therefore, to improve competency in the new global environment and to upgrade business capabilities for SMEs are key success factors of long-term development of Taiwan economy. The prevalence of Electronic Commerce (e-commerce) originates from computer-based office and networking facilities that has been noted as a fundamental tool for improving the competency of the contemporary business environment (Parker, 1996; Guimaraes & Armstrong, 1997; Ghosh, 1998). For SMEs, implementing e-commerce is expected to create operational efficiency while it is also considered an external interface for communicating with existing and potential customers. Furthermore, e-commerce provides infrastructures to link SMEs with larger firms in collaborative design or manufacture of products.

E-commerce is a cutting edge business practice for today which could become a significant global economic element in 21st century (Clinton & Gore, 1997). Mention e-commerce and high-profile Internet stars such as Amazon.com, Yahoo! Shopping and eBay come to mind. However, e-commerce existed well before consumers' widespread adoption of the Internet. Many researchers or industrial practitioners separate electronic trading into two very different segments of the e-commerce market: business to consumer (B2C) or the sale of goods, services and content to individuals; and business-to-business (B2B) or the buying and selling of goods, services and content among enterprises.

Lawrence et al. (2000) note that e-commerce is the buying and selling of information, products and services via the Internet. Four perspectives have been adopted by them, namely from a communications perspective, business perspective, service perspective, and online perspective. The term commerce is also viewed by some as transactions conducted between business partners (Turban et al., 2000). The term electronic commerce seems to be fairly narrow, and many prefer the term e-business. It refers to a broader definition of EC, not only buying and selling but also servicing customers and collaboration with business partners, and conducting electronic transactions with an organisation.

Similarly there are many definitions of e-commerce. Some people include all financial and commercial transactions by electronic data interchange (EDI), electronic funds transfers (EFT), and other credit/debit card activities. Others focus e-commerce on retail sales to consumers for which the order, payment, or distribution take place on public networks such as the Internet. Some people separate eBusiness from e-commerce that limits the former to buying and selling activities of retailers and consumers, not including other business process encompassed by the latter, such as servicing customers, collaborating with strategic partners and communicating with other firms.

The Taiwanese government has been promoting its global logistic strategy for economic development, which stresses supply chain integration by bridging information flows among overseas enterprises, domestic large firms, and local SMEs. Government projects related to this strategy are intended to anchor SMEs' growing needs in linking B2B e-commerce with large firms. A supply chain consists of multiple partnerships (Gentry, 1996) and, therefore, a business network of partners is an important concept for successful supply chain relationships. Handfeld and Nichols (1999) identify two major flow components of the supply chain: materials and information. From a business-process perspective, it highlights the role of integration of business processes from end user to original suppliers.

Handfeld and Nichols (1999) define supply chain management as the integration of all activities associated with the flow and transformation of goods from new materials, through to the end user, as well as associated information flows, through improved supply-chain relationships to achieve a sustainable competitive advantage. Mentzer et al. (1999) refer to the relationships to include business functions and the tactics across these firms within the supply chain, which consists of multiple firms within network formation. This suggests that supply chain management is the management of interfirm relationships such as collaborative partners, suppliers and customers, and contemporary B2B e-commerce will need to utilise information systems to build up these relationships.

IMPACTS AND BARRIERS OF B2B E-COMMERCE ON TAIWANESE SMEs

With their relatively small scale, SMEs are significantly affected by the overall economic environment. In Taiwan, most firms are SMEs. There are 1,078 million SMEs, 98.18% of the total numbers of firms. Between them, they have 7.4 million employees and account for 77.67% of the total work force (See Appendix 2). Those SMEs have their own business networks and vertical integration channels which rely on supply chain management to cooperate with suppliers, buyers, and collaborative manufacturers so as to integrate their resources and gain competitive advantages. Even so, many of them recently face big competitions from the neighbouring countries such as Mainland China, Singapore, Malaysia, and South Korea, especially after joining WTO. Some of these countries have cheaper labour forces and the rest have good product quality and advanced technologies. Added to this are the problems of reduced overseas orders and investment associated with worldwide economic recession. As to B2B e-commerce, the post WTO impacts are as follows:

Computer-Based Informatisation Process Need to Be Accelerated

Though the Taiwanese government has promoted e-commerce development in enterprises to gain competitive advantage and efficiency for about five years, those who have been actively setting up infrastructures are still large firms and most are in Information Technology or Telecommunication Industries. SMEs have been around 97-98% of the total numbers of firms in Taiwan (Taiwanese SMEs, White Pages, 2002) and are the portion which have conservative attitude in such investments for e-commerce. Most of the firms which have planned to do so are still in the initiative steps.

Nevertheless, SMEs which depend on global supply market will face more direct competition and customers' demand. In order to link up with the global market, informatisation process needs to be accelerated through further infrastructure implementation. SMEs are mostly used to doing business with traditional communication channels via telephone and facsimile. Without adapting to new business trading practice using B2B e-commerce, they face the danger of being squeezed out by competitors from neighbouring countries.

Need for Supply Chain Integration

This issue can be looked at from two angles. First, Taiwan has become a global manufacturing and designing centre for information technology products during the past decade. This advantage binds the relationships between Taiwanese firms and other global brands such as Dell, Intel, and HP and provides large local firms and many SMEs business opportunities. And it is part of the tools to cope with the serious competition for global market from neighbouring countries. Second, the Taiwanese government has given up its policy of restricting outward investment to US$50 million in mainland China for each case. The new policies have opened more spaces for Taiwanese firms to set up manufacturing plants in mainland China and the current trend permeates from traditional to high-tech industries. It will come with a logistics management model of "receiving orders in Taiwan, manufacturing in China, and exporting to global market" which has been adopted by some of SMEs and large firms already.

Taiwanese firms have been noted for their specific forms of collaboration known as "business networks" (Chen, 2001), which means a group of firms collaborate with each other in certain scopes and boundaries of supply chains. The interfirm dynamics and interaction will affect interfirm linkages with the passage of time (Gulati, 1999; Wang & Heng, 2002). Liu and Brookfield (2000) believe that effective inter-firm networks have been an important competitive advantage during the last decade for Taiwanese and Japanese firms, especially SMEs. Shifting their manufacturing bases into mainland China involves reallocation of business networks and cross-strait supply chain integration. Bridging their interfirm collaborations and inter business-units communication through B2B e-commerce has become a serious issue

Barriers of SMEs in Implementing B2B E-Commerce

To overcome the new challenges, SMEs, given their scant resources, will need to form strategic alliances. Their problems represent an attractive market. Hence, Application Service Providers such as IBM, Epson, and HP in Taiwan have targeted this market since 2000. However, from government research data in Taiwan obtained by surveying 233 firms (Table 1), there were 24.8% of SMEs which implemented or planned to implement e-commerce systems comparing 36% of large firms. In the normal business network structure, one large firm (core firm) links up with many SMEs.

Another survey (Table 2) by the Taiwanese Ministry of Economic Affairs, Small and Medium Enterprises Administration shows that SMEs need more help in computer-based management and e-commerce than the rest.

From the two sources above, it is clear that SMEs do face certain difficulties in implementing e-commerce when compared with large firms. They are as following:

1. Huge sunk costs need to be invested. Unless used for reducing transaction cost only, B2B e-commerce might not be able to help SMEs to establish brand name in the e-marketplace. They still need to spend money to build up reputations like other large firms.
2. B2B e-commerce can increase the efficiency of business processes. Nevertheless, it raises the performance requirements of the physical

Table 1. Survey of firm sizes and e-commerce systems implementations.

Firm Sizes and E-commerce Implementation		
Firm Sizes	**Not implemented**	**Planned or Implemented**
Large firms	64 (64.0%)	36 (36.0%)
SMEs	100 (75.2%)	33 (24.8%)
Total	164	69

Sources: Small and Medium Enterprises White Pages 2000, Ministry of Economic Affairs, Taiwan

Table 2. Survey of SMEs needs for guidance from government.

Needs for Government Guidance	Numbers	Percentage
Computer-based Management	843	27.82
E-commerce	522	17.22
General Management	1043	34.42
Financing & Business Loan	476	15.7
Quality Improvement	57	1.88
Assisting Strategic Alliances	89	2.93

Sources: Ministry of Economic Affairs, Small and Medium Enterprises Administration, Taiwan
Surveying period: 1/7/2002 ~ 31/12/02

business processes such as distribution, inventory control, and other after-sales services. Once B2B e-commerce had been implemented, SMEs might not have the capabilities to fulfill these requirements compared to core firms in the business networks.

3.   SMEs have less resources and funds to invest in related information systems. Because they have fewer resources to train their staffs or recruit people to implement it, they eventually find it difficult to install and upgrade the information systems needed to link up with large firms.

4.   SMEs are unwilling to share their internal information while larger firms normally differentiate confidential and public information carefully. This would discourage SMEs from constructing some infrastructures of B2B e-commerce such as EDI (Electronic Data Interchange) and B2Bi (Business to Business Integration), which have potentials to leak unsecured information. This matter is of grave concern to many small firms because they may only possess few key business processes or products as their competitive advantages.

5.   As information systems at the enterprise and inter-organisational level become more and more complicated, SMEs normally lack knowledge and technical support for strategic planning and systems maintaining B2B e-commerce. In particular, it needs to embed existing business process in supply chain management. Because SMEs have fewer resources to train their staffs or recruit people to implement it, they eventually find it difficult to install and upgrade the information systems needed to link up with large firms.

6.   There are more varieties of databases, platforms and applications among SMEs. It results in lack of standard interfaces and information formats which are needed to avoid data redundancy and system errors. It also indicates that the internal information systems development in SMEs

varies, which may affect the absorptive capabilities (Cohen & Levithal, 1990) for B2B processes.

7. From business network point of view, linkages among SMEs are not in stable collaborative mode. SMEs are pragmatists (Liu & Brookfield, 2000) and they shy away from new investment of interorganisational systems especially when there is not short-term return of investment. Besides, core firms and the affiliate firms might not have similar appreciation of B2B e-commerce since the switching costs and business opportunities in the network centre and its edge may be different. Though SMEs have less resources and capabilities, they are more flexible in terms of their core competency — they are more prepared to change their product line, business process, or other partners.

Information systems providers have struggled to penetrate SMEs market where beneath the stable surface there is still turmoil. Taiwanese SMEs have found barriers to set up and choose adequate information systems to achieve strategic positions in the business networks of complete supply chains. While short-term advantages have allowed SMEs to thrive, the trend of informatisation, the needs for collaboration, and governance of core firms would eventually force them to opt for B2B e-commerce. After all, the questions will be what to choose, how to do it, and when to implement it.

PROJECTS AND POLICIES OF GOVERNMENT SUPPORT

The Taiwanese government has realised the difficulties of e-commerce for industries during the last ten years and its supports have played a great role in the past. The supports can be traced back to as early as 1993 when the Ministry of Economic Affairs (MOEA) introduced advanced technology and cooperation programs as past of the "Economic Revitalization Program" (2002 Development of Industries in Taiwan). Governmental resources have then been made available, according to the need of each case to help businesses resolve problems and accelerate technology development and transformation of both traditional industries and high-tech Industries. There are at least four departments in MOEA and two government funded institutes (Appendix 4) which are currently involved with e-commerce promotion and upgrading of Taiwanese enterprises. They are the Industrial Development Bureau (IDB), Small and Medium Enterprises Administration, Department of Industrial Technology, and Department of Commerce.

Rather than supervising most business or technical activities, funded by MOEA, two non-profit organisations were funded — Institute of Information Industry and Corporate Synergy Development Center. The first one has become a backbone of research and development for Taiwan's information industry sector, while the second is continuously helping industries to develop collaborative systems in designing manufacturing, and optimising supply chain. Given their specific missions, many government projects are required to be implemented through them. They play the role as bridging government policies (mostly from MOEA) and private sectors in the areas of Information Technology research and e-commerce development (Figure 1).

Projects for E-Commerce Infrastructures and Environment

The Industrial Development Bureau (IDB) has developed the "Automation and Information Application Plan for Manufacturing Industry" so as to create an environment for industry automation and the application of e-commerce, and to construct an effective supply-chain with optimal supply/demand mechanisms. The plan intends to achieve the following goals by 2004: (1) to promote at least 70 industrial chain systems for the building and improvement of e-commerce among around 5,500 businesses; (2) to complete assistance to at least 250 businesses for their automation and e-commerce, and to help businesses promote, apply, and install automation and e-commerce technology; and (3) to promote advisory and site visit services for e-commerce.

Figure 1. Relationships of government units for e-commerce project implementing.

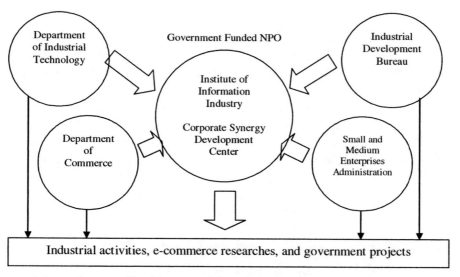

Source: Information sorted by this research from Taiwanese government projects

The department of Small and Medium Enterprises Administration also started a project in 1999 to promote industrial information database installations, which is believed to help accelerating B2B e-commerce process. Twenty-eight industries had been selected with 17 systems providers to build up business information in the database of these industrial associations. A typical example is Taiwan Bicycles Exporters Association (TBEA) which under the supervision of Small and Medium Enterprises Administration has built up an e-market place (http://www.biketrade.org.tw/news/e-index.htm) that it provides business information and opportunities for suppliers, manufacturers, and exporters. In the project of "2002 Guidance for Consultancy and Diagnosis of SMEs Informatisation Process," Small and Medium Enterprises Administration inaugurates a service team to promote learning by SMEs in application, quality management and knowledge management in broadband networking surroundings. In order to stimulate B2B e-commerce activities for SMEs, the department of Small and Medium Enterprises Administration further constructed a website called "SMEs Information Center for Governmental Procurement" which helps SMEs in getting business from governments and provides legal counsel through its webpage.

From research by Institute of Information Industry, there are 61.6% of Taiwanese firms utilising the Internet in doing business in 2002, an increase of 17.2% over the previous year (Institute of Information Industry, 2002). It also indicates that firm size is a major factor rather than different industries and areas. What is interesting is that the rate of small enterprises grows from 29.9% to 54.9% and medium enterprises from 51.4% to 67.5%. This suggests that e-commerce infrastructure has been greatly improved in Taiwanese SMEs during 2001-2002.

Roles of Government Funded Non-Profit Organisations

One example of project implementing through Institute of Information Industry is "The Commerce Automation Project" (Appendix 4). Its main objects are to initiate B2B and B2C e-commerce environments such as research on new business models, human resources, legislation and strategic alliances which can make firms achieving Quick Response/Efficient Consumer Response (QR/ECR) (Figure 2). First of all, the Department of Commerce formed this idea in 1999 and then the Institute of Information Industry has facilitated this process to assist 30 industries and 30,000 firms in starting e-commerce in 2000. In its fourth year, it is still an ongoing project. The two non-profit organisations are now the main agencies to promote governmental plans of e-commerce.

Projects for Linking Global and Local Supply Chains – Examples of Information Industry

Another famous project which focuses on Supply Chain Integration for B2B e-commerce is "Informatisation Promotion Projects for Information Industry."

Figure 2. Commerce Automation project.

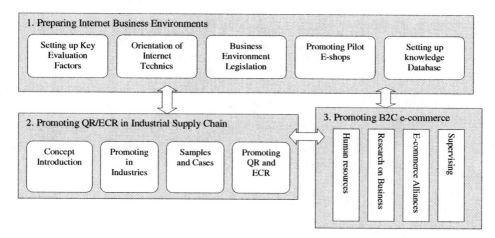

Source: Department of Commerce, Ministry of Economic Affair

Widely known in Taiwan as another name "A/B Plans" (Table 3), it was designed by the Department of Industrial Technology and again completely implemented in 2001 by the Institute of Information Industry.

There are 15 large firms currently building up systems such as ASUS, Inventec, Mitac, MSI, and Twinhead which link up with 3,948 IT components manufacturers so as to implement B2B e-commerce from procuring to manufacturing processes (Din, 2002a). It typically reflects the business capability in adaptation that Taiwanese firms managed to achieve as part of their competitive advantages in Original Equipment Manufacturing (OEM) and Original Design Manufacturing in the past. With the strong support by government and technology development (Taiwan has become the third largest exporting country of IT products in the world during last decade), firms have adjusted their relationships with local large firms and international enterprises to Original Design Logistics (ODL) and Global Logistics (GL). It means that firms have to take care of the process from designing and manufacturing to delivering for the needs of business customers. In these changing phases, the Taiwanese Information Industry works closely with those global brand owners. Tight collaboration and synchronised operations become major successful factors and essential requirements in the supply chain systems.

Therefore, three functional models have become important in the B2B e-commerce processes. They are: (1) e-procurement which includes online order exchange, order confirmation, and forecast data exchange; (2) e-quality assurance systems which can allow business customers to check real time situations in the production lines and thus to control product qualities; (3) e-Room, which

Table 3. Contents of A/B plans in IT supply chain integration.

Project Items	Description	Firms Involved
Plan A	Bridging the supply chains in between Taiwanese IT suppliers and International Buyers.	IBM (with 20 suppliers), Compaq (with 10 suppliers), and Hewlet Packet (with 12 suppliers), etc.
Plan B	Linking collaborative supply chains for large firms (core firms in business network) which have annual revenues more than 10 billion NT dollars. It targets the goal to further bridging domestic SMEs in IT supply chain.	There are 15 large firms currently building up systems such as ASUS, Inventec, Mitac, MSI, and Twinhead which respectively link with 3,948 IT components manufacturers so as to implementing B2B e-commerce from procuring to manufacturing processes.

is a communication and information sharing system that allows more than one firm to discuss issues on-line. Those efforts have made Taiwan the first overseas country linking e-procurement systems with IBM.

After the successful experiences of A/B plans, C/D/E plans have been on the stages since September 2001. They focus on the further enhancement of supply chain integration by including financial institutes (finance flow) and logistics firms (goods flow). Based on XML technology, those plans are expected to complete in 2004 so as to let firms exchange common information about payments, account integration, and financial accommodations. In the meantime, an international standard (RosettaNet) is introduced for tracking and tracing information for the flow of goods. Currently it has nine banks and 10 other large IT enterprises and involves those SMEs associated with them. Through those plans, the Taiwanese government wishes to create the first industrial supply chain integration in the world by using the IT industry as an example. Ideally, traditional industries like the steel industry, textile industry, plastic industry, and machinery industry are expected to be in the next steps of supply chain integration for B2B e-commerce after the completion of the implementation of the IT industry

Difficulties Encountered within Business Network Boundaries

Whereas the above plans have brought clear benefits to the large firms involved (Ding, 2002b), there are still criticisms from those firms involved — especially those SMEs linking with large firms. They are in the business network boundaries of an entire supply chain which have less resources and business capabilities (Wang & Heng, 2002a). Difficulties have been identified in the following areas that deter enterprises from bridging their collaborative SMEs through the systems:

1. *Difficulty of systems standards integration* — RosettaNet standard has been adopted in A/B plans, however, for those Taiwanese SMEs it is an immense burden since they lack the IT human resources and budget to implement.

2. *Conflicts with existing Enterprise Resource Planning (ERP)* — domestic firms own all types of ERP systems. Many of them constructed the systems with local Application Service Providers (ASP) and some of them only have certain models designed to fit their specific needs and business process. Hence, they are not fully compatible with ERP of other large firms and overseas enterprises in the functions, procedures, and data format.

3. *Different concept of ordering automation* — Most large firms have more than one or two business units such as Note Book, Desktop PC, and Mobile Automation. Most of them run different operation models in linking with their collaborative manufacturers. Redundant efforts have become inevitable in this case and many SMEs have had problems in keeping up with their core firms in the business network.

4. *Different perceived benefits and absorptive capability (Cohen & Levithal, 1990)* — Perceived benefit is an important incentive (Saunders & Clark, 1992; Son, Narasimhan, & Riggins, 1999) for B2B e-commerce. In this issue, large firms indeed enjoy more efficiency in their business processes after project implementing. However, to those SMEs, their environments and business opportunities have undergone more changes than expected, thereby creating uncertainty after the huge investment. Supply chain integration might not bring equal perceived benefits to firms with different sizes. It weakens the resolves of many SMEs in going ahead with future plans. Different degrees of implementation also cause the imbalance of absorptive capability in utilising B2B systems.

SUGGESTIVE STRATEGIES FOR ASSISTING B2B E-COMMERCE PROMOTION

B2B e-commerce is the bringing together of individual entities so that they can work and function as a single entity, especially in supply chain integration. An integration solution must be able to bring together diverse systems to work in a cooperative manner. This is accomplished by defining which internal data and processes should be shared, or made available, to other services. Making the data and processes of a particular service available to external parties is the first step to integrate with other business functions and services. Electronic integration along with free flow of information among the supply chain partners opens up a wide range of business opportunities (Clark & Lee, 1997).

Nonetheless, implementation is not always easy. There may be resistance because integration may not provide equal benefits to all partners and as time passes an existing business network formation/boundaries may change. Once a solution is deployed, additional business drivers might emerge from external issues. This latent demand will be revealed as the integration solution is seen to deliver the expected benefits. Any integration solution must be able to support the intrinsic business network features within its boundaries - both by extending the existing architecture, and also through the smooth rollout of new logic processes and control parameters (Wang & Heng, 2002b). Based upon existing projects and the above analyses, there are several suggestions for governments that can help to bridge the gaps of Taiwanese SMEs in implementing B2B e-commerce.

Creating E-Government Portal

For potential overseas customers, the Taiwanese government can further strengthen the information integrity by constructing government portals — central websites which links to industrial databases (Figure 3), related associations and other government departments. It can be further divided into three categories:

1. *E-commerce Portal for International B2B Trading* — allow overseas business customers to find potential suppliers and partners in Taiwan. Also, information about export laws and channels should be found through the links;
2. *E-commerce Portal for Domestic Business Opportunities* — it can create interfirm visibilities and enhance collaborations for Taiwanese SMEs. They are expected to find business opportunities, human resources, financial support, and government policies through this portal;
3. *E-commerce Portal for Cross-Taiwan Strait Business Opportunities* — Mainland China is one of the major export and outward investment countries for Taiwan (Appendix 3). Because of having the same language and similar cultures, there are thousands of Taiwanese firms and many of them keep business on both sides of the strait. There is a need to open an official channel for those firms and thus help them to keep the business models of receiving overseas orders in Taiwan. Websites in English have to be maintained with the same qualities and quantities of updated data. It will require government to form a special team with government resources in order to fulfill those ideas.

Integrating Industrial Databases with Projects of Supply Chain Management

To handle the greater complexity of B2B e-commerce, SMEs require the functionality to conduct regular conversations with potential suppliers, to look

Figure 3. Integrating industrial databases and supply chain management for B2B.

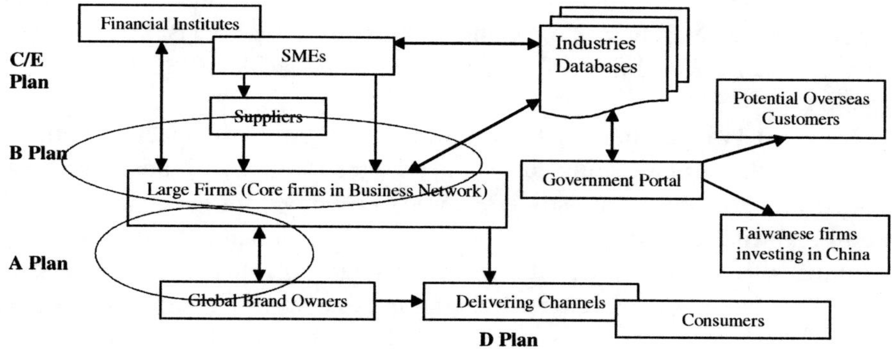

Source: *This research*

into non-price factors, to develop multiple collaborations, and to opt for competitive tools for complex situations. Although the Small and Medium Enterprise Administration promotes B2B e-commerce for SMEs, many firms still run business by traditional ways without using industrial databases set up by government. Those well constructed databases need to have regular updating and maintenance so as to have latest business news and more useful links. With the completed A/B plans and ongoing C/D/E plans in supply chain integration, those industrial databases should be further integrated in supply chain management of the information industry and other industries (Figure 3). It will increase supply chain visibility, hence reduce costs in planning, inventory carrying, forecasting, and outsourcing.

Promotion Business Network Strategies in Governmental B2B E-Commerce Projects

Referring to Italian industries as examples, Benedetti (1999) points out that a complete supply chain has multi-paths and business networks. In fact, Taiwanese industries have the similar situation (Ding, 2002b) which accounts for the fragility of supply chains (Wang & Heng, 2002b). A business network, which consists of information flow and goods flow, might link core firms (Banerji & Sambharya, 1998), suppliers, collaborative designers, original equipment manufacturers (OEMs), systems vendors (brokers), and finance service providers. Advocated by Wang (2001), Christiaanse, and Markus (2002), strategic network theory is one of the important factors for B2B e-commerce which has been neglected for a long period. Successful B2B e-commerce implementation needs congruence with firms that it includes by having clear goals, an acceptable interface, affordable costs among participants, and perceived benefits, etc.

Therefore, the network members have to participate and react by following the characteristics of their business network, for example, the interfirm linkage (Hong, 2002) network formation (Wang & Heng, 2002a), binary trading relationship (Damsgaard & Truex, 2000), and ownership structure (Baldi & Borgman, 2001) in order to sustain and maximum the benefits of B2B e-commerce utilisation.

There are two perspectives of looking at it. First, SMEs need to adopt B2B e-commerce with capable interfaces and adapters to link with business network members but not simply choose EDI, XML, or other techniques so as to maintain systems stability. Based on this analysis, trade-offs in installation priorities and procedures have to be clarified since SMEs lack resources. Second, through outstanding business processes by business network stakeholder analyses, optimum solutions for systems planning will become manifest. For instance, in order to reduce the time for goods delivery, a firm might investigate other forms and interfaces of systems in other firms or find out corespondent departments of other organisations for the purpose of optimum processes, and thus get financial transactions down properly and efficiently.

To help themselves in successfully implementing B2B e-commerce, firms will have to understand the key characteristics of the stakeholders in the business network, to combine system flexibilities with stabilities, to work out strategies at the business network level and to take account of external environment changes. The success of doing so will not only rely upon the government's support but also the attitude of core firms in the business network. In the meantime, core firms and large firms are suggested to ordain and initiate the standards, interfaces, and platform used with the Institute of Information Industry as well as the smaller firms to consider the network theory to develop their information systems and B2B e-commerce strategy.

One rationale is to maximise benefits with minimum sunk costs and risks. Consequently, government projects should be designed by explicitly considering the analysis of business network environments and strategies. The firms which are involved in the "Informatisation Promotion Projects for Information Industry" are currently categorised into three types according to their sizes. Nevertheless, different classification schemes may affect supply chain integration. The examples can be the topologies of business networks formed by members' business flows (Liu & Brookfield, 2000), absorptive capabilities (Cohen & Levithal, 1990), and resources interdependency (Gulati et al., 2000). Analyses of the characteristics of Taiwanese business networks can help the government's projects to provide more appropriate and applicable solutions for different types of firms — especially those SMEs.

CONCLUSION

B2B e-commerce is generating much interest in many businesses, as it is an area where substantial operational and strategic benefits can be achieved. The collection, creation, management, and communication of information are critical to the efficiency, effectiveness, and competitive advantage of any supply chain (Son et al., 1999; El-Ansary et al., 1996). Nevertheless, the implementation processes need to fit the diversified needs of different firms with unified leading mechanisms.

Taiwanese SMEs have contributed to make Taiwan a global manufacturing centre and created a well-known image of "made in Taiwan" in the past. Though joining the WTO has brought new challenges to SMEs, perhaps even threatening their survivals, it also brings opportunities to upgrade their industrial structures and gain healthier managements. Success in implementing B2B e-commerce is not only dependent on the firms' level of preparation but also on environmental readiness provided by government. Compared with large firms, SMEs have relatively less resources and capabilities. The Taiwanese government has started early in setting up strategic directions and projects in promoting e-commerce development for industries. In order to provide competitive benefits both for SMEs and large firms, they should actively utilise government supports in projects, funds, and human resources to augment what they lack.

By building up a unique government portal, integrating industrial databases with government projects by business network analysis, technical development, and identifying appropriate needs and goals, the government can actively assist those firms to speed up their B2B e-commerce process, thereby linking them with both domestic and global supply chains.

REFERENCES

2002 Development of Industries in Taiwan. (2002). Industrial Development Bureau, Ministry of Economic Affairs.

Banerji, J. & Sambharya, R. B. (1998). Effect of Network Organization on alliance Formation: A Study of Japanese Automobile Ancillary Industry. Journal of International Management. 4(1), 41-57.

Benedetti, T. E. (1999). Industrial districts of Italy: Local-Network Economies in a Global-Market Web. Human System Management. 18, 65-68.

Chen, C. H. (2001). Organisational teams and the boss: the development of organisational ability for Taiwan Enterprises. Taichung, Taiwan: Tunghai University. (In Chinese.)

Choi, S. Y., Stahl, D. O. & Whinston, A. B. (1997). The Economics of Electronic Commerce. Indianapolis, IN: Macmillan.

Clark, T. H. & Lee, H. (1997). EDI Enabled Channel Transformation: Extending Business Process Redesign beyond the Firm. International Journal of Electronic Commerce. 2(1), 7-22.

Clinton, W. J. & Gore, A., Jr. (1997). A Framework for Global Electronic Commerce. Retrieved from the World Wide Web: http://www.iitfnist.gov/electonic /ecomm.htm.

Cohen W. & Levithal D. (1990). Absorptive Capacity: A New Perspective on Learning and Innovation. Administrative Science Quarterly. 35, 128-152.

Damsgaard J. & Truex, D. (2000). Binary Trading Relations and the Limits of EDI Standards: the Procrustean Bed of Standards. European Journal of Information systems. 19, 173-188.

Din, H. M. (2002a). Inaugurating the Informatisation Process to International Supply Chain – A/B Plans for IBM, Compaq and HP. eBusiness Executive Report. 35, 69-73. (In Chinese.)

Din, H. M. (2002b). Creating Electronic World by Embedding Network to Network. eBusiness Executive Report, 35, 74-83. (In Chinese.)

El-Ansary, S. A. I. & Coughlan, A. T. (1996). Marketing Channel. 5th ed. Englewood Cliffs, NJ: Prentice Hall.

Ghosh, S. (1998, March/April). Making Business Sense of the Internet. Harvard Business Review.

Guimaras, T. & Armstrong, C. (1997, March). Exploring the Relations between Competitive Intelligence, IS Support, and Business Change. Competitive Intelligence Review, 9.

Gulati, R. (1999). Network Location and Learning: The Influence of Network Resources and Firm Capacities on Alliance Formation. Strategic Management Journal. 20, 397-402.

Gulati, R., Nohria, N. & Zaheer, A. (2000). Strategic Networks. Strategic Management Journal, 21(3), 203-215.

Hong, I. B. (2002). A New Framework for Interorganizational Systems Based on the Linkage of Participants' Roles. Information & Management, 39, 261-270.

Lawrence, E., Corbitt, B., Fisher, J., Lawrence, J. & Tidwell, A. (2000). Internet Commerce: digital models for business. Second edition. Singapore.

Liu, R. J. & Brookfield, J. (2000). Stars, Rings and Tiers: Organisational Networks and Their Dynamics in Taiwan's Machine Tool Industry. Long Range Planning, 33, 322-348.

Novack, R. A., Langley, C. J., Jr, & Lloyd, M. R. (1995). Creating Logistics Value: Themes for the Future. Oak Brook, IL: Council of Logistics Management.

Parker, M. (1996). Strategic Transformation and Information Technology. Upper Saddle River, NJ: Prentice Hall.

Saunders, C. S. & Clark, S. (1992). EDI Adoption and Implementation: A Focus on Interorganizational Linkages. Information Resources Management Journal, 9.

Son, J. Y., Narasimhan, S. & Riggins, F. J. (1999). Factors Affecting the Extent of Electronic Cooperation between Firms: Economic and Sociological Perspectives. Proceedings of the 20th International Conference on Information Systems, Charlotte, NC, pp 550-560.

Turban, E., Lee, J., King, D. & Michael, H. (2000). Electronic Commerce: A Managerial Perspective. International Edition. NJ: Prentice-Hall.

Wang, Y. C. & Heng, M. S. H. (2002a). A Kaleidoscope Approach in Exploring Information Systems Flexibility and Stability for B2B Integration. Proceedings of the 7th United Kingdom Academy Conference of Information Systems. Leeds Metropolitan University, UK.

Wang, Y. C. & Heng, M. S. H. (2002b). Boundaries of business network in Supply Chain: breaking SMEs' barriers in implementing Business-to-Business Integration. Proceedings of the 4th International Conference of Electronic Commerce, HK.

GOVERNMENTAL/INDUSTRIAL WEBSITES

Bike Trading e-Market Place. Retrieved from the World Wide Web: http://www.biketrade.org.tw/news/e-index.htm.

Government Procurement Link. Retrieved from the World Wide Web: http://gpl.moeasmea.gov.tw.

Institute of Information Industry. Retrieved from the World Wide Web: http://www.find.org.tw/.

Taiwanese Bike Exporters Association. Retrieved from the World Wide Web: http://www.tbea.org/.

Taiwanese Ministry of Economic Affairs. Retrieved from the World Wide Web: http://www.moea/gov.tw/.

APPENDIX 1

Definition of Small and Medium Enterprises in Taiwan

Size Industries	Small and Medium Enterprises		Small Enterprises
	Principle	**Exception**	
Manufacturing Construction Mining Quarrying Agriculture, fishing, lumbering	*Total Asset less than NT 80 millions*	*Not more than 200 permanent employees*	*Not more than 20 permanent employees*
Utility Supplying General Commerce Transportation/Logistics Telecommunication Financing industry Service Industry	*Revenue less than NT 100 millions per fiscal year*	*Not more than 50 permanent employees*	*Not more than five permanent employees*

According to the Amendment of Enterprises Legislation NO893420202 Ministry of Economic Affairs, Taiwan

NT = New Taiwanese Dollar
Exchange Rate on 14/12/2002
USD : NT = 1: 34.69
AUD : NT = 1 : 19.6

APPENDIX 2

Industrial General Statistics, Taiwan, 2001

Table 1. Firm sizes and ratios of 2001.

Items \ Size	All Enterprises	Large Enterprises	SMEs
Numbers	1,098,185	20,023	1,078,162
Percentage %	100.00	1.82	98.18
Increase Rate %	0.64	−4.36	0.73
Number of Workers	9,382,540	1,133,794	7,287,766
Percentage %	100.00	12.08	77.67
Increase Rate (%	−1.09	0.78	−1.58
Number of Employed Workers	6,726,627	1,129,270	4,636,377
Percentage %	100.00	16.79	68.93
Increase Rate %	−0.22	0.75	−0.59
Sales NT Million	24,108,790	17,267,226	6,841,565
Percentage %	100.00	71.62	28.38
Increase Rate %	−7.67	−6.89	−9.58
Domestic Sales NT Million	17,812,606	12,270,992	5,541,613
Percentage %	100.00	68.89	31.11
Increase Rate %	−7.57	−6.15	−10.57
Direct Export NT Million	6,296,729	4,996,345	1,300,385
Percentage %	100.00	79.35	20.65
Increase Rate %	−7.95	−8.67	−5.08

Table 2. Numbers of SMEs — Sorted by industries from 1998 ~ 2001.

Industries Size	Total	Fishing and Agriculture	Mining Quarrying	Manufacturing	Utility Supplying
98 Total	2,275,384,787	3,905,074	3,145,576	764,595,293	33,172,214
SMEs	690,778,099	1,454,111	2,521,825	232,394,334	412,608
Ratio	30.36	37.24	80.17	30.39	1.24
99 Total	2,385,093,485	4,270,766	3,507,287	806,777,090	34,206,586
SMEs	690,511,197	1,342,862	2,821,356	229,229,403	442,194
Ratio	28.95	31.44	80.44	28.41	1.29
00 Total	2,611,248,898	3,957,980	3,125,657	926,916,528	37,601,474
SMEs	756,661,746	1,431,949	2,492,366	253,988,396	481,232
Ratio	28.98	36.18	79.74	27.40	1.28
01 Total	2,410,879,018	3,206,359	2,852,431	789,796,791	44,226,685
SMEs	684,156,458	1,308,015	2,145,558	218,565,633	483,636
Ratio	28.38	40.79	75.22	27.67	1.09

Sources: 2001 White Paper on Taiwanese Small and Medium Enterprises, Department of SMEs Development, Ministry of Economic Affairs, Taiwan

APPENDIX 3

Economic Statistics of Taiwanese Firms' Outward Investment

Cross-Taiwan Strait investment statistics

Years	Approved by Ministry of Economic Affair				Data Announced by P.R.C (Mainland China)		
	Quantities (Cases)	Money (100 Million USD)	Average Investment (100 thousand USD)	Percentage of Total Outward Investment (%)	Quantities (Cases)	Negotiated Amount (100 Million USD)	Actual Amount (100 Million USD)
1991	237	1.74	73.48		? 3, 884	? 35.37	? 11.05
1992	264	2.47	93.56	21.78	6, 430	55.43	10.50
1993	1, 262	11.40	90.33	40.71	10, 948	99.65	31.39
	(Amended)8, 067	20.28					
1994	934	9.62	103.02	37.31	6, 247	53.95	33.91
1995	490	10.93	223.00	44.61	4, 778	57.77	31.62
1996	383	12.29	320.95	36.21	3, 184	51.41	34.75
1997	728	16.15	221.78	35.82	3, 014	28.14	32.89
	(Amended) 7 ,997	27.20					
1998	641	15.19	236.97	31.55	2, 970	29.82	29.15
	(Amended) 643	5.15					
1999	488	12.53	256.72	27.71	2,499	33.74	25.99
2000 1-5	256	8.02	313.28	37.02	.1-3 581	1-3 8.81	1-3 4.11
Total	22 ,390	152.97	68.32	39.60	44,535	454.09	245.36

Sources: Investment Commission, Ministry of Economic Affairs (Taiwan)/Ministry of Foreign Trade and Cooperation (China)

APPENDIX 3 (continued)

International Trading Ranking Table 2002 January to October (in USD)

TOP 14 COUNTRIES	Rank	Total Value Amount	(%)	Rank	Export Amount	(%)	Rank	Import Amount	(%)
UNITED STATES	1	37,431,816,304	18.681	2	22,202,731,056	20.737	2	15,229,085,248	16.322
JAPAN	2	32,358,812,398	16.150	3	9,981,988,475	9.323	1	22,376,823,923	23.983
HONG KONG	3	26,849,759,367	13.400	1	25,418,388,777	23.741	14	1,431,370,590	1.534
CHINA	4	14,068,342,026	7.021	4	7,698,734,650	7.191	4	6,369,607,376	6.827
SOUTH KOREA	5	9,547,463,134	4.765	6	3,128,448,433	2.922	3	6,419,014,701	6.880
GERMANY	6	6,720,616,486	3.354	8	3,069,985,139	2.867	5	3,650,631,347	3.913
SINGAPORE	7	6,550,497,802	3.269	5	3,569,205,920	3.334	8	2,981,291,882	3.195
MALAYSIA	8	6,084,364,526	3.037	9	2,610,704,941	2.438	6	3,473,659,585	3.723
PHILIPPINES	9	4,775,460,873	2.383	13	1,662,587,970	1.553	7	3,112,872,903	3.336
NETHERLANDS	10	4,319,192,086	2.156	7	3,098,396,136	2.894	16	1,220,795,950	1.308
AUSTRALIA	11	3,717,673,262	1.855	14	1,307,717,484	1.221	9	2,409,955,778	2.583
THAILAND	12	3,706,825,773	1.850	11	1,906,094,776	1.780	13	1,800,730,997	1.930
UNITED KINGDOM	13	3,512,083,216	1.753	10	2,385,276,153	2.228	17	1,126,807,063	1.208
INDONESIA	14	3,380,817,086	1.687	16	1,238,002,063	1.156	10	2,142,815,023	2.297
TOTAL VALUES		200,369,684,087	100.000		107,067,249,385	100.000		93,302,434,702	100.000

Source: Directorate General of Customs, Ministry of Finance, Taiwan

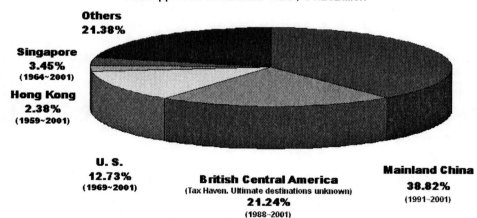

TAIWAN'S APPROVED OUTWARD INVESTMENT
(Cumulative till 2001 -- Various Starting Points)
RECIPIENT'S AMOUNT AS PERCENTAGE OF TOTAL
Total Approved Investment = US$ 51.23Billion

Others 21.38%

Singapore 3.45% (1964~2001)

Hong Kong 2.38% (1959~2001)

U. S. 12.73% (1969~2001)

British Central America (Tax Haven. Ultimate destinations unknown) **21.24%** (1988~2001)

Mainland China 38.82% (1991~2001)

Sources: Investment Commission, Ministry of Economic Affairs, Taiwan, R.O.C., December 2001.
Graph: Department of Economic Affairs, Mainland Affairs Council, Executive Yuan, R.O.C., December 2001.
2-2 Chi Nan Road, Sec. 1, 17/F, Taipei, Taiwan, R.O.C.
TEL: 886-2- 23975589   FAX: 886-2-23975281   URL:www.MAC.GOV.TW   E-MAIL:macst@mac.gov.tw

APPENDIX 4

Examples of Government Departments and Institutions Related to E-Commerce Development of Taiwanese SMEs

Government Departments	Main Responsibilities	Projects Related to SMEs (2001 -2002)
Ministry of Economic Affairs, Department of Commerce	Formulation of commercial policy and regulations, Registration management (eg. trade mark), Material adjustment and commodity price management etc.	The Commerce Automation Project
Ministry of Economic Affairs, Department of Industrial Technology	Strengthening industrial technology policy plans (including industrial technology policies research), and Promoting international scientific and technological cooperation etc	IT Application Promoting Project
Ministry of Economic Affairs, Small and Medium Enterprises Administration	The assistance and assessment toward small and medium enterprises; the investigation and study of small and medium enterprises; the improvement of operation and management and short-term loan for use as revolving fund supplement matters etc.	Guidance for Consultancy and Diagnosis of SMEs Informatisation Process
Ministry of Economic Affairs, Industrial Development Bureau	To formulate policies, strategies and other industrial development measures; to promote industrial advancement; to develop and manage industrial parks; to formulate financial and tax measures for industrial development; to prevent industrial pollution, provide guidance on industrial safety, and regulate industries; and to monitor general industrial affairs.	Automation and Information Application Plan for Manufacturing Industry ; Statute for Upgrading Industries

Sources: Sorted from Taiwanese government websites

APPENDIX 4 (continued)

Government Funded Organisations		
Institute of Information Industry	Institute for Information Industry (III) started from an ideal that was commonly shared by the Ministry of Economic Affairs and several private enterprises and its main task is to Improve the productivity and competitiveness of all industries through the use of IT.	Perspective Networking Technics for e-commerce – by advanced e-commerce technology laboratory
Corporate Synergy Development Center	Promoting Corporate Synergy Development; Assisting enterprises for B2B e-commerce development and IS infrastructure implementation; Researching related technologies and strategies, etc.	Industrial Information Technology development for Corporate Synergy (The Fourth Year)

Sources: Sorted from Taiwanese government websites

SECTION III:

POLICY PUSH AND MONITORING

Chapter XII

Providing Information
for Business:
Government Strategy for the
Online World

Tanya Castleman, Deakin University, Australia

Marina Cavill, Deakin University, Australia

ABSTRACT

Governments assume a major role in providing information resources for business as a way of promoting national development. This has proven to be a much more demanding task than one might suppose, given the diversity and complexity of business needs and the limitation of government resources for undertaking the task. This chapter will: (1) identify the challenges posed for government online business information strategies, (2) discuss research relating to the information strategy of one Australian government agency to support export development among small business, and (3) set out a framework for government online information provision in a diverse industry context. Coordination of the many government information services remains a challenge, especially among different levels of government. Well-designed strategies can improve the usability of online information and the efficiency of government information services.

INTRODUCTION

The power of the Internet to deliver information and services online offers an opportunity for governments to support businesses and the economies they serve. This is an important issue, both for government economic development strategies and to help them meet the rising public expectations of online service provision (Carberry & Steins, 2000; Symonds, 2000; Public Management, 2000). The economic importance of a strong, viable business sector, especially a strong and viable small business sector with its potential for employment and export generation, makes it imperative that government agencies provide encouragement, leadership and effective support. Governments undertake a wide variety of initiatives to achieve these ends and online information provision is one of many such initiatives. Individuals and firms moving into a new and unfamiliar field of activity are increasingly using information resources provided over the Internet. Many small to medium-size enterprises (SMEs) may turn initially to a government agency for business-related information, in part because they lack the confidence and financial resources to engage private consultants at the initial stages of the planning process.

Providing the necessary information poses a significant challenge for government. Enterprises vary in size, resources, management expertise and awareness of the kinds of assistance they might access. The information required to answer each inquiry cannot be too generic if it is to be relevant. It is essential that the answer be structured to meet the needs of the inquirer. Customised advice to individual enterprises would have a maximum impact but it is too costly for government agencies to employ the necessary personnel with a high level of expertise. Thus, governments must strike a balance between offering individual advice and the need to keep service costs contained.

Government business information strategies must be oriented to a number of issues:

- *Complexity:* business operations have become increasingly complex and demanding, with greater product specialisation, globalisation, legal requirements and competition. To give detailed information about this complexity is beyond the capability of governments, but failure to acknowledge and describe it could have unfortunate consequences for individual businesses and whole sectors of the economy.
- *Diversity:* the range of business activities, markets and operations confronts information providers, including government, with a major task of dealing with a high level of diversity. Addressing the information needs of one sector or type of business may well fail to address those of other business types.
- *Relevance:* government information needs to be relevant, both to the specific business activities of each user and to the context in which they

operate. This means that the format and medium of information must be easy to find, assimilate and apply.

- *Efficiency and integration:* governments' business information material must be delivered efficiently, not only in the initial cost of provision but in the maintenance and updating of information. This dictates simplicity and avoidance of duplication in provision, using other reliable information sources (including industry and other government sources) to the maximum while maintaining the quality of information provision. The task of integration between channels for one government is challenge enough; to integrate across different levels of government and between governments is especially problematic. Some degree of duplication is likely to develop in a multi-layered system, which may create both inefficiency and confusion.
- *Impact and reciprocity:* each government information channel (e.g., a web site) will depend on its profile and recognisability for impact. Business users should recognise the site as a rich and trustworthy one, easy to find and navigate. To achieve this, some publicity and reciprocal links with other sites are highly advantageous. This recognition is difficult to achieve with the plethora of sites, layers of government and competing "brands" of government information provision. While governments may be trusted sources of information, they must first attract users, many of whom operate in a commercial context and tend to draw their information from existing commercial information sources, both private and public.

To meet these challenges, many governments have established online portals to provide information and links to other sources of business information.

Information portals, the most common form of information provision by governments on the Internet, are provided at various levels including whole-of-government portals which give the user access to a wide array of government activities with links to specific sections of government, often through links to ministries or departments (see, for example http://www.fed.gov.au). The richness of these high level portals is sometimes obscured by the complexity and magnitude of the operations of the government and the user may become lost or overwhelmed by the sheer volume of information available. When links to non-government sites are included, a sense of disorientation may result. Effective navigation of the site will depend on the user's familiarity with the structure of government administration and the operation of the various departments and instrumentalities which are subject to periodic name changes and reorganisation. While whole-of-government portals are a good format for providing information about the operations of government, this is not optimum for providing information relating to a particular area of activity, especially one in which a variety of government organisations have an interest. To address this, many governments have developed nested portals which provide specific, collected information about a major activity, including business support.

This chapter explores the initiative of one government agency in developing a portal to assist businesses to develop their export activities and associated e-commerce activities. This example highlights issues that an effective government information strategy should consider and the ways in which it might best use the Internet and its abundant resources to achieve its information goals, including the goal of assisting users to access specialised and even individual advice when it is required.

AUSTRALIA'S MOVE ONLINE

Governments in Australia have attached a high priority to developing strategic online information dissemination to support business, especially the small and medium enterprises which comprise a major part of the economy (ABS, 2002). The Commonwealth (national) government underwrote this thrust with its Government Online strategy, launched in 2000, in which it mandated a move of "all appropriate government services" to online delivery by 2001 (Government Online, 2000). State governments have developed parallel online policies and service provision. Steady work has been undertaken since that time to achieve this move with a burgeoning government web presence and increasing richness of information provision and functionality.

Government strategy for business development includes the increased development of export and international trade and the use of e-commerce to facilitate that development. This dual agenda has had Commonwealth government support (DFAT, 1999) and state governments have supported it in their own regions. A strong export economy enabled by electronic business processes is a key part of the "Information Economy" (NOIE, 2002) from which Australia is well positioned to benefit, being among the advanced nations in terms of key measures of Internet infrastructure, penetration and activity. A national survey of small businesses in 2002 (Pacific Access, 2002) reported that Australia had reached:

*   Record levels (79%) of small businesses and (94%) of medium businesses with PCs connected to the Internet, which are starting to plateau. Of these, 82% were using the Internet to look for information, products, or services with a further 8% planning to do so within 12 months.
*   Record levels (94%) of small businesses connected to the Internet using email.
*   Record levels (46%) of small businesses reporting they had a home page; with another 16% expecting to establish a home page in the next 12 months.

However, in comparison with larger Australian businesses and SMEs in some other countries, Australian small businesses have been relatively slow to adopt e-commerce. Of those using the Internet for business communications, only a fraction do any form of e-commerce such as taking orders and receiving payments. Almost 50% of small businesses did not see e-commerce as having any particular relevance to their business at that time. Many small businesses have little interest in e-commerce, specifically in buying and selling over the Internet and have a limited appreciation of the benefits of moving online and the costs and process of doing so (NOIE, 2000, p. 11). To Australian governments, which have been pursuing a range of strategies to encourage small business to use the Internet and increase international trade activity, such findings are of continuing national concern, although the issues small businesses face in moving online have been widely reported (see DFAT, 1999; Poon & Swatman, 1999; Corbitt & Kong, 2000; Levy & Powell, 2002; Lawrence & Hughes, 2000).

Against this backdrop, the Victorian government's VicExport site was developed primarily to provide small businesses with information to help them with export, but in doing so included online information about e-commerce as well. Thus, it is an example both of an online information initiative and an initiative to promote e-commerce.

THE VicExport
INFORMATION INITIATIVE [1]

The Victorian State government has for some time provided services to help businesses develop and participate in international trade, assisting firms already trading across borders to improve their performance. The Government has pursued a range of initiatives to encourage Victorian businesses to adopt e-commerce, both for domestic and international trade. Promoting e-commerce for export (EC4X) encourages the use of advanced online business techniques to lift the state's trade performance.

Prior to the Government's move online it dispensed export information primarily by the provision of printed material. This made revision and update of the material both difficult and expensive. In addition, the available information was not structured to facilitate its effective utilisation by inquirers who did not know exactly what information they were seeking. The Government believed that using the Internet could solve the problem of providing cost-effective export information to the target audience. They developed the VicExport web site to provide a comprehensive checklist of export issues. From this list, inquirers can access information which is relevant to their own specific needs and level of awareness.

The *VicExport* web site (http://www.export.vic.gov.au) provides access to a repository of information on all aspects of export. Its purpose is to:

- increase export awareness in the general community,
- encourage firms who have export potential to trade internationally,
- assist existing exporters to improve their export performance, and
- avoid ill-advised, under-resourced and premature ventures into international trade.

The site added a section on e-commerce in 2002 to help exporters develop EC4X. The information it contains is structured to provide a logical progression through the various stages of export development from initial consideration of export potential to the finalisation of contracts and export expansion. VicExport avoids duplication by using links to the web sites of other agencies able to assist in export development. In this way, the VicExport portal offered an opportunity to improve the quality and cost-effectiveness of information provision about export and e-commerce.

The site is openly available but is primarily designed to assist SMEs with little or no exposure to international markets. An important aim is to provide information for enterprises in regional and rural areas where access to this type of information is limited. The site uses the interactivity of the Internet to allow the inquirer independently to develop a preliminary export strategy specific to their business either on or offline. The department estimated the site saved over 1,600 hours of face-to-face counseling by departmental staff in the 18 months after its launch. Its positive impact on the Victorian economy cannot at this stage be gauged, but it was followed by a marked increase in the number of small to medium-size enterprises showing interest in taking products and services into international markets. This trend is also evident from the increased number of direct contacts from users of the site seeking further advice on export and referral to export service providers.

The Government estimated conservatively that its saving from the site was in the order of 60% less time spent in export counseling; 20% improvement in service levels and 10% decrease in operating costs mainly associated with reduced costs of printing export information material. Overall costs have been contained to existing levels despite increased workflows and higher levels of customer service. A further benefit of the site is its use as an easy reference resource for departmental staff who may have little or no personal experience of international trade.

It has to be acknowledged that no matter how comprehensive the information provided by *VicExport* and no matter how innovative the means of delivery, most SMEs will ultimately require specific and ongoing support in the form of individual counseling and advice. The information that *VicExport* provides must be viewed as a starting point on the road to e-commerce implementation and the successful move into international markets. To work effectively, a site such as *VicExport* must provide information that matches the needs of exporters and potential exporters. To do this, they must know:

- the information needs of SMEs involved with EC4X,
- what resources are available to provide that information accurately and efficiently, and
- the appropriate mix of online and individual assistance for EC4X and how this can be structured into the government strategy.

The dual goal of increasing export trade and e-commerce use raised issues about how this could best be achieved and what role the government ought to play in this development. Earlier research (Castleman & Cavill, 2000, 2001) examined the experiences of companies which were successful in EC4X and identified their needs in a number of areas. To support the government's EC4X initiative, the research reported here looked more specifically at the information strategy and, in particular, the state government strategy, to help SMEs move into EC4X.

Investigation of the EC4X Information Needs of SMEs

In November 2001 the Victorian Department of State and Regional Development (now the Department of Innovation, Industry and Regional Development) contracted us to conduct an investigation of the information and support needs of SMEs engaged in EC4X and to advise on the EC4X content for the *VicExport* web site (Castleman & Cavill, 2002).

The project entailed an interview survey of 25 SMEs currently using or contemplating using EC4X in order to identify the issues confronting them in export development and the use of e-commerce. In the course of the interviews, a level of detail about business operations emerged which provided an understanding of the wider context of EC4X development. To provide a range of business types, we drew up a sampling framework to select businesses in four categories, depending on their level of export and e-commerce activity.

We adopted the following criteria for this framework:

- *Established export activity* was indicated by regular and planned provision of goods or services in an international market, even if that business accounted for only a small part of the business. The proportion of export share of the business ranged from 100% (two companies) to 5% (two companies) with an average of 49% of business activity devoted to export among the companies. Seventeen companies were established exporters.
- *Established e-commerce activity* was less easy to define because of the variable nature of the use of e-commerce technologies. Most businesses were online, used email and had a static web site, but this did not indicate

Table 1. Levels of export and e-commerce activity in survey sample (N = 25).

E-Commerce activity

		Established	Developing
Export activity	Established	**Group 1: n = 11** Exporting and using E-Commerce to a significant degree	**Group 3: n = 6** Significant level of export activity but not using E-Commerce to a significant degree
	Developing	**Group 2: n = 4** Significant levels of E-Commerce use but not exporting regularly	**Group 4: n = 4** Not engaged in either export or E-Commerce to a significant degree but actively considering both

active e-commerce use. We considered a business to have established e-commerce if it was able at least to take orders and provide customer service via its web site or if it used more sophisticated applications for either business-to-business or business-to-consumer interactions. Fifteen companies had established e-commerce activity.

• A company was classified as *"developing"* export or e-commerce if they were considering these activities seriously but did not meet the criteria listed above.

Table 1 shows the distribution of participating companies into four groups according to their export and e-commerce activity.

The participating businesses varied in size, although all were small or medium businesses. The average number of employees in the 25 businesses was 28 and the mean annual turnover of the 16 businesses willing to divulge this information was $5.3 million. They were located in both metropolitan and regional areas of the state. Nine of the 25 businesses had a number of branch offices, including six with offices located overseas. Their business activities were diverse, including manufacturing, services, retail, wholesale and logistics.

Besides interviewing members of the companies, we conducted interviews with eight representatives of industry and regional business organisations. This provided confirmation of the SME interviews and another valuable perspective on the issues.

Study Findings

The interviewees gave a detailed account of their move into export, e-commerce and EC4X. Both established and beginner exporters overwhelmingly cited expansion and diversification of their market base as the main reason for moving into export. This was important to businesses for many different reasons, for example: to overcome troughs and peaks in local markets, to expand the risk base, to provide improved cash flows, to reach markets for goods that the domestic market alone could not absorb and to achieve economies of scale in production.

The main reason given for developing e-commerce was the ability to reach new customers and to achieve internal efficiencies. However, only a small percentage of companies were able to conduct business transactions from their web sites. The reasons appear to be a general lack of information technology expertise within the businesses, limited resources, and uncertainty about e-commerce applications. This is especially a problem in rural areas where expert advisors and mentors often are not readily accessible.

The analysis of the factors important in EC4X adoption highlights the importance of personal contacts, attending trade fairs, and taking part in trade delegations. As earlier reports commented, "while the Internet provides excellent means of doing business quickly once a link has been established, the process of establishing a relationship between buyer and seller and developing trust and mutual respect remains a critical foundation for the business relationship, just as it has always been" (DFAT, 1999, p. 58). Often it is only after establishing these international business contacts that E-Commerce becomes critical to a business, allowing it to develop and maintain these relationships and to move into international markets.

Several businesses commented that in order to trade internationally it had become essential for them to use e-commerce. It helps SMEs maintain personal relationships and realise internal cost efficiencies by streamlining operations. It can also open up new markets through international electronic marketing.

Established exporters reported their reliance on networks and personal contacts and when the beginner exporters were asked how they would determine if they were export-ready the majority indicated that they would have to check out the market personally by paying a visit, attending international exhibitions or trade fairs, and making contacts with local agents. They would be guided partly by the level of interest they had from overseas as well as by their own market research. Several also mentioned that they would need to ensure that they had adequate infrastructure to deal with exports — such as an appropriate web site, reliable transport logistics, and knowledge of the documentation requirements.

Table 2. Information required to launch or extend EC4X.

	Number of mentions
Export information	
International markets	16
Import-export regulations	16
Contacts with trading partners and agents abroad	12
Financial matters including payments and currency	4
Local customs and business practices	6
Logistics	3
E-Commerce information	
IT and related technical matters	11
Website design and designers	8
Better general knowledge about E-Commerce	7
Costs of going online	4
Online finance and banking	4
Electronic marketing	4
Online security	4
	N = 25

Requirements for EC4X Information

We asked the interviewees what information they required to help them begin or to develop EC4X. The responses for both export and e-commerce information are tallied in Table 2. This not only indicates the scope of information needed, but the mixture of generic and specific information. For example, seven interviewees (beginning e-commerce users) wanted general information about what e-commerce was and what applications were available and eight wanted information about how to find a web designer at a very specific level. Sixteen mentioned import-export regulations and 12 wanted to find specific contacts.

This list to some extent masks the range of specific and general information required. The level of specific information about regulations, for example, varied. For example, some reported a need for very detailed information about customs requirements, while others needed information relating to their industry or their specific product.

Sources of EC4X Information

Not only were we interested in discovering the type of information SMEs needed in order to embark on EC4X, we also wanted to find out where they turned to find that information. This factor would provide useful feedback on the channels which would assist SMEs most effectively in the future.

All 17 established exporters ranked personal contacts including export agents as their main source of export information. Government organisations (10) and industry associations (eight) were the next ranked. Both established and potential exporters associated the Commonwealth government with export information. Potential exporters ranked state and federal government information sources as most likely to be useful followed by private providers (e.g., shipping agents and export agents).

The pattern of e-commerce information provision was very different. Sources of e-commerce information mentioned by e-commerce users were primarily IT providers and consultants (eight of the 15) followed by online sources (six). Five said there was no suitable information available at the time they were developing e-commerce.

For the companies in the early stages of e-commerce development (who said their needs included general knowledge about what it was and what it could do), private providers were by far the highest ranked information source followed by industry associations. They were unaware of the EC4X information available from State government sources.

Respondents provided further insights about the pros and cons of accessing information from these sources. Personal relationships turned out to be a very highly rated source of information. These included contacts established at times of personal visits overseas or at trade shows, information provided by customers or people who had experience in export, freight forwarders, import agents, regional export development officers. While people seem to be happy to look up much of the export information online, often there is no substitute for personal mentoring and one-to-one information transfer. A number of respondents emphasised the importance of combining research and networking, using both channels to gain a good knowledge of the area and business opportunities. However, some businesses are still not confident that they are using the Internet effectively to find information such as the export code for an unusual product. They want a personal contact to follow up. Some respondents mentioned the usefulness of the individual help they had received from Business Victoria's export advisers who provided personalised advice and "someone to hold your hand." Personal contacts overseas were also of great value.

Several respondents commented that information from Commonwealth government sites was too generic to meet their needs beyond a certain point and that they needed to go further. Business organisations both in Australia and internationally such as national Business Councils and Chambers of Commerce, employer and industry organisations, local business organisations and business service providers provide useful sources of advice for many industries. However, not all industry groups are yet online, and not all can provide dependable, comprehensive export advice.

Courses and workshops were not rated very highly, either because they were too costly and time consuming to attend or because they were too generic and not focused enough. E-commerce beginners sought information from IT professionals and liked to speak to people who had already introduced e-commerce into their business. They preferred individual advice sessions and mentoring from these groups. However, several participants mentioned difficulties in finding reliable and trustworthy sources of local e-commerce advice, indicating that not all such practitioners are good or impartial sources of information. This echoes findings from earlier studies (Castleman & Cavill, 2000 & 2001; Castleman, Cavill & Parker, 1999) that pointed to the problems in the capabilities and business practices of some IT and Internet consultants and the difficulties that companies had in assessing their ability to provide high quality e-commerce services. Good strategic advice about e-commerce is also difficult to source from providers concerned primarily with IT.

The high number of mentions of personal contacts is notable. Certainly personal contacts are likely to be more enduring (in many cases long-term relationships) and more memorable than official information sources. Thus even among relatively established exporters with some e-commerce readiness, individual contacts remain a significant element of their export business. A government information strategy should not try to replace these sources but to provide general information which enables small businesses to make good decisions about choosing private providers.

Channels for EC4X Information Delivery

Having identified the range of EC4X information needs and the relevant sources of that information, a key issue for the study was the preferences the respondents had for the delivery of that information. What channels and what mix of channels would be most effective in getting the information to the users? How can this be done cost effectively?

Each respondent was asked to evaluate the format in which export information was provided. The results summarised in Table 3 shows the number of respondents who indicated the format was very useful.

Online information was endorsed as the most useful, although there were some limitations to relying entirely on online provision. The high ranking given

Table 3. Assessments of formats of export information provision.

	Designations as "Very Useful"	Rank
Online information; websites	19	1
Individual advice sessions	17	2
Printed brochures	12	3
Workshops and training courses	11	4
	N=25	

to individual advice sessions is consistent with the strong approval of face-to-face and personal contact as a good information source. Although the need for printed material is not as important as it was before the spread of the Internet and businesses going online, there is still evidently a need for printed information within an overall information and support strategy. While workshops and seminars were cited as a source of export information, they did not rate as highly as other sources. The explanation seems to be that SMEs have limited finances and time available; workshop attendance requires both. Some have attended workshops and have found that they were too generic and did not address the issues of concern to them. Many prefer to find the information online and to be advised of courses on specific topics.

The representatives of industry associations confirmed that personal contacts and networking were likely to provide the most useful source of information for export. Trade missions, local agents and distributors were seen to be particularly useful. They also noted that individual mentoring assistance, particularly in regard to export documentation would be very valuable. Training courses were viewed as useful, providing they could be provided at a low cost and were specific to the SMEs' needs. The relevance of these findings is that online information is seen as useful but it needs to be linked to other information sources (printed materials) and needs to facilitate personal contacts and linking with business contacts.

Asked to evaluate the format in which e-commerce information was provided, both groups ranked interactive sessions (individual or workshop sessions) as more useful than general information, with printed information being ranked as the least useful format. However, usefulness should not be confused with cost-effectiveness. The higher ranking given to individualised and interactive sessions does not mean that they should replace general information provided online. Established e-commerce users ranked workshops and training courses as the second most important source of information, while beginner e-commerce users ranked online information sources higher. This is partly a

Table 4. Assessments of formats for e-commerce information provision.

	Number of designations as "Somewhat or Very Useful"	Rank
Individual advice sessions	18	1
Online information; websites	16	2
Workshops and training courses	15	3
Printed brochures	13	4
	N=25	

reflection of the information that was online around 1997 when most of the established users introduced e-commerce compared with the information that is now available online.

KEY ELEMENTS OF AN ONLINE BUSINESS INFORMATION STRATEGY

Governments have an important role to play in the provision of business information and they will increasingly use the Internet to do this effectively. We argue that they should focus on the provision of generic information about export and electronic commerce as they cannot realistically provide all the detailed information needed for diverse industries and destination countries. However, without links to the more specific information and pointers about how to use these links, the value of the government efforts will be undermined. The links to more specific information will typically be to industry information sites.

Even access to specific online information will not be sufficient if there is not also some support for locating individualised sources of advice. Some kind of guidance to help smaller companies find those individual sources would be useful, given the evidence that these connections remain critical in the development of EC4X. Governments need to be cautious about appearing to recommend private providers, but they may help by suggesting business directories and headings in those directories under which the right kinds of people can be found as well as suggesting criteria for selecting such providers and the pitfalls to avoid.

Government online information strategies should provide generic information along with guidance about how to access more specific information at various levels. In Table 5 we have set out an example showing the elements of an information strategy for one issue (customs regulations) that will affect wine exporters. There are many other issues for which a similar table could be constructed for this group. Wine exporters need access to general information about customs regulations but also more detailed information about export labelling that applies specifically to wine. They are likely to need yet more specific information about how to label their wine for a particular exporter or a particular market.

The general information about customs can be provided on a government web site (in this case, the Commonwealth government would provide that information with links to State government web sites). By following links to the relevant industry associations (in this case the Australian Wine and Brandy Corporation), the exporter can find details about the particular regulations for the export of wine (and of no interest at all to exporters of auto parts). Information about e-commerce can be structured along the same lines. General information

Table 5. Aspects of and integrated EC4X information strategy — an example from the wine industry.

	Export	E-Commerce
Information Needs		
Generic	Customs regulations	Web-based logistics tracking
Specific	Wine export labelling	Online documentation for wine industry
Individual	Wine labelling for a particular importer	Proprietary online logistics systems
Information Sources		
Generic	Australian Customs Service	Department of Transport and Regional Services
Specific	Australian Wine and Brandy Corporation - Export Grid	Australian Wine and Brandy Corporation – Wine Export Approval System
Individual	Suitable export agents	Shipping agents with IT capability
Information Delivery		
Generic	Government websites	Government websites
Specific	Industry websites	Industry websites
Individual	Individual import/export agents

Government and industry export advisors; referrals | Individual shipping agents |

on the government site about logistics and web-based tracking could link to specific information that related to the documentation needs of wine exporters provided on an industry web site. For individual-level advice, these sites refer to potential individual information providers, whether they are government, industry associations or private providers. The development of reciprocal links between these various sources will dramatically increase their usability and effectiveness.

An information strategy that gives primary focus to Internet sources also needs to link to people not online and to more individualised sources of advice and networks. A promotion strategy must also include other channels to heighten the profile of the online site. Multiple channels will need to be maintained for some time yet, perhaps indefinitely. It is imperative to coordinate the online information service with other information sources, while moving the balance gradually toward the Internet as yet more companies go online.

The *VicExport* strategy is designed to provide an informative, efficient web site which points exporters to e-commerce information and other more specialised information sources. Many easily-navigated links between the export and e-commerce material and between the general and specific levels will help support SMEs developing EC4X.

CONCLUSION

This chapter has outlined the challenges that governments face in providing effective information supported by online resources. First, they must gain the attention of the businesses which need to access the information. Thereafter, the information must be provided to address the complexity and diversity of the potential users, neither confusing them with excessive and irrelevant detail nor giving them only bland, superficial information that is of little use. An effective online business information strategy will be structured to point users to increasingly specific and more detailed information, often provided by other organisations such as the industry associations that cover the area in question. These organisations are sources of current, specific and relevant information that governments will find it difficult to locate and maintain. Effective information provision also leads business owners to find personal contacts and individualised information and advice, but only after they have accessed much of their information online and are able to take better advantage of the specific advice.

Efficiency of service provision is important, given the limited funds that governments have for this purpose and the broad group of users they must serve. Part of this efficiency derives from links to good quality sites outside the government, including other governments, which give more specific information. Traditionally, governments have been obliged to provide information for their own constituents but web sites do not limit use that way. As a result there is considerable overlap, duplication and sometimes confusion. Greater cooperation and integration between government service providers and better coordination with private sector sources, including industry associations, would improve efficiency and reduce users' confusion. The VicExport site is a good example of a government portal based on such principles. Ultimately, more extensive information coordination and cross-referenced links would benefit all parties. Although not easy to achieve, this is the form of information provision that would make most ·sense from a user's as well as the providers' point of view. Governments are in a good position to take the lead in achieving it.

REFERENCES

ABS (Australian Bureau of Statistics). (2002). Small Business in Australia. Catalogue No. 1321.0. Commonwealth of Australia. Canberra. AGPS.

Carberry, J. & Steins, C. (2000, Nov/Dec). G2B Web Sites. *Tech Trends*, 20-24.

Castleman, T. & Cavill, M. (2000). Supporting E-Commerce for Export: Australian and international initiatives. *Proceeding of CollECTeR 2000. Fifth CollECTeR Conference on Electronic Commerce,* Brisbane, Queensland, Australia (December 13-14).

Castleman, T. & Cavill, M. (2001). Voices of experience: Developing Export Capability Through E-Commerce in Australian SMEs. *The 14th Bled Electronic Commerce Confere*nce, Bled, Slovenia (June 25-26).

Castleman, T. & Cavill, M. (2002, February). *Facilitating Victorian Business Use of E-Commerce for Export (EC4X).* Study commissioned by Department of State and Regional Development. Victoria.

Castleman, T., Cavill, M. & Parker, C. (1999, September). *Issues in the Use of E-Commerce by Australian Exporters.* Report to Austrade.

Corbitt, B. & Kong, W. (2000). Issues Affecting the Implementation of Electronic Commerce in SMEs in Singapore. *Proceedings of the 13th Bled Electronic Commerce Conference,* Bled, Slovenia (pp. 474-494).

DFAT (Department of Foreign Affairs and Trade). (1999). *Driving Forces on the New Silk Road.* The Use of Electronic Commerce by Australian Business. Commonwealth of Australia.

Government Online (2000, April). *Government Online - The Commonwealth Government's Strategy.* Department of Communications Information Technology and the Arts.

Lawrence, J. & Hughes, J. (2000). Internet Usage by SMEs: A UK Perspective. *Proceedings of the 13th Bled Electronic Commerce Conference, Bled, Slovenia* (pp. 738-753).

Levy, M. & Powell, P. (2002). SME Internet Adoption: Towards a transporter model. *Proceedings of the 15ᵗʰ Bled Electronic Commerce Conference, e-Reality: Constructing the e-Economy,* Bled, Slovenia (pp. 507-521).

NOIE (National Office of the Information Economy). (2000). *Taking the Plunge 2000: Sink or Swim.* Retrieved from the World Wide Web: http://www.noie.gov.au/publications/NOIE/SME/SinkorSwim2000.pdf.

NOIE. (2002, April). *Australia's Information Economy: The Big Picture.* Report Prepared by the Allen Consulting Company and Monash University. Retrieved from the World Wide Web: http://www.noie.gov.au/projects/framework/Progress/IE_Aust/start.htm.

Pacific Access. (2002, July). *Yellow Pages® E-Business Report. The Online Expereince of Small and Medium Enterprises.* Retrieved from the World Wide Web: http://www.sensis.com.au/Internet/static_files/smeiypbibi_jul02.pdf.

Poon, S. & Swatman, P. (1999). An exploratory study of small business Internet commerce issues. *Information & Management,* 35, 9-18.

Public Management. (2000). A guide to e-government and e-commerce. *Public Management,* 82(7), 1.

Symonds, M. (2000). Government and the Internet - The next revolution. *The Econom*ist, 355(8176), 3.

VicExport. (n.d.). Retrieved from the World Wide Web: www.export.vic.gov.au.

ENDNOTES

[1]   Information about the VicExport initiative and export advice to small business was generously provided by Les Terrill, Senior Project Manager - Business Information Services, Victorian Department of Innovation Industry and Regional Development.

Chapter XIII

Government Promotion of E-Commerce in SMEs:
The Australian Government's ITOL Program

G. Michael McGrath, Victoria University, Australia

Elizabeth More, University of Canberra, Australia

ABSTRACT

As in many other countries, the take-up rate of e-commerce in Australian SMEs has been poor. The Australian Government has attempted to address this (in part) through its "Information Technology On-Line" (ITOL) program — a program that aims to accelerate the adoption of e-commerce through the provision of seed funding to on-line projects proposed by industry-based consortia. Some 81 projects have been funded so far and, in this paper, we review progress to date. While there have been some outstandingly successful projects, others have floundered. Provision of adequate project resources, together with effective change and relationship management, were identified as key critical success factors.

INTRODUCTION

What we are witnessing in contemporary organizational life are the opportunities wrought by technological changes, most recently through web-based technology and the Internet. These shake traditional foundations of organizing and the very nature of organizations. New challenges are, therefore, confronting management across a diverse array of industries and government, and offer the likelihood, through economically viable new options, of new paradigms for organizational life, practices and processes, models, and relationships (Feeny, 2001).

There is widespread agreement, however, that the impact of on-line technologies has been very uneven, with a relatively small number of individuals and (particularly) companies quick to take advantage of new opportunities. This applies particularly to SMEs, a sector of the Australian economy where over one million companies provide jobs for almost five million members of the workforce (approximately 28% of the total Australian population). Yet, according to the Boston Consulting Group (2001), take-up of e-commerce by Australian SMEs is very slow — even by world standards. This is somewhat surprising given that, according to most studies undertaken (e.g., NOIE, 2001; Boston Consulting Group, 2001), Australia rates very highly by international standards with regard to the percentage of its population connected to the Internet. It is also a matter of considerable concern for the Australian Government.

Reasons identified for the slow take-up of e-commerce among Australian SMEs include: a lack of strategic awareness; lack of technical knowledge; mistrust of technology; the "what's in it for me" syndrome; high costs; and immediate, competing pressures (Boston Consulting Group, 2001). Another study (NOIE, 2001) suggests that among the major impediments to e-commerce up-take by small businesses are the lack of access to information and ICT skills, and the lack of practical experience in preparing, appreciating and applying a business case for e-commerce.

This is consistent with international experience. For example, Fife and Pereira (2002) demonstrate that lack of capital and skilled personnel, the high cost of e-commerce applications, and the need to re-engineer SMEs' core business processes remain as the most challenging impediments to the adoption of e-commerce applications by SMEs. For example, they point out that most estimates put the cost of establishing a web site at around $US15-17,000. Furthermore, in a recent survey of small businesses in the UK, 48% of respondents said that they did not have web sites and did not understand the potential benefits that might flow from e-commerce applications. In addition, only 50% of SMEs with web sites were using them to sell goods and services. In the US, 62% of SMEs reported not having web sites and only 12% were using them for on-line sales. The same research notes that since SMEs are part of some 80% of the supply chains of large corporations, these SMEs would require a re-engineering of their core business processes so that both SMEs and large corporations can realize e-commerce-generated cost savings (Fife & Pereira, 2002).

In an attempt to address these problems, the Australian Government has established its *Information Technology On-Line (ITOL)* program. This $13-million program provides seed funding for diverse on-line activities, with the aim of encouraging and hastening e-commerce take-up among Australian organizations — particularly SMEs. ITOL commenced in 1996 and, in this chapter, we report on a two-year study where we reviewed the program, its funded projects, collaborative arrangements between project consortia, problems and obstacles, and success measures. In this chapter, we focus mainly on the degree to which the program might be judged to have been successful (or otherwise) and the related issue of problems encountered. We also pay particular attention to relationship management — a critical issue, given that a fundamental feature of ITOL is its emphasis on collaboration between and among companies and other stakeholders.

ITOL PROGRAM

The ITOL Program (NOIE, 2001) aims to accelerate Australian adoption of e-commerce solutions by providing seed funding for diverse activities that encourage collaborative industry based projects, enhancing adoption of B2B practices across a wide range of industry sectors, especially by clusters of SMEs. It also aims at fostering awareness and strategic take-up of innovative e-commerce solutions within and across industry sectors, in order to deliver sustainable economy-wide returns and contribute to increased competitiveness. Since the program began in 1996, ITOL has already provided $7.5 million (in seven funding rounds) to support 81 innovative e-business projects across a diverse range of industry sectors and geographic regions. The extension of the program will see over $13 million in additional funding available to the program through 2006.

The range of projects is impressive and cluster around the following categories:

- *Applied solutions* – projects designed to use on-line technology to provide solutions to everyday problems (e.g., Livestock Exchange Online).
- *Data warehouse* – projects that will make industry information easier to access for businesses and consumers (e.g., Australian Tourism Data Warehouse).
- *Industry network* – projects designed to establish extranets for a specific industry or sector (e.g., Screen Industries Online).

- *Portal* – projects designed to encourage an industry or a region to move on-line by providing a specific facility (e.g., Water Industry Alliance Portal).
- *Supply chain management* – projects designed to improve the flow of products and services (e.g., Office Products E-Commerce Network (OPEN)).
- *Security solutions* – projects designed to develop technologies to address security concerns (e.g., Patient Centred Data using Smart Cards).
- *Standards setting* – projects primarily designed to establish common standards for a particular industry (e.g., E-Hub: The Electrical & Data Cabling Industry EC Initiative).
- *Others* – projects for training or e-commerce research (e.g., Electronic Commerce for SME Exporters).

National Office for the Information Economy (NOIE) CEO John Rimmer (ITOL Workshop, 29/3/01) explained his vision for NOIE as a key focal point in coordinating, advising and providing leadership for the Australian Government's consideration of Information Economic Issues. He emphasised the adoption of e-business and on-line systems within government and the development of an innovative supply side industry. He regarded the ITOL program as a *"catalyst for e-business adoption in the community,"* stressing the importance of a learning approach in projects, building capabilities and skills, broader learning in e-commerce for the wider community, and as an investment in Australia's future. Another NOIE Branch Manager, Phil Malone (ITOL Workshop, 29/3/01) emphasised NOIE's role as a broker and facilitator.

A recent report by Boston Consulting Group (2001) was positive in its assessment of ITOL, suggesting that:

> *Government policy to assist business adoption is off to a good start. NOIE has taken some excellent steps, and the government is rated highly in its "light touch" approach to regulation. ... The ... ITOL program to assist the private sector in exchange development ... is a welcome step. .... Government's role in e-business adoption is two-fold: to facilitate, where possible, the private sector's rapid adoption of e-business; and to ensure that government itself comes on-line quickly and efficiently. In both of these areas, Australia has enjoyed strong early leadership.*

As we shall see, the results of our own study were somewhat more mixed, with some extremely successful projects, some abject failures and many more where the "jury is still out."

STUDY METHODOLOGY

In our study, we aimed to address the following questions:

- To what extent have ITOL projects proved to be successful?
- What do the ITOL projects reveal about critical success factors for e-commerce projects?

The study took approximately two years to complete and was conducted during 2001/2002. We used key concepts from knowledge management, organization studies and resource-based perspectives, and employed both quantitative and qualitative methods including:

- A literature review covering areas such as e-commerce, collaboration, strategic alliances, new organizational forms, diffusion of technology, organizational knowledge and learning, and critical success factors.
- A review of similar grant programs in other countries.
- Analysis of ITOL project files.
- Participation in ITOL Peer Workshops.
- Interviews with key NOIE/ITOL personnel.
- Content analysis of publications such as government reports, company profiles, and relevant web sites.
- A survey sent to all 67 ITOL grant recipients with a response rate of 52%. The survey incorporated questions around the background of projects funded, the nature of collaboration, achievements, obstacles and outcomes, and comments on NOIE support.
- In-depth interviews, both face-to-face on site, and tele-conferenced, each of approximately two hours duration with a representative group of 27 projects across each of the five funding rounds. These involved both successful and unsuccessful projects and those that were completed and ongoing. These were taped with permission and transcribed for analysis. The selection criteria related to innovation, degree of success (as rated by survey respondents), e-commerce readiness, collaboration experience, measurable community benefits, and scale and diversity.
- Quantitative data analysis of survey responses and qualitative data analysis of interview data.

In this research, success was defined in terms allied to that emphasised by Douma et al. (2000): *"as the degree to which ... partners achieve their alliance objectives."* Failure was defined in terms of not meeting objectives, although in some cases objectives had been modified or changed with experience and, in others, objectives had not been completely met because time and/or funding had run out. It is important to note, however, that, in a wider sense, a lack of success did not necessarily imply total failure, in that the ITOL program was structured such that all participants could benefit from the experiences of others through knowledge-sharing processes.

Among some of the problems encountered during the research were the following:

- Some difficulty in getting up-to-date contact addresses for old ITOL projects, given that several of those in charge of completed projects had moved on to other jobs and could no longer be located. In addition, a number of the consortia for the different projects had disbanded or the partners were no longer in contact with each other.
- Some of those involved in the different projects claimed heavy workloads prevented them from participating in the research.
- Responses to both the survey and interview questions had to be assessed in light of the fact that grant recipients were probably reluctant to "bite the hand that was feeding them." To attempt to counter this, anonymity protocols were devised and rigorously enforced. Also, additional sources were referenced in cases where apparent inconsistencies were noted.

In the remainder of this paper, we focus mainly on findings related to project success and factors that influenced the same.

SOME KEY FINDINGS
Project Success Levels

On the surface, with 74.3% of survey respondents claiming to have met or exceeded their original goals, this is an excellent result. However, a degree of caution in interpreting these raw figures is warranted. Specifically: (1) we suspect the success rate among the 48% of grant recipients who did not return the survey might be considerably lower — particularly as we could not locate some recipients and some consortia had disbanded; and (2) as noted previously, self-interest should not be discounted (particularly with a number of respondents stating that they intended to apply for further funding). We should also note that many goals were fairly modest, relating (for example) to the establishment of a very basic infrastructure on which future project phases might build. This is perfectly understandable given the average level of funding support was only of the order of $90,000 and that most projects were still in a very early phase. However, it does mean that the survey response to this question says little about critical success factors such as eventual buy-in by intended users, measurable business and community benefits, etc.

Table 1. Extent to which project goals were achieved.

Survey Question: To what extent has the consortium met project goals and achieved desired outcomes?	
	%
Barely met original goals	17.1
Satisfactorily met desired goals and outcomes	62.9
Exceeded original objectives	11.4
No response	8.6
Total	100.0

Some projects, however, have achieved indisputable commercial success, a good example being TradeData. TradeData provides an information service to business and governments based on detailed up-to-date information on thousands of traded products. The data is sourced from Customs declarations. Using advanced data-mining techniques, the system supplies valuable market information on the size and price structure of markets, it can assess market shares, identify market opportunities, and can assist in assessing the effectiveness of its customers' market strategies. The facility was established in the mid-1990s — as a joint undertaking of Victoria University's Centre for Strategic Economic Studies and the Department of Applied Economics. Following the award of an ITOL grant in 1997, development was undertaken that enabled the organization to develop and test its technology, leading to the spin-off of its commercial arm in 2000. The commercial venture is now self-sustaining and both its customer base and the range of its operations continue to expand. One of the company principals believes the ITOL grant was critical:

> *Without this [ITOL grant], we probably wouldn't be in the position we are now in... [It] has revolutionised our business... we can do all sorts of new analysis that we couldn't have done or even contemplated before... It's given us a twenty-fold increase in performance, [which] was all theory until this project (Interviews, 2001).*

TradeData is by no means alone. Other ITOL projects that have achieved commercial success include the Water Industry Alliance Portal (designed to promote commercial cooperation between South Australian SMEs involved in the water industry), the Australian Tourism Data Warehouse (an on-line tourism destination and marketing services application) and My Southwest (a portal, sponsored by the local Chamber of Commerce, designed to promote the South West region of Western Australia). More detail on the first of these ventures is presented later in the chapter.

Figure 1. Project motives.

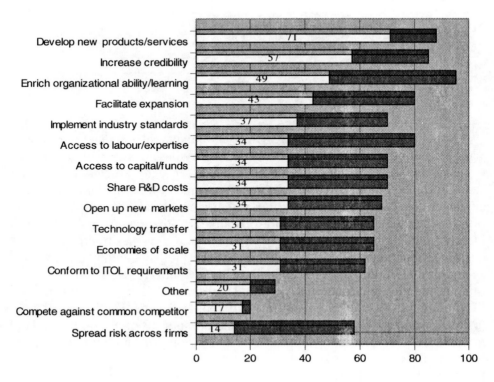

□	Major
■	Minor

Project Motives

Many of the consortia included members who were industry associations, technology providers, and business enterprises. In most (80%) of the projects surveyed, collaboration for the project was initiated by the principal grant recipient. In a number of cases (20%), the consortium partners had worked together before. Partners were generally (54%) based in both metropolitan and non-metropolitan areas, in single or multiple Australian States. There were three projects whose consortium members were based in non-metropolitan areas exclusively and only one project surveyed that had a global scope or links to partners outside Australia. The notion of "co-opetition" (Ordanini & Pol, 2001) was brought to life in 30% of the projects surveyed where members of the consortium were collaborating with their competitors. The primary contribution of project partners was in the form of "knowledge and expertise" with most of the principal grant recipients providing project management support.

As is illustrated in Figure 1, the following were cited as the most important motives for establishing the consortium: (1) to develop new products or services (71%); (2) to increase credibility (57%); (3) to enrich organizational ability and learning (49%); (4) to facilitate regional or international expansion (43%); and (5) to implement industry standards (37%). Surprisingly, 77% said they did not form their consortium to effectively compete against a common competitor. Our findings provide some support for Yeshekel et al.'s (2001) theoretical explanations for parties entering strategic alliances: namely, to create synergistic and competitive advantages through expanding an organization's resource base; and to build an organization's skills and capacities through acquisition of specialized and vital knowledge from other organizations.

Project Schedules

At first glance, there is an apparent inconsistency here: specifically, 74.3% of respondents stated that they met or exceeded their project goals (see Table 1), yet 51.4% of the same respondents reported significant delays (Table 2). In interviews, the reason for this discrepancy became apparent: namely, many of these projects were classed more as infrastructure development, research and development or "proof of concept" exercises. As such, project schedules and milestones did not assume the same importance as they might in mission-critical, mainstream information systems developments.

Table 2. Extent to which project milestones were met.

Survey Question: To what extent was the project able to meet most of its milestones?	
	%
With significant delays	51.4
As planned	31.4
Ahead of schedule	8.6
No response	8.6
Total	100.0

Table 3. Most significant type of problem encountered.

Survey Question: What type of problem most influenced the outcome of your project?	
	%
Operational	25.7
Technology	25.7
Relationship	14.3
Change management	22.9
Standards	0
No response	11.4
Total	100.0

Problems Encountered

From Table 3, it is apparent that operational, technology and change management problems were considered (roughly) equally culpable when assessing reasons for difficulties encountered (leading to missed milestones and objectives not realized). Operational problems include aspects such as funding and resourcing difficulties; technical problems cover hardware, software and data communications difficulties; and change management problems include end-user resistance and lack of interest, resistance to innovation, power-political factors and the like. As implied, relationship problems refer to difficulties in managing consortia relationships and standards problems include difficulties encountered in setting and conforming to agreed standards (and, in some cases, even finding appropriate standards). When these broad categories are broken down further, however, a somewhat different picture emerges. That is, respondents were asked whether or not they encountered specific types of problems and (partial) results are presented in Figure 2.

From Figure 2, we can see that the major problems encountered were estimating and securing resources. Also a lack of time to devote to projects was rated the fourth most serious problem. Thus resourcing issues were clearly the most problematic and, understandably, this was most evident in projects where little progress had been made. Also, in many cases, it was evident that there had been a very substantial under-estimation of the effort (at the coalface) required to bring potential end-users (particularly SMEs) on-board and provide them with required levels of ongoing support. For example:

I mean a lot of it was done marvellously well. Technically the project management and everything else at the more senior levels

Figure 2. Percentage of projects encountering problems.

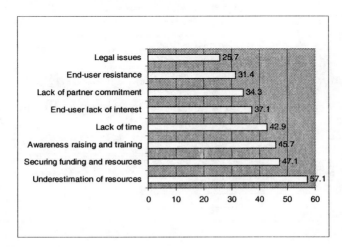

of cooperation …. But then once they got down to the point at which they had to bring in the [SMEs] and get buy-in there, that's where the whole thing fell down. … There's a need for a more independent third party, sitting in the middle, who can put the effort in and almost wear the white coat between the parties. … There might be industry associations … [but] they still don't drill down to this stage of going out and doing the hard work and making things happen (Interviews, 2001).

Preparing information systems so that they could interface with the project infrastructure (particularly database schema consistency) was a problem area mentioned by many interviewees, even though standards issues were not rated much of a problem in survey responses (see Table 3). However, almost all interviewees stated that they had greatly under-estimated the time they would have to devote to their targeted end-users. Not surprisingly then (Figure 2), we can see that end-user change management problems (lack of interest and resistance, and awareness-raising and training) ranked just behind resource issues in terms of difficulties encountered.

A few project participants raised the issue of underpricing or not costing services and the problem that things that were provided for free were not valued and appreciated. As one interviewee noted in hindsight:

people's perception of the value of something is clouded by how much they've had to pay for it… . It might have been a harder sell to get people to pay a subscription fee … but we would have picked up people who genuinely wanted to take advantage of what the technology offered (Interviews, 2001).

Finally, in our survey responses, problems faced in managing consortia relationships were not ranked all that highly in comparison to the other broad problem categories (Table 3). However, from Figure 2, we can see that lack of partner commitment and legal issues ranked six and eight (out of a total of 26 problem types) among survey respondents. These are definitely relationship management issues and, while not completely reflected in our survey results, the whole area of effectively forging and managing collaboration was consistently brought up by interviewees as one of *the* most critical success factors for ITOL projects.

RELATIONSHIP MANAGEMENT

As Paul and Antonio (2001) have noted, the most prevalent leadership flaw in e-business initiatives is a failure to nurture and manage the change that new economy business models create. Inter-organizational collaboration is absolutely intrinsic to e-commerce initiatives and clearly one of the strengths of the ITOL program comes from its insistence on projects being implemented by multi-partner alliances or consortia. As the survey results showed, the majority (69%) believed project outcomes were better achieved because of collaboration and sharing of resources. Yet one interviewee (2001) emphasised the *"complex matrix of collaboration."* Nowhere was this more evident than in the highly successful South Australian Water Industry Alliance Portal project.

The portal (http://www.waterindustry.com.au) has changed the culture of the water industry in South Australia. Here there is a most interesting mix of government and private sector participants where (Interview, 2001) *"the only way to work was to produce an alliance with an independent broker."* It is claimed that the alliance is *"... the only type in the world — a purely commercial cluster (not individual associations) and not technologically driven" (Interview, 2001).* With 170 financial member companies and a preponderance of SMEs lacking export skills, the alliance has members collaborating and sharing resources and IP and joint bidding for projects. The philosophy of the alliance is *"providing integrated solutions"* (Interview, 2001).

The Water Industry Alliance formed in 1998 includes 170 South Australian-based companies and related organizations seeking to develop their export markets, or wishing to form strategic alliances with other water-related organizations in Australia and offshore. The Alliance is focused on networking and dissemination of strategic information on emerging and current business opportunities. Member companies are encouraged to join together in strategic alliance teams to tender for specific projects.

Figure 3. Water industry alliance structure.

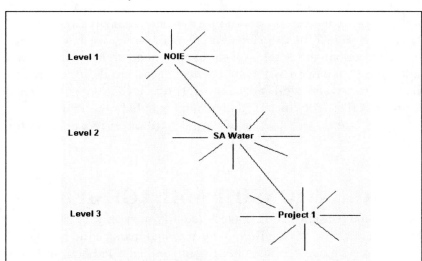

The Water Industry Alliance portal is exceptional in that it was not simply designed for information dissemination. It was specifically aimed at promoting on-line collaboration. By using the portal as a focal point for reviewing business opportunities and for communicating with each other, the alliance members are able to form business clusters that enhance their competitiveness and ability to offer innovative cost-effective solutions to customers in Australia and overseas. The portal is industry-driven and was identified as a priority need by the alliance members.

Figure 3 shows the various levels of networking and collaboration happening in this project. As the diagram shows, NOIE is the central facilitator (at Level 1) and, in the early stages of the project (grant application preparation and evaluation), is right at the centre of most activity. But later when the grant is approved, NOIE's involvement diminishes and its facilitation role is taken over by the project consortium (or SA Water at Level 2). Finally, when different consortiums are formed and win projects, SA Water's role is reduced to what is essentially, a watching and monitoring brief.

One further point we should note here is that, while effective collaboration at all levels is essential, the role of SA Water in facilitating and maintaining alliances was absolutely critical — and, indeed, in our view this was the single most important critical success factor with respect to this project. Furthermore, their role extended way beyond provision of the portal, the generation of content and signing up alliance members — with one especially important activity being their vigorous promotion of regular, informal, social get-togethers where alliance members could establish ties and friendships not generally feasible in a purely virtual world.

It was clear that in this case the right person was put in charge of the alliance, a project manager who was most effective at building relationships (on-line and face-to-face), establishing a working trust among consortium members, and weaving the fine balance between conflict and consensus. The project revealed the benefits of well-managed networking and relationship-building partnering practices and mindsets rather than a focus purely on transactions. Moreover, there was a real understanding of interdependence, of one organization's fate linking with a myriad of others in co-creating and utilizing opportunities (Conlon & Giovagnoli, 1998). Finally, the project avoided what Davies (2001) has claimed is the major reason alliances fail — that of opportunistic behaviour.

ITOL PROGRAM: FUTURE CHALLENGES

In spite of its achievements to date, there are a range of issues ITOL (and its sponsor, NOIE) must confront.

Funding

Clearly, there was some concern across the projects about the level of funding NOIE provided. For instance:

> *There is never enough money in ITOL grants to get full buy-in from organizations. Project management investment is needed from organizations." Or, "... the income we are generating is just only barely able to sustain the administration itself. So from the educational and marketing point of view, our funds are really very limited. ... We need to do more marketing than we can afford for our sustainable budget to grow" (Interviews, 2001). Another contends, "What NOIE or the Federal Government has to realize ... is that in order for community portals to become sustainable, first of all they have absolutely to be funded for two to three years minimum; three to five years would be really good" (Interviews, 2001).*

There were several instances where people were actually working on a voluntary basis because of inadequate funding levels. But despite the long hours and the countless in-kind contributions that they put in, many of those interviewed feel rewarded as evident in the following quote:

> *... The [money] that NOIE provided initially was in no way enough for us to do what they asked us to do. ... I haven't been paid for any of the work that I've done for the last year. Now the reason why I've stuck in there is because I really believe in this" (Interviews, 2001).*

For those projects already overtly successful, the broader issue of access to capital externally, in order to realise the potential originally backed by ITOL, was a growing concern. For example, in one successful pilot project that could have delivered industry-wide benefits had it received additional support for project expansion, the former project manager said:

> *I think we did meet the minimum requirement but I didn't feel it was an accomplishment. I think we failed extensively to deliver an effective ... portal for industry. ... I think we...delivered it, but in the lighter sense. The pity about the whole thing is that, you know, the gust of the thing was there and [if there was] just a little bit more effort, more money for the sums, something really good could have come out of the whole thing (Interviews, 2001).*

There were others issues of concern, such as: to what extent NOIE was actually focused on innovative e-commerce. One group suggested that NOIE was *"backing certain styles, that is, imposing an answer and backing quick fixes"* (Interviews, 2001) instead of backing projects that were in for the long haul. The same group also felt that projects were *"all done like orphans"* (Interviews, 2001), and that there were many similar projects that were not innovative and merely reinventing the wheel. The view was that, while understanding the context of political agendas, NOIE must take a macro view of the economy and understand its key leverage points so that the projects it supports can tackle some key areas and cause a ripple effect for the wider community.

Networking

It was thought that NOIE should be a facilitator of personal networking, enabling learning among the ITOL projects. In addition, some felt they had had little connection with NOIE staff aside from funding news. Still others, who received only part of the amount they requested, suggested that there should be:

> *"Better communication about decision parameters and outcomes of grants. ... NOIE should employ staff to communicate with projects" (Interviews, 2001).*

One interviewee (2001) suggested that NOIE:

> *"...take [something like] $120,000 out of the funding pool to employ two people whose responsibility could be to keep in touch with the coordinators of 16-18 funded projects, even if it was only on a monthly or bi-monthly basis. Just to get a five-minute report, and to have a conversation every now and again." Still another said, "We would welcome greater involvement with ITOL on a project level and for them to have a greater understanding of what exactly is going on. ... We'd love to see them down here more often ... getting involved" (Interviews, 2001). The same project team encouraged NOIE staff to "go out in the field and actually touch and see some of the participants" (Interviews, 2001).*

Concern was expressed that ITOL grant money was spent and that NOIE gets little for its efforts. Consequently, some interviewees (2001) suggested that *"NOIE should better capitalise on the investment"* and continue the innovations commenced by helping open doors for the projects in both Commonwealth and State Departments. Within such sentiments, a view was expressed that NOIE *"should provide pathways to further capital required" (Interviews, 2001).* This echoed the sentiment that there should be a better payback to NOIE mentioned by quite a few respondents. For example:

> *"NOIE should promote the results of the projects and understand where the benefits could be applied ... helping other agencies" (Interviews, 2001).*

Knowledge Sharing

The issue of better sharing of knowledge and learning gained was raised. For example:

"... the whole program was fantastically useful .... We certainly see a situation wherein anybody who has received monies should be basically obliged to share their information freely with others. We certainly don't want to see duplication of efforts and people reinventing the wheel if it can be avoided. We think that should be a very fundamental part of the system in the future" (Interviews, 2001). Or, "Good if ITOL and scarce resources used the experience now to enhance the new projects ... [there are] common themes in challenges undertaken. ... See NOIE doing more networking" (Interviews, 2001).

A more pragmatic approach to the learning issue came from another interviewee (2001):

Overall I am very supportive of ITOL but I think it is quaint and it fills a niche and it is more successful than it isn't, but for all the wrong reasons. Because if you look at almost all of the ITOL projects, you could find a reason to fail them all, and some more than others ... . [But] these people are developing Australian knowledge and technology and even though it fails, it doesn't — because these people learn, their way of thinking changes ... . So the money in itself is not enough to make things happen but it is enough money to make other people change to make things happen. That's why I think ITOL is such a success. It takes away the squabbling and [encourages people]...to cooperate.

There was also the other side of learning and education emphasised, the need for better publicity:

"There's probably ... not a high recognition of NOIE in the industry... you've really got to explain what NOIE is all about" (Interviews, 2001). One project team notes, "...there's a whole range of things out there that presents an interesting opportunity for a national showcase. ... [Give] a bit of emphasis on Australian made. ... It's so important for our IT industry to have somebody championing our own product development" (Interviews, 2001).

The same project team provided a more concrete example by suggesting that instead of presenting ITOL projects by funding rounds on NOIE's web site, the successful ones should instead be showcased to give others a greater degree of understanding as to what the project is all about and what its deliverables are.

This would minimize duplication of efforts, enhance knowledge sharing and facilitate networking.

Operational Concerns

There were, however, some issues raised about NOIE's understanding of its clients. As one interviewee (2001) mentioned, *"NOIE doesn't know who the audience is."* The same interviewee expounds:

> *I think that despite all their submission guidelines and reporting procedures and everything, NOIE sometimes does not get right who the people they are giving the money to. ... What I'm saying is if you get somebody in there who is a bit of a megalomaniac with regards to the money, then you have a power situation, and then you've got problems in making it work. So my advice ... is to have a [closer] look at the submission, who's written the submission, and who it is aimed at"* (Interviews, 2001).

One project leader suggested that NOIE put more effort into properly assessing the viability of consortia applying for grants but concedes that this is not an easy task since *"talk is really cheap, and you can get plenty of it out there"* (Interviews, 2001).

Setting up the appropriate review processes for the projects before, during, and after was an issue raised by some project personnel. For instance:

> *"And I think from an ITOL point of view, this should be part of all ITOL things. There should be some discipline so that they have a common way of recording this nebulous thing called 'in kind"* (Interviews, 2001).

CONCLUSION

E-commerce is having major impacts on our global social world, with a key influence in the way organizations and governments configure, manage, and run their businesses. Often this requires a change of paradigms, of routines, and challenges to the traditional status quo and power domains. Recognizing the power of the information economy and knowledge as a key ingredient for competitive advantage at a national level, the Australian Government (as have others, such as Singapore) has promoted e-commerce practices through its ITOL financial assistance program. While there have been a number of specific successes as outlined in the paper, perhaps the most overwhelming general success has been in the education of business and the broader community to the notion of e-commerce and the vital competence of effective organizational collaboration — without which new organizational learning and knowledge are harder to achieve. This helps the Government's broader agenda of moving

Australia to a position where businesses and consumers alike are well-placed to take maximum advantage of technological advances as they emerge. As such, the catalytic role of the Government in the e-commerce field has proved a crucial one.

REFERENCES

Boston Consulting Group. (2001). *BCA E-Business Roundtable.* Sydney: Business Council of Australia.

Conlon, J. & Giovagnoli, M. (1998). *The Power of Two.* San Francisco: Jossey-Bass.

Davies, W. (2001). *Partner Risk: Managing the Downside of Strategic Alliances.* IN: Purdue University Press.

Douma, M., Bilderbeek, J., Idenbur, P. & Looise, J. (2000). Strategic Alliances: Managing the Dynamics of Fit. *Long Range Planning.* 33, 579-598.

Feeny, D. (2001). Making Business Sense of the E-Opportunity. *MIT Sloan Management Review,* 42(2), 41-51.

Fife, E. & Pereira, F. (2002). Economic, Social and Cultural Factors Affecting the Adoption of E-Commerce Applications in Small and Medium Enterprises: A Cross-Country Comparison. *Proceedings of the 24th Annual Pacific Telecommunications Conference (PTC'2002).* Honolulu, (January 13-17, pp. 1-8).

NOIE (2001). B2B E-Commerce: Capturing Value Online. Retrieved from the World Wide Web: http://www.noie.gov.au/publications.

Ordanini, A. & Pol, A. (2001). Infomediation and Competitive Advantage in B2B Digital Marketplaces. *European Journal of Management,* 19(3), 276-285.

Paul, L. & Antonio, F. (2001). 12 Rules to Avoid E-Business Failure. *E-Business Advisor,* 19(1), 38-42.

Yeheskel, O., Shenkar, O., Fiegenvaum, A., Cohen, E. & Geffen, I. (2001). Cooperative Wealth Creation: Strategic Alliances in Israel Medical-Technology Ventures. *Academy of Management Executive,* 15(1), 16-25.

About the Authors

Brian J. Corbitt, PhD, is pro vice chancellor (Online Services)/ vice president at Deakin University, Melbourne, Australia. He is responsible for the integration of systems that support Deakin's commitment to online support for teaching and learning. He is also a chair professor of Information Systems and was head of School in the School of Information Systems at Deakin University in Melbourne (2001-2002). He had previously been JADE professor of e-commerce at Victoria University of Wellington (2000-2001). Prior to that, Professor Corbitt taught Information Systems and Management at the University of Melbourne in the Department of Information Systems and at Monash in the Department of Management. He was also head of College, International House in the University of Melbourne. This followed a successful career as a high school teacher and Principal in Victorian High Schools. His research specializes in electronic commerce and IT policy development, analysis and implementation, in the impact of culture on information production and interpretation, and in business modelling and electronic commerce trade relationships, and knowledge management and e-learning in tertiary institutions. His published research includes over 120 scholarly publications in journals and books and includes joint authorship of four books. The body of work also includes reports to public and private agencies on smart cards, implementation of electronic commerce in SMEs in Australia, on intranets and on electronic commerce policy implementation. He has a great deal of experience in the implementation of e-commerce solutions in developing countries, especially Thailand and Malaysia, and in the implementation of EC in Singapore. He has also been responsible with the Ministry of Economic Development for the writing and launch of the e-commerce policy for New Zealand and currently planning for implementation of that policy via applied programs for all levels of industry. Professor Corbitt has completed a five year consultancy to the Thai Ministry of University Affairs on management reform and change in the Thai public university sector through the TASEAP Project. This work has resulted in delivery of a two day seminar on SMEs and e-commerce for the Thai Ministry of Commerce and the Institute of SMEs in Bangkok. He has also been consulting to New Zealand and Australian companies on the development and implementation of B2B exchanges applicable to SMEs.

Nabeel A. Y. Al-Qirim is a lecturer of IS, a module coordinator of eBusiness IT and a researcher (path) in the School of Computer and Information Sciences, Faculty of Business, Auckland University of Technology (AUT), Auckland, New Zealand. He has a Certificate (Education), bachelor's in Electrical Engineering, Post Graduate Diploma in Information Systems (Honors with distinction), MBA, and PhD. His research interests and publications are in IT and eBusiness in small business, SCM, mobile business, telemedicine and eBusiness in NGOs and in SMEs in developing countries. He is the editor of *Electronic Business in Small to Medium-Sized Enterprises: Frameworks, Issues, and Implications* and co-author of the book, *eBusiness, Government & Small and Medium-Sized Enterprises: Opportunities and Challenges.* He worked in the IT industry for 12 years as a consultant and in managing total IT solutions with international companies: IBM, Compaq, Data General, Group Bull, and Siemens Nixdorf.

* * *

Olayele Adelakun is an assistant professor of MIS at DePaul University Chicago, Illinois (USA), School of Computer Science, Telecommunication and Information Systems. His research focuses on IT outsourcing, ERP systems implementation, and information systems quality and evaluation. He has conducted case studies in both medium size companies and multinational companies in Finland and the US. He was the chairman of the 2001 and 2002 IT outsourcing conference and the moderator of the 2003 offshore outsourcing panel discussion at DePaul University. He has also given several executives presentation. He has published over 30 articles in conferences, books and journals. He holds an MS in Information Processing Science from University of Oulu, Oulu, Finland and PhD in Information Systems from the Turku School of Economics and Business Administration, Turku, Finland.

Don Amoroso is associate professor of Information & Decision Sciences at San Diego State University, USA. He is coordinator of the Information Systems Group and teaches classes in information systems, Web development, and strategy formulation with executive MBA students. He manages the hiring and evaluation of part-time faculty members, curriculum development and other academic programs. Prior to his appointment at SDSU, Dr. Amoroso worked with GE Capital as a director of enterprise solutions and with Solista/GartnerGroup as a consulting partner. He has authored 53 articles and proceedings, written five books, presented at more than 45 professional conferences and venues, and managed the Information Systems Department while at the University of Colorado, Colorado Springs. He has published in journals such as *Journal of Management Information Systems, Data Base,* and *Information & Management.* Dr. Amoroso has been director of the Pacific Research Institute for Information Management and Systems (PRIISM) with the goal to disseminate information technology findings in Asian-based organizations. He has been mini-track chair for the Hawaii International Conference on Systems Sciences from 1992 through present and is track chair for the current AMCIS Conference on Social Issues in Information Systems. He was inducted into the Who's Who Worldwide in 1995 for contributions to international organizations changing the distribution of technology information within the Pacific Rim. Donald received his bachelor's degree in Accounting and Finance from Old Dominion University in 1980 and his MBA and PhD from the University of Georgia in 1984 and 1986, respectively.

Suzanne Bergin-Seers is the research coordinator of the Small Business Research Unit and has been involved in research activity concerned with small business for six years. During that time she has tendered for and managed many industry and government commissioned projects as well as academic research. She has published in international journals and has presented research papers at national and international conferences. Suzanne has undertaken research projects in a range of areas including quality management, information technology, trade, training and support needs and legislative requirements.

Piet Boekhoudt is a scientific researcher and project manager at the Telematica Instituut, The Netherlands. He holds a master's degree and PhD in Applied Mathematics from the University of Twente and has been appointed as an assistant professor at the University of Maastricht from 1989 to 1998. At the Telematica Instituut he has been involved in a number of scientific and applied projects in areas such as business and e-business process (re)engineering and application service providing (ASP). He is currently leading the ASPect project on the introduction of ASP to Dutch small and medium-sized enterprises.

John Breen is an associate professor in Accounting and head of the Small Business Research Unit at Victoria University of Technology, Australia. He has been involved in small business research activity for more than 10 years, with particular interest in education and training issues. He is a past president of the Small Enterprise Association of Australia and New Zealand (SEAANZ) and a member of the Small Business Centre of Excellence of CPA Australia. John is currently working on a project with growth businesses and another investigating the most appropriate form of communicating information to small firms.

Deborah Bunker is a senior lecturer in the School of Information Systems, Technology and Management (SISTM) at the University of New South Wales (UNSW), Australia. She is the director of Publications for Australasian Association of Information Systems (AAIS) and is on the editorial board for the *Australian Journal of Information Systems*. She has been a guest editor for the electronic journal, *Philosophical and Conceptual Foundations of Information Systems* and is secretary of IFIP TG8.6 on Transfer, Diffusion and Implementation of Technology. Deborah has research interests that cover the management and diffusion of electronic commerce technologies in small and large businesses in relation to institutional culture. Deborah also has wide-ranging experience as a senior consultant within the IT industry in the finance, transport, insurance and government sectors in projects that have included change management, end-user system development, human resource and financial system development and implementation and open systems architectures.

Stephen Burgess (MBus, RMIT; PhD, Monash) is a senior lecturer in the School of Information Systems at Victoria University, Melbourne, Australia. He has a bachelor's degree in Accounting and a graduate diploma in Commercial Data Processing, both from Victoria University, Australia; an MBus (Information Technology) from RMIT, Australia, and a PhD at Monash University, Australia, in the area of small business to consumer interactions on the Internet. His research and teaching interests include the use of IT in small business, the strategic use of IT, B2C electronic commerce and management IT education. He has recently edited a book through Idea Group Publishing, *Managing Information Technology in Small Business: Challenges and Solutions*. Stephen is a cofounder of the new research group and IRMA Special Research Cluster on Small Business and Information Technology (www.businessandlaw.vu.edu.au/sbirit/) and a Research-in-Progress chair at the ISOneWorld conference (www.ISOneWorld.org).

Gordon Campbell (BEc, Monash; BArts, Melb; BEd, La Trobe; MArts, Charles Sturt) was a lecturer in Management at Victoria University, Australia. His research interests include the measurement and ranking of communication skills in Australian organisations. He contributed to the text *Communication Skills in Practice* and to the *Communication Skills Workbook* as well as authoring the popular *The Little Black Book*, both editions of which have been instrumental in the improvement of oral presentation and written skills of Victoria University's students. Gordon has carried out consultancy work for a number of state and local government organisations in Australia.

Sten Carlsson is a Doctor of Philosophy (PhD) and senior lecturer in Information Systems at Karlstad University (Sweden), specializing in learning, communication and competence issues in systems development. He heads the research group "Systems Development for Learning Organizations." His special interest springs from practical experience of systems development, in both public organizations and private companies. Sten runs a research project on electronic business together with small and medium-sized enterprises (SMEs) in the Karlstad region within the scope of a large venture called Wermland E-Commerce market. He is connected to the multi-disciplinary Human IT research centre and has participated in CENS (Centre for Service to Business) — both of his projects working to improve the contacts between the university and local companies. Sten has laid the foundations for the industry board that is related to the subject of Information Systems.

Tanya Castleman is professor of Information Systems at Deakin University (Australia) and director of research in the School of Information Systems. The main focus of her research is the organisational and social aspects of information and communication technologies, especially the Internet and e-commerce. Her research is practically-oriented and she has conducted a broad range of research and consultancy projects. Tanya has published internationally on issues including: the adoption and implementation of e-commerce by small and medium enterprises, employment implications of e-commerce applications, the Internet and regional sustainability, ICT in health and human service delivery and government electronic service delivery.

Marina Cavill is a research consultant in the School of Information Systems at Deakin University, Australia, and has extensive experience as a commercial consultant in the area of information technology, regional development and SME use of technology. Marina has been involved in many research and consultancy projects involving telecommunications and communuity needs and issues in e-commerce use for small business. Much of her work has been oriented to government policy and community development. Marina worked for nine years with Telstra as a senior researcher and business development manager and for 10 years in local government as a strategic planner.

Stephen B. Chau initially graduated from the University of Tasmania (Australia) with a BEc. He returned to the university some time after to complete an Honors degree in Computing and a Doctoral degree from the School of Information Systems. His PhD explored the utilisation of e-commerce amongst a range of Australian SMEs. Currently Stephen is working as a research fellow with the School of Information Systems in the Smart Internet CRC. Prior to returning to post-graduate studies Stephen worked as an IT consultant in several large corporate and government agencies. Stephen maintains an interest in the use of e-commerce by SMEs and organisational change facilitated by Internet communication technologies. He has written a number of Australasian and International academic publications on the subject electronic commerce and SMEs.

Freek Ebeling is a scientific researcher and project manager at the Telematica Instituut, The Netherlands. He holds a master's degree in Computer Science. At the Telematica Instituut he has been involved in a number of scientific and applied projects, carrying out research in the following areas: innovation, scenario planning, mobile technology, services and applications. He is currently leading the iMPact project on the introduction of electronic marketplaces to Dutch small and medium-sized enterprises.

Michael S.H. Heng is associate professor of Information Systems and assistant director of the IS Doctoral School at the University of South Australia. His current research interests include globalization, IS strategy, e-business, IS development and open source software. He is an associate editor of the *Journal of Electronic Commerce Research*, and co-program chair of Pacific Asia Conference on Information Systems 2003. His publications have appeared in *Information & Organization, Information Systems Journal, Journal of Strategic Information Systems, Information & Management* and *Akademika*.

Leo Tan Wee Hin has a PhD in Marine Biology. He holds the concurrent appointments of director of the National Institute of Education, professor of Biological Sciences in Nanyang Technological University, and president of the Singapore National Academy of Science. Prior to this, he was director of the Singapore Science Centre. His research interests are in the fields of marine biology, science education, museum science, telecommunications, and transportation. He has published numerous research papers in international refereed journals.

Maria-Eugenia Iacob is a scientific researcher at Telematica Instituut (The Netherlands) since July 2000. She holds a PhD in Mathematical Analysis from the University Babes-Bolyai of Cluj-Napoca, Romania. She also worked for this university, from 1990 until 2000, as an assistant and then associate professor in the Department of Computer Science. At Telematica Instituut she has carried out research in several projects in the areas of business and e-business process (re)engineering (GigaPort, Refmod and iMPact) and of information systems architectures (ArchiMate).

Murray E. Jennex is an assistant professor at San Diego State University (USA) and president of the Foundation for Knowledge Management (LLC). Dr.

Jennex specializes in knowledge management, system analysis and design, IS security, and organizational effectiveness. He has managed projects in applied engineering and business and information systems development and implementation. His industrial and consulting experience includes nuclear generation, electrical utilities, communications, health services, and governmental agencies. Dr. Jennex is the author of numerous publications on knowledge management, end user computing, international information systems, organizational memory systems, and software outsourcing. He holds a BA in Chemistry and Physics from William Jewell College, an MBA and an MS in Software Engineering from National University, and an MS in Telecommunications Management and PhD in Information Systems from the Claremont Graduate University. Dr. Jennex is also a registered professional mechanical engineer in the state of California.

Dawn N. Jutla is an associate professor in Sobey School of Business at Saint Mary's University (Canada) and in Canada. She holds a doctorate in Computer Science, has worked in the Information Technology field for the past 18 years, and presently teaches, researches, consults, and authors in the area of e-business. She is the co-author of more than 40 publications in the computing, information system, electronic business, and e-government areas including refereed conference papers, journal articles, and book chapters. She also speaks frequently at international venues. She is co-author of the book, *e-Business Readiness: A Customer Focused Framework* (published in the Addison Wesley Information Technology Series). Her latest works are in e-privacy and knowledge management.

Robert MacGregor is senior lecturer and head of Discipline in Information Systems at the University of Wollongong, Australia. His research expertise lies in the areas of information technology (IT) and electronic commerce (e-commerce) in small to medium enterprises (SMEs). He has authored a number of journal and conference publications examining the use and adoption of IT in SMEs. Rob is also the editor of the *Australian Journal of Information Systems* and was conference chair of the Australian Conference of Information Systems in 1992. In his spare time, Rob writes music. His most recent work is the symphony "Alba."

Monika Magnusson is a PhD student at the Department of Information Technology, Karlstad University, Sweden. She is conducting research in the area of electronic commerce. Her main research interests are small business adoption of e-commerce, implementation methods, and change management in connection to e-commerce. She is participating in several research projects on electronic commerce, one of them particularly addressing small and medium-sized enterprises. Monika Magnusson is giving courses in Information System Development and Analysis of Change on the undergraduate level.

Muhammad Mahmood is senior lecturer in the School of Applied Economics, Faculty of Business and Law, Victoria University, Melbourne, Australia. He has a PhD from the University of Melbourne. His research interests include international trade and industrial organization. Dr. Mahmood has published in international journals and has co-authored a book, *International Business and Australia*. He has also contributed to edited books. Dr. Mahmood has lectured or served as a visiting scholar at numerous universities including Melbourne University, Sheffield Hallam University and Greenwich University. He has worked in economic research and statistics areas in a number of Australian Federal Departments in Canberra.

G. Michael McGrath gained his PhD from Macquarie University and is currently professor of Information Systems at Victoria University, Melbourne, Australia. He has more than 30 years experience in the IT industry — mostly at Telstra, Australia, where he worked in a variety of senior positions. His current research is focused mainly on database integration, strategic alliances, and applications of IT in the tourism industry. In recent years he has conducted research and consultancy work for Telstra, IBM, Centrelink, the ADF and NOIE (National Office for the Information Economy). He has authored over 80 refereed journal and conference papers.

Elizabeth More is deputy vice-chancellor of the University of Canberra, Australia. She holds a PhD from the University of NSW and has published widely, both locally and internationally, in the field of organisation studies, particularly in the areas of organisational communication, culture, change, communications technology, and policy. Her current research focus is on inter-organizational collaboration, strategic alliances, networks, and e-commerce communities. She is a member of the NSW Government's Council on the Cost and Quality of Government; a member of the Board for the Australian Centre for Advanced Computing and Communications; and a member of the ACT Government's Knowledge Economy Board.

Sushil K. Sharma is currently assistant professor in the Department of Information Systems & Operations Management, at the Ball State University, Muncie, Indiana (USA). He received his PhD in Information Systems. Dr. Sharma has a unique distinction of having been conferred two doctoral degrees. Prior to joining Ball State, Dr. Sharma held the associate professor position at the Indian Institute of Management, Lucknow (India) and visiting research associate professor at the Department of Management Science, University of Waterloo, Canada. Co-author of two textbooks in Information Technology (*Programming in C* and *Understanding Unix*), Dr. Sharma's research contributions have appeared in many peer-reviewed national and international journals, conferences and seminars' proceedings. Dr. Sharma's primary teaching and research interests are in E-Commerce, networking environments, network security, ERP systems, database management systems, information systems analysis & design and knowledge management. Apart from teaching and guiding students for various innovative IS-related topics, Dr. Sharma has wide experience consulting in information systems and e-commerce area and has served as an advisor and consultant to several government and private organizations including World Bank funded projects. Dr. Sharma has also conducted number of executive development programs for the corporate world and Government organizations on e-commerce, networking environments, and database-related subjects.

Robert Sims (Master of Business; Bachelor of Economics, Monash) is currently senior lecturer in the Dept. of Accounting and Finance, Victoria University of Technology, Australia. His interests include accounting, and IT. Sims has many years experience in university administrative roles, more recently in the establishment/management of off-shore masters and undergraduate programs. He has 20 years experience with small businesses as an accountant/advisor and extensive experience as a consultant to private and public sector organizations.

R. Subramaniam has a PhD in Physical Chemistry. He is an assistant professor at the National Institute of Education in Nanyang Technological University and honorary secretary of the Singapore National Academy of Science. Prior to this, he was acting head of Physical Sciences at the Singapore Science Centre. His research interests are in the fields of physical chemistry, science education, theoretical cosmophysics, museum science, telecommunications, and transportation He has published several research papers in international refereed journals.

Paul Turner is an honors graduate of the School of Oriental and African Studies, University of London. He has a master's degree in Information Systems and a doctoral degree from the School of Informatics, City University, London. Prior to joining the School of Information Systems, Paul was a research fellow at CRID (Computer, Telecommunications and Law Research Institute) in Belgium where he worked on a variety of European Commission projects in the field of electronic commerce, telecommunications and intellectual property rights. Paul's strong research focus in the field of electronic commerce has continued in his work as senior research fellow at the University of Tasmania, Australia. For two years, Paul was also research manager for the Tasmanian Electronic Commerce Centre (www.tecc.com.au). Paul is currently the SME coordinator for the Smart Internet CRC.

Lejla Vrazalic is a lecturer in Information Systems at the University of Wollongong, Australia. She was awarded the University Medal in 1999. Her research interests are in the areas of human computer interaction (HCI) and e-commerce. As part of her PhD, Lejla is developing a usability testing method based on Activity Theory which can be applied to the evaluation of web sites. Lejla is also currently involved in developing training programs for new researchers.

Yu Chung William Wang is a course coordinator/lecturer in the Department of Management Information Systems, Yuan-Pei University of Science and Technology, Taiwan. With the experiences of being a telecom and computer engineer, he is currently supervising research groups in Taiwan in the field of B2B integration, interfirm dynamics, and information strategy. Focusing on the interaction and business network boundaries, his researches also relate to systems analysis, B2B e-commerce, and supply chain management for both large firms and SMEs.

Nilmini Wickramasinghe (PhD, MBA, Graduate Diploma Management Studies, BS, AmusA (piano) AmusA (violin)) After graduating from The University of Melbourne, Australia, with a Bachelor of Science in Mathematics and Computing, Nilmini completed her MBA at Melbourne Business School. In August 1995 she accepted a full scholarship to undertake PhD studies with Michael Ginzberg at Case Western Reserve University, Ohio (USA). During this time she was involved with many research projects focusing on health care issues. She was awarded her PhD in Management Information Systems in April 1999. On the completion of her PhD, Dr. Wickramasinghe returned to Australia where she was a senior lecturer Business Information Systems at The University of Melbourne, Australia, in the Faculty of Economics and Commerce. Currently, she is an assistant professor in the Computer and Information Science Department at the James J. Nance College of Business Administration at Cleveland State University, Ohio (USA). She teaches Information Systems at the undergraduate and graduate levels in particular, Knowledge Management as well as e-commerce and m-commerce, IT for Competitive Advantage and Organizational Impacts of Technology. She is currently carrying out research and is published in the areas of management of technology, in the field of health care as well as focusing on IS issues especially as they relate to knowledge work and e-business. She can reached at n.wickramasinghe@csuohio.edu.

Anne Wiggins (a.wiggins@lse.ac.uk) is currently researching her PhD at the Department of Information Systems of the London School of Economics and Political Science. The main focus of her research has been the strategic implications of e-business on SMEs in the UK in light of EU policy initiatives. She also holds an undergraduate degree from the University of Sydney and a master's degree from the University of London's Birkbeck College. As a consultant in the field of IT she has worked for public and commercial organisations in the US, Australia and the UK.

Index

NEW from Idea Group Publishing

- **The Enterprise Resource Planning Decade: Lessons Learned and Issues for the Future**, Frederic Adam and David Sammon/ ISBN:1-59140-188-7; eISBN 1-59140-189-5, © 2004
- **Electronic Commerce in Small to Medium-Sized Enterprises**, Nabeel A. Y. Al-Qirim/ ISBN: 1-59140-146-1; eISBN 1-59140-147-X, © 2004
- **e-Business, e-Government & Small and Medium-Size Enterprises: Opportunities & Challenges**, Brian J. Corbitt & Nabeel A. Y. Al-Qirim/ ISBN: 1-59140-202-6; eISBN 1-59140-203-4, © 2004
- **Multimedia Systems and Content-Based Image Retrieval**, Sagarmay Deb ISBN: 1-59140-156-9; eISBN 1-59140-157-7, © 2004
- **Computer Graphics and Multimedia: Applications, Problems and Solutions**, John DiMarco/ ISBN: 1-59140-196-86; eISBN 1-59140-197-6, © 2004
- **Social and Economic Transformation in the Digital Era**, Georgios Doukidis, Nikolaos Mylonopoulos & Nancy Pouloudi/ ISBN: 1-59140-158-5; eISBN 1-59140-159-3, © 2004
- **Information Security Policies and Actions in Modern Integrated Systems**, Mariagrazia Fugini & Carlo Bellettini/ ISBN: 1-59140-186-0; eISBN 1-59140-187-9, © 2004
- **Digital Government: Principles and Best Practices**, Alexei Pavlichev & G. David Garson/ISBN: 1-59140-122-4; eISBN 1-59140-123-2, © 2004
- **Virtual and Collaborative Teams: Process, Technologies and Practice**, Susan H. Godar & Sharmila Pixy Ferris/ ISBN: 1-59140-204-2; eISBN 1-59140-205-0, © 2004
- **Intelligent Enterprises of the 21st Century**, Jatinder Gupta & Sushil Sharma/ ISBN: 1-59140-160-7; eISBN 1-59140-161-5, © 2004
- **Creating Knowledge Based Organizations**, Jatinder Gupta & Sushil Sharma/ ISBN: 1-59140-162-3; eISBN 1-59140-163-1, © 2004
- **Knowledge Networks: Innovation through Communities of Practice**, Paul Hildreth & Chris Kimble/ISBN: 1-59140-200-X; eISBN 1-59140-201-8, © 2004
- **Going Virtual: Distributed Communities of Practice**, Paul Hildreth/ISBN: 1-59140-164-X; eISBN 1-59140-165-8, © 2004
- **Trust in Knowledge Management and Systems in Organizations**, Maija-Leena Huotari & Mirja Iivonen/ ISBN: 1-59140-126-7; eISBN 1-59140-127-5, © 2004
- **Strategies for Managing IS/IT Personnel**, Magid Igbaria & Conrad Shayo/ISBN: 1-59140-128-3; eISBN 1-59140-129-1, © 2004
- **Beyond Knowledge Management**, Brian Lehaney, Steve Clarke, Elayne Coakes & Gillian Jack/ ISBN: 1-59140-180-1; eISBN 1-59140-181-X, © 2004
- **eTransformation in Governance: New Directions in Government and Politics**, Matti Mälkiä, Ari Veikko Anttiroiko & Reijo Savolainen/ISBN: 1-59140-130-5; eISBN 1-59140-131-3, © 2004
- **Intelligent Agents for Data Mining and Information Retrieval**, Masoud Mohammadian/ISBN: 1-59140-194-1; eISBN 1-59140-195-X, © 2004
- **Using Community Informatics to Transform Regions**, Stewart Marshall, Wal Taylor & Xinghuo Yu/ISBN: 1-59140-132-1; eISBN 1-59140-133-X, © 2004
- **Wireless Communications and Mobile Commerce**, Nan Si Shi/ ISBN: 1-59140-184-4; eISBN 1-59140-185-2, © 2004
- **Organizational Data Mining: Leveraging Enterprise Data Resources for Optimal Performance**, Hamid R. Nemati & Christopher D. Barko/ ISBN: 1-59140-134-8; eISBN 1-59140-135-6, © 2004
- **Virtual Teams: Projects, Protocols and Processes**, David J. Pauleen/ISBN: 1-59140-166-6; eISBN 1-59140-167-4, © 2004
- **Business Intelligence in the Digital Economy: Opportunities, Limitations and Risks**, Mahesh Raisinghani/ ISBN: 1-59140-206-9; eISBN 1-59140-207-7, © 2004
- **E-Business Innovation and Change Management**, Mohini Singh & Di Waddell/ISBN: 1-59140-138-0; eISBN 1-59140-139-9, © 2004
- **Responsible Management of Information Systems**, Bernd Stahl/ISBN: 1-59140-172-0; eISBN 1-59140-173-9, © 2004
- **Web Information Systems**, David Taniar/ISBN: 1-59140-208-5; eISBN 1-59140-209-3, © 2004
- **Strategies for Information Technology Governance**, Wim van Grembergen/ISBN: 1-59140-140-2; eISBN 1-59140-141-0, © 2004
- **Information and Communication Technology for Competitive Intelligence**, Dirk Vriens/ISBN: 1-59140-142-9; eISBN 1-59140-143-7, © 2004
- **The Handbook of Information Systems Research**, Michael E. Whitman & Amy B. Woszczynski/ISBN: 1-59140-144-5; eISBN 1-59140-145-3, © 2004
- **Neural Networks in Business Forecasting**, G. Peter Zhang/ISBN: 1-59140-176-3; eISBN 1-59140-177-1, © 2004

Excellent additions to your institution's library! Recommend these titles to your Librarian!

To receive a copy of the Idea Group Publishing catalog, please contact 1/717-533-8845,
fax 1/717-533-8661,or visit the IGP Online Bookstore at:
[http://www.idea-group.com] !
Note: All IGP books are also available as ebooks on netlibrary.com as well as other ebook sources.
Contact Ms. Carrie Skovrinskie at [cskovrinskie@idea-group.com] to receive a complete list of sources
where you can obtain ebook information or IGP titles.

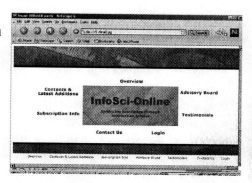